한국 인권문제

제 사안 2

한국 인권문제

제 사안 2

| 머리말

　일제 강점기 독립운동과 병행되었던 한국의 인권운동은 해방이 되었음에도 큰 결실을 보지 못했다. 1950년대 반공을 앞세운 이승만 정부와 한국전쟁, 역시 경제발전과 반공을 내세우다 유신 체제에 이르렀던 박정희 정권, 쿠데타로 집권한 1980년대 전두환 정권까지, 한국의 인권은 이를 보장해야 할 국가와 정부에 의해 도리어 억압받고 침해되었다. 이런 배경상 근대 한국의 인권운동은 반독재, 민주화운동과 결을 같이했고, 대체로 국외에 본부를 둔 인권 단체나 정치로부터 상대적으로 자유로운 종교 단체에 의해 주도되곤 했다. 이는 1980년 5·18광주민주화운동을 계기로 보다 근적인 변혁을 요구하는 형태로 조직화되었고, 그 활동 영역도 정치를 넘어 노동자, 농민, 빈민 등으로 확대되었다. 이들이 없었다면 한국은 1987년 군부 독재 종식하고 절차적 민주주의를 도입할 수 없었을 것이다. 민주화 이후에도 수많은 어려움이 있었지만, 한국의 인권운동은 점차 전문적이고 독립된 운동으로 분화되며 더 많은 이들의 참여를 이끌어냈고, 지금까지 많은 결실을 맺을 수 있었다.

　본 총서는 1980년대 중반부터 1990년대 초반까지, 외교부에서 작성하여 30여 년간 유지했던 한국 인권문제와 관련한 국내외 자료를 담고 있다. 6월 항쟁이 일어나고 민주화 선언이 이뤄지는 등 한국 인권운동에 많은 변화가 있었던 시기다. 당시 인권문제와 관련한 국내외 사안들, 각종 사건에 대한 미국과 우방국, 유엔의 반응, 최초의 한국 인권보고서 제출과 아동의 권리에 관한 협약 과정, 유엔인권위원회 활동, 기타 민주화 관련 자료 등 총 18권으로 구성되었다. 전체 분량은 약 9천여 쪽에 이른다.

2024년 3월

한국학술정보(주)

| 일러두기

· 본 총서에 실린 자료는 2022년 4월과 2023년 4월에 각각 공개한 외교문서 4,827권, 76만 여 쪽 가운데 일부를 발췌한 것이다.

· 각 권의 제목과 순서는 공개된 원본을 최대한 반영하였으나, 주제에 따라 일부는 적절히 변경하였다.

· 원본 자료는 A4 판형에 맞게 축소하거나 원본 비율을 유지한 채 A4 페이지 안에 삽입하였다. 또한 현재 시점에선 공개되지 않아 '공란'이란 표기만 있는 페이지 역시 그대로 실었다.

· 외교부가 공개한 문서 각 권의 첫 페이지에는 '정리 보존 문서 목록'이란 이름으로 기록물 종류, 일자, 명칭, 간단한 내용 등의 정보가 수록되어 있으며, 이를 기준으로 0001번부터 번호가 매겨져 있다. 이는 삭제하지 않고 총서에 그대로 수록하였다.

· 보고서 내용에 관한 더 자세한 정보가 필요하다면, 외교부가 온라인상에 제공하는 『대한민국 외교사료요약집』 1991년과 1992년 자료를 참조할 수 있다.

| 차례

정 리 보 존 문 서 목 록					
기록물종류	일반공문서철	등록번호	15902	등록일자	2000-05-04
분류번호	701	국가코드		보존기간	영구
명 칭	한국 인권문제 관련 사안, 1990-91. 전2권				
생 산 과	서구1과/국제연합과	생산년도	1990~1991	담당그룹	
권 차 명	V.1 1990-91.2월				
내용목차	* 아시아워치 인권보고서 및 휴먼라이트 워치 연례보고서 포함				

0001

Retreat from Reform

Labor Rights & Freedom of Expression in South Korea

An Asia Watch Report
November 18, 1990

Retreat from Reform

Labor Rights & Freedom
of Expression in South Korea

An Asia Watch Report
November 18, 1990

0003

Retreat from Reform

Labor Rights & Freedom
of Expression in South Korea

Despite the South Korean government's June 1987 promise of reforms, there is a wide desparity between the rhetoric of democracy achieved and the reality of the Roh government's retreat from reform.

The government continues to violate the workers' right to elect their own leaders and take collective action. Riot police are frequently used to break up strikes and workers' rallies.

The government employs the stringent National Security Law to arrest its critics and advocates of unification with North Korea. Publishing houses are raided and "objectionable" materials confiscated. Writers, publishers and editors are rounded up. Military and civilian security agencies engage in domestic surveillance.

Asia Watch urges the Bush administration to drastically revise its current policy of "silent diplomacy" and to use its leverage as a major ally and trade partner to condemn human rights abuses and promote needed reforms.

0004

Retreat from Reform

Labor Rights and Freedom
of Expression in South Korea

An Asia Watch Report
November 18, 1990

485 Fifth Avenue
New York, NY 10017-6104
(212) 972-8400
(212) 972-0905 Fax

1522 K Street, NW, #190
Washington, DC 20005-1202
(202) 371-6592
(202) 371-0124 Fax

• November 1990 by Human Rights Watch
All Rights Reserved.
Printed in the United States of America.

ISBN 0-929692-75-6
Library of Congress Catalog Card Number: 90-85381

The Asia Watch Committee

Asia Watch was formed in 1985 to monitor and promote in Asia observance of internationally recognized human rights in. The chairman of Asia Watch is Jack Greenberg and the vice-chairpersons are Orville Schell and Nadine Strossen. Sidney Jone is the executive director. Mike Jendrzejczyk is Washington Director. Patricia Gossman, Robin Munro and Ji Won Park are research associates. Jeannine Guthrie, Joy Lewis and Mary McCoy are associates.

Human Rights Watch

Human Rights Watch is composed of the five Watch Committees: Africa Watch, Americas Watch, Asia Watch, Helsinki Watch, and Middle East Watch.

Executive Committee

Chairman, Robert Bernstein; Vice Chairman, Adrian W. DeWind; Members; Roland Algrant; Lisa Anderson; Peter Bell; Dorothy Cullman; Jonathan Fanton; Jack Greenberg; Alice H. Henkin; Stephen Kass; Marina Kaufman; Jeri Laber; Aryeh Neier; Bruce Rabb; Kenneth Roth; Orville Schell; Sophie C. Silberberg; Gary Sick; Nadine Strossen.

Staff

Executive Director, Aryeh Neier; Deputy Director, Kenneth Roth; Washington Director, Holly J. Burkhalter; California Director, Ellen Lutz; Press Director, Susan Osnos; Counsel, Jemera Rone; Business Manager, Stephanie Steele; Women's Rights Project Director, Dorothy Q. Thomas; Prison Project Director, Joanna Weschler; Research Associate, Allyson Collins; Orville Schell Fellows, Richard Dicker, Robert Kushen, Dinah PoKempner.

Executive Directors

Africa Watch	Americas Watch	Asia Watch
Rakiya Omaar	Juan E. Mendez	Sidney R. Jones

Helsinki Watch	Middle East Watch
Jeri Laber	Andrew Whitley

0006

TABLE OF CONTENTS

0007

0008

I. INTRODUCTION

In June 1987, the government of South Korea embarked on a path of political reform. The tentative moves towards political openness came toward the end of the rule of President Chun Doo-hwan, whose administration had been marked by human rights abuses, ranging from the Kwangju massacre in 1980 to imprisonment and torture of critics and opponents and heavy-handed repression of the press.[1]

Massive protests in the spring of 1987 attracted a wide cross-section of the South Korean population and led to government acceptance of an eight-point reform proposal issued by Roh Tae-woo (then chairman of the ruling Democratic Justice Party) on June 29, 1987, calling for direct presidential elections and other reform measures. In October, a newly amended constitution was approved in a national referendum. Besides the provision on elections, the constitution also included provisions strengthening protection of individual rights and empowering the legislature to hold public hearings on issues of national importance.

On December 16, 1987 South Koreans went to the polls for the first time in sixteen years to directly elect a new president. The opposition was split, unable to agree on a single candidate. Roh Tae-woo was elected with a plurality of 36.7 percent of the votes. In his inaugural address on February 25, 1988, President Roh declared, "The day when freedoms and human rights could be slighted in the name of economic growth and national security has ended. The day when repressive force and torture in secret chambers were tolerated is over."[2]

Two months after Roh took office, elections to the National Assembly took place in April 1988. For the first time the ruling party had a minority of seats in the legislature, while three other parties held a majority. The opposition asserted its newly-won power by initiating investigations and public hearings into the corruption and human rights abuses committed by former President Chun Doo-hwan. Numerous close associates and relatives of Chun were eventually arrested and jailed on corruption charges. In a controversial move, Chun was allowed to avoid prosecution by apologizing publicly for his past misdeeds and going into internal exile, where he remains as of the date of this publication.

In 1988, reacting to opposition pressure and the focus of the world's media in anticipation of the Olympic Games in Seoul in September, Roh proceeded to implement some of the other promised reforms, including elimination of many of the restrictions placed on the press, amendment of laws regulating trade unions, and the release of hundreds of political prisoners.[3] Important as those changes were, some things remained unchanged.

---

[1] On May 18, 1980 demonstrations for democratic reform and against martial rule in the city of Kwangju (South Cholla province) were brutally put down by riot police and special airborne troops. In three days of barbarity, including beating, stabbing, and mutilating of unarmed and defenseless civilians, thousands were seriously injured and at least 2,000 were killed. Asia Watch, *Human Rights in Korea*, (January 1986), pp. 36-43. This report surveys human rights violations of the early-mid 1980's in South Korea. *See also* Asia Watch, *A Stern, Steady Crackdown: Legal Process and Human Rights in Korea*, (May 1987) and *Assessing Reform in South Korea*, (October 1988).

[2] *Korea Times*, February 26, 1988.

[3] For details on the prisoner releases, *see Assessing Reform in South Korea*, pp. 13-14.

1

0009

All the political parties initially expressed support for reforms and discussions took place in 1988 between the opposition parties and the Democratic Justice Party to hammer out a reform program. But disagreements and competition between the parties led to a failure to eliminate the repressive laws and practices that characterized the Chun Doo-hwan government. Most significantly, they failed to amend most of the laws used to restrict freedom of expression, association and assembly. Roh vetoed amendments of the labor laws approved by parliament. The National Security Law (NSL), a broadly worded law providing stiff penalties for anyone accused of supporting or benefitting an "anti-state organization," remained on the books and continued to be used to arrest government critics. The Law on Assembly and Demonstration, which allows the government to ban a wide range of gatherings, also remained in force (although it was amended in March 1989). The Agency for National Security Planning, historically involved in domestic surveillance and interrogation of political opponents as well as espionage cases, had no new legal limits put on its activities. And although fewer than before, incidents of torture and mistreatment of detainees continued to be reported.

By the end of December 1989, the parliament was at an impasse, with the opposition political parties refusing to pass the national budget. In a surprising move, the presidential Blue House issued on December 16, 1989 an 11-point statement outlining a new agreement reached by the four political parties. President Roh and his ruling party agreed to persuade Chun Doo-hwan to return from internal exile and testify on corruption and abuse of power charges before the National Assembly. Roh also agreed to persuade two key military figures -- who had helped Chun come into power and whom the opposition held responsible for the 1980 Kwangju massacre -- to resign from their public offices. Finally, Roh agreed to seek compensation for those the government admitted were killed or injured during the 1980 Kwangju massacre. He also promised to cooperate in passing local autonomy election laws and amending the National Security Law and the Law on Agency for National Security Planning. But the "grand compromise," as the December agreement was dubbed, and the hope for reform that it engendered were short-lived.

In January 1990, two parties in the National Assembly which were previously considered opposition parties merged with the Roh's Democratic Justice Party to form the Democratic Liberal Party (DLP). The merger followed secret negotiations with the Reunification Democratic Party, headed by Kim Young-sam, and the New Democratic Republican Party, led by Kim Jong-pil. Kim Young-sam, who had been an important opposition leader for more than ten years, became the executive chairman of the new party. This left Kim Dae-jung as the leader of the sole opposition group, the Party for Peace and Democracy. The huge new DLP effectively controls more than two-thirds of the seats in the legislature. The leaders of the new party blamed competition between the four parties for the failure to enact structural reforms which would have led to democratization and reunification, including action on the National Security Law. They claimed the new party would not be hindered by such inter-party squabbles, yet none of the promised reforms were carried out by the new party.

By mid-1990, it was clear that South Korea's path to democratization was going to be neither smooth nor rapid, as various groups in Korean society tested the government's willingness to implement reforms and found it lacking. Since early 1989, thousands of people -- writers, editors, publishers and others -- have been arrested and prosecuted for expressing views contrary to those of the government on reunification between North and South Korea or for engaging in personal pro-unification diplomacy through unauthorized travel to North Korea. This crackdown took place despite President Roh's *Nordpolitik* declaration in July 1988 that it was time to stop treating North Korea as the enemy and that the government wanted to promote contacts across the demilitarized zone.

Likewise, the labor movement, taking advantage of Roh's announced reforms, began to agitate for increased wages and the right to form "democratic unions." In addition to strikes and other labor activity by industrial workers, unions sprang up among teachers in public and private schools and within the broadcasting and newspaper publishing industries. On January 20, 1990, blaming the labor movement for threatening the economy, the government announced a tough crackdown. Strikes were crushed with riot police. Many labor activists were arrested. Dissident labor publications and writers were banned.

The gap between the government's stated commitment to reform and its actual practices widened. The number of political prisoners, one indicator of this gap, continued to rise. There were nearly 1,400 political prisoners in South Korea as of the end of July 1990.[4] Nearly half of the political prisoners were workers and labor activists. Reforms in the security and labor laws were stalled. Rather than facilitating the smooth operation of the National Assembly, the merger of the political parties only led to further friction and division. The DLP unilaterally passed twenty-six bills in July and disbanded parliamentary investigations into past abuses. In protest, all of the non-DLP legislators resigned and refused to participate in National Assembly proceedings.

In early October, the limits of democratization were brought into sharp focus when an agent in the Defense Security Command (DSC), the military's counterintelligence agency, publicly revealed the existence of an extensive spying program that kept at least 1,300 politicians, labor leaders, academics, religious leaders, journalists and others under regular surveillance.[5] President Roh, who had once been the head of DSC, immediately fired his defense minister and the head of the Defense Security Command but replaced them with his loyalists. As one respected publication noted, the new appointments "appear cosmetic rather than substantial."[6] Kim Dae-jung, frustrated with affecting change through the parliament, began a hunger-strike to demand political reforms, including an end to the political surveillance. His strike ended on October 20.

Taken together, these laws and measures against individuals and organizations advocating reunification or involved in collective trade union action provide a telling indictment of the Roh administration's failure to protect fundamental human rights in South Korea.

---

[4] Minkahyop, *Detainees in Connection with the Current Situation*, as reported by *Hankyoreh Shinmun*, August 4, 1990. Minkahyop is an organization of families of political prisoners. *See* chapter 2, footnote 31 and accompanying text. This figure encompasses all those believed to have been arrested for committing politically-motivated offenses, regardless of whether those are considered to be criminal offenses or acts of violence. Asia Watch calls for the unconditional release of only those persons who have neither engaged in or advocated the use of violence.

[5] "The evidence [including files and computer disks] ... appears to be the first to contradict repeated assurances by President Roh Tae-woo that the armed forces would not get involved in politics. The politicians [under surveillance] include Kim Young-sam, until this year a prominent opposition figure but now executive chairman of the ruling Democratic Liberal Party, and Kim Dae-jung." *The New York Times*, October 8, 1990. The 1,300 included some 140 politicians, 550 dissidents, 250 workers and labor activists, 27 members of Chunkyojo, 160 student activists, 120 religious leaders, 60 professors, 27 journalists, and others. All names were published on October 6, 1990 in *Hankyoreh Shinmun*. Many of the persons mentioned in this report are named in the list, including: Moon Ik-hwan, Kim Keun-tae, Jang Myung-guk, Koh Un, Lee Bu-young (Chonminnyon), Kim Huon-jang, Hong Song-dam and persons associated with the newspaper *Hankyoreh Shinmun* (chapter 2); Yun Yong-kyu and Lee Bu-young (Chunkyojo) (chapter 3); Dan Byung-ho (chapter 4); Kwon Yong-mok (chapter 5); and members of the press unions discussed (chapter 6).

[6] Shim Jae-hoon, "Old Habits Die Hard," *Far Eastern Economic Review*, p 28.

3

0011

•   •   •   •   •   •   •

This report is divided into ten chapters. Chapter 1 examines political developments in South Korea since the last Asia Watch report, *Assessing Reforms in South Korea*, published in October 1988. Chapter 2 examines the ways in which freedom of expression has been restricted through application of the National Security Law, controls on the press, and arrests of opposition leaders, publishers, writers and others. Chapter 3 provides an overview of the labor movement, an analysis of the repression it has faced since President Roh took office, and an examination of both the legal safeguards protecting workers and the ways they are violated. Chapters 4, 5, 6, 7 and 8 are case studies of how certain labor rights are violated in particular industries or professions, including the Hyundai group, the teaching profession, and the broadcasting and newspaper publishing industry. The report concludes with a chapter on recommendations to the South Korean government and a chapter on the U.S. role and government policy toward South Korea.

This report was written by Edward J. Baker, a member of the Asia Watch Committee; Mike Jendrzejczyk, the Asia Watch Washington director; and Ji Won Park, Asia Watch research associate. They visited South Korea from June 5-17, 1990 and interviewed government officials and a wide range of non-governmental authorities and contacts, including lawyers, labor activists, domestic and foreign press correspondents, academics, and human rights monitors. Most of the interviews took place in Seoul; the delegation also visited Ulsan, site of the giant Hyundai company plants, and Taegu, where they visited a political prisoner. The report is based on information gathered during the June mission, as well as research before and after it.

We would like to thank all those who gave generously of their time, energy and expertise to assist with the mission and with this report. We are especially grateful to Mr. Cho Young-rae, a respected human rights lawyer and friend, who reminds us all that concern about human rights is based upon a basic compassion for one's fellow men and women. He guided us but would not allow us to abdicate the responsibility of forming our own impressions and conclusions about the state of human rights in his country.

4

0012

II. VIOLATIONS OF THE RIGHT TO FREEDOM OF EXPRESSION

Despite its rhetoric and repeated commitments to reform, the Roh government continues to imprison publishers, labor activists, writers, political opponents, advocates of reunification with North Korea and others who to exercise their right to freedom of expression. Government control over the press and publishing industry has eased, but self-censorship is widely practiced. Foreign correspondents have limited access to information, and the broadcast media are largely owned and operated by the state.

The Unification Debate and the National Security Law

Under Roh Tae-woo, it has become much more difficult to prosecute people just for their pronouncements on domestic affairs, and much is now said in public and in private, in the National Assembly and in the press, which once might have landed the speaker in prison. One obvious example: Kim Dae-jung, while functioning as the head of a political party and a member of the National Assembly, has constantly criticized the government in terms at least as harsh as those which led to his being sentenced to death under the National Security Law in 1980.

As the permissible scope for critical political discussions has broadened, the taboo subjects fall into two broad areas: advocacy of unification and criticism of the policies which have led to economic growth at the expense of worker rights. Those speaking out on these subjects can still be arrested under the National Security Law.

The National Security Law (NSL) gives the authorities broad powers to arrest and imprison anyone accused of forming, participating in, or benefitting an "anti-state organization." According to the NSL, such an organization, whether based in South Korea or abroad, is one whose purpose is to "assume a title of the government or disturb the state" or an organization operating "along the lines of the communists."[7]

Over the years, the National Security Law (NSL) has been widely used to imprison people who, according to the government, visited North Korea, met North Koreans or alleged North Korean agents abroad, expressed support for North Korea or views similar to North Korean positions, listened to North Korean broadcasting, or possessed North Korean or other Marxist books. Conviction under the NSL can result in long prison sentences or the death penalty. Despite the fact that all the political parties have agreed since 1988 that it should be revised, the NSL remains the most frequently used instrument of repression against government dissenters in South Korea. Thirty-three percent of the political prisoners as of June 1990 were detained under the National Security Law.

The law was first enacted in November 1949 and has been amended several times, most importantly in 1980 when the Anti-Communist Law was repealed and several of its key provisions were incorporated into the NSL.[8] In an April 1990 decision on two key provisions of the NSL, Articles 7(1) and 7(5), the South Korean Constitutional Court recognized that the law raised problems and that it was subject to abuse, yet still found the provisions constitutional and merely recommended limited application

---

[7] Quoted from Article 3 of the NSL. Amnesty International, "Revision of the NSL and of the Law on the Agency for National Security Planning," AI Index: ASA 25/25/90 (May 1990)

[8] Ibid. The Anti-Communist Law was promulgated in 1961 to counter communist insurgencies and infiltration.

5

0013

in cases where there was "explicit harm to national security, existence or the basic order of free democracy."[9]

On July 7, 1988, President Roh made a declaration in which he proposed an end to confrontation and an increase in contact between South and North Korea and a willingness to bring North Korea into the international community.[10] Many groups and individuals responded with proposals for contacts with the North and some even made contact. One was the Association of Writers for National Literature which proposed to meet with its North Korean counterpart at Panmunjom, the truce village at the demilitarized zone which divides North and South.[11] A second was Chonminnyon, a nationwide coalition of dissident groups, including artists', farmers' and workers' organizations, which was founded in January 1989 to campaign for freedom from foreign (i.e. American) influence, democracy, economic justice and reunification of Korea. At its inaugural meeting it proposed a conference to be attended by "representatives of all walks of life" in the North, the South and abroad.[12] Efforts to hold the conference led to the arrest of several Chonminnyon leaders.

Newspaper editors and political activists also tried to take advantage of the new *Nordpolitik*. Professor Lee Young-hee and some of his colleagues at *Hankyoreh Shinmun* allegedly attempted to arrange for a group of *Hankyoreh* reporters to visit North Korea to write feature articles for the paper. He was arrested, tried and given an 18-month suspended sentence in September 1989 after he had spent five months in prison.

The Roh government's response to these and other cases has made it clear that old habits die hard. After initially responding positively and helpfully to the Association of Writers for National Literature's proposal, the government backed away, then banned the proposed meeting and arrested the chairman of the executive committee, Ko Un, a well-known poet. Other members of the committee were indicted without detention. Eventually Ko was convicted and given a suspended one-year sentence for violating the National Security Law.[13] Lee Bu-yong and other leaders of Chonminnyon were arrested in April 1990 for violating the NSL, the Law on Assembly and Demonstration, and in Lee's case also the labor laws for interfering in a labor dispute as a "third party."[14] They were sentenced to one-year and two-year terms. Lee was sentenced in October to two years' imprisonment and then was released.

Those who visited North Korea without government permission fared worse. Reverend Moon Ik-hwan, a well-known political activist; Im Su-kyong, a leader of Chondaehyop, a nationwide alliance of student organizations; and Representative Suh Kyong-won, an opposition party member of the National Assembly, all made separate trips to North Korea in the spring and summer of 1989 which were not authorized by the government. All three and several of their associates were arrested, tried, convicted and

---

[9] Article 7, para.1 prohibits "benefiting an anti-state organization by praising it, encouraging it, siding with it, or through other means." Para. 5 deals with "importing, disseminating, buying or selling, etc. documents, drawings or other means of expression" for purposes benefiting or supporting "anti-state organizations." The court ruled that these provisions were "qualifiedly constitutional if rightly applied." Yonhap, April 2, 1990, in FBIS, same day.

[10] *Korea Herald*, July 8, 1988.

[11] *News from Asia Watch*, "Update on Human Rights Concerns in South Korea," July 26, 1989, p. 3; Amnesty International, *Urgent Action*, April 18, 1989.

[12] Amnesty International, "South Korea: Return to 'Repressive Force and Torture?'" p.6.

[13] Baker memo; "Update on Human Rights Concerns," p. 3; "'Repressive Force and Torture?'" p. 21.

[14] *See* chapter 3 for discussion of the labor laws, including the ban on "third-party interference."

6

0014

sentenced to substantial terms of imprisonment under the NSL. On appeal, the Supreme Court reduced Im's sentence to five years, but it confirmed Reverend Moon's seven-year sentence. Representative Suh is serving fifteen years.[15] On October 20, 1990, Reverend Moon was released for reasons of "poor health." The government denied that there was any connection with North Korea's demand for the release of the prisoners tried for visiting the North, which threatened to impede North-South talks. The others sentenced with him remained in prison.

In contrast with the treatment of these individuals, Chung Ju-yong, the founder and head of the Hyundai Group, who also visited North Korea in early 1989, has suffered no ill consequences. The government said, however, that Chung had obtained prior permission to travel to the North.

Reverend Moon's trip spurred the creation of an investigatory body which had a brief but active existence. In April 1989 representatives of the various South Korean security agencies were temporarily grouped into the Joint Security Investigations Headquarters (JSIH). Ostensibly formed to investigate persons in connection with Reverend Moon's trip, its mandate was far broader. The JSIH became a key element in April in a governmental "crackdown on rising militant forces."[16] At a meeting of security officials, President Roh called for tough measures to root out alleged violent leftist revolutionary forces from schools, publishing houses, religious groups, and the labor movement. The Culture and Information Minister was quoted as saying his ministry would "tighten its control over the publication of leftist ideological books."[17] In the first month of operation, the JSIH arrested 234 people, booked 215 others without detention, put 88 on a wanted list, and seized 11,471 publications from 460 bookstores.[18] Another source, the Korean Association for the Publishing Culture Movement, reports that in one three-month period in 1989, the Joint Security Investigations Headquarters organized "the most extreme suppression of the press in Korean history [and] had publishers arrested each week."[19] Those arrested, indicted or sought by JSIH agents included advocates of democracy and unification, labor activists, publishers, booksellers, writers, and others.

The JSIH was officially disbanded in June, although arrests of dissidents under the security laws continued. In the publishing sector alone, according to the Korean Association for the Publishing Culture Movement, 43 people were arrested for suspected violations of the National Security Law, and all were found guilty.[20]

The pattern of repression continued in 1990. As of the end of July 1990, there were said to be 1,379 persons "detained in connection with the current situation," i.e. arrested for having committed

---

[15] Yonhap, January 25, 1990, in FBIS, January 29; Yonhap, February 10, 1990, in FBIS, February 12; Yonhap, June 8, 1990, in FBIS, June 11; Reuters, June 11, 1990; Seoul Domestic Service, February 5, 1990, in FBIS, same day; Yonhap, June 11, 1990, in FBIS, June 13.

[16] *Korea News Review*, April 15, 1989, p. 3.

[17] *Ibid.*, p. 5.

[18] "Update on Human Rights Concerns."

[19] Korean Association for the Publishing Culture Movement, *The Sixth Republic and Suppression of the Press*, (published in Korean in Seoul, June 8, 1990), pp. 5-6.

[20] See Appendix 4. Arrested publishers are almost always found guilty of having violated the National Security Law but are released some months later after being given suspended sentences.

7

0015

politically-motivated acts. Of the total, 435 were detained under the National Security Law. Approximately 438 were workers and union activists, and 25 were involved in publishing.[21]

National Security Law Cases

One of those arrested was Hong Song-dam, chairperson of the Kwangju chapter of the Korean National Artists Federation (Minminyon). Hong's main offense was sending a photographic slide of a large mural he painted, along with several other artists, to Pyongyang, North Korea. There it was displayed at the 13th World Festival of Youth and Students in July 1989. The mural, entitled "A History of the National Liberation Movement," depicts some scenes of popular movements in Korea from the late 19th century through the 1980 Kwangju uprising. Hong was also charged with leaking state secrets by sending books and magazines to North Korean sympathizers in Europe to pass on to North Korean artists. A third charge was that he met with North Korean agents in Germany and received funds for and instructions to set up the Korean National Artists Federation.

On June 1, 1990 the Seoul Appellate Court confirmed the seven-year sentence handed down by the Seoul District Criminal Court for violation of the National Security Law (NSL). Seven years is the maximum sentence allowed under Article 7 of the NSL prohibiting production and distribution of "documents, drawings or any other means of expression" which "praise, benefit or encourage" North Korea.[22] In September 1990, the Supreme Court ruled on Hong's case, reversing one charge against him and finding him guilty of the other charges; it sent his case back to the appeals court for retrial.[23]

Hong alleged at his initial trial that he had been tortured during his three weeks of detention by the Agency for National Security Planning. A forensic pathologist on the faculty of the Seoul National University testified that he had found evidence of torture when he examined Hong while he was still in detention.

On June 18, 1990 the Seoul Appellate Court also upheld the seven-year sentence of another prominent dissident, Kim Hyon-jang, head of the International Relations Bureau of Chonminnyon.[24] Kim's offense also involved expression which the government disliked. He was convicted under the NSL for sending facsimile messages to Hanmint'ong, an association of Korean residents in Japan which was declared an "anti-state organization" by the South Korean Supreme Court in the late 1970's. Hanmint'ong was one of several organizations abroad to which Kim sent appeals for support for a campaign to demand an independent autopsy and investigation into the suspicious circumstances surrounding the May 1989 death of a Kwangju student activist, Lee Chol-kyu. The authorities alleged that Hanmint'ong sent a contribution of $1,200 in response.[25]

---

[21] Minkahyop, *Detainees in Connection with the Current Situation*, as reported by the *Hankyoreh Shinmun*, August 4, 1990. *See* chapter 1 of this report, footnote 5.

[22] Amnesty International, "South Korea: Hong Song-dam: Seven Years' Imprisonment for Sending Paintings to North Korea," February 1990; North American Coalition for Human Rights in Korea, *Korea Update*, Issue No. 100, July-August 1990, p. 22.

[23] The court said there was no evidence to prove that Hong knew that the person he contacted in Germany was a North Korean agent and dismissed his conviction on an espionage charge. *Korea Herald*, September 26, 1990.

[24] Kim, a free-lance writer and human rights activist, was previously jailed from 1982-1988 on charges of violating the National Security Law. He had been wanted by the authorities for circulating documents on the Kwangju massacre.

[25] *Korea Update*, p. 22.

0016

Kim Keun-tae

Kim Keun-tae is a chairperson of the Executive Committee of Chonminnyon and a prominent leader of the opposition movement.[26] His case illustrates the use of both the National Security Law and the Law on Assembly and Demonstration, another security measure frequently used to control dissent and restrict freedom of expression.

On September 29, 1990, Kim Keun-tae was sentenced to three years in prison on charges filed in connection with demonstrations on May 9, 1990 by at least 100,000 people, protesting the formation of the new government party.[27] Many people, including Kim, expressed the fear at that time that the new Democratic Liberal Party, holding more than the required two-thirds of the National Assembly seats, would act to amend the constitution to establish a cabinet system thus allowing President Roh to remain in power after his current single five-year term ending in 1992.[28] The demonstration led to a firebomb attack on the U.S. Information Service building in downtown Seoul, a frequent target of anti-American protests. About 40,000 riot police were mobilized and as many as 1,900 demonstrators were briefly detained by the police. Kim was arrested on May 14 and indicted on June 9, 1990 under the National Security Law and the Law on Assembly and Demonstration.[29]

It appears that Kim was arbitrarily singled out because of the influential role he was playing in the movement to unify the opposition, since he was the only person prosecuted for a serious offense in connection with the May 9 demonstrations. Asia Watch believes that Kim was arrested simply for exercising his right to freedom of expression. In response to concerns raised by Asia Watch in meetings in June with the Ministry of Justice, and in correspondence, the government changed the stated reason for Kim's arrest, saying he was charged not only in connection with the May 9 rally, as his arrest warrant indicated but also with other violations of security laws.[30] Specifically, the Ministry said he was charged with violating the NSL by reading, at the organization's inaugural rally in January 1989, Chonminnyon's charter which advocated reunification. It is not at all clear how Kim's activities at the rally were "aiding the enemy," as the government alleged. especially when an official announcement made well after the rally in June 1989 cited the findings of government investigators who uncovered no evidence to link

---

[26] Kim has a long history of opposing the governments of Roh Ta-woo and Chun Doo-hwan. He was detained from 1985 until mid-1988 for his involvement in the National Youth Alliance for Democracy and his role in organizing anti-government demonstrations. He was severely tortured during the initial interrogation. *See* Asia Watch, *A Stern, Steady Crackdown*, pp. 78-89. He and his wife, Inn Jae-keun, also a leading human rights activist, were awarded the Robert F. Kennedy Human Rights Award for 1987.

[27] For descriptions of the demonstrations, *see New York Times*, May 10, 1990, p 1 and UPI, May 10, 1990, *New York Times*, May 14, 1990, p. 6. Kim was sentenced to a three-year prison term by the Seoul District Criminal Court on September 29, 1990. Yonhap, September 29, 1990, in FBIS, same day.

[28] The Democratic Liberal Party was formed in January by the merger of the governing Democratic Justice Party, Kim Jong-pil's New Democratic Republican Party (a conservative "opposition" party), and Kim Young-sam's Reunification Democratic Party. *See* Chapter I for additional details and background.

[29] *Korea Times*, June 10, 1990.

[30] Asia Watch wrote to Minister Lee Jong-nam, August 6, 1990, raising questions about Kim's trial and the charges against him. Lee Sun-woo, Director of the Human Rights Division, Ministry of Justice, replied for the government. The case was raised with Lee Sun-woo and other Ministry officials on June 15, 1990 by the Asia Watch mission.

9

0017

Chonminnyon with the "enemy" (i.e. North Korea), though some of its members have been arrested for trying to make contact with individuals in the North.[31]

In addition, Kim was accused of participating in several protest activities in 1989 and 1990 (including the May 9 demonstration) in violation of the Law on Assembly and Demonstration. Kim's alleged violations of this law included failing to report the assemblies 48 hours in advance as the "sponsor" is required to do, although it is not clear why the government considers Kim the sole "sponsor" of these protest activities.[32] Failure to report properly is punishable by up to two years in prison or a fine of two million won (US$2860). The law was amended in March 1989 considerably reducing the penalties for violating it. For example, failure to report properly was previously punishable by up to seven years in prison and a three million won fine (US$4290). In addition, any assembly "feared to conspicuously cause unrest" was previously prohibited. The changed law specifies there has to be a "clear and present danger" of a threat to public order.[33] Before the amendments were made, the law was used to prevent opposition demonstrations from taking place, and they continue to be used by the authorities to restrict the exercise of freedom of speech by preventing or breaking up peaceful anti-government demonstrations.[34] In a letter to Asia Watch, the Justice Ministry maintained that "the National Security Law and laws governing public assembly and rally have been enacted to regulate freedom of speech and freedom of assembly to protect national security" and insisted they do not violate the "basic essence" of Kim's freedom guaranteed by Korean law.[35]

Kim Keun-tae's case went to trial on July 20, 1990 and lasted only about five minutes. Kim refused to participate in the proceedings, characterizing his arrest "as a political reprisal for [his] criticism of the ruling group" and stated he could no longer recognize the state's authority to mete out punishment. He withdrew from the courtroom and was informed by the judge as he left that his walkout would be "tantamount to accepting all the evidence presented by the prosecution."[36] After he left the courtroom, the prosecutor asked the court to sentence him to seven years imprisonment to be followed by a seven-year's suspension of his civil rights. Asia Watch raised questions about the proceedings in a letter to the Ministry of Justice and expressed concern that the court may have violated Kim's right to the presumption of innocence, as guaranteed in South Korean domestic and international law.[37] In response, the government denied that the judge made the statement attributed to him and said it would be up to the court to rule on the basis of the evidence presented regardless of the position taken by Kim and his

---

[31] "Aiding the enemy..." quoted from Justice Ministry letter, Ibid. The announcement was made in connection with the dissolution of the Joint Security Investigation Headquarters. Korea Herald, June 18, 1989.

[32] Law on Assembly and Demonstration, Article 6(1). The South Korean government claims that Kim somehow "instigated" acts of violence which allegedly took place in connection with protest activities in February 1990, April 1990, and May 1990. Letter from Lee Sun-woo to Asia Watch, September 11, 1990.

[33] Law on Assembly and Demonstration, Article 19(2).

[34] See Freedom of Expression, pp. 38–40; Asia Watch, Assessing Reform in South Korea, (October 1988), pp. 37–39.

[35] Letter from Lee to Asia Watch, September 11, 1990.

[36] Account of the trial, confirmed to Asia Watch by Kim's attorneys, is from the Hankyoreh Shinmun, July 23, 1990, p. 19.

[37] Asia Watch letter, August 6, 1990: "Under international law, the state has the burden of proof regardless of whether the defendant chooses to participate in the trial. The court may have violated Kim's right to presumption of innocence by accepting the probative value of the prosecutor's evidence before the court had the opportunity to weigh it." The presumption of innocence is guaranteed in Article 14(2) of the ICCPR and Article 27(4) of the 1987 Constitution.

10

lawyers.[38] In keeping with his refusal to stand trial, Kim has refused to appeal. The prosecutor has appealed for a heavier sentence and an appeal has also been made by the defense in the name of one of Kim's lawyers.

Freedom of Expression and the Labor Movement

If those seeking reunification with North Korea have experienced the limits on freedom of expression, so have the leaders and members of South Korea's independent trade unions. The growth of the labor movement stimulated the creation of new periodicals and magazines dealing with labor issues, as well as a weekly newspaper (*Nodongja Shinmun*, literally translated as *Workers' Newspaper* but also known as the *Korea Labor News*). But like the independent unions themselves, the labor publications and the individuals associated with them have been targeted by the authorities for sustained and harsh repression. The suppression of labor publications is evidently aimed at stifling further growth and mobilization in the independent trade union movement by hindering the free and open exchange of information, news and ideas.

Asia Watch has compiled information on a number of cases of labor publishing companies and/or individuals associated with them, although these are only a fraction of the nearly eighty such cases of persons arrested during the Sixth Republic (Roh Tae-woo's presidency) for their publishing activities.[39] Asia Watch obtained information about cases of labor activists labelled by the authorities as "leftists" and "radicals" because they allegedly possessed "pro-communist" or pro-North Korean books or literature.

Dawn (Stone Pagoda (Suktap) Publishing Company)

Jang Myung-guk is the founder of the Stone Pagoda (Suktap) Labor Research Institute. In October 1988, the Stone Pagoda Publishing Company, affiliated with the labor institute, began issuing *Dawn*, a periodical dealing with labor issues. Jang, 43, contributed articles addressing issues of economic class, social stratification, women's concerns and other matters. Active in the labor movement for twenty years, he authored the well-known book, *Explanation of Labor Laws*, which was published in 1982 and has sold 400,000 copies. In March 1989, Jang went into hiding for thirteen months. In the May 1990 issue of *Dawn*, Jang contributed articles that critically examined the present and future direction of the labor movement. Arrested on June 19, 1990, he was indicted on August 8 under the National Security Law (NSL) and the labor law ban on "third-party interference" in labor disputes.[40] His trial began on October 19, 1990. The NSL charges under Articles 7(1) and 7(5) stem from articles Jang wrote in *Dawn*.

---

[38] Lee letter to Asia Watch, September 11, 1990: "The court stated that in order for the prosecution to prove Mr Kim's crimes [sic], each evidence admitted must be examined and explained by Mr. Kim or his lawyers.... The presiding judge cannot simply rule that the defendant is guilty just because he refused to examine and comment on the evidence presented by the prosecution Mr. Kim will receive a fair trial on the charges brought against him."

[39] *See* Appendix 4.

[40] For details on the "third-party interference" charge against Jang, see chapter 3.

11

Nodong Haebang Munhak (Nodong Munhak)

The Nodong Munhak Company (Labor Literature Company) began publishing its *Nodong Haebang Munhak* (Labor Liberation Literature) magazine in March or April 1989.[41] In publishing the magazine, its editors said, "Our goal is to maintain a clear line on behalf of the labor class."[42] They added that the magazine was mainly intended for a readership consisting of union activists and reporters covering the labor scene.[43] The editors pledged "to make their magazine a guardian for the working class, a moderator of independent labor movements, and an essence of poignant literature of labor issues."[44]

In May 1989, *Nodong Haebang Munhak*'s publisher, Kim Sa-in, and its editor, Im Kyu-chan, were arrested in May 1989 in connection with an article on the Kwangju massacre published in the magazine's May issue. On September 18, 1989, they were found guilty and were each sentenced to two years' imprisonment and deprivation of civil rights. Their sentences were suspended for three years.

In December 1989, *Nodong Haebang Munhak* was ordered by the authorities to suspend publication for three months. On January 11, 1990, Kim and Im were arrested again by the Agency for National Security Planning (ANSP) and held under the National Security Law for allegedly defaming President Roh in their December issue. Im was sentenced on May 1, 1990 to two years' imprisonment and deprivation of civil rights; his sentence was suspended for two years.

ANSP agents also raided the magazine's office and the homes of the magazine staff members and confiscated 46,000 copies of the magazine.[45] Security agents were also reported to be seeking several other contributors to the magazine, including the author of the offending article who wrote it under the pen name Pak No-hae (short for Nodong Haebang). Pak, 31, is believed to be a poet from Chollanamdo reportedly famous for satirical verses and prose about harsh working conditions of workers. Among his writings is a piece published in the magazine's October issue entitled "Our Love, Our Wrath" which criticizes the semi-autobiography of Kim Woo-choong, chairman of one of Korea's largest conglomerates, the Daewoo group.[46]

Kim Ta-jong, also a publisher of the *Nodong Haebang Munhak*, was arrested in February 1990 in connection with the May – December 1989 issues of the magazine. He had previously been arrested in March 1989 for publishing "A Philosophy of National Liberation."

Together with Farmers

Kim Chun-ki, publisher of *Together with Farmers* was arrested around June 26, 1989. According to the New York-based Committee to Protect Journalists, the magazine published articles criticizing the government's agricultural policies and the influence of the United States on the South Korean economy.

---

[41] The June 1990 report by the Korean Publishing Culture Movement Association; International PEN, *Writers in Prison Committee Report*, September 1990.
[42] *Korea Herald*, February 24, 1989.
[43] *Korea Herald*, February 24, 1989.
[44] *Ibid.*
[45] *Korea Herald*, January 13, 1990.
[46] *Korea Times*, January 13, 1990, in FBIS, January 18, 1990.

12

0020

In late 1989, Kim was sentenced to two years' imprisonment under the National Security Law for disseminating and publishing materials that "praised" North Korea. Lee Sam-haeng, a writer for *Together with Farmers* was also arrested; he was released on a suspended sentence.[47]

Choe Yun-yong

Choe Yun-yong, 29, a labor activist, was accused of receiving a "seditious" book on communist organization tactics from a member of the audience during an October 16, 1988 performance of a play that was performed to raise money for a workers' library on the Kyongbuk National University campus in Taegu. Choe was accused of displaying the "pro-communist" book at the office of the Progressive Political Union in Pisan-dong and photocopying it in order to disseminate information on communist tactics. He was arrested on May 21, 1989, convicted of violating the National Security Law and sentenced to six months' imprisonment and deprivation of civil rights for the same period. Choe appealed his case to the appellate court but on February 3, 1990 he was given a heavier sentence--10 months' imprisonment plus one year's civil rights suspension. In the ruling, presiding judge Son Che-hui reportedly said, "We cannot allow his actions committed in the name of academic freedom to overthrow the free democratic system, even though we admit that freedom of thought is one of the basic rights that should be guaranteed fully."[48]

Inchon Labor Activists

In April 1990 eight labor counselors were arrested and three others booked for alleged violation of the National Security Law for teaching the *juche* (self-reliance) theory to workers. (*Juche* is the name of North Korean President Kim Il-sung's "self-reliance" ideology.) The National Police Headquarters accused the men of setting up a labor counselling center in Inchon in November 1988 and teaching the North Korean ideology to workers at five companies, including Daewoo Heavy Industries, Haitai Confectionery and Jindo Industries. Investigators also confiscated 300 articles on *juche* and other "illegal" publications containing the texts of North Korean radio broadcasts.[49]

Kim Hong-shin

Kim Hong-shin, a well-known novelist was fired from his job in June 1990 for speaking out about the police mistreatment in April 1990 of striking unionists at the Korea Broadcasting System (KBS). During his radio program at a KBS-owned station, Kim announced over the air that he had watched a video showing police violence against striking KBS workers and that he could not remain silent about it. He added that if he were prohibited from broadcasting after he made his statement or if the radio station were retaliated against, then South Korea could not be a democracy. The KBS management pulled Kim off the air.[50]

---

[47] *See* Appendix 4.
[48] *Korea Times*, February 4, 1990, in FBIS, February 6, 1990.
[49] The names of the men were not published. *Korea Herald*, April 13, 1990, in FBIS, same day.
[50] Interview with labor activist in Seoul, June 1990. Kim's case reportedly received wide press coverage in South Korea. Also *see* chapter 7.

13

0021

Freedom of Expression and the "Conversion" System

Another group in South Korea which faces violations of freedom of expression consists of prisoners convicted under the National Security Law and the Anti-Communist Law who are pressured to sign statements formally "converting" to anti-communism and recanting their allegedly pro-communist beliefs. Requiring prisoners to sign "conversion" statements violates their rights to freedom of expression and freedom of conscience as guaranteed by the International Covenant on Civil and Political Rights and Article 19 of the South Korean Constitution.[51]

A ranking system exists in the South Korean prisons. As an inmate serves his sentence, he moves up the ranks and is afforded better treatment, such as more frequent family visits and correspondence, as well as the possibility of being considered for parole commutation or inclusion in a presidential amnesty. Prisoners convicted under the National Security Law are not included in this ranking system unless they sign a conversion statement. Signing such a statement, however, does not necessarily guarantee improved treatment.[52]

Family members are pressured to convince prisoners to sign conversion statements, and there have been reports of ill-treatment of long-term prisoners who refuse to convert. In September and October 1989, inmates at several prisons staged hunger strikes; among their demands was a call for the abolition of the conversion system.[53]

Suh Sung, a former political prisoner who spent nineteen years behind bars and was released on parole in February 1990, provided Asia Watch with information on 57 political prisoners, all refusing to convert, held at Taejon Prison. According to Suh, 51 of them are serving life sentences. Twenty-five are between 60 and 70 years old; ten are over 70. Three prisoners have served 40 years behind bars, and 20 have spent more than 30 years in prison. Many of them are now reportedly in failing health with little hope of being released. Suh said beatings and other forms of physical and psychological pressure were employed over the years to coerce the prisoners to convert.[54]

Press and Publishing

In his inaugural address on February 25, 1988, President Roh admitted that critics had often accused his predecessors of stifling free expression "in the name of national security." When he took office, Roh ended regulations for overt censorship of the daily press, which under the Chun administration had included specific, detailed guidelines on what could and could not be published, and the press often contains articles critical of the government.

---

[51] "Everyone shall have the right to freedom of thought, conscience and religion...No one shall be subject to coercion which would impair his freedom to have or to adopt ... beliefs of his choice." Article 18, ICCPR; "All citizens shall enjoy freedom of conscience." Article 19, Republic of Korea Constitution.

[52] See *Assessing Reform* and Amnesty International, "South Korea: Long-term Political Prisoners," December 1989. The requirement to sign conversion statements was also confirmed to Asia Watch by Suh Joon-shik, chairman of Minkahyop (families of political prisoners) in an interview, Seoul, June 1990.

[53] *Ibid.*

[54] Suh Sung is the only prisoner convicted under the NSL known to have been released before the end of his sentence despite his refusal to convert. For details of his imprisonment, *See* Suh Sung, "Nineteen Years Behind Bars: My ordeal as a political prisoner in South Korea," *Asahi Monthly*, May 1990.

14

0022

According to publishers interviewed by Asia Watch, publishing companies are no longer required to register with the government and to submit manuscripts to the Ministries of Culture and Information before they are put on sale.[55] Both requirements had been used as a censorship tool to control the content of publications.[56] Books and periodicals which could not have been published before June 1987 are now published. Under the Chun administration, some 650 books were banned. The ban on 431 titles on this list was lifted in October 1987, and the decision in the cases of 181 others was entrusted to the courts. In addition, there are new guarantees and protection of the right to freedom of expression contained in the 1987 South Korean constitution and in the International Covenant on Civil and Political Rights (ICCPR) to which the Roh government acceded in July 1990.[57]

The problems that remain with censorship of the press stem largely from the fact that many of the most conscientious journalists were fired under government pressure during the Park and Chun years, and the habit of self-censorship has become ingrained. Self-censorship continues in part because of uncertainty about the consequences of ceasing it. *Hankyoreh Shinmun*, an outspoken opposition newspaper which employs many of the formerly dismissed journalists, continues to have trouble attracting corporate advertisers because "its lower income readership and politically committed coverage have branded it a newspaper of the militant working class and radical fringe."[58] The danger of being seen to support *Hankyoreh Shinmun* was underscored in 1989 by the arrest and conviction of editorial board member Professor Lee Young-hee, and by a July 12 police raid of the newspaper's offices to confiscate photographs and documents a reporter had allegedly received from National Assemblyman Suh Kyung-won after his trip to North Korea.[59]

Since 1987, reporters have been given greater access to information. But the existence of a small elite of media personnel with close proximity to those in power has been, since the time of Park Chung-hee,[60] an obstacle to accuracy in reporting, reinforcing the trend toward self-censorship. After thirty years of dictatorship, a "yardstick" measuring what was acceptable to the government has been internalized in the minds of many journalists.

---

[55] The Ministry of Culture and Information was divided in beginning of 1990 into two separate ministries.

[56] *See* Asia Watch, *Freedom of Expression in the Republic of Korea*, August 1988, pp. 37-38. However, despite the lifting of these requirements, an informed person told the Asia Watch delegation that advance copies of books still have to be filed with the relevant ministries: books with the Ministry of Culture and periodicals with the Information Ministry. Interview in Seoul, June 1990.

[57] Article 18 of the constitution guarantees the right of all citizens to "freedom of conscience"; Article 37(2) protects the freedoms of speech, press and assembly. Article 19 of the Universal Declaration of Human Rights specifies, "This right includes freedom to hold opinions without interference and to seek, receive and impart information and ideas through any media regardless of frontiers." Article 19 of the ICCPR provides similar guarantees. South Korea ratified the ICCPR with four reservations, none of which applied to this article. The ICCPR allows for "certain restrictions" in these rights, under law, "for the protection of national security or of public order...." (3)(b). The Korean constitution, in an almost identical provision, says the rights of citizens are to be restricted only "when necessary for national security, the maintenance of law and order or for public welfare;" but it adds, "Even when such restriction is imposed, no essential aspect of the freedom or right shall be violated." 1987 Constitution of the Republic of Korea, Article 37(2).

[58] Shim Jae-hoon, "A Different Drummer," *Far Eastern Economic Review*, August 23, 1990, p. 26.

[59] *See* below for details of cases of Lee and Suh. For details on the raid, see *News from Asia Watch*, "Update on Human Rights Concerns in South Korea," July 26, 1989, p. 3.

[60] Park Chung-hee was South Korea's president from 1961 until 1979.

15

0023

Access to information with respect to the civilian and military intelligence agencies and high government officials, remains restricted. Reporters, particularly cameramen and photographers, are still sometimes beaten by the police while trying to cover demonstrations. For example, a Yonhap news agency photographer and another photographer from *Hankyoreh Shinmun*, plus two others from local dailies were beaten by police while covering a demonstration in Inchon. The Yonhap photographer was trying to photograph riot police running to arrest demonstrators. He was reportedly swept up by the police squad who threw him to the ground, ten police officers trampled on him and beat him with truncheons. The other journalists were beaten when they tried to intervene.[61]

Related to the problem of journalists' access to official sources of information is the informal system of bribes reportedly paid by government ministries to the reporters assigned to cover them. Members of the press corps reportedly receive envelopes containing money -- termed *chonji* -- on a periodic basis from the ministries they cover. We were told that the sum given to the reporters varies; a former journalist said that the money is even allocated in some of the ministries' budgets as a "public relations expense." Many of the journalists we spoke with frowned upon acceptance of *chonji* and agreed that the practice should be discontinued, but there appears to be little prospect of this. In fact, we were told that newspapers calculate the ministries' bribes as part of journalists' salaries; the only exception was *Hankyoreh Shinmun*, which maintains a company policy of refusing to accept *chonji*.[62]

Foreign Correspondents

Foreign correspondents based in South Korea have special problems with respect to access to news and official sources. The Press Freedom Committee of the Seoul Foreign Correspondents Club (SFCC) believes that the attitude of officials "has always been to keep [foreign correspondents] from, rather than to help us obtain, information."[63] At the same time, we were told it was easier for a foreign correspondent to obtain an interview with certain ministers, for example. In addition, the assistant foreign minister holds a briefing each Friday at the Seoul Foreign Correspondents' Club.

Since 1987, the SFCC and the Korea Overseas Information Service (KOIS), a government agency, have engaged in a dialogue on restrictions on access imposed on the foreign media. This ongoing dialogue has been chronicled in the "Press Freedom Report" column of *The Seoul Correspondent*, the SFCC's in-house newsletter. In the June 1988 "Press Freedom Report," Joe Manguno, reporter for the *Asian Wall Street Journal* and then chair of the SFCC's Press Freedom Committee, observed, "Personal hazards, censorship and poor access to government information continue to present obstacles to foreign media working in South Korea." A Reuters correspondent had been severely beaten on April 13, 1988 by guards of former President Chun Doo-hwan while trying to cover a press conference for "local media

---

[61] *Korea Herald*, February 28, 1989. *See also* June 1988, March/April 1989, May 1989 issues of *The Seoul Correspondent*, an in-house newsletter of the Seoul Foreign Correspondents Club.

[62] *Far Eastern Economic Review* reported on August 23, 1990, "Following overseas publicity, news organizations have posted circulars banning acceptance of money or favor by journalists. But the movement has had only limited success, according to newsroom sources...(the) technique is reportedly favored by the political parties and government ministries, which so far failed to disband their notoriously cozy 'press clubs' despite criticism from within the profession and the public." "Watching the Watchdog," p. 25.

[63] Interview with Joe Manguno, *Asian Wall Street Journal*, in Seoul, June 1990.

16

0024

only," and a cameraman from Visnews, a British news organization, was hit and seriously injured by a tear gas grenade while covering a demonstration.[64]

Access to information remained a key problem. Manguno cited the following in his June 1988 report:

-- Lack of access to venues open to the Korean media, such as the presidential Blue House, Kimpo Airport VIP lounges, and even portions of President Roh's public inauguration ceremonies;
-- Restricted access to information from and about the government, particularly regarding political matters;
-- Arbitrary decisions, such as allowing print reporters at events barred to photographers or prohibiting tape recorders at events that are open to video cameras with sound.

The SFCC petitioned and met with various government and party officials to discuss their concerns. At a meeting with the SFCC in August 1988, one month before the Seoul Olympics, KOIS officials pledged to resolve the problems of foreign media access within a month's time. As of April 1990, the Press Freedom Committee remained dissatisfied with the limited measures the KOIS had taken to ostensibly fulfill their promise.[65]

The Broadcast Media

The government's tight control over the broadcast media is described in chapter 7. The Korea Broadcasting System, which has a near monopoly over television and radio, is wholly owned and operated by the state. It need only be noted here that in June 1990, a complicated and controversial White Paper was issued by the government proposing a fundamental restructuring of the South Korean broadcasting industry. It introduced the notion of privately-owned companies, as well as regional broadcasting systems and other major changes in television and radio. The White Paper called for the breakup of the two existing broadcasting systems. Stocks in the new, wholly privately-owned companies would be limited to no more than 30 percent to be owned by any individual or group. The large conglomerates would not be permitted ownership, nor would anyone associated with a conglomerate be allowed to own stock.[66]

It is not yet clear how the reorganization will proceed, or what the implications will be for freedom of expression in South Korea.

---

[64] Attacks against foreign journalists have also been carried out by demonstrators. In a March 1989 report to the SFCC's annual meeting on press freedom, Manguno wrote that SFCC had begun issuing its own armbands to members of the foreign media. He said this was necessitated by "the government practice of issuing armbands to foreign journalists -- and slipping the same foreign journalists armbands to government agents so they could get close to demonstrators and protestors. That resulted in growing mistrust by protestors of anyone wearing the government armbands.... [Since the issuance of the new armbands,] incidents of abuse dropped dramatically."

[65] See SFCC Press Freedom Report for details.

[66] Far Eastern Economic Review, Ibid.; Korea Herald, June 29, 1990.

17

0025

III. VIOLATIONS OF WORKER RIGHTS

Under Roh Tae-woo's administration, labor union activity and government repression of workers have both risen dramatically. Workers have seen the more open political atmosphere as an opportunity to make long-suppressed demands for better wages and working conditions; the government has seen the increasingly militant labor movement as both a threat to economic growth and evidence of a growing leftist ideology which imperils national security. In the clashes that have ensued, both sides have used violence. In some cases, the use of an appropriate level of force by police in controlling demonstrations may arguably have been justified.[67] But Asia Watch is concerned about a range of techniques used by the government to curb the labor movement which violate fundamental human rights. These include laws which curtail the exercise of freedom of assembly, association and expression, and arrests of workers under those laws; tacit condoning of the use by companies of goon squads to break strikes, often resulting in serious injury to workers; excessive use of force by riot police to break up workers' rallies and strikes; and physical abuse of workers in detention.

Background

Until June 29, 1987, the government's program to promote economic growth depended upon tight restrictions on the labor movement, aimed at keeping workers docile and wages low. (One scholar estimates that the hourly wage of a Korean industrial worker in the beginning of 1987 was 11 percent of his or her American counterpart and less than that of a worker in Japan, Taiwan or Hong Kong.)[68] From the time of Park Chung-hee, successive governments have regarded unions as inherently left-wing institutions; the restrictions were thus also aimed at keeping communism out of the work place.

No independent unions were allowed under President Chun Doo-hwan. Existing unions, which were virtually company-controlled, were required to join the Federation of Korean Trade Unions (FKTU), the only legal nationwide federation of trade unions, which was closely tied to the ruling Democratic Justice Party. Some of the largest corporations in the country, such as the Hyundai conglomerate, allowed no unions at all. A strict trade union law placed severe constraints on the rights to form a union, engage in collective bargaining, or take other kinds of collective action.

The institution of the *chaebol*, or conglomerate, contributed to the difficulties faced by the labor movement. Run in a hierarchical, often authoritarian manner by the founder or his family, these massive enterprises such as Hyundai, Samsung, or Daewoo used appeals to Confucian values and patriotism to demand from their workers long hours, high production levels and total obedience.

---

[67] The United Nations Code of Conduct for Law Enforcement Officials, adopted by the General Assembly on December 17, 1979, stipulates: Art. 3 "Law enforcement officials may use force only when strictly necessary and to the extent required for the performance of their duty." Commentary (a) "This provision emphasizes that the use of force by law enforcement officials should be exceptional; while it implies that law enforcement officials may be authorized to use force as is reasonably necessary under the circumstances for the prevention of crime or in effecting or assisting in the lawful arrest of offenders or suspected offenders, no force going beyond that may be used."

[68] Walden Bello and Stephanie Rosenfeld, *Dragons in Distress*, The Institute for Food and Development Policy (San Francisco: 1990), p. 24.

19

0026

Roh Tae-woo did not mention labor rights specifically in his Eight Point Reform Program of June 29, 1987. But the theme of that program, democratization, seemed to give a green light to all sectors in society to participate more actively in the political system, and workers were no exception. The June declaration became the impetus for an explosion of labor union activity, focused heavily on improving wages and working conditions, which as of October 1990 showed no signs of letting up.

Workers at the various Hyundai companies formed unions within days of the 1987 declaration. Teachers, who as public sector employees were forbidden by law to form unions at all, began to organize. Workers in the news media took the opportunity to demand that curbs on editorial freedom be lifted. In January 1989, Chonminnyon, the opposition political coalition, was inaugurated with the participation of labor leaders. These labor leaders moved to form a second federation of unions, Chonnohyop (Council of Korean Trade Unions), directly challenging the FKTU's legitimacy. Chonnohyop was formally inaugurated in January 1990.

The government response to the unprecedented wave of strikes and demonstrations, often involving violence, was initially muted. In 1987 and 1988, it is true, thousands of workers were arrested under the Law on Assembly and Demonstration and labor laws, but the government tended to leave the work of strike-breaking to company goons called *kusadae* ("company defense corps") rather than trying to intervene directly.

By the beginning of 1989, however, the government was becoming increasingly frustrated at its inability to curtail labor unrest. The government was also fearful that Chonnohyop's emergence -- as a coordinating body for the new, independent unions and alliance between workers and the dissident and student movement -- would further fuel the labor unrest anticipated with the spring collective bargaining negotiations. In April, amidst the escalating labor unrest and Chonnohyop's call for a general strike on May 1, the Joint Security Investigation Headquarters (JSIH) rounded up hundreds of union leaders and labor activists.[69] The new labor activity became not just a public order issue but an ideological one as well. As the Chun administration had blamed "radicals" for labor unrest, President Roh also indicated the need to "set stern measures to root out leftist elements from the labor movement."[70] In June, the government stepped up its campaign against the labor movement and began blaming the workers' "excessive" wage demands and strikes for the country's "gloomy" economic forecast of 7.5 percent growth in GNP for 1989. To forestall additional labor disputes over wage increases, the government said that all wage increases from then on would "be curbed at 10 percent or less."

By the beginning of 1990, the government's campaign against the workers was in full swing. Having fostered a widespread sense of economic crisis, on January 20, the government unveiled a package of tough policies aimed at curbing the labor movement. It called for ending illegal labor strikes by mobilizing police. The government move had widespread public support. An Economic Planning Board survey showed that nearly 90 percent of those polled thought the economy was in crisis, and half put the blame on strikes and excessive wage hikes.[71]

---

[69] The JSIH, composed of civilian and military security officials, was formed to investigate dissident organizations in the aftermath of Reverend Moon Ik-hwan's trip to North Korea. *See* chapter 2.

[70] *Korea News Review*, April 15, 1989, p. 3.

[71] *Korea News Review*, January 27, 1990, p. 13. The date of the survey was not given.

20

0027

But if the public supported the new measures, workers criticized them as "an effort to turn back the clock to the dark era of the past."[72] The effect of the new policies was to make labor disputes even more violent than before. When riot police intervened in the labor dispute at Hyundai Shipyard in April 1990, over 600 workers were arrested and two policemen and four workers were injured. The raid, in turn, sparked violent street demonstrations by the workers who clashed with the police. Similar violence took place when security forces clashed with members of Chonnohyop following its inauguration on January 22.

It turned out there was no economic crisis after all. Perhaps worried by a fall in the stock market caused by government-induced concern about the economic situation, President Roh declared in a televised address on May 7, "It is wrong to think we have an economic crisis on hand.... The real problem is that a pervasive sense of anxiety is making the situation more troublesome than it actually is."[73]

Laws Placing Restrictions on Worker Rights

At the same time that the Roh government was deciding to intervene more forcefully in labor disputes, it was trying to gain membership in the International Labor Organization (ILO).[74] Those efforts are ironic given that South Korea's domestic labor laws violate the fundamental principle of the right to freedom of association contained in the ILO's constitution.[75]

The three key laws in this regard are the Trade Union Law and the Labor Disputes Adjustment Law, both of which were promulgated in 1953, and the Law on Assembly and Demonstration, promulgated in 1962. The Trade Union Law and the Labor Disputes Adjustment Law were most recently amended in November 1987; the Law on Assembly and Demonstration in 1989.

Right to Form Unions

The Trade Union Law, the relevant articles of which appear in Appendix 2, restricts the right to form unions. Workers are not permitted to form a union whose potential "membership is the same as the already existing trade union" or if it is "deemed to hamper the normal operation of the already existing trade unions."[76] These provisions effectively outlaw any alternative to the company-sponsored unions or union federations existing at the time of Chun. They were used, for example, in January 1990 to declare Chonnohyop illegal.

Likewise, public servants, a category which includes government personnel, public school teachers at all levels, maintenance workers, and other miscellaneous state employees, cannot form a union unless

---

[72] *Ibid.*, p. 3.

[73] As quoted in the *Wall Street Journal*, May 8, 1990, p. A21.

[74] A country may become a member of the ILO by: 1) getting two-thirds of the votes at an ILO conference, including two-thirds of the votes of government delegates or 2) first becoming a member of the United Nations and then communicating to the Director-General of the ILO its formal acceptance of the obligations under the ILO Constitution. ILO Constitution, Art. 1(2) and (3). South Korea had observer status with the ILO and was attempting to gain membership in the United Nations, as of October 1990.

[75] "Declaration Concerning the Aims and Purposes of the International Labor Organization" (also known as the Philadelphia Declaration), *Constitution of the International Labor Organization and Standing Orders of the International Labor Conference* (Geneva: International Labor Office, January 1988), pp. 22-23.

[76] Art. 3(5).

0028

"stipulated separately by a Law."[77] No such law has been enacted. This provision, reinforced by the Civil Service Law,[78] violates an ILO convention which notes the special need for unionization in the public sector, and it has been used to declare illegal an independent teachers union called Chunkyojo. Repression against that union is described in chapter 4.[79]

Independence of Unions

The independence of unions, a corollary of freedom of association and one specifically guaranteed by the ILO Convention on Freedom of Association and Protection of the Right to Organize, is undermined in South Korea by the Trade Union Law. By terms of that law, workers who wish to form a union must receive prior authorization by relevant Labor Ministry authorities. In order to get that authorization, the workers must submit a report which contains information, among other things, on the proposed union's by-laws, membership and background of leaders. The administrative authority may refuse to certify the union based on the information contained in its report.[80] Contrary to international standards which provide for the union's autonomy, "union by-laws are subject to amendment, cancellation or supplementation by the administrative authority."[81] Government authorities may also investigate the union's internal documents when it deems necessary[82] and impose ceilings on allocation of dues.[83] Unions are prohibited from engaging in political activity.[84]

"Third-Party Interference" and Freedom of Expression

Unions are also forbidden to seek advice from a "third party." "Third-party interference," banned by both the Trade Union Law and the Labor Disputes Adjustment Act,[85] is one of the most controversial provisions in Korean labor laws and has been used to arrest hundreds of trade unionists and labor activists and prevent any organized effort to educate workers about their rights. It places severe constraints on freedom of expression. "Third parties" are defined by the Trade Union Law as:

> Persons other than a worker who has actual employment relations with the employer, or a concerned trade union, or other persons having legitimate authority under law....[86]

---

[77] Trade Union Law, Art. 8. *See also* Republic of Korea Constitution (November 1987), Art. 33(2).

[78] Art. 6.

[79] It should be noted that Korea is not alone in prohibiting teachers from forming unions. In the U.S., any teacher can legally belong to a union, but not all states allow collective bargaining. Thirty-three states have laws recognizing teachers' collective bargaining rights; in three other states, contracts are legally enforceable though there is no state law. Many states that allow collective bargaining rights impose restrictions and sanctions on strikes. American Federation of Teachers, Research Department, Washington, D.C.

[80] Trade Union Law, Arts. 13-15. The term "administrative authority" refers to the proper government authority to which unions and employers must submit all required documents and notices, as described in Appendix 2.

[81] Trade Union Law, Arts. 16 and 21.

[82] Trade Union Law, Art. 30; penal provisions in Art. 47.

[83] Trade Union Law, Art. 24.

[84] Trade Union Law, Art. 12.

[85] Trade Union Law, Art. 12(2), penal provisions in Art. 45(2); Labor Disputes Adjustment Law, Art. 13(2), penal provisions in Art. 45(2).

[86] Trade Union Law, Art. 12(2).

These third parties

shall not engage in an act of interference for the purpose of manipulating, instigating, obstructing, or otherwise influencing the concerned parties in the establishment or dissolution of a trade union, joining or withdrawing from a trade union, or in collective bargaining with the employer.[87]

The provisions against "third-party interference" in both the Trade Union Law and the Labor Disputes Adjustment Law were enacted in 1980 during a period of severe labor repression to prevent two church-related organizations, the Urban Industrial Mission and the Catholic Workers Movement from educating and organizing workers.[88] They have been used repeatedly since then. For example, in June 1990, Jang Myung-guk, the publisher of a labor magazine, was arrested under the "third-party interference" provision for a series of articles on the labor movement in South Korea (see chapter 2). In March 1989, the National Assembly amended the Trade Union Law and the Labor Disputes Adjustment Law to permit labor advisers and lawyers to advise workers without violating the "third-party" ban. The amendments were vetoed by President Roh.

Collective Bargaining and Strikes

The Trade Union Law and the Labor Disputes Adjustment Law also allow for a degree of government control over collective action that is unacceptable by ILO standards. Collective bargaining, for example, must be conducted at the enterprise level; a collective agreement is not valid beyond the individual enterprise level unless determined otherwise by the administrative authority.[89] The administrative authorities "may order changes or nullification of a term in collective agreement when the term is improper in violation of laws."[90]

The right to strike is severely constrained. Labor disputes are permitted under the Labor Disputes Adjustment Law (as amended in November 1987), as long as they concern working conditions such as wages, hours, welfare, dismissals or treatment of workers. However, "No act which suspends, discontinues or obstructs the normal maintenance and operation of safety protection facilities, of factories, work places or any other workshops shall be regarded as an act of dispute,"[91] and the administrative authority can order the suspension of acts falling under those categories. In addition, the government announced in January 1990 that strikes on "political issues," such as the release of jailed unionists, appointments of management and personnel, and relocation plans were prohibited, as were sympathy strikes. In announcing the decision, the official noted that these provisions are not legally binding but that labor

---

[87] But a federation of unions or the industrial federations affiliated with the concerned unions shall not be regarded as a "third party." This latter provision exempts the Federation of Korean trade unions from being considered an illegal "third party" in labor disputes. Republic of Korea Ministry of Labor, *Labor Laws of Korea* (Seoul, 1989), p. 5. Translation altered slightly after consulting original Korean text.

[88] Asia Watch, *Human Rights in Korea*, p. 185.

[89] The binding force of a collective agreement beyond the individual enterprise level is described in Trade Union Law, Art. 38.

[90] Trade Union Law, Art. 34(3).

[91] Art. 13-2.

23

0030

offices reportedly were ordered to refer to them.[92] According to figures provided by the Labor Ministry in February 1990, nearly 70 percent of the 1,107 labor disputes in 1989 were deemed illegal.

Before the union can engage in a strike, it must notify the administrative authority of a labor dispute[93] and then wait out the "cooling-off" period.[94] Additionally, the Minister of Labor "may render a decision for an emergency adjustment, in case an act of dispute is related to public interests, or it is of large scale or specific character, and that because of such act of dispute ... might impair the national economy or endanger the daily life of the general public."[95]

Strike-breaking

The government has used or condoned several methods of strike-breaking which are in violation of international standards on freedom of association and freedom of assembly. One is the use of special units of police in civilian clothes, called *baikgoldan* (literally translated as the "white skull brigade," a derogatory term) to forcibly break up strikes. A second is the practice of charging striking workers under a provision of the Criminal Code prohibiting "interference with business." A third is the use of *kusadae* (company goon squads) which the government appears to condone.

A company will most often call in the *baikgoldan* during the "cooling-off period." A union must notify the authorities and the company of its plan to strike.[96] Thereafter, it has to wait until the "cooling-off period" has elapsed before striking.[97] To discourage workers from going through with the strike, a company will call in the police and complain about the workers. The company can file a written complaint or, more simply, dial "112" on the telephone, the emergency number that South Koreans call to report crimes.[98] Regular police respond when ordinary crimes are reported. When a report concerns a labor problem, however, the *baikgoldan* are dispatched to the work site to harass, intimidate, and arrest the workers. The police authorities also summon workers for questioning.

Arresting striking workers on charges of violating the criminal code provision barring "interference with business"[99] has been one of the most commonly used strike-breaking methods since mid-1989.[100]

---

[92] It had always been the government's stance to prohibit strikes over such matters. The formal announcement, however, was made on January 20, 1990 after a high-level meeting. *See* chapter 4, Chonnohyop. There is no inherent ban on strikes over issues such as management appointments in international standards and laws; they are protected as a form of free association. Though such strikes are not prohibited by law in the U.S., they would be in violation of most contracts, and striking workers would not be protected by U.S. labor laws.

[93] Labor Disputes Adjustment Law, Art. 16.

[94] *Ibid.*, Art. 14.

[95] *Ibid.*, Art. 40(1). In such instances, the act of labor dispute in question must be suspended immediately. Art. 41.

[96] Labor Dispute Adjustment Law, Art. 16.

[97] Labor Dispute Adjustment Law (LDAL), Art. 14. The "cooling-off period" is 10 days for regular businesses, 15 for "business of public interest," as defined in LDAL, Art. 4.

[98] "119," similarly, is the number to report fires; "113" to report spies.

[99] See Appendix 3 for list of unionists imprisoned under this legal provision.

[100] The Republic of Korea Criminal Code Article 314 provides that: A person who interferes with the business of another .... by the threat of force, shall be punished by penal servitude for not more than five years or by a fine not exceeding twenty-five thousand Hwan [won] ($US3570)." There is no comparable law in the U.S., but under certain circumstances, unions on strike can be restrained by a court injunction from organizing picket lines or other

24

0031

A person may be arrested for posing a "threat of force," as opposed to express use of force, while interfering in the business of another. Workers who did nothing more than to sing or beat on drums while on strike have been arrested under this law.[101] For example, in April-May 1990, ten striking workers at Taehwa Dyeing Company in Taegu were arrested for beating drums outside of the plant. All were charged with "interference with business," but only one worker was additionally charged with committing physical violence.[102]

The *kusadae* function as another form of strike-breaker. Hired and trained by the individual companies, these goon squads serve as virtual corporate armies and are believed to have links with government security officers. They have been responsible for beatings, kidnappings and other forms of violence against workers. One instance of *kusadae* violence at Hyundai attracted nationwide attention and led to the arrest and prosecution of those involved (see chapter 5). But for the most part, the goons are allowed to operate with impunity. A Labor Ministry spokesman stated that companies had been told to stop using *kusadae*, but the Ministry's admonitions do not seem to have been effective.[103]

Preventing Worker Rallies

Workers are prevented from holding and participating in demonstrations and rallies which authorities consider constitute a "clear and present danger" to public order. For example, in November 1989, the government denied Chonnohyop permission to hold a rally saying that it feared violence by the participants.

In most instances, workers will hold the demonstration regardless of official approval. If the government is aware that the workers will hold a demonstration, the riot police are dispatched to blockade the rally site (and other possible alternate sites) in advance to prevent the participants from gathering. Additional riot police are deployed at railway stations, the bus terminal and other key strategic locations to turn back those coming from other areas to participate in the rallies.[104] If the demonstration is still held, rally participants are rounded up *en masse* by riot police who sometimes employ excessive force. Nearly all of those arrested are detained and sentenced under special summary proceedings authorized by the Minor Offense Punishment Act. Those accused of being the leaders or organizers of the demonstrations are formally arrested and charged under the Law on Assembly and Demonstration.

---

strike activity, under penalty of arrest.
[101] Interviews in Seoul, June 1990.
[102] Interview in Seoul, June 1990.
[103] Interview in Seoul, June 1990.
[104] *Korea Times*, January 23, 1990, in FBIS, January 26, 1990.

0032

IV. CHONNOHYOP

Chonnohyop (Council of Korean Trade Unions) was inaugurated in January 1990 despite a government ban and outstanding arrest warrants against its leaders.[105] It emerged in response to restrictions on the labor movement and quickly became one of the foremost targets in the government's suppression of that movement. Its rallies were blocked, its leaders imprisoned, and its member unions harassed.

Background

At the time of its inauguration, 600 member unions and 190,000 workers belonged to Chonnohyop. Its membership was comprised of the independent unions formed since July 1987 which sought an alternative to the pre-existing Federation of Korean Trade Unions (FKTU).[106] These unions set up links at the regional level, and in December 1988 formed the National Council of Regional and Industrial Trade Unions Association (NCRITUA). Representatives of these unions announced in February 1989 their plan to form Chonnohyop.[107] In October 1989, NCRITUA decided upon a platform that emphasized economic demands including increased wages, a 44-hour work week, and improved working conditions. They also called for the amendment of labor laws and cooperation with dissident organizations.[108]

Beginning in early November 1989, the government took steps to control Chonnohyop which was to be formally inaugurated January 22, 1990. The Labor Ministry stated that it would form an inter-ministry committee to cope with labor disputes.[109] The special committee, chaired by the vice minister of labor, would analyze the causes behind the labor unrest. The Labor Ministry reportedly also decided to conduct regular investigations of 500 firms which had been embroiled in labor unrest more than three times in the previous three years or whose labor unions had links with dissident labor organizations.

In mid-January at a meeting held at Chongwadae (the Blue House) with President Roh Tae-woo presiding, key cabinet ministers discussed a package of measures termed "countersteps to achieve industrial peace and to stabilize wages."[110] President Roh told his key ministers that "labor problems should be coped with resolutely at an early stage and forces behind illegal disputes should be subject to stern punishment."[111]

After the meeting, the Labor Ministry announced a new set of guidelines restricting the scope of "legitimate" collective action. There were four key guidelines. First, unionized workers would not be

---

[105]   For details on its inauguration, *see Asian Labour Update*, February-April 1990, p. 9.

[106]   FKTU has 7,000 member unions numbering 2 million members.

[107]   *Korea Times*, February 24, 1989, in FBIS, March 3, 1989.

[108]   *Chungang Ilb*, January 23, 1990, in FBIS, March 14, 1990. Chunkyojo (Korean Teachers and Educational Workers Union), the Technical Specialists' Union, and the Freight/Transportation Workers Union maintain observer status in Chonnohyop.

[109]   *Korea Herald*, November 1, 1989.

[110]   *Korea Herald*, January 20, 1990 in FBIS, January 24, 1990.

[111]   *Korea Herald*, January 21, 1990, in FBIS, January 24, 1990.

27

0023

allowed to stage legal strikes if they put forth "political demands," such as the release of their imprisoned union leaders, resignation of certain executives, or opposition to appointment of presidents or senior company officials. Second, unions would be prohibited from staging sympathy strikes in support of striking workers at other sites of the same company. Third, striking workers would not be paid. And fourth, workers could not launch collective actions against relocation plans.

According to the Labor Ministry, these guidelines were not legally binding, but labor offices were reportedly ordered to refer to them.[112]   Other official measures reportedly planned included mobilizing the police, either with or without the request of the companies involved, at the onset of an "illegal" strike. Labor Minister Choi Young-chul said that the government would consider invoking emergency powers if unrest at key industries became serious.[113]

On January 20, 1990, two days before the inauguration, the government officially banned Chonnohyop. Arrest warrants were issued for key Chonnohyop leaders who were accused of violating the Law on Assembly and Demonstration, the ban on "third-party interference" in labor disputes and "interference with normal operations of business." Although Chonnohyop was formally inaugurated on as planned,[114] the government's actions had their intended effect: fifty to sixty member unions dropped out of Chonnohyop.[115]

The Legal Issue

The ban on Chonnohyop was based in part on Article 3(5) of the Trade Union Law which prohibits the formation of a union at any level that would compete for membership with a preexisting union.[116]   Korean law recognizes three levels of union: the company union, the single industry federation (such as the Korean Metalworkers Federation) and the cross-industry federation. Until Chonnohyop's emergence, the FKTU was the only federation in the country to consist of both company and industry-wide unions. Chonnohyop broke that monopoly; the government feared that it would compete for membership with FKTU and that any such competition would only further fuel labor disputes.

Asia Watch believes that Article 3(5) itself restricts the right to freedom of association and should be repealed. The ban on Chonnohyop is in clear violation of international standards which safeguard the right to establish and join federations.[117]   International standards also state, "The acquisition of legal personality by workers'...federations and confederations shall not be subject to conditions" that infringe on the workers' right to freedom of association.[118] Chonnohyop's leaders, however, challenged the ban on other grounds. The federation claimed that it was a consultative committee, not a national union

---

[112] *Korea Herald*, January 21, 1990.

[113] *Korea Herald*, January 20 and 29, 1990.

[114] Dan Byung-ho was elected chairman. Forty-two Central Committee members appointed, including nine vice-chairmen among whom were Kim Young-dae, Chairman of the Seoul Association of Workers' Unions (also chair of the Chonggye apparel labor union); Choi Dong-sik, Chairman of Inchon Association of Workers' Unions; and Kwon Yong-mok, Chairman of the Hyundai unions in Ulsan. *Korea Herald*, January 21, 1990.

[115] Interview in Seoul, June 1990. Also, *Korea Times*, February 7, 1990 in FBIS, February 12.

[116] *See* Appendix 2 for text of the law.

[117] "Workers' ... organizations shall have the right to establish and join federations and confederations." Art. 5, ILO Convention (No. 87) concerning Freedom of Association and Protection of the Right to Organize, adopted by the General Conference of the ILO July 9, 1948 and effective July 4, 1950.

[118] Art. 7, ILO Convention 87, cited above.

28

0034 .

federation and, therefore, did not need to register or obtain government certification in order to operate legally.

Right to Assembly

One of the ways in which the government has suppressed Chonnohyop has been to deny its members the right to assemble. The police blocked a November 12, 1989 rally planned by Chonnohyop to promote their right to organize and to demand the release of Choe Tong-shik, 28, the chairman of Chonnohyop's Inchon chapter. On the next day, 47,000 Chonnohyop-affiliated workers from 95 companies staged one-day or half-day strikes to protest what they alleged was police suppression of their legal union activities.[119] The authorities said they had blocked the rally because they feared violence by the participants, although an FKTU-organized rally had been permitted to take place at the same site only a week before.[120]

Chonnohyop was forced to change its inaugural site to the Suwon campus of Sunggyunkwan University because the originally planned site, Seoul National University, was blocked off by police.[121] But even at the new site, the rally was aborted after 20 minutes as some 600 riot police, firing tear gas, charged into the campus to break it up.[122]

On March 18, Chonnohyop held rallies in five big cities, including Seoul, Inchon and Taegu. Some 15,000 riot police were mobilized around the country to prevent the rallies. Yonsei University, the original site for the protests, was sealed off by riot police, who were posted on roads and outside subway stations around the campus. The police detained a total of 1,552 protesters.[123] According to the same news report, all except seven were released on the following day with admonitions. Four were referred to summary courts, and three were still being questioned as of June 1990.

Arrests

The government has tried to inhibit the new federation's activities by arresting its leaders. According to Amnesty International, 136 persons were arrested at Chonnohyop's January 22 inauguration rally.[124] Dan Byung-ho, the federation's chairman who had been wanted by the police since December, managed to evade arrest that day. But at the beginning of February, the National Police Headquarters (NPH) announced that it had ordered all police stations around the country to arrest Dan "by every means available" before March 3. Special investigation squads were reportedly set up at police stations, and special probing teams planned to make house-to-house searches. Temples, churches, inns and apartment houses for bachelors were also to be searched.[125] On February 28, Dan was arrested during an on-the-

---

[119] *Korea Herald*, November 18, 1989. The figure was provided by the Labor Ministry.

[120] Yonhap, December 13, 1989, in FBIS, same day.

[121] *Korea Herald*, January 23, 1990.

[122] *Korea Herald*, January 23, 1990. Police were also reportedly deployed around railroad stations and bus terminal to turn back those coming from other areas to participate in the Chonnohyop rally. *Korea Times*, January 23, 1990, in FBIS, January 26, 1990.

[123] Yonhap, March 19, 1990 in FBIS, March 20, 1990.

[124] Amnesty International, ACT 73/03/90 March 1990.

[125] *Korea Times*, February 7, 1990, in FBIS, February 12, 1990

spot check on the street.[126] In July, he was convicted under the Law on Assembly and Demonstration and sentenced to one-and-a-half years' imprisonment.

On May 3, the prosecutor's office announced the names of thirty-two Chonnohyop leaders and heads of Chonnohyop-affiliated unions who were being investigated or sought for arrest.[127] Fourteen Chonnohyop leaders were on a wanted list, including Kim Yong-tae, acting president, Hyon Chu-ok, vice president; Kim Hak-tu, auditor; and Choe Tong-sik, secretary-general.[128]

Harassment of Member Unions

To further erode support for Chonnohyop, on February 1, 1990 the Ministry of Labor launched a fifteen-day probe into 160 member unions of Chonnohyop to find out whether they misappropriated funds for "ideological purposes."[129] According to the Trade Union Law, "When it is deemed necessary, the Administrative Authority may have the accounting status or other necessary documents of the trade union submitted for investigation."[130] Anyone violating that provision may be jailed for up to three months and fined.[131]

On March 13, the government arrested Kim Un-im and Kim Young-sun, leaders of the union at Samsung Pharmaceutical Industrial Company for refusing to hand over union office papers to the authorities.[132] Hanyang University Hospital union leader Cha Su-yon, who had twice refused to submit union papers to the authorities, evaded arrest that day. But as of early October, she was also under arrest for violation of the Trade Union Law. The labor authorities began a probe of 24 independent unions with significant roles in Chonnohyop. The leaders of 13 of the 24 unions were accused of violating the Trade Union Law. When some of the leaders under investigation refused to submit the requested documents, they were arrested.[133]

The prosecutors' office also announced that it had booked chairmen of some fifty trade unions, most of whom belonged to Chonnohyop. They were charged with violating the labor laws by obstructing the government's investigations into their union's internal affairs.[134]

---

[126] *Korea Herald*, March 1, 1990.

[127] *Korea Herald*, May 4, 1990, in FBIS, same day.

[128] Other Chonnohyop activists being investigated or sought for arrest were: Choe Yong-min, president of the Kangwon Industrial Company union; Kim Pyong-oh, president of the Hyosung Machinery Company union; Kim Kyong-man, a leader of the Dalim Motor Company union; Kim Chong-hun and two other leaders of the Tongil Company union. Eleven others had already been arrested for their membership in or affiliation with Chonnohyop.

[129] *Korea Times*, February 2, 1990, in FBIS, same day.

[130] Art. 30.

[131] Article 47, Trade Union Law states: "Any person who, in violation of the provisions of Article 30, failed to submit the required documents or filed false report, or who refuses, obstructs or obviates investigation, shall be subjected to an imprisonment for the term not exceeding three months or a fine for the amount not exceeding 200 thousand *won*."

[132] Yonhap, March 14, 1990, in FBIS, same day.

[133] *Korea Times*, March 14, 1990, in FBIS, March 16, 1990.

[134] Yonhap, March 14, 1990, in FBIS, same day.

May Day Response

In March, to protest the suppression of their rallies, Chonnohyop decided to stage a walkout on May Day. By the end of March, however, member unions of Chonnohyop decided not to walk off their jobs. Instead, it planned to stage a "reduced commemorating ceremony" and to co-sponsor several cultural events on that day with the rival FKTU. It also showed a flexible stance on its demand for 23.3 percent pay increase.[135] A spokesman for the independent workers' federation said, "Chonnohyop leaders reached the conclusion that flexible and multilateral strategies are the only way to obtain its long-term goals."[136]

Subsequent developments at Hyundai Heavy Industries and the Korean Broadcasting System changed that stance. Following raids by riot police to break up the strikes at Hyundai and KBS, Chonnohyop called for a nationwide general strike on May 1.[137]

---

[135] *Korea Times*, March 31, 1990, in FBIS, April 3, 1990.

[136] *Ibid.*

[137] Workers' day in South Korea is commemorated on March 10. The government refuses to recognize May Day, which was banned in mid-1950s by the Syngman Rhee government. This year, the government intended to partially lift the ban on May Day celebrations In a compromise agreement with union leaders, the government said it would allow a rally in a Seoul gymnasium on May 1 in exchange for the cancellation of all other outdoor and indoor celebrations. Yonhap, April 12, 1990, in FBIS, same day. [137]

31

0037

V. HYUNDAI

Background

The Hyundai Group, founded in 1947, produces most of Korea's automobiles and ships and a variety of other industrial products. Twelve of its 45 subsidiaries, including Hyundai Engine, Hyundai Shipbuilding, Hyundai Motors and Hyundai Heavy Industries, are located in the port city of Ulsan and employ some 70,000 people.

Hyundai's fortunes got a mammoth boost in the late 1970s when President Park Chung-hee embarked on a new economic strategy favoring heavy and chemical industries (HCI). Its rapid growth was due in part to the economic incentives that accompanied the new strategy but also to its policy of keeping wages low and hours long. Hyundai's authoritarian founder, Chung Ju-yung, is said to run the congolmerate like a "boot camp," demanding regulation uniforms and haircuts and absolute obedience from his workers.[138]

If the HCI strategy catapulted Hyundai into the forefront of Korea's economic development program, it also meant that Hyundai workers would be at the forefront of the labor movement when controls on union organizing were eased in 1987. The first union at a Hyundai company was formed at Hyundai Engine on July 4, 1987, only five days after Roh Tae-woo's democratization declaration.

Workers at other Hyundai firms in Ulsan soon followed suit, and in August 1987, unions at the 12 Ulsan-based firms formed an Association of Unions at Hyundai to coordinate their efforts. The man they elected chair, Kwon Yong-mok, founder of the path-breaking union at Hyundai Engine, became one of the most important trade union leaders in South Korea and was in and out of jail ever after. Hyundai management tried to control the new unions through bribes, threats, and infiltration. At Hyundai Heavy Industries, for example, the company conceded in August 1987 to workers' demands for recognition of rank-and-file elected union leaders. But only a few weeks later the same union leaders were arrested and held responsible for the workers' riot at Ulsan City Hall. While they were in jail, Hyundai managed to fill their union positions with more pliable individuals. When they sought to regain their jobs and union offices after their release, they set off a chain of events which led to collective actions. The company and the government aggravated the situation by blaming only the "militant" faction for the labor unrest, jailing the leaders once again and setting the stage for the massive industrial actions that characterized the next three years.

Independent Unions and Dismissals

The right to an independent union and the right not to be dismissed for engaging in union activity are essential components of freedom of association. ILO conventions, for example, state that workers shall be protected from acts of anti-union discrimination, including acts calculated to "cause the dismissal of

---

[138] Walden Bello and Stephanie Rosenfeld, *Dragons in Distress*, The Institute for Food and Development Policy (San Francisco: 1990) pp. 29, 41.

0038

or otherwise prejudice a worker by reason of union membership or because of participation in union activities outside working hours...."[139]

In the Hyundai disputes, with rare exceptions, the government, using provisions of the Trade Union Law, acted in concert with Hyundai management to curb those rights. A pattern was established in August 1987 during the first violent clashes between the new unions and the government. Key elements of the pattern were as follows: workers would demand higher wages, better working condition, and, after the first strikes, the release of arrested union leaders and reinstatement of workers dismissed for their participation in strikes. The companies would either refuse (which led to collective actions) or agree to negotiate. Failure of the negotiations would also lead to collective action. The government would declare such action "political" and therefore illegal, riot police would be called in, workers and police would clash, and union leaders would be arrested or dismissed. Their arrest would lead to new demands for their release or reinstatement, and a whole new chain of events would begin.

The August 1987 Clash

Because the August 1987 clash set the pattern for subsequent disputes, it is worth noting in some detail. That month, after Hyundai refused to recognize the new unions at the twelve Hyundai firms or their Association of Unions at Hyundai, some 40,000 workers went on strike in Ulsan, and Hyundai imposed lock-outs at six of its firms.[140] The government, still committed to the democratization process, intervened on behalf of the workers. Appearing at a strikers' rally held on August 19, Labor Vice Minister Han Jin-hee announced that the government had managed to persuade the Hyundai Group to recognize the worker-elected unions and the new association. He also promised that the government would not punish those who played key roles in the labor disputes and that the issue of wage increases would be settled by September 1.[141]

Although Hyundai initially denied that there had been an agreement, it agreed to recognize the association. Hyundai also agreed to secure recognition for the newly-elected independent union at Hyundai Heavy Industries.[142] But the wage negotiations became deadlocked, provoking strikes and violence at four of the Hyundai firms, Hyundai Heavy Industries, Mipo Dockyards, Precision and Motors. According to news accounts, on September 3 about 300 workers, mostly from Hyundai Heavy Industries, stormed Ulsan city hall, set cars on fire and ransacked offices.[143] The government arrested nearly 300 strikers, including fifteen union leaders at Hyundai Heavy Industries.[144] Domestic human rights monitors and opposition politicians charged that the government was exaggerating the level of violence to justify the crackdown.[145]

---

[139] International Labor Organization, "Convention Concerning the Application of the Principles of the Right to Organize and to Bargain Collectively," Article 1.

[140] *Korea Herald*, August 18, 1987; *see* articles of the same date in *The New York Times, Washington Post*, and the *Los Angeles Times*.

[141] Yonhap, August 19, 1987, in FBIS, same day.

[142] *New York Times*, August 19, 1987; Yonhap, September 2, 1987, quoted in FBIS, same day.

[143] *Korea Herald*, September 3, 1987; *Washington Post*, September 3, 1987; *New York Times*, September 4, 1987.

[144] *Washington Post*, September 4, 1987; *Korea Herald*, September 7, 1987; *Los Angeles Times*, September 5, 1987.

[145] *Korea Herald*, September 4, 1987; *New York Times*, September 7, 1987, also noted that the Korean government, abetted by the South Korean press, exaggerated the level of violence by the striking workers.

34

0039

The government had no hesitation about charging the strikers with violations of the law, and the Hyundai management equally readily sacked those charged, then claimed that as they were no longer workers at the firm, they could not hold union positions. The government and Hyundai management together made two not fully successful attempts to use the arrests as a pretext for replacing the union leaders with more pro-company individuals.

In the first attempt, on September 10, 1987, Hyundai Heavy Industries requested that the Ulsan City administration order the disbandment of the present union leadership.[146] The company stated that fifteen of the union's twenty leaders, including union president Lee Hyong-kon, were in jail in connection with the September 3 violence, and it refused to negotiate with the "interim" leadership of the union. The city denied the request stating that the company's reasons were insufficient. As 5,000 workers protested the company's move,[147] Hyundai made a second request a day later. This time city officials reversed themselves, reportedly at the Home Ministry's instructions,[148] and forwarded their decision upholding Hyundai's request to the Kyongsangnam-do provincial government and its Labor Committee for a final decision.

On September 17, the Kyongsangnam-do Labor Committee voted to order the reelection of current labor leaders, and the next day, the Kyongsangnam-do provincial government issued an administrative order to Lee Hyong-kon, in police custody, for the reorganization of the union leadership.[149] When the Labor Committee's decision was handed down, the workers voted to protest it. They turned down a proposal to resume operations by September 21 because, the union stated, the proposal "includes non-recognition of the current labor union leadership."[150]

On September 19, Hyundai Heavy Industries reversed its earlier position and met with ten members of the union's interim leadership.[151] They reached a four-point agreement in which management agreed to try and secure the release of the jailed unionists, who would be allowed to return to work upon their release. Work resumed three days later.

The second attempt was aimed at one individual in particular. Kwon Yong-mok was arrested in November 1987 for his role in leading the August protests. Hyundai Engine workers began a movement to secure his release, but the company responded by dismissing two other union leaders at Hyundai Engine. Kwon himself was dismissed on February 4, 1988 after a district court sentenced him to a one-year prison term, suspended for two years, on charges of leading protests.[152] On February 15, a district court ruled that Kwon could not be a candidate for president of the union at Hyundai Engine because he no longer worked for the company. The next day the workers at Hyundai Engine elected him anyway.

---

[146] *Korea Times*, September 11, 1987, in FBIS, same day.

[147] *Korea Herald*, September 12, 1987.

[148] *Korea Times*, September 12, 1987, in FBIS, September 15. In contrast, the National Police Headquarters (NPH) stated on September 15 that it opposed replacing the current union leadership "as it may aggravate the protracted labor strife... [and] that the government order is sure to backfire and aggravate public opinion." *Korea Times*, September 16, 1987, in FBIS, same day. The NPH asked the Kyongsangnam-do Labor Committee not to order the disbandment.

[149] *Korea Times*, September 18, 1987, in FBIS, same day.

[150] *Korea Times*, September 18, 1987, in FBIS, same day.

[151] Yonhap, September 22, 1987, in FBIS, September 23.

[152] *Korea Herald*, March 1, 1988.

0040

The company refused to recognize the new union leadership because it included Kwon. He in turn challenged the company's position, stating that his dismissal could not be effective until a higher court ruled on his appeal. On February 26, hundreds of Hyundai Engine workers protested and began a sit-down strike. The next day, Hyundai Engine was forced to suspend its operation. Kwon and some 90 fellow workers barricaded themselves in the fifth floor of the Hyundai Engine company's office building, vowing to stay there until the company recognized the new union leadership. On March 16, the company requested negotiations with them. Kwon and two other union leaders went down to talk with the management. But word spread among workers outside of the building that Kwon had been kidnapped by company officials.[153] The workers protested, and in the ensuing confusion a security guard for the company was hit on the head and killed with a stone thrown from the roof of the building.[154] At this point Kwon and the other two union leaders stopped the negotiations and rejoined the protestors. The police accused Kwon of having incited the workers and immediately launched a manhunt to apprehend him. On March 27, Kwon was arrested once again. The protest petered out, and the workers returned to work.[155]

More Arrests and Dismissals

In December 1988, more strikes broke out at Hyundai Heavy Industries and lasted 128 days. The strike was crushed with a massive show of force by riot police. Nearly 700 workers were rounded up, but most were released after questioning.[156] Some were sentenced to short prison terms and dismissed from their jobs. In response to work slowdowns protesting the dismissals, however, Hyundai eventually reinstated them.

Six of the arrested workers from Hyundai Heavy Industries were in danger of being sentenced to longer terms. The company acceded to worker pressure and pledged to ask the prosecution to seek lesser sentences for them. When the trials were over, one worker was released and five were given sentences ranging from two and one-half to three years' imprisonment. But at the appeals hearings before the Pusan Appellate Court in February 1990, the prosecution requested that the sentences be increased. The prosecution demanded that Kim Chin-kuk, a former union vice president, be sentenced to five years in prison, three more years than it had demanded in lower court.[157] The prosecution demanded an eight-year sentence for O Chong-sae, also a union leader, although it had previously demanded a two-year sentence.[158] The workers believed that the company reversed its earlier pledge and used its influence to persuade the prosecution to demand tougher sentences.[159] Some 20,000 workers staged a walkout in protest, and the next day, refused to go back to work. The company complained to the police that the workers were "interfering with the normal operation of business."[160]

---

[153] Ogle, p. 244.
[154] *Korea Herald*, March 17, 1988.
[155] Although it is unclear when Kwon was released from jail, he addressed workers at a gathering held on April 1, 1989, after the 128-day strike was broken up. For this, he was once again sought for arrest on the charge of "third-party interference." Kwon was in hiding for 11 months before being arrested in March 1990. *See* section on "third party interference" in chapter 3.
[156] *Korea Times*, April 2, 1989, in FBIS, April 4.
[157] *Korea Herald*, February 8, 1990, in FBIS, February 13, 1990.
[158] *Ibid.*
[159] *Korea Herald*, February 8, 1990, in FBIS, February 13.
[160] "Interference with the conduct of business" is a violation of Article 314 of the Criminal Code. *See* chapter 3.

36

Lee Young-hon, the newly elected union leader at Hyundai Heavy Industries who called for the walkout, asked the workers to go to Pusan to protest the sentencing. Anticipating that the police might try to prevent a demonstration in Pusan, Lee himself decided to travel there the day before. But he was stopped at a roadblock and arrested under an outstanding arrest warrant. The next day, while some 4,000 workers protested in front of the court in Pusan against Lee's arrest and the anticipated sentencing of the six others, the judge entered the courtroom, read off the sentences, and left the room. The workers called for a new strike.

During March-April 1990, all twelve of the Hyundai Group's Ulsan firms struck in rotation. The vice-chairman on strike participated in the demonstrations, and each chair was then, in turn, arrested. Most were charged with "interference with normal operations." Again, the arrests seemed to be a way of preventing top union leaders from engaging in organizing efforts.

The April 20 arrest of U Ki-ha, senior vice-chairman of the union at Hyundai Shipbuilding, sparked the shipyard workers' anger and provoked a spontaneous strike action.[161] They were joined by workers from the Heavy Industries, Motors, and other sections of Hyundai as well as by workers from non-Hyundai companies in Ulsan whose union leaders had also been arrested. On April 28, more than 10,000 riot troops raided the Heavy Industries, clashed with strikers and detained nearly 700 workers.[162] Sympathy strikes broke out. At the Hyundai Shipyards, 100 workers staged a hunger strike atop a huge shipbuilding crane to demand the release of their co-workers and the withdrawal of the riot police. Their hunger strike continued until the end of May when normal operations resumed at all the Hyundai companies. The storming once again of the world's largest shipyard by riot police sparked international headlines and editorials. *The New York Times* queried: "Is this the new democratic South Korea?"[163]

Use of Goon Squads *(Kusadae)*

Links between *kusadae* and government security forces were conclusively demonstrated in what has come to be known as the "James Lee Terror Incident" involving one of Hyundai's goons. Evidence of the links hardly came as a surprise. Contact between management of the *chaebols* (conglomerates) and police is known to be close, and the Korean intelligence organization reportedly includes the Committee to Combat Labor Insurgency, originally set up by the Korean Central Intelligence Agency and maintained by its successors.[164] Perhaps because of the severity of the violence in the James Lee case and Lee's status as a permanent legal resident of the U.S., this case is one of the few where the perpetrators were arrested and prosecuted. In most cases, the goons go free.

James (Yun-sop) Lee, a forty-year-old Korean-American, was hired by some Hyundai executives in January 1989 to train some 100 "pro-management" Hyundai workers and launch a violent assault

[161] Reuters, April 27, 1990. The Shipbuilding section employees 8,000 persons.
[162] Reuters, April 30, 1990.
[163] "Stutter-step Democracy in Korea," *New York Times* editorial, May 4, 1990. The editorial warned that the government's "violent assaults on labor" had steadied the shaky stock market but risked "setting off a dangerous backlash." The *Times* also observed that "in light of the importance of U.S. economic and military ties with Korea, any threat of a return by Seoul to the discredited repressive ways of the past is a legitimate cause for U.S. concern."
[164] Bello and Rosenfeld, *Dragons in Distress*, p.33

against the union leaders.[165] On January 8, Lee and a group of thugs went to a meeting of Hyundai union leaders and brutally beat those present. Afterwards, about thirty of them raided the offices of an organization of fired Hyundai workers and supporters called the Association of Dismissed Hyundai Workers. There they beat up five persons, including Kwon Yong-mok. Kwon's right arm was so severely broken in the attack that bone had to be removed from his hip to repair it.

Chon Chang-su, one of the workers seriously injured that night, reportedly said that "the attackers carrying about 20 torches [sic] ... dragged him and his colleagues outside their room, forced them to place their heads on the ground before taking pictures and beating them."[166] Other victims said that the attackers shouted "Kill the bastards" while beating them with baseball bats. The attackers also beat them when they refused to chant "Our father is Kim Il-sung," as ordered.[167]

James Lee's involvement came to light when one of the assailants was caught and eight others surrendered to the police.[168] Kim Nam-so, one of the arrested goons, told the police that he purchased wooden sticks including four baseball bats for the assault. Lee admitted that he gave Kim 400,000 won (about US$570) to carry out the attack in order "to discipline militant workers who 'inflict much harm' on a majority of shipyard workers."[169]

Curiously, all of the nine arrested were identified by the company as current or former "labor representatives" at Hyundai companies. The nine claimed that "neither management nor outside forces were involved in the incident."[170] A police investigation revealed, however, that top level management at Hyundai was directly responsible for the assault as well as subsequent attempts to cover up the high-level involvement. Han Yu-dong, a managing director in charge of personnel management at the Hyundai Group's Planning Office, had ordered three buses to transport the *kusadae* to the site of the assault. He was later charged with planning it.[171] To Yong-hoe, director of the Hyundai Group Human Resources Development Institute, was also questioned by police. The nine attackers had a meeting with To before their surrender to the police, according to the investigators.[172]

On January 17, members of the National Assembly's Labor Committee went to Ulsan to investigate the assaults. In the course of their investigation, they uncovered evidence of direct police complicity. According to an account in the *Korea Herald*, Sergeant Lee Sang-gu, chief the Ulsan Police Station's Sangbuk substation, said that on January 8 at 1:30 a.m., the night of the assaults against Hyundai unionists, he stopped three buses which had their license plates covered with tape. He ordered James Lee out of one of the buses and questioned him. Lee then telephoned Superintendent Kim Yong-gap, the intelligence chief at the police station. Sergeant Lee said he did not know what James Lee had said to

---

[165] *Korea Herald*, January 10, 1989; *see also Korea Times*, January 10, 11, and 18, 1989, in FBIS, January 18, 1989; Yonhap, January 11, 12, and 18, 1989 in FBIS, January 18, 1989. Lee's activities on behalf of Hyundai and Samsung are also discussed in Ogle, pp. 245-251 and pp. 254-5.

[166] *Korea Herald*, January 10, 1989.

[167] *Korea Herald*, January 10, 1989. Kim Il-sung is the president of the DPRK (North Korea).

[168] A source close to the Hyundai union told Asia Watch that the Hyundai Group had paid James Lee four million *won* (US$5,700) to carry out the attacks because he was known to have "a good technique for breaking things up." We are, however, unable to verify the figure. Interview in Ulsan, June 1990.

[169] *Korea Herald*, January 11, 1989.

[170] *Korea Herald*, January 10, 1989.

[171] *Korea Herald*, January 15, 1989.

[172] *Korea Herald*, January 11, 1989.

38

0043

Kim but that he had let the buses pass on Kim's orders. According to the account of the National Assembly investigation, Kim was quoted as having said to Sergeant Lee: "You must keep secret what happened at the police box because police may be suspected of intervention in the case."

Superintendent Kim admitted that he ordered Sergeant Lee to let the buses pass but said that "since Lee Yun-sop [James] gave his identity," he "assumed that those on board were trying to hold talks with militant unionists."[173]

James Lee received a prison term of one year after a trial in April 1989.[174] He was released in January 1990 and has resumed goon squad activity in Inchon, although we have no information as to who his current employers are. Others also received minor sentences. Han Yu-dong, a Hyundai company executive was sentenced to one year for his involvement in the assault.[175] Kim Nam-so, one of the key assailants, received the longest sentence of one year and six months' imprisonment.[176] Thirty-one other workers who took part in the assault were given suspended sentences and released.

Kidnappings

The *kusadae* have also been responsible for kidnappings of union leaders. Kim Hyong-kwon, a leader of the Hyundai Heavy Industries union, told a reporter for the *Christian Science Monitor* that some 30 company-hired men tried to kidnap him in September 1987.[177] Kim said that he had gone to the headquarters of another Hyundai union when suddenly a "gang of about 30 company goons burst in, grabbed him, hustled him into a waiting van." Workers witnessing this incident rushed to the van and rescued Kim and grabbed seven goons. They took the seven to the police; six of them were released due to lack of evidence.

In May 1988, So Chong-hui, a 37-year-old assistant manager at the Hyundai Engineering and Construction Company, was kidnapped by goons hired by the Hyundai Group. According to reports in the *Korea Herald*, So had been attempting to form a trade union for white collar workers at Hyundai, and Hyundai executives were pressuring him to give up his efforts.[178] On May 6 he was abducted by five persons outside a saloon in Yongdong after meeting with Choi Che-dong, a Hyundai director. At home in Seoul on May 11, So said that he had been kidnapped by five people, blindfolded and driven to an inn in Mokpo where he had been held for five days. According to So, the kidnappers told him that they had

---

[173] *Korea Herald*, January 18, 1989. On January 20, the National Police Headquarters announced that Superintendent Kim would be removed from his position, and possibly fired after the prosecution completed its investigation. The prosecution, in the meantime, announced that it would seek an arrest warrant for Kim for not taking any action to prevent the incident when he knew a clash was imminent. Prosecutors said that Superintendent Kim received a tip ten hours before the attack that the Hyundai workers were planning to hold the meeting at a particular bungalow, and he had even dispatched his subordinate Senior Patrolman Kim Tu-hwan to monitor their activities. Ulsan police chief Senior Superintendent Kwon Chung-su was also removed from his position by the National Police Headquarters. The prosecutors said that Kwon would be arrested if it was found that he had been notified of a possible clash but failed to take any action. *Korea Herald*, January 21, 1989.
[174] *Korea Herald*, April 25, 1989.
[175] *Korea Herald*, April 25, 1989.
[176] *Ibid.*
[177] "South Korea Unions: A Potent Voice Shaping Democracy Debate," *Christian Science Monitor*, September 21, 1987.
[178] *Korea Herald*, May 11, 1988.

39

been paid 17 million *won* (US$24,300) by an unnamed person. His abductors forced him to write a letter of resignation and freed him when he complied.[179]   Hyundai president Chun Hun-mok denied any involvement of Hyundai officials in the kidnapping, but among the ten persons who were convicted and drew light sentences on July 30 for their roles in the abduction were two company officials: Kang Myung-gu, chief of the Hyundai Construction Company's General Affairs Department and Choi Che-dong, a company director.[180]

Treatment of Detained Unionists

In addition to the violations of their freedom of association, Hyundai workers have also had to face physical abuse and ill-treatment in detention. The Hyundai unionists arrested in connection with the April-May 1990 strikes were reportedly mistreated both at the Ulsan Nambu Police Station and the Pusan Pre-trial Detention Center where they were being held as of June 1990. [181]

Ulsan Nambu (South Section) Police Station

Normally, prisoners awaiting trials are kept in pre-trial detention centers, but Ulsan does not have one. Hence, the Hyundai workers were kept in the lock-up facilities at the Nambu Police Station along with common criminals, who reportedly extorted "entrance fees" from the unionists in the form of clothes and other goods brought by their family members. [182]   If the unionists refused, the criminals would beat them. But even if they paid the "entrance fee," they were beaten, albeit less severely.

Relatives of the detained workers felt that at best the police had lost control of the situation in the lock-up or were "like the monkey who closes his eyes." At worst, the families feared the police were encouraging or abetting this practice. When the family members initially complained to the police, they were told that extortion of "entrance fees" was a standard practice in the jail and that the unionists should simply handle it by paying up.

Not satisfied with the police response, members of the Family Association of Imprisoned Hyundai Workers picketed outside the main Hyundai complex gate for ten days in May to protest the mistreatment of workers and the violence in the police lock-up facility.[183]   On May 28, the association released a statement on the prison conditions. The protest and the statement generated publicity on national television, thereby attracting the attention of the police officials. The chief investigator called the families and asked them why they were making trouble. He told them that they should try to resolve the problem without creating so much trouble.   Yet the outside pressure had some effect.   Within a day of the association's public statement, on May 29, the workers were given a separate room where they could eat by themselves.   In South Korean prisons, as in most other prisons, meals are centrally prepared and

---

[179] *Korea Herald*, May 12, 1988.

[180] *Korea Herald*, May 22, 1988.

[181] Information gathered in Ulsan and Seoul, June 1990. Asia Watch has raised the following cases with South Korean officials and their responses are noted in this section. We also raised these cases with the U.S. Embassy officials in Seoul; their responses are noted in the U.S. policy chapter.

[182] Interview in Ulsan with the workers' families, June 1990.

[183] The Association was formed in May 1990 after the most recent strikes were broken up and union leaders jailed. It is composed primarily of women whose husbands, sons or brothers are imprisoned. Its predecessor was called the Association of Dismissed Hyundai Workers.

40

portions allocated by inmate-workers. Before the measure, the common criminals prevented the unionists from getting their share of the food. But now they could eat in peace and supplement their diet by buying private food without fear of having it snatched away.[184]

The common criminals continued to extort goods from the workers, however. After the chief investigator met with the protesting family members on May 29, he instructed the clerk not to accept packages brought for the workers. This angered the common criminals. They blamed the families for the discontinuation of the goods and, in retaliation, beat the jailed workers.[185] In one incident in early June, the workers were beaten during the regular visiting hours, forcing officials to abruptly halt all visits for half an hour. The unionists were reportedly refused access to medical care after they were beaten.

All persons awaiting trial in South Korea fall under the jurisdiction of the Justice Ministry. However, Lee Sun-kil, Director of the Security Division at the Justice Ministry, maintained that the violence against the unionists detained at the Ulsan police station was not his division's responsibility.[186] The internal affairs of the police stations fall under the jurisdiction of the Ministry of Home Affairs, he said.

Cho Chu-nam: Beating in Prosecutor's Office

Another account of abuse involves a Hyundai worker named Cho Chu-nam. All of the following information comes from a source who asked to remain anonymous. In May 1990, Cho, a union official, was beaten in the presence of a prosecutor for his refusal to sign a prepared statement on the charges against him. Cho was in the office of Chung Pyong-t'ae, Ulsan regional prosecutor No. 330, when he was asked to sign the statement. When he refused, Choi Chong-gi, prosecutor Chung's clerk, beat him. Chung, who was present throughout, then told Cho to cross out the parts of the statement he did not agree with and sign it. When Cho crossed out everything of importance, he was forced to stand with his hands in the air for one hour. Afterwards, when he still refused to sign a statement that was satisfactory to the prosecutor, he was beaten again. This time, the clerk stomped on Cho's head five times with his boots and kicked Cho in the mouth, causing swelling and lacerations. Cho was unable to eat for three days. Although Cho was also promised medical attention, he did not receive any.

When Cho's relatives found out about the beating and complained about the mistreatment, his case was moved to another prosecutor's office in Yangsan. The beating was not investigated. Chang Yun-suk, the Director of the Prosecution Division at the Justice Ministry, said that he was unaware of the incident.[187] He stressed that such mistreatment was forbidden by law, but said that if the clerk had hit Cho, he must have done so for a reason.

---

[184] The prisoners are permitted to spend 1,000 won/day (US$1.50) on private food.

[185] The Asia Watch delegation accompanied several Hyundai family members to the Ulsan Nambu Police Station and observed the procedures and conditions for visits. Visiting conditions are the same for all detainees at the police station. Regular visiting hours are 10 a.m.-noon and 2-4 p.m., Monday through Friday; on Saturday, 2-4 p.m.; no visits allowed on Sunday. Visitors are usually allowed 3-5 minutes per visit and speak to the prisoner over an interphone. Dark glass windows with bars separate the prisoners from their visitors making it possible only to see the outline of the person on the other side of the glass. While there are barriers between the prisoners and their visitors, nothing separates the prisoners from each other on their side of the visiting room.

[186] Interview in Kwachon, June 1990.

[187] Interview in Kwachon, June 1990.

41

0046-

Asia Watch requested that Cho's case be investigated, and we reiterated our appeal in a July letter to Lee Sun-woo, the Director of the Human Rights Division at the Ministry of Justice. Lee responded:

Cho Chu-nam was arrested on May 13, 1990 for leading the Hyundai Heavy Industry illegal strike and violent demonstration. After an investigation at the Ulsan police, he was transferred to the Pusan District Prosecutor's office. During the prosecutor's investigation, he was shown his statement prepared by the clerk Choi Chong-gi. As he requested some corrections to be made, he was allowed to make the corrections himself. The statement prepared by the clerk was an official document and damaging it constituted a criminal offense. However, while he was making corrections, he drew a diagonal line from left to right and damaged the entire document despite the clerk's attempts to stop him. Thus, the clerk kicked the chair once. Cho protested it, pushing the clerk and causing a disturbance. During the process of trying to stop the disturbance, he fell down, his face striking the desk, and received minor injury on his lips. The injury was not visible on that day, but there was a little swelling on the following day. He never requested any treatment. As the injury was not serious enough to require any treatment, the prosecutor did not suggest any treatment. This incident did not occur during the process of obtaining an involuntary confession.[188]

Pusan Pretrial Detention Center

Because of the overcrowded facilities in Ulsan, some Hyundai workers awaiting trial were held at the Pusan Pretrial Detention Center. At the beginning of June 1990, some 44 prisoners there staged a hunger strike to protest the treatment of Hyundai workers being tried in Masan. (At that trial, the workers had been led into the courtroom handcuffed and roped to one another, in contrast to the normal procedure of using only one method of restraint.) The hunger strikers were beaten and put into punishment cells. On June 7, the prisoners' relatives and their supporters demonstrated in front of the prison. According to one of the family members, they were demanding an end to the violence in prison, no tying together of prisoners when they go to court, and outside medical examinations for the prisoners who had been beaten.[189] The authorities showed that they were sensitive to publicity about the mistreatment of imprisoned Hyundai workers because the vice warden reportedly apologized to the demonstrators and ordered the prisoners transferred to their regular cells.

Kim Nam-suk, a Hyundai union executive, participated in the hunger strike. He was reportedly beaten so severely, including having his back trampled on by the guards, that he could not move at his waist. His attorney, a member of the Pusan branch of Lawyers for a Democratic Society (Minbyun),[190] requested that Kim be hospitalized.

The Justice Ministry's Director of the Security Division told Asia Watch that Kim was not in any way mistreated.[191] He said that Kim was moved from Ulsan to Pusan in handcuffs and his wrist may have been somewhat chafed as a result, but he denied that Kim was beaten. Hunger strikers, he said, are

---

[188] August 1990 letter addressed to Edward J. Baker, Asia Watch board member and member of the delegation to South Korea.
[189] Interview in Ulsan, June 1990.
[190] Minbyun is an association of lawyers working on human rights cases.
[191] Interview in Kwacheon, June 1990.

42

0047

never beaten. Chang Yun-suk. Director of the Prosecution Division, said that Kim's family and attorney were lying and what they told Asia Watch was a complete fabrication. He said that Kim admitted that there had been no problem, apologized to the police and resumed eating.

The Justice Ministry confirmed that more than 40 prisoners at Pusan Pretrial Detention Center had conducted a protest on June 1, 1990.[192] The Ministry stated that "there was some physical struggle between the prisoners and the guards" as the protest was "suppressed with force." However, "no prisoner was beaten or injured." Kim Nam-suk "refused to cooperate while being transferred" from Ulsan to Pusan. He "received a little scratch on the wrist" as he was being handcuffed but neither he nor his lawyer ever requested treatment and Kim therefore received none" according to the Justice Ministry.[193]

---

[192] August 1990 letter from Lee to Baker.
[193] Ibid.

0048

VI. CHUNKYOJO

Repression of the South Korean labor movement is not just directed at industrial workers. Public school teachers, who are part of the civil service, and private school teachers, who are treated as if they were civil servants, have been arrested and dismissed for activities in support of an independent union called Chunkyojo. This is an acronym for the Korean Teachers and Educational Workers Union. Chunkyojo members have been accused of being communists; all applicants for teaching positions are now interviewed about their political beliefs and activities, past and present, and whether they intend to join the new union. An affirmative response to the latter can lead to disqualification.

Background

Chunkyojo was launched on May 28, 1989 despite a legal ban on collective action by public sector employees and the arrest and dismissal of 100 union organizers less than two weeks earlier. It was the first independent teachers' union in almost 30 years. Such a union had been formed once before in 1960, but despite a membership of 20,000, then one-fifth of the teaching profession, it lasted less than a year. In 1961, it was declared illegal by Park Chung-hee and harshly suppressed.

In the intervening two decades before Chunkyojo was established, the only organization representing the interests of teachers was the government-sponsored Korean Federation of Education Associations (KFEA), which included administrators as well as primary and secondary school teachers and which was more a professional association than a trade union. Teachers, as civil servants, were barred from collective action by both the South Korean constitution, the National Civil Service Act and the Private School Law.

The flowering of the labor movement that followed Roh's June 1987 declaration, however, affected the teaching profession as well. In September 1987, a voluntary organization called the National Teachers' Association began advocating reforms in the educational system and improved working conditions for teachers. The teachers wanted more democratic operation of the schools as well as flexibility in choosing their teaching materials. At a conference in February 1989, participants decided they needed a full-scale union and resolved to establish Chunkyojo.

While the preparations were underway for Chunkyojo's inauguration, the Education Ministry announced that it would deal severely with any teachers involved in organizing the union. On May 16, two days after a Chunkyojo convention, the government convened a high-level meeting of the vice ministers of Education, Culture and Information, Home Affairs, and Labor, the under-secretary of the Agency for the National Security Planning and the vice director of the Public Prosecutors' Office. They decided to dismiss and arrest the 100 leading organizers of the union.[194]

Despite these threats and intimidation, Chunkyojo was launched on May 28, 1989 at a rally at Yonsei University. Riot police were mobilized to block the site of the rally, and 1,082 teachers and students of teachers' colleges were arrested.

---

[194] Yonhap, May 16, 1989, in FBIS, May 17, 1989.

45

0049

The four general principles of Chunkyojo are as follows:

1. We firmly unite to establish the autonomy and specialty of education and to realize democracy in education.

2. We strive to improve the socio-economical status of teachers, to acquire the civil rights of teachers and to improve the educational environment.

3. We stand in the vanguard of realizing nationalistic, democratic and humane education for pupils to lead their own independent life as citizens of [a] democratic society.

4. We cooperate with every organization in our country and [every] world-wide teachers' organization which supports liberty, peace and democracy."[195]

The union stated its determination to undertake activities to achieve these goals and to win the teachers' rights "to organize, negotiate and act collectively through revising the laws concerning education."[196]

In November 1989, clearly in response to the challenge from Chunkyojo, the official KFEA became the Korean Federation of Teachers Association (KFTA). But the name change meant little. Dues for the KFTA continued to be deducted automatically from teachers' salaries; the leadership continued to be chosen from retired government bureaucrats, with the president approved by the Ministry of Education. And the KFTA had no more bargaining power than its predecessor.

Suppression of Chunkyojo

Since their union was founded, Chunkyojo members have lobbied unsuccessfully for its legalization. Members have conducted hunger strikes and sit-down strikes, started signature and petition campaigns, staged cultural performances, launched support committees, organized massive rallies and demonstrations and even threatened mass resignation in protest at government actions against them. As a result, thousands of Chunkyojo members from public and private schools were arrested, detained or dismissed from their jobs because of their involvement in union activities. On a single day, July 9, 1989, more than 1,900 teachers were reportedly detained under the Law on Assembly and Demonstration for attempting to take part in a rally in Seoul. The rally site, according to the Yonhap news agency, was blocked by some 12,000 riot police, and the demonstrators were stormed by 1,500 police.[197]

More than 80 teachers have been jailed for violating the Civil Service Law. Among them was Yun Yong-kyu, president of Chunkyojo, a physical education teacher at Junnam Physical Education High School. He was arrested on June 9, 1989 and charged with violating the Civil Service Law; six months later, he was sentenced to a one year jail term. He was released at the end of June 1990. A list of other teachers arrested appears in the Appendix 3.

---

[195] "The General Principles of Chunkyojo," in Chunkyojo, *Movement for Genuine Education*, Appendix 1, p. 27.
[196] *Ibid.*
[197] Yonhap, July 10, 1989, in FBIS, July 11, 1989.

Some 1,500 Chunkyojo members have been dismissed from their jobs. Many have filed appeals for reinstatement with arbitration committees but only a few have been successful. In December 1989, a district court in Kochang ordered the reinstatement of two private school teachers because the judge ruled that none of their activities "had harmed social order or education."[198] In June and July of 1990, Chunkyojo initiated a nationwide petition campaign for the reinstatement of the dismissed teachers. The government responded by threatening to dismiss or arrest the leaders of the campaign, despite guarantees of the right to petition the government contained in South Korea's Petition Law and the Constitution.[199] Not only have teachers been dismissed, but high school students have been expelled or even arrested for protesting the dismissal of their teachers. In September 1989, a Yangjong High School student was reportedly suspended from school for two weeks for writing "I support the teachers in Chunkyojo" in her test paper.

The Education Ministry decreed in August 1989 that all applicants for teaching positions in public schools must be interviewed on their views on political issues and Chunkyojo. In a break with the previous practice of automatically giving jobs to graduates of state-run teachers colleges, more than 250 prospective teachers underwent interviews conducted by the Seoul Board of Education. The interviews included questions about the applicants' past political activities and inquired as to whether they would join Chunkyojo upon becoming teachers. According to government officials, 18 persons were disqualified because of their past links with the student movement, and 46 applicants did not show up for the interviews.[200]

Support of Chunkyojo not only has disqualified applicants for teaching jobs but may affect applicants to teachers' colleges as well. In October, the Education Ministry issued new guidelines for those applying to teachers' colleges. Unlike other college applicants, they were now required to submit recommendations from their high school headmasters and records of their school activities "in what appears to be a government preemptive measure to wed out dissident students that may be involved in the union movement after becoming teachers."[201]

In August 1989 the Ministry of Education ordered university officials not to reappoint Chunkyojo-member professors unless they quit the union. According to Chunkyojo, more than 400 college professors had joined the union, but it was not known how many would be affected by the new order. According to the prevailing law, full and associate professors at state universities must have their contracts renewed every six years, and assistant professors every three years. The re-employment statute had come under wide criticism in the past because the government had used it to expel dissident professors from college campuses; now the government was criticized for using it as a means to suppress the dissident union. But the Education Ministry maintained that it was "natural" for college professors to be dismissed for their membership in Chunkyojo as their counterparts in elementary and secondary schools faced the same punishment.[202]

In addition to those arrested or dismissed, others have reportedly been transferred to less desirable, remote villages and islands in retaliation for their pro-union activities. A teacher in Seoul, for example,

---

[198] Amnesty International, March 17, 1990, ASA 25/10/90.
[199] Korea Herald, July 4, 1990.
[200] Korea Herald, August 8, 1989.
[201] Korea Times, October 8, 1989.
[202] Korea Herald, August 3, 1989.

was reportedly sent to a distant mountain village; another was transferred from Kwangju in the south to a northeastern province near the demilitarized zone.

A Chunkyojo official told Asia Watch of alleged mistreatment of teachers detained after the attempted July 9, 1989 demonstration in Seoul. Although the level of mistreatment varied in local police stations around the city, he said that detained teachers, male and female, who refused to hand over their citizens' ID cards, were often stripped and subjected to body searches. Some male teachers were so severely abused they required hospitalization; they were then re-arrested upon their release from the hospital. Mistreatment was said to be particularly harsh at a detention center in the northern section of Seoul. One person held there was beaten and sent to the hospital, then re-arrested when he was discharged. He was convicted and given a suspended sentence. Four teachers were subsequently charged and physically detained; 47 were indicted without physical detention and 6 were tried in the summary courts.[203]

The Legal Issues

The Law on Assembly and Demonstration (LAD), described in chapter 2, has also been most frequently used against the teachers. Lee Bu-young, for example, was convicted of violating the Law on Assembly and Demonstration. Lee, 43, acting president of the Chunkyojo and a teacher in Seoul, was arrested on July 13, 1989 on charges of organizing illegal rallies. In October, he was sentenced to an 18-month jail term, suspended for two years. Teachers who participate in Chunkyojo-organized demonstrations, rallies, sit-in protests and even hunger strikes have been arrested under the LAD. Most have been released after a short period of detention and a trial in summary court.

Teachers, however, have faced a particular problem because of ban on public sector workers. The South Korean constitution guarantees that "workers shall have the right to independent association, collective bargaining and collective action."[204] However, the Constitution limits that right by stating that "only those public officials who are designated by law shall have the right of association, collective bargaining and collective action."[205] This right has never been granted to teachers.

As noted by a legal scholar who compared South Korea's domestic laws with international labor standards, teachers are among a whole class of civil servants whose rights are abridged:

Employees of state-owned commercial enterprises are not prohibited from unionizing in South Korea, but the authorization contemplated in article 31 of the Korean Constitution has never been granted for most civil servants, a class comprising not only government personnel but also school teachers at all levels ... The effect of this restriction is to deny the right to unionize to large numbers of workers who could not be said to occupy administrative jobs in the government proper.[206]

---

[203] *Movement for Genuine Education*, p. 32.
[204] Constitution of the Republic of Korea, Art. 33(1).
[205] Constitution of the Republic of Korea, Art. 33(2).
[206] James M. West, "South Korea's Entry into the International Labor Organization: Perspectives on corporatist labor law during a late industrial revolution," *Stanford Journal of International Law*, v. 23, no. 2, (1987), p. 509.

48

0052

In addition to the constitutional restriction, Article 66 of the National Civil Service Act bars civil servants, including public school teachers, from taking collective action, thus prohibiting their participation in trade union activity.[207] In March 1989, amendments to the Trade Union Law which would have nullified the prohibition on union organizing by public sector employees were passed by the National Assembly. President Roh, however, vetoed them.[208]

In April 1990, the South Korean Supreme Court considered the constitutionality of the government's ban on organizing by public school teachers in the case of Won Yong-man. Won, a former teacher at Haksong Middle School in Wonju, was arrested in June 1989 for attempting to organize a branch of Chunkyojo.[209] The Supreme Court upheld the provision of the Civil Service Law in question. Justice An U-man said that Chunkyojo could not be considered as legitimate even though the union members are pursuing the democratization of education and "true education," or Chamkyoyuk.[210] (*See* page 50 for further details about *Chamkyoyuk*.)

The Supreme Court's decision apparently conflicts with international labor standards. As West observed, "The pertinent International Labor Organization (ILO) standards have been consistently interpreted as rejecting a public/private distinction as determinative of associative rights."[211] Moreover, the international trend, reflected in the ILO norms, is shifting away from blanket restrictions on public sector organizational rights. The ILO Labor Relations (Public Service) Convention (No. 151), for example, notes the special need for unionization in the public sector.[212]

Private school teachers are also banned from organizing under Arts. 55 and 58 of the Private School Law. The first article stipulates that private school teachers are to be treated as public school teachers.[213] The second article states: "(A teacher may be dismissed from office) when he joins political movements or labor movements or ... agitates the students to support or to oppose any political party."[214]

---

[207] National Civil Service Act, Art. 66: "Prohibition of Collective Action: Civil servants may not take collective action for labor movement purposes or other purposes outside of public duty." The law was promulgated in 1963 and amended in 1986. *1989 Popjun* (Code of Laws).

[208] Trade Union Law, Art. 8: "Restriction on Formation and Membership of Trade Unions: Workers may organize or join a trade union at liberty. In case of public officials, however, the right shall be stipulated separately...." *Labor Laws of Korea*, Republic of Korea Ministry of Labor (1989), p. 4.

[209] *Korea Herald*, April 12, 1990. Won had been sentenced to two-year prison term, which was later reduced to a 1 million *won* [US$1430] fine.

[210] *Ibid*.

[211] West, p. 508.

[212] ILO Convention No. 151, Part II "(Protection of the Right to Organize): "Public employees shall enjoy adequate protection against acts of anti-union discrimination in respect of their employment... (in respect of acts calculated to) -- (a) make the employment of public employees subject to the condition that they shall not join or shall relinquish membership of a public employees' organization; (b) cause the dismissal of ... a public employee by reason or membership ... or because of participation in the normal activities of such an organization." International Labor Office, *International Labor Conventions and Recommendations, 1919-1981* (Geneva, 1982), p. 26.

[213] Private School Law, Art. 55: "The provisions concerning the duties of the teachers of national and public schools shall apply *mutatis mutandis* to the duties of the teachers of the private schools." (Promulgated in June 1963). *Laws of the Republic of Korea*, v. 1, p. 11150).

[214] Private School Law, Art. 58.1(4).

49

0053

In a case pending before the South Korean Constitutional Court in mid-1990, private school teachers were arguing that these provisions violate their constitutional right to freedom of association as well as to organize and bargain collectively. Although the courts have thus far upheld the government's position on the legal status of Chunkyojo, the Democratic Liberal Party introduced a Special Law Concerning the Status of Teachers during the June-July 1990 special session of the National Assembly. The bill designated the KFTA as the sole, officially recognized association representing teachers, thus emphasizing the illegal status of Chunkyojo. The bill also did not grant the KFTA collective bargaining rights. Wide criticism forced the government to shelve the bill, but it is expected to come up for debate in a future session of the National Assembly.

Chamkyoyuk (True Education)

Chunkyojo's chief aim is *Chamkyoyuk*, the establishment of democracy and autonomy in teaching. The elements of this aim include revision of textbooks and curricula, an improved educational environment and improved working conditions.

In September 1989, Chunkyojo teachers filed a case with the Constitution Court challenging the constitutionality of Article 57 of the Education Act which gives the Education Ministry the exclusive authority to write or review textbooks used in primary and secondary schools. Teachers were concerned that these textbooks contained historical distortions and reflected the political bias of previous dictatorships.[215] While a decision has yet to be rendered in the case, the authorities reportedly agreed that revisions were needed to the curriculum and to some textbooks. The Education Ministry announced that until the textbook revision was completed sometime in 1990, teachers would be free to depart from those texts which did not reflect the government's recent improvement in relations with communist countries or ignored the abuses of the Chun Doo-hwan government.[216] In addition, the Education Minister reportedly told the National Assembly's Education-Information Committee, which met to discuss the Chunkyojo controversy, that the government would push for legislation to "enhance the status of school teachers and improve their working conditions," and the Ministry would "actively" accommodate the teachers' demand for "democratic and rational" school operations and revisions in the curriculum.[217]

Improving the student-teacher relationship is a fundamental part of their aim to improve the educational environment. In September 1989 the Education Ministry reported that 126 secondary students nationwide committed suicide for academic reasons during the 1988 school year.[218] Chunkyojo believes that over 200 students kill themselves each year.

---

[215] As recently as June 1990, in a seminar sponsored by the Presidential Advisory Commission on Education Policy, a Seoul National University professor noted, "Schools of all levels had been instilling rigid anti-communist ideas into the minds of the growing generation for the last four decades." *Korea Herald*, June 28, 1990. He added that there needed to be new guidelines on how subjects like reunification and North Korea should be treated, "Under these guidelines and subsequent limits, teachers and professors should be allowed to conduct their classes in their own way."

[216] Amnesty International, March 17, 1990, ASA 25/10/90.

[217] These demands for enhanced status and democratic operations of schools were to be met, he said, in the delayed Special Law Concerning the Status of Teachers. *See* "The Legal Issues" section, *supra*; *Korea Herald*, August 10, 1989.

[218] Twenty killed themselves after their parents severely scolded them for their poor academic performance; seven were afraid of fierce competition over college entrance.

50

Chunkyojo also demands improved working conditions. Teachers' salaries in South Korea are below those of other clerical jobs and some blue-collar jobs such as cab drivers. As of mid-1990, an average teacher with five-year experience earns 437,000 *won* (US$624) per month for teaching a minimum of five classes a day.[219] Classrooms are overcrowded. The Education Ministry exercises near complete control over the entire educational system. It recruits and promotes teachers, has the power to dismiss and transfer them, and selects all their teaching materials.

---

[219] *Far Eastern Economic Review*, July 27, 1989.

51

VII. BROADCASTING AND PRESS UNIONS

Unions in the broadcasting and newspaper publishing industries have challenged the government's restrictions on collective action by striking over personnel decisions, issues of editorial independence and censorship. They have demanded a greater voice in the running of their industries.

A series of strikes, both legal and illegal, have taken place since June 1987, when Roh Tae-woo's promised reforms included a pledge to expand press freedom. The most dramatic confrontation between the unions, management and the government took place at the Korean Broadcasting System (KBS) in April 1990 when thousands of riot police broke up an "illegal" sit-in by employees at the headquarters of the giant TV and radio system.

Asia Watch takes no position on the specific grievances raised by the broadcasting and press unions. It maintains, however, that workers in the newsrooms and broadcasting studios have every right to freely express their views without fear of being arrested or forcibly silenced by riot police.

Background

Since the Republic of Korea was established in 1948, successive governments have maintained tight rein on the nation's press. Chun Doo-hwan's administration was accompanied by a particularly harsh suppression of the press. In 1980 alone -- as part of his "purification movement" against "undesirable and corrupt elements" of Korean society -- Chun fired and banned from writing 683 members of the press from some 40 newspapers and broadcasting stations; banned 172 periodicals on charges of obscenity and creating social confusion; closed 617 publishing firms; closed a Seoul-based daily newspaper; permitted only one newspaper per province; closed down two major news agencies and several smaller agencies and forced them to merge into the Yonhap News Agency.[220] Two independent broadcasting stations were merged into the state-run Korean Broadcasting System (KBS), which also took over 70 percent of Munhwa Broadcasting System stocks.[221]

In December 1980, the government enacted the Basic Press Law which then became the legal basis for government censorship of the press and the broadcasting industry. The Basic Press Law required publishers to be licensed by the state and to submit two advance copies of their publications to the Ministry of Culture and Information.[222] Periodicals could not be edited or published at branch offices. All journalists were required to have a press card to have their works published.

Broadcasters had to submit records of broadcasts to the Ministry of Culture and Information. The Korean Broadcasting Commission, whose members were appointed by the South Korean President, had broad powers over personnel and editorial decisions.

---

[220] Asia Watch, *Human Rights in Korea* (January 1986), p 289. Yonhap News Agency is a cooperative company, structured much like the Associated Press, with member companies represented on the board of directors. Currently about half of Yonhap's stocks are owned by KBS and MBC.

[221] *Ibid*.

[222] *Ibid.*, p 290.

53

Those who protested the government's censorship were dealt with harshly.[223]   But until early 1985, "there had been very few instances of government action against the media since 1980 for the simple reason that the media has learned the limits of government tolerance and has policed itself."[224] For its part, the Ministry of Culture and Information issued hundreds of daily, written guidelines to the news media.[225] The guidelines dictated which stories and photos the news media should cover or ignore and how certain sensitive stories should be treated. The practice of issuing written guidelines ceased only after Roh Tae-woo's June 29, 1987 declaration. In November 1987, the National Assembly repealed the Basic Press Law and replaced it with two new laws, one governing periodicals and the other governing broadcasts.

Broadcasting Media

There are five television channels and some 50 radio stations in South Korea. Broadcasting has been the most tightly controlled mass media, with KBS having a near monopoly on the industry.[226] Wholly owned and operated by the state, KBS broadcasts over three television channels and owns 25 radio stations. KBS also owns 70 percent of the stocks in the Munhwa Broadcasting Corporation (MBC) which has one television channel and operates twenty radio stations. A much smaller company, the Christian Broadcasting System (CBS) operates four radio stations. CBS was restricted only to religious programming until September 1987, when it was permitted to begin airing news broadcasts.[227]

Political control over the industry was traditionally maintained through presidential appointments to key posts. By the time Chun Doo-hwan left office, the last five presidents of KBS and MBC had been his former secretaries.[228] Appointments to the chief regulatory agency of the industry, the 12-member Korean Broadcasting Commission (KBC), established in 1980, were and continue to be controlled by the President.

The November 1987 Broadcast Law ostensibly guaranteed an end to government interference in the broadcasting industry. But it retained the earlier provision empowering the President to appoint the heads of broadcast networks and members of KBC. The new law also appeared to strengthen the role of the Commission in programming and management decisions. The networks were required to submit details of daily broadcasts to the Commission and the Minister of Culture and Information. The Commission was also authorized to deliberate basic programming issues and to approve or disapprove the contents of programs.

During the upsurge of labor activism after June 1987, two large and powerful media unions emerged at MBC and KBS to challenge the Commission and the management's control over the broadcasting media. Both unions -- beginning in July 1987 at MBC and in April 1990 at KBS --

---

[223] *Ibid.*, p. 290.
[224] *Ibid.*
[225] "Guiding the Press,'" *Index on Censorship*, May 1987, pp. 28-36. Also see *Human Rights in Korea*, p. 291.
[226] *See Freedom of Expression in the Republic of Korea*, jointly published in August 1988 by Asia Watch, International Human Rights Law Group and American Center of International PEN. For background on the 1980 media merger, *see* pp. 19-20.
[227] *Freedom of Expression in the Republic of Korea*, pp. 19-20, p. 67.
[228] *Los Angeles Times*, August 17, 1987.

54

0057

asserted their strength through a series of strikes and protests to demand fair and impartial broadcasting and editorial independence.

Munhwa Broadcasting Company (MBC)

The union at the Munhwa Broadcasting Company (MBC) is one of the strongest in the media industry; 950 of MBC's 1,800 employees are members of the union. Beginning in July 1987, they carried out three strikes which, over the course of three years, elicited concessions from the government and management on issues of editorial independence, most notably expanding the union's role in the system of appointing high-level officials at the network.

On July 16, 1987, approximately 100 journalists staged a 12-hour stoppage of news coverage to press for their demands, including greater freedom of the press and the reinstatement of hundreds of journalists who had been dismissed from their jobs over the past several years.[229] A number of photographers and journalists joined in the protest.[230] The striking journalists said they would work only under conditions that allowed fair and impartial reporting. Ranking MBC executives reportedly promised that the network would devote itself to fair reporting.[231]

The union conducted a second strike a year later. In June 1988, they began negotiations on guarantees for fair reporting, demanding the resignation of the MBC president and establishment of a system for nominating chief editors that would ensure editing functions would not be influenced by the management. In late August, after a series of unsuccessful attempts to settle, the union decided to strike. The Minister of Culture and Information accused the union of calling an illegal strike because it did not observe the fifteen-day cooling-off period mandated for a "public utility."[232]

The MBC strike threatened to disrupt coverage of the upcoming Olympic Games in Seoul, and the management relented. Hwang Sun-pil, the government-appointed president (and a former spokesman for Chun Doo-hwan) submitted his resignation. In addition, seventy percent of MBC's ownership that had been previously in the hands of KBS was transferred to a newly-established, private Broadcast Culture Foundation.[233] The Foundation's board of directors, composed of ten persons, would include one to be chosen by the union.[234]

In September 1989, over eighty percent of the 1,150 unionized workers at MBC voted to strike to demand a larger role in selecting key editors and program producers. The union also began talks with

---

[229] Kyodo, July 16, 1987, in FBIS, same day.

[230] At the beginning of February 1988, the union at MBC filed a petition with the Seoul Labor Committee protesting the management's January 29 transfer of Shim Chae-chol, a union member and staff reporter at the Foreign News Desk to the Business Department. The union alleged that the transfer was aimed at suppressing union activities. Journalists Association of Korea issued a statement demanding management stop "intentional and systematic" activities aimed at curbing labor activities. *Korea Herald*, February 4, 1988.

[231] *Korea Herald*, July 18, 1987.

[232] *Korea Herald*, August 27, 1988. *See* Appendix 3, Trade Union Law, Article 14.

[233] Kyodo, August 28, 1988, in FBIS, August 23, 1988. The other 30 percent of the stock is owned by the Chung-Soo Foundation, named for former President Park Chung-hee and his wife Yook Yong-soo. The exact nature of this foundation is not clear.

[234] The remaining nine members are chosen as follows: four by the Korean Broadcasting Commission, four by the-then existing four political parties, and one by management.

55   0058

management on appointment procedures for directors of programming, news, and technical divisions, proposing a direct voting system for the three core directors. But management rejected the notion of a voting system, and subsequently turned down a series of alternative proposals for nomination or arbitration procedures to appoint the directors. Negotiations broke down, and on September 8, the union walked out.

The next day, MBC union president Kang Song-ju and four other union officials were charged with engaging in an illegal strike. The Labor Ministry accused the workers of violating the Labor Disputes Adjustment Law by failing to observe the required 15-day cooling-off period. The government also objected to a work stoppage on August 31-September 1 by more than 700 workers who took their monthly leave *en masse*.

The strike lasted until September 19, when management recognized the workers' demand for a voice in key management appointment decisions. The staff of the three departments (news, programming, TV technical division) would vote and recommend two or more candidates for the director-level positions, with the final selection to be made by the MBC president. Furthermore, by majority vote, a panel made up of six members -- three each from the union and the management -- could request the dismissal of high-ranking officials at the network.

The agreement set an important precedent for collective action in the broadcasting industry, demonstrating that a union could win significant concessions on decisions on editorial appointments from management and the government.[235]

Korean Broadcasting System (KBS)

Nearly a year after the MBC union formed, the KBS union was established on May 20, 1988. In contrast to the MBC union, the KBS union maintained a good relationship with the network officials, including then-network president, Suh Young-hoon. Suh was considered sympathetic to the free press movement, and the union grew rapidly during his tenure. He was forced to resign, however, in December 1989, after allegations of financial irregularities surfaced at the network.[236]

On April 9, 1990 Soh Ki-won was appointed as the new head of KBS by President Roh Tae-woo.[237] He had close connections with the government, including a position as press secretary to former

---

[235] On September 21, 1990, MBC unionists staged an overnight sit-in strike to protest the company's dismissal a week earlier of two union leaders, including union chairman and city-desk reporter Ahn Song-hil. The unionists also passed a no-confidence measure against the network's president. *Korea Times*, September 23, 1990 in FBIS, September 24; *Korea Herald*, September 22, 1990. The reasons for the dismissals and the outcome of the sit-in strike are not clear.

[236] The Board of Audit and Inspection announced that KBS had spent more than 4 billion *won* (US$5700) illegally in 1989. With fictitious documents, KBS paid 4,032 million *won* (US$5760) to its employees, 3 billion *won* (US$4290) as allowances for overtime work and 1,032 million *won* (US$1470) as holiday bonuses, according to the Korea Herald. Payments were made in line with a labor-management agreement reached in December 1989 but KBS altered the date of the agreement to December 16 from December 23 to pay 1,702.4 million *won* ($US2430) in special allowances to its employees from December 18 to December 31. In June 1989, it also illegally spent 1,377 million *won* (US$1970) in that manner. The Board findings were expected to go to the Ministry of Information for actions against the KBS president and other management officials. *Korea Herald*, February 27, 1990. We understand from our interviews in Seoul that Suh had been under pressure to resign even before the financial scandal "surfaced."

[237] It was known as early as in February that Soh would be appointed as KBS president.

56

President Park Chung-hee. As president of the pro-government newspaper, *Seoul Shinmun*, he had a reputation for union-busting and censorship and had reportedly ordered company employees to throw out workers engaged in a peaceful sit-in strike at the paper. The KBS union vigorously opposed Soh's appointment,[238] viewing it as part of the government's plan to strengthen its control over the state-run network[239] by revising the broadcast laws.

The appointment sparked a dramatic confrontation between the union, management and the government. There is no question that Soh's appointment was an assertion of government determination to control the media. There is also no question that the appointment of a company president *per se* would not be considered a legitimate issue for collective bargaining in many countries, including the U.S.

Ha Un-sung, a KBS union official interviewed by Asia Watch, described a sit-in strike that began on April 10 with a peaceful blockade to prevent Soh from entering the KBS building.[240] But on April 12 Soh managed to evade the blockade and gain access to his office on the sixth floor. Some 200 surprised and angry workers went up to his office via the fire escape and tried to get in, using a rope to remove the doorknob when they found the doorway locked from the inside.

They encountered a large group of KBS officials with offices on that floor, and 20 to 30 company security guards blocking the hallway leading to Soh's office. The unionists asked all the company officials to leave peacefully in order to avoid a confrontation. When the managers refused, the workers moved them, one by one, out of the way. At the same time, several hundred riot police and *baikgoldan*, summoned by Soh, appeared and filled up the middle of the hallway, ordering the workers to disperse. The workers sat down, sang and shouted slogans, until the police after an hour began to forcibly disperse them. Some, including Ha, were reportedly beaten. But in general the police, aware that they were being filmed by the unionists, exercised restraint. As demonstrators came down the stairway, they were forced to walk between two columns of policemen leading them to police buses. A total of 117 union members were detained and transported to local police stations.

At the police stations, the demonstrators were treated politely, according to Ha. (KBS unionists we spoke with noted that there is generally a higher level of respect in South Korea for journalists than for ordinary workers and believe that for this reason, they tended to receive better treatment by the police.)

But there were some reports of police abuse. Kim Chum-suk, editor of the union's paper, told us that the police kicked him in the shins and bent his fingers back when he was arrested on April 12. Lee Won-hu, a vice-president of the KBS union, was reportedly beaten severely on April 11 and sustained head injuries. He was hospitalized for ten days. The authorities threatened to arrest him if he returned to "Democracy Plaza," the lobby area on the second floor of the KBS headquarters where the workers assembled for protest actions.

---

[238] Yonhap, April 13, 1990 in FBIS, April 17.

[239] We were also told that the KBS board of directors were indirectly threatened to support Soh's appointment. The KBS board of directors are chosen by the government appointed Korean Broadcasting Commission. Han Un-sa, a television and drama writer and a KBS board member, reportedly disclosed that the board was indirectly pressured and intimidated to accept Soh's selection without discussion. Han protested the closed procedure and another board member, Lee In-ho, a professor at Seoul National University, urged all the board members to resign in protest, but none did.

[240] Interview with Asia Watch, June 8, 1990, at the KBS union office.

At the police station Ha and others learned from an early evening news broadcast that other KBS employees were refusing to work in protest against their colleagues' arrests. But the 9:00 p.m. newscast was abruptly halted and replaced with another program. Only later did Ha discover the reason for the interruption: ten reporters had staged a silent strike in the newsroom to demand airing of the labor unrest at KBS, standing behind the anchorman though out of the range of the cameras. By 9:13 p.m., when major news items had all been covered and there was still no mention of the KBS strikes, the anchor and the news production people walked off in the middle of the live newscast. In fact, while Ha and his colleagues were being detained, the police intervention had prompted over 500 KBS unionists to take part in an overnight sit-in strike at the KBS headquarters to demand their colleagues' release and Soh's resignation.

On April 13, the union held a general meeting, and more than 3,000 union members from all departments except the transmission section decided to go ahead with work stoppages until Soh resigned. Some 350 managing staff members at lower levels also demanded Soh's resignation and the release of all detained union members.[241]

On April 17, the government's Information Minister, Choe Pyong-yul, ordered the KBS workers back to work:

> The entire KBS staff should be enlightened to the public indignation stemming from the prolonged blockade of information and the act of holding broadcasting hostage for their struggle. The union's refusal to broadcast since April 12 is an obvious violation of the law and a virtual walkout.

Soh Ki-won had been chosen and taken office through a legal process, he asserted, and was therefore the legitimate head of the network.

The stand-off over Soh's appointment continued to generate controversy, with the government on the defensive. Home Minister An Ung-mo testified before the National Assembly's Home Affairs Committee and defended the decision to deploy -- at Soh Ki-won's request -- riot police at KBS headquarters. The Culture and Information Committee of the National Assembly also debated the KBS incident.[242] No one questioned the fact that the KBS strike was illegal under Korean Law: the KBS union did not file notice or wait out the cooling-off period, and the walk-out did interfere with normal operations. At the same time, 47 out of 72 bureau chiefs of the KBS issued a joint statement expressing full support for the efforts of the KBS workers and criticized Soh's "rash" mobilization of the police.

KBS executives called on employees to return to work and also urged the government revise the current system of appointing the KBS president to safeguard the independence and neutrality of the public network. "No punitive measures should be taken against employees for joining the massive walkout," they declared, adding that all bureau chiefs would resign with the normalization of broadcasting. Kang Won-yong, head of the Korean Broadcasting Commission reportedly discussed the situation in separate meetings with Soh Ki-won and KBS union representatives.[243]

---

[241] Yonhap, April 13, 1990.
[242] Yonhap, April 18, 1990, in FBIS, same day.
[243] *Korea Times*, April 18, 1990, in FBIS, same day.

58

0061

MBC and its 19 affiliated provincial networks held an emergency meeting and decided on April 18 to stage a work boycott in support of the KBS union:

> The government's appointment of Soh as KBS president and Soh's resort to police force to quell the protest are an obvious sign of attempting to keep under the government control the broadcasting networks and to suppress mass media once again.[244]

But the government continued to resist the mounting pressure and criticism. On April 23, the ministers of Home Affairs, Justice, Labor and Information issued a joint statement threatening to take even tougher action:

> If the KBS labor union continues to trample on the public's right to know and continues unlawful acts, the government cannot help taking all necessary measures in order to restore order at any cost...This is not a legal labor movement designed to improve working conditions. This is a challenge to the government's right to manage personnel and is an illegal collective action.[245]

They also dismissed the charge that Soh was appointed as KBS president to keep the nation's broadcast media under government control.[246] The government referred to guidelines issued in January by the Labor Ministry. Though not legally binding, they stated specifically that unionized workers were not allowed to stage a legal strike over personnel decisions such as the resignation of certain executives or appointment of presidents or senior company officials.

A compromise agreement negotiated by KBS union leaders and management was rejected, late on April 30, by a union membership vote because it did not stipulate Soh's resignation as a precondition for ending the sit-in strike. Around midnight, approximately 2,000 riot police stormed the KBS headquarters, arresting 333 journalists, producers and other workers.[247] The police raid -- just two days after the massive assault on striking unionists at the Hyundai shipyards -- made international headlines and conveyed the image of a government determined to maintain control over the media at virtually any cost.

On May 1, over 100,000 workers affiliated with Chonnohyop (the "illegal" national union federation) staged strikes at more than 50 work places, in part to protest the police raid on KBS strikers.[248] The Korean Federation of Press Unions, composed of unions in print and broadcasting media, called for an unprecedented industry-wide work stoppage in solidarity with the KBS workers and the jailed KBS staff members. Both the MBC and CBS unions launched sympathy strikes.[249] Editorials by most major newspapers generally supported the workers and criticized the government for its use of

---

[244] Yonhap, April 18, 1990, in FBIS, April 19. An emergency solidarity committee at CBS was also considering a production boycott to support the KBS workers.

[245] Yonhap, April 23, 1990, in FBIS, same day. On January 20 of this year, the Labor Ministry had announced new, although not legally binding guidelines restricting the scope of collective action. Specifically, the guidelines stated that unionized workers were not allowed to stage a legal strike over personnel decisions such as the resignation of certain executives or appointment of presidents or senior company officials.

[246] Ibid.

[247] Reuters, May 1, 1990; Associated Press, May 1, 1990.

[248] Reuters, May 1, 1990.

[249] Yonhap, May 3, 1990 in FBIS, same day.

the riot police to break up labor disputes. The government responded by threatening to arrest 30 more KBS staff workers on charges of "interference with business."[250]

By May 3, most of the 6,500 KBS workers had returned to work. But about 1,000 union members stayed away, and there were continuing reports of brief skirmishes with a force of 2,000 riot police deployed at KBS headquarters. Pak Chu-sang, head of the Management Workers Association, joined other KBS union leaders in an agreement on May 11 to drop Soh's resignation as a precondition to returning to work.

Normal operations at KBS resumed on May 18, but hundreds of riot police remained stationed in and around KBS headquarters as a visible reminder of the state's tough anti-labor policy. In mid-June, the Asia Watch delegation observed heavy anti-riot equipment, police buses, barbed wire barricades, and a fenced-off field with tents and other supplies in an area adjoining the KBS building.

In addition, we were told that security agents tapped the phones at the KBS union office (situated in the basement of the broadcasting headquarters), and subjected the office to constant surveillance. We also heard reports that the telephone conversations of unionists' relatives were monitored by the police as part of their search for union leaders whom they sought to arrest or wanted for questioning.[251]

Print Media

Journalists at *Hanguk Ilbo* were, in October 1987, the first to form a union at a newspaper. Workers at other newspapers followed suit after the repeal of the Basic Press Law in November 1987. As the *Far Eastern Economic Review* noted:

> As if to shake themselves loose from the trauma of the past, journalists took to celebrating their new freedom with a vengeance. Strikes, protest marches, newsroom sit-ins and even scuffles with riot policemen all marked the drive to unionize the profession.

> As a result, militant trade unions have been organized at almost every newspaper and television company. The few newsrooms that have held out against unionization have done so only with the consent of their employees.[252]

In April 1988 a consultative body of press unions was formed with 14 trade unions represented. An industry-wide federation, the Korean Federation of Press Unions (KFPU), was established in November 1988 with membership of 13,000 media workers from 41 member unions. KFPU's primary goal was to "contribute to social democratization through achieving perfect editorial freedom."[253] It designated 1989 as "The Inaugural Year for Press Liberation" and dedicated itself to press liberalization,

---

[250] Yonhap, May 3, 1990, in FBIS, same day.

[251] The police raids on April 12 and April 30 resulted in the arrest of over 500 KBS union members. Most were released after a short period of detention. Union leaders were also subsequently arrested or placed on wanted lists. See appendix for names of those being held as of late June, 1990 on charges of "obstructing business." KBS trials were scheduled to begin in early July.

[252] Shim Jae-hoon, "Watching the Watchdog," *Far Eastern Economic Review*, August 23, 1990, p. 24.

[253] Interview with Lee Seh-yong, Director of Domestic and International Relations, KFPU, in Seoul, June 1990.

60

0063

including advocacy of editorial independence and democratization in the media.[254] As of October 1990, KFPU had approximately 16,000 members from 53 affiliated-unions.

"Democracy in the newsroom" was a chief objective of KFPU member unions, as reporters demanded a greater voice in the selection of editors. At *Hankyoreh Shinmun* the editors are elected directly by the newsroom employees. After one or two years, newsroom staff can choose to veto their continued tenure in editorial positions. The staff at *Chungang Ilbo* also elect their managing editors.[255] In 1989 at least one business newspaper closed down rather than agree to union demands for control over all newsroom appointments.[256]

Other press unions also demanded, through collective actions, the right to have a say in the selection of editors. As the following cases indicate, the results have been mixed:

-- The union at *Hanguk Ilbo* and its seven sister newspapers and magazines went on a six-hour strike on June 16, 1989 after failing to reach agreement with the management.[257] The union demanded the right to elect managing editors and editorial executives of each publication, plus increased wages and bonuses. Only through direct elections of the managing editors by the staff, the union said, would the publications have editorial independence.[258] The company agreed to most of the union's demands. The management currently selects the editors but the union must ratify appointments.

-- The union at *Seoul Shinmun*, a newspaper owned jointly by the Finance Ministry and the state-run Korean Broadcasting System, went on strike at midnight on September 22, 1989 upon expiration of the mandatory 10-day "cooling off" period. The management and union had been negotiating since July over the key demand of the union for the right of the staff to approve or reject the appointment or dismissal of managing editors.[259] The strike ended on October 19 with a compromise agreement; the company managers agreed to inform the unions in advance of editorial appointments.

On October 8, more than 500 non-union workers at *Seoul Shinmun* held a rally in support of management, vowing "to protect the company and continue to produce newspapers despite the labor union-called walkout." (Of 1,400 employees at the paper, 730 belonged to the union.) The day before the rally, some 300 non-union members, including company executives, reportedly stormed the paper's newsroom and drove out about 100 members on strike, using force. Seven workers, including Kim Yong-won, the union's vice-president, were attacked and injured. Company president, Soh Ki-won, filed complaints with the police against seven union leaders for "obstructing company

---

[254]*See* "Activity of the KFPU: Media Labor Union Movement and Democracy," *Inha Times*, September 10, 1990.
[255]*Ibid.*
[256] "Watching the Watchdog," p. 24.
[257] Yonhap, June 16, 1989, in FBIS, same day.
[258] *Hanguk Ilbo* employees organized the first journalists' union in October 1987. *Korea Herald*, October 31, 1987.
[259] *Korea Herald*, September 24, 1989.

0064

operations." The union, in turn, protested against the company president and executives for ordering what they called illegal anti-labor acts.[260]

-- In October 1989, a year after a union was formed at the Yonhap News Agency, members voted to go on an indefinite strike after failing to settle disputes with the management. One of the central issues was the independence of editors from the management.[261] The strike lasted for nearly three weeks and ended with a compromise agreement acceding to the workers' demand for a voice in choosing editors, though a procedure for doing so has reportedly not yet been established. Yonhap is structured as a cooperative with member companies represented on the board of directors. The board chooses the president of the company who, in turn, selects the editors.

---

[260] *Korea Times,* October 10, 1989, in FBIS, October 17, 1989. In April 1990 Soh Ki-won was appointed president of the Korean Broadcasting System.

[261] *Korea Herald,* October 13, 1989.

VIII. ORIENT ELECTRONICS

"If this problem [with mercury poisoning] is not solved, it will affect the next generation. We must do something about it or the health of the next group of workers will be threatened in the same way. We have to draw the line...."

--Orient Electronics worker

In May 1990, workers in a legally recognized union at Orient Electronics, Ltd., a small company in Seoul, went on strike over issues of worker health and safety related to alleged mercury poisoning. The resulting labor dispute, which ended with an agreement in July, illustrated the narrow range of permissible issues over which workers can engage in collective actions. Complaints about violent attacks on the strikers by company officials were ignored by the police.

Background

The Orient Electronics Company was founded in 1971 with U.S. investment to manufacture mercury switches used in telephone exchange devices. Since 1987, the company has been owned and operated by a Korean-American, Kang In-ho.

A union was organized at Orient in March 1989, affiliated with the Korean Metalworkers Federation; as of June 1990 most of the work force (34 out of 55 persons) were members. Most of the production workers were young single women in their 20's some as young as 18 years of age. High school students, we were told, were employed by the company on the night shifts. There was no safety committee at the plant; such a committee was reportedly not required by law in factories with fewer than one hundred employees.

The workers we spoke with said that when they were hired, no one explained to them the risks and hazards entailed in handling a dangerously toxic substance, nor were they properly trained or provided with protective clothing. There has been a constant turnover of personnel at the plant; none of the current employees had worked there for more than two years.[263]

The workers experienced apparent symptoms such as pain in the eyes, difficulties in breathing, headaches, memory loss, and insomnia, which they suspected might be connected with the hazardous substances in the factory. Two workers underwent medical tests at their own expense. One of them was Han Young-kwon, 23 years old, the vice-president of the union. His test results, and that of his colleague, indicated high levels of mercury in the urine and blood.[264] He worked in the "activating room" where mercury is activated by heat and is often scattered in all directions when a glass is broken. (Mercury is injected into the glass in the previous step of the production process.) Workers do not wear special suits and are reportedly exposed directly to the mercury vapors. When we visited in June, Han was seriously ill, suffering from high blood pressure and other maladies.

---

[263] On June 13, the Asia Watch delegation interviewed a group of twenty Orient employees (nineteen women and one man) The president of the union was reportedly too ill to meet with us.

[264] Han's initial test results: 77.02 mg/l of mercury in urine, 11.72 mg/100 ml in blood.

In April 1990, alarmed by the implications of these results for the rest of the work force, 11 workers underwent tests with expenses shared between themselves and the union. Nine of the eleven were told their levels of chronic mercury poisoning were far above international standards for mercury exposure; five of them tested above South Korean standards, which allow for a greater level of exposure.[265] In May, two of the workers were acknowledged by the Ministry of Labor to have an occupational disease and thus became eligible for compensation and free medical care.

Issues in the Labor Dispute

This revelation set off a series of labor disputes which pitted the workers against management over occupational health and safety issues.[266] The outcome has potentially profound implications for the health and safety of the workers, as well as the union's ability to effectively agitate on their behalf within the framework of existing labor laws.

The workers' right to freedom of association was violated initially when the company refused to recognize the results of a union election on March 22, 1989. The government did nothing to protect the workers' rights to carry out collective actions, as guaranteed by Korean law and conventions of the International Labor Organization, or to stop the company from intimidating and harassing Orient's striking employees. Asia Watch was particularly concerned about allegations of beatings by the company's directors, and the failure of the police to investigate and prosecute those responsible even after official complaints were filed by the workers and union.

The Orient workers went on strike on May 15, 1990 to demand medical testing, compensation for those injured by mercury poisoning, improved working conditions, increased wages, and an inspection of the plant environment by occupational and medical specialists. In advance of the strike, they complied with legal requirements for the filing of a notice of dispute and a mandatory 10-day "cooling-off" period.[267] Shortly before the strike began, there was a union election, but the company refused to recognize the newly-elected union leaders. In mid-May, two employees were hospitalized for symptoms of mercury poisoning and treated at the expense of the Ministry of Labor. The remaining workers refused treatment as a way of pressuring the company to cover the costs of testing all of the employees for mercury exposure.[268]

---

[265] The World Health Organization (WHO) has recommended a standard of 0.05 mg/m^3 of mercury vapor in the air, as have the American Conference of Governmental Industrial Hygienists and others. Mercury in its vapor form is extremely easy to inhale and absorb and can be quickly absorbed through the skin. Medical consultants for Physicians for Human Rights (PHR) (Dr. Howard Hu, professor of Occupational Medicine at Harvard School of Public Health and Dr. Michael Kosnett, Clinical Instructor of Medicine at the University of California at San Francisco) reviewed records provided to them by Asia Watch about the Orient Electronics case. Based on the data provided, they concluded that it is likely that at Orient the levels of exposure to mercury vapors in the air exceeded this standard. PHR's consultants also noted that the current Korean Ministry of Labor air exposure standard of 0.1 mg/m^3 permits exposure twice as high as the standards recommended by WHO and enforced in the U.S. by the U.S. Occupational Safety and Health Administration. "Permissible Exposure Limits for Hazardous Substances," Ministry of Labor Notice 88-69, effective from March 1, 1989.

[266] Dong-a Ilbo reported on May 10, 1990: "Laborers Group Mercury Poisoning: Nine workers are ill with headaches, two hospitalized."

[267] A report in Dong-a Ilbo on May 17, 1990 was entitled: "Their Complaint Is: 'Shaking Our Fists We Demand Environmental Improvements.'"

[268] Interviews with Orient workers, in Seoul, June 13, 1990.

64   0067

On May 15 the workers set up eating and sleeping accommodations inside the factory, in accordance with the Labor Dispute Adjustment Act prohibiting strikes outside the concerned place of business. But they were informed by a police officer from the Kuro South (Nambu Station) that it was illegal for them to sleep in the plant or to use a butane gas burner for cooking. The workers then conducted a sit-in strike inside the plant. On the second day of the strike, while they were singing and banging drums, they were evicted by the company managers, who reportedly beat them as they left the factory. The beatings continued outside. One of the injured women said she required two weeks of treatment in the hospital for injuries to her eye.[269] Han, the union's vice-president, complained to us of continuing problems with his legs as a result of the beatings.

The pattern of beatings at the hands of the company managers continued at least until early June; the last such incident reportedly took place on June 8. Throughout the strike the union says it tried to negotiate with management, but the president of the company refused to meet with them. Instead, they say, he ordered his managers and directors to beat and harass them to discourage them from continuing the strike. Towards the end, more sophisticated tactics of violence were utilized: the workers allege they were kicked in the abdomen in order to avoid leaving easily detectable marks of abuse.

Complaints were filed by the workers with the police, naming the persons responsible for the violence, but no investigations were undertaken or arrests made.[270] In addition, on one occasion, a plainclothes police detective from the Seoul South Station intelligence section reportedly witnessed a beating but did not intervene to stop it.[271]

Meanwhile, the ill workers were plagued by continuing health problems. At one stage they were sent to a clinic recommended by the Labor Ministry, but the union did not feel confident in the clinic's diagnoses or in their ability to be impartial and independent.[272]

Government Response

Asia Watch raised the Orient Electronics case with the Labor Ministry and with U.S. embassy officials in Seoul. We were assured that the allegations of abuse by the management and the role of the police in the dispute would be investigated. To date, we have received no response from either South Korean or U.S. officials.

---

[269] Medical diagnoses of those injured in the beatings indicated multiple contusions, abrasions, and conjunctival hemorrhage -- issued by Kuro Clinic, May 16, 1990.

[270] Charges of physical violence were filed with the Seoul District Police Headquarters, South Section Branch, on May 21, 1990, naming the company managers involved: Koh Kyung-il, Bae Jung-hee, and Oh Pyong-am.

[271] A separate complaint was filed by the union on May 20, 1990 against a police officer, Mr. Choi, alleging misconduct and abuse of power to forcefully stop a legitimate strike.

[272] According to Pak Suk-un, director of the Labor Human Rights Center, Seoul, "Doctors belonging to an institution recognized by the Labor Ministry have been suspected of unfairness by the workers...(because) these doctors tend to acknowledge a worker's occupational disease only when the results of blood or urine tests exhibit a level beyond the criteria fixed by the Ministry... In some cases, therefore, they do not acknowledge an occupational disease even when the worker has clear symptoms of it. Moreover, workers think that these physicians are strongly influenced by the Ministry of Labor or companies, which do not want the problem of occupational disease or unsanitary working environment to be publicized widely." Report to Physicians for Human Rights, July 18, 1990.

65

On July 9, 1990 an agreement was reached between Orient and the union, providing for special diagnostic tests of the workers to be conducted by the Korean University Environmental Medicine Research Institute (recommended by the company), an inspection of the work place to be carried out by the Seoul National University Graduate School of Public Health (recommended by the union), and some wage increases.[273]

The Labor Ministry and the police have a responsibility to protect the rights of workers, including their right to engage in labor disputes and collective actions free of harassment or physical violence. Asia Watch has urged a thorough, independent investigation into the complaints filed by the Orient employees against the company management and police and prosecution of those responsible for any physical violence committed against the strikers.

---

[273] Before the agreement, the workers told us they earned 6,400 won (US$9.15) per day and were requesting an increase of 1,700 won (US$2.43). They also were seeking an increase of 3,000 won (US$4.29) in their monthly travel allowance of 7,900 won (US$11.29). According to the *Korean Times*, October 21, 1990, in October the Ministry of Labor recognized that four more workers had an occupational disease including the union's vice president. The *Hankyoreh Shinmun*, September 21, 1990, reported that 24 other workers had examinations. None were found to have the degree of mercury poisoning necessary to be judged to have an occupational disease and thus to be eligible for compensation and medical treatment from the Ministry of Labor. Four were to be monitored because they might develop an occupational disease. As of mid-October, the inspection of the work place had not taken place. A labor activist assisting the union noted that this is the second time the company has failed to keep its agreement to have an environmental survey conducted. The Minister of Labor referred the Orient case to the prosecution which levied a fine on September 17, 1990 of 300,000 won ($US429) against the company in a summary proceeding under the Industrial Safety and Health Law for failure examine the work place environment and failure to have the workers examined.

66

0069

IX. CONCLUSIONS AND RECOMMENDATIONS

The South Korean government, despite its promised reforms, continues to deny the fundamental rights of workers, labor organizers, writers, publishers, opposition leaders and others. It punishes many of those who attempt to exercise freedoms of expression and association guaranteed to them under domestic and international law. Its crackdown on labor has been particularly severe, as the administration of President Roh has attempted to blame economic difficulties on labor unrest and agitation. There are strict limits on the rights of workers to organize unions and engage in peaceful collective action and collective bargaining. Efforts to reform Korea's labor laws have been resisted by Roh's government.

Asia Watch recommends to the South Korean government the following urgently needed measures and reforms:

1. All persons being detained under the National Security Law or the Law on Assembly and Demonstration solely for the exercise of the peaceful expression of their beliefs, such as Kim Keun-tae, Hong Song-dam, and Kim Hyong-jang, should be promptly and unconditionally released.

2. The vaguely-worded National Security Law should be amended to prevent its frequent use to punish or prevent peaceful expression and dissent. Police and prosecutors should cease abusing the Law on Assembly and Demonstration to restrict free expression by preventing or suppressing peaceful protests.

3. The practice of pressuring prisoners sentenced under the National Security Law to sign "conversion" statements should be abolished.

4. Trade unionists and labor activists detained solely because of peaceful trade union activity, including those on trial or imprisoned charged with "third-party interference," "interfering with ordinary business," or violations of the Law on Assembly and Demonstration, should be released. Among those who should be released are Jang Myung-guk, Kwon Yong-mok and Dan Byong-ho. Allegations of mistreatment of arrested workers, such as those held at the Ulsan police station and Pusan Pretrial Detention Facility, should be fully investigated and steps should be taken to ensure they are not subjected to beatings, harassment or other forms of ill-treatment.

5. The labor laws should be reformed to bring them into line with international standards and South Korean constitutional guarantees of workers' rights to independent association, collective bargaining and collective action. The Trade Union law should be amended to allow independently-formed trade union federations, such as Chonnohyop, to freely function. Provisions of the Labor Dispute Adjustment Law and Trade Union Law prohibiting "third party interference" should be abolished, workers should have the right to associate freely and seek assistance from labor educators, advisors, lawyers and others. The laws governing public sector employees should be changed -- specifically the National Civil

Service Act, Trade Union Law, and Private School Law -- in order to recognize the right of both public and private teachers to form their own trade unions.

6. The South Korean government should undertake a thorough, public and independent investigation of the violent activities of the *kusadae* (company goon squads). Where such squads are found to have engaged in assaults on workers seeking to carry out peaceful trade union activity, they should be disbanded.

7. The practice of using *baikgoldan* (teams of special non-uniformed police) to break strikes should be ended. Allegations of police or company violence -- as in the case of Orient Electronics Ltd. -- should be fully investigated and prosecuted by the authorities, as vigorously as they prosecute workers engaged in alleged acts of violence. This is crucial to restore the role of the government as a neutral mediator in labor disputes.

8. The South Korean government should refrain from interfering with the internal operation of legally elected unions, by using arrests of union leaders as a pretext for dismissing them from their jobs, thus rendering them ineligible for union positions, or employing riot police and the threat of violence to suppress peaceful trade union activities. The rights of workers in the broadcast and newspaper industries to express their views and carry out peaceful collective actions in accordance with international standards should be fully respected and upheld by the government.

68

0071

X. U.S. ROLE AND GOVERNMENT POLICY

As a military and political ally, trading partner, and major investor, the United States has played a crucial role in the Republic of Korea since before its foundation. The U.S. could bring significant pressure to bear on the government to protect freedom of expression, freedom of association and other basic human rights and to fulfill the promises of reform made in 1987.

U.S. Government Policy

The U.S. State Department *Country Report on Human Rights Practices for 1989*, published in February 1990, praises South Korea for "moving away from its authoritarian past" and for "making great strides towards attaining full democracy." It points to releases of some political prisoners in 1988 and a "boisterous free press" as examples of such progress, while at the same time it criticizes the increasing use of the National Security Law and the Law on Assembly and Demonstration to repress dissidents. It also notes the failure of the government to implement promised reforms in these laws. (As noted in chapter 2, the Law on Assembly and Demonstration was amended in March 1989, but abuse of the law continues.) Despite these, and other continuing human rights violations, the State Department concludes that "on balance Korea remains a much more tolerant and open society" than in the past.

In view of the massive crackdown on trade unions, stalling of promised legal reforms, and continued restrictions on free expression, these conclusions seem overstated.

On the question of trade union rights and the right of association, the report describes the lack of progress towards reform of the Trade Union Law and Labor Dispute Adjustment Act, noting that President Roh had vetoed several amendments. Most significantly, the report comments only very briefly on the government's crackdown on trade unionists, with a four-sentence reference to the Hyundai strike, the Seoul subway strike,[274] and the teachers union dispute. It provides no details on the massive use of force to suppress strikes or on the number of arrests of trade unionists (with the exception of noting that forty teachers had been arrested as of early September). It concludes with the ambiguous statement that in 1989 "the Government began to take a more active role in labor-management disputes."

In surveying South Korea's observance of the right to organize and bargain collectively, the State Department says that "many major employers are strongly anti-union" and mentions that in several cases company goon squads have been used to beat up union organizers and intimidate workers. The State Department observes, correctly, that the authorities have "not been effective in investigating such incidents," but again the report provides no specifics.

The Asia Watch mission, in discussions with U.S. embassy officials in Seoul, raised several of the cases documented in this report, including those of Kwon Yong-mok, Cho Chu-nam, and Kim Nam-suk, as well as the plight of the Orient Electronics workers. The embassy's first secretary in the political section and its part-time labor attache agreed to make private inquiries about the cases with relevant

---

[274] A Seoul taxi company employee was reportedly killed by company goons, or by "anti-union workers," as the Korean authorities concluded Department of State Country Report on Human Rights Practices for 1989 (February 1990), p 897.

69

0072

government officials and said that the embassy had an "active interest" in bringing up incidents of abuse at every opportunity. As of October 1990, we had not been informed of the outcome of any such inquiries.

The embassy also acknowledged that the South Korean government's policy on labor issues was headed in the "wrong direction." However, U.S. government officials in Seoul stated it was current U.S. policy to raise human rights concerns only through quiet diplomatic channels. These officials firmly rejected the notion that the U.S. embassy should be publicly outspoken about human rights abuses or that it should demonstrate its concern about detainees subjected to abuses by seeking to visit them. We specifically asked for review of the existing stated policy of refraining from visiting any political prisoners.[275]

· Finally, the embassy was reluctant to consider sending observers to political trials or trials of trade union leaders as a way of indicating U.S. concern that trial procedures are fair and legal according to international standards.

Asia Watch suggested that the U.S. government's restriction of its comments on human rights problems to "quiet diplomacy" might be a factor contributing to rising anti-Americanism -- marked, for example, by violent attacks on the U.S. Cultural Center in Seoul in May 1990 and a firebomb attack on the U.S. cultural center in Kwangju on June 11, 1990. Although the first secretary, who described himself as the embassy's anti-Americanism specialist, conceded that the failure of the U.S. government to speak out publicly about human rights at the time of the Kwangju massacre in 1980 was a major cause of the rise of anti-American feelings in the 1980's, he rejected the argument that continuing this approach was a mistake. He insisted that a more vocal, public policy would ostensibly reinforce the perception that the U.S. government is "omniscient" and "omnipotent" and should be responsible for solving South Korea's problems. Another State Department official in Washington, D.C. defended existing policy with a different argument: It is a "new day" in South Korea and "we can't interfere with their problems."[276]

This policy is politically short-sighted. It ignores the fact that the U.S. is widely perceived in South Korea as firmly aligned with the government of President Roh Tae-woo and its policies, and this perception contributes significantly to anti-American feelings. (This has made the U.S. a ready target for so-called "extremist violence," which in turn has provided a pretext for further repression.) Such an approach also fails to express what should be unequivocal U.S. government policy of support for democratic reform and the protection of basic rights of freedom of expression, association, and free trade union activity. Governments change their policies not only through private pressure but through public stigmatization. At a time when Korea is seeking to become a member of the United Nations, the U.S. should use Korea's desire for international acceptance to publicly press for improvements in the human rights situation.

The attitude of U.S. officials in Seoul reflects the overall Bush administration policy toward human rights in South Korea. Throughout 1989 and 1990 the Bush administration stated that it was committed to human rights and democratic reforms in South Korea. But its failure to comment publicly

---

[275] Asia Watch made this request earlier in a letter to Mr. Raymond Burghardt, Deputy Chief of Mission, on April 9, 1990 following a meeting with him in Washington, D.C. on March 11, 1990.

[276] Interviews with Lynn Turk and Jeffrey Goldstein, U.S. Embassy, Seoul, June 14, 1990; Roberta Chew and Spence Richardson, U.S. State Department, Office of Korean Affairs, May 16, 1990.

70

0073

and forcefully when the number and severity of human rights violations increased sent the opposite signal to the South Korean government and people.[277]

The administration repeatedly failed to take advantage of strategic opportunities to comment publicly on specific human rights abuses, such as the meetings between President Bush and President Roh on February 27, 1989, and the visit to Seoul by Vice President Quayle on September 19, 1989. On June 6, 1990, another meeting between President Roh and President Bush took place at a particularly opportune moment, following Roh's "summit" meeting in San Francisco with Soviet President Gorbachev, at which there were discussions of steps towards reunification and improved relations between North and South Korea. It was also shortly before a special legislative session was due to begin in Seoul during which reforms in the National Security Law, the labor laws, the broadcasting commission, and various other laws relating to human rights were reportedly scheduled to be taken up. Asia Watch publicly urged the administration to use the occasion to press the South Korean government to implement legal reforms, including revisions of the National Security Law, and to release those imprisoned for non-violent political activity. No reference whatsoever to human rights was made by President Bush or the State Department as far as could be determined from the published accounts of the talks.

U.S. Trade Policy and Labor Rights

Legislation enacted by the U.S. Congress in 1984 links certain U.S. trade benefits to the recipient governments' respect for internationally-recognized labor rights. Section 502 (b)(8) of the Trade Act denies a recipient country preferential treatment under the Generalized System of Preferences (GSP) if that country "has not taken or is not taking steps to afford internationally recognized workers' rights." In addition, Congress made observance of interna·.·nally recognized rights, such as the rights of association, organization and collective bargaining, a condition for insurance and investment guarantees provided to U.S. companies investing abroad under the Overseas Private Investment Corporation (OPIC). In addition, OPIC is mandated by Congress to "take into account ... all available information about observance of and respect for human rights and fundamental freedoms" in countries receiving OPIC assistance.[278]

In 1988, imports from South Korea into the U.S. totalled $20.2 billion. In 1989, $19.7 billion worth of goods were exported to the U.S., making this country one of South Korea's most important trade markets.[279]

Asia Watch presented testimony on South Korea before the U.S. Trade Representative during the review of GSP in October, 1987. At that time, following an Asia Watch mission to South Korea from June 27 to July 14, we were encouraged by indications that labor reform might be promoted by a program of government liberalization, but we also expressed the concern that "such reform will have negligible impact on labor rights in the absence of an official, and continuing, commitment to end abusive and illegal practices."[280] Asia Watch's testimony urged the U.S. Trade Representative to assess progress in the implementation of a number of measures to determine South Korea's eligibility under the GSP law. These

---

[277] Human Rights Watch, *The Bush Administration's Record on Human Rights in 1989* (December 1989), pp. 243-8.

[278] Section 239(i) of the Foreign Assistance Act.

[279] The U.S exported $10.6 billion to South Korea in 1988 and $13.5 billion in 1989, *Official Statistics*, U.S. Department of Commerce, July 26, 1990.

[280] Asia Watch testimony, p. 3.

0074

included reforms in the Trade Union Law and Labor Dispute Adjustment Law; an end to the official harassment, intimidation and mistreatment of labor organizers; and no further prosecutions of workers and labor groups for exercising their rights to peaceful expression and association.

South Korea graduated out of the GSP program on January 1, 1989 due to the increase in trade volume beyond the legal limit entitling South Korea to GSP benefits and not because of any improvement in their treatment of workers. However, OPIC continues its program in South Korea, notwithstanding the labor rights abuses.[281]

Role of the U.S Congress

The South Korean government's suppression of trade unionists and denial of their human rights has been a matter of concern for many members of the U.S. Congress, despite the erroneous assumption on the part of some that the human rights situation has improved dramatically under President Roh and does not require close scrutiny.

Congressional offices have been active on behalf of trade unionists in South Korea. On March 9, 1990, the Congressional Working Group on International Labor Rights, a bipartisan group of fifty U.S. senators and representatives, wrote to South Korean officials about the deterioration of labor rights in South Korea. They expressed concern about restrictions on Chonnohyop (Council of Korean Trade Unions) and arrests of its leaders, and they urged an end to the government's crackdown "which clearly violates the rights of Korean workers to participate in peaceful union activities."

A separate letter signed by ten U.S. senators[282] was sent to President Roh on June 14, 1990. In particular, they criticized the government's infringement of the basic right of unionists to take collective action in the cases of Hyundai Heavy Industries and the Korean Broadcasting System. Furthermore, they warned, "Regulations to limit or prevent the formation of trade unions or restrict collective bargaining... may contravene laws requiring countries receiving loan [guarantees] from the Overseas Private Investment Corporation to extend to their workers internationally recognized worker rights." The appeal was covered in the Korean press.[283]

Congressional hearings on democratization in South Korea and the status of North-South relations were held on July 26, 1989, before the House Subcommittee on Asian and Pacific Affairs. At that hearing, Deputy Assistant Secretary of State for East Asia and Pacific Affairs, William Clark, Jr., said, "While there remain some elements of the past to be overcome...the American people can and do warmly applaud the progress which has been made" towards democratization.

---

[281] In 1989, over $80 million in OPIC guarantees were given to U.S. investors in South Korea. This declined steeply in 1990 due to a ceiling imposed by the OPIC board of directors, which was recently lifted.

[282] Senators Kennedy, Leahy, Harkin, Levin, DeConcini, Mikulski, Kerry, Burdick, Conrad, and Akaka.

[283] *Hankyoreh Shinmun*, June 16, 1990.

72

The Role of U.S. Investors and Companies

American companies and direct investors are heavily involved in the South Korean economy, taking advantage of low wages, high productivity and skills level, high profits,[284] and an anti-union environment. While Japan is the largest foreign investor, the U.S. comes second with total investments of $1.9 billion in 1989.[285] The infusion of American capital and technology has been crucial to South Korea's economic growth. U.S. investors thus should be able to play an important role in promoting respect for labor rights.

U.S. companies operating in South Korea are most active in the heavy-industries manufacturing sector.[286] Many started in the 1960's as small operations, as in the electronics field, with 100–200 employees. According to a representative of the American Chamber of Commerce in Seoul to whom we spoke, approximately 200 of the 348 member companies in the Chamber are U.S. companies, including the largest and most powerful.[287] The balance are Japanese, South Korean and European. He said that 90 percent of U.S. companies are now unionized. The Chamber has a labor committee, and the organization sees its role as explaining labor standards and obligations under South Korean law to U.S. companies, assisting in the development of positive labor-management relations, and lobbying on behalf of business interests.[288] The Chamber's representative characterized unionization as a "fact of life" which companies should accept and said that labor relations at U.S. companies in South Korea were "for the most part, relatively smooth." (We asked for statistics on the number of strikes and disputes at U.S. companies, but he was unable to provide that information.) He acknowledged, however, that there have been "problems" and alluded specifically to the 1987–88 strike against Motorola Company[289] and to the Pico Korea Ltd. dispute.[290]

The Pico dispute has followed a pattern similar to other disputes involving foreign investors who have responded to labor unrest by pulling up stakes and leaving the country without fulfilling their legal obligations in the process.[291] During wage negotiations in February 1989, Pico Korea, a subsidiary of a Pico Products, cable T.V. component manufacturer headquartered in Syracuse, New York, closed down its South Korea operations and left the workers empty-handed, without back pay and benefits to which they were entitled. According to Pico workers interviewed by Asia Watch, on March 22, 1989 about 300 people went to the American Chamber of Commerce's offices in Seoul to ask their assistance in contacting

---

[284] George Ogle, *South Korea: Dissent within the Miracle* (to be published in December 1990), Zed Books, London and distributed by Humanities Press International in the U.S.) Remittances in 1986 to U.S. businesses from Korean operations were approximately $368 million, according to the U.S. embassy.

[285] Bureau of Economic Analysis, U.S. Department of Commerce, statistics for year-end 1989.

[286] Ogle: These include automobile, transportation equipment, machinery and chemicals.

[287] Among the Chamber's members are: Westinghouse Electric (Asia), AT&T Far East, Bank of America, Citibank, Goodyear Korea, Litton Korea, Texas Instruments Korea. *1990 American Chamber of Commerce Directory*.

[288] According to the Spring 1990 Introduction to the *American Chamber of Commerce Directory*, its aims include activities to "represent and relay the opinions and positions of the American business community to the Korean government ... (and) to U.S. government officials." The U.S. ambassador is the Chamber's honorary president; he meets monthly with the organization's board of governors, p. 3.

[289] Repeated attempts to organize a legal union at Motorola, a major U.S. company with over 5,000 employees, were resisted by the company and ended tragically with the self-immolation of a worker.

[290] Interview with Jeffrey Jones, attorney and a vice-president of U.S. Chamber of Commerce, Seoul, June 14, 1990.

[291] *See e.g.*, the 1982 case of Control Data Company, Asia Watch, *Human Rights in Korea*, (January 1986), pp. 197–199.

0076

the president of Pico Korea, Ltd., although Pico is not a member of the Chamber. The police came in to remove them, workers were repeatedly beaten and 17 were ultimately hospitalized. This violent incident was heavily covered in the media.

Trade unions in the U.S. have taken an active interest in the case. Several U.S. unions supported a tour of Pico workers in the U.S. and organized a picket line at the convention of national cable TV in Atlanta, Georgia. AFL-CIO President Lane Kirkland, on April 25, 1990, condemned Pico's violation of workers' rights and wrote to the South Korean government urging the Labor Ministry to initiate a lawsuit against Pico in South Korea.[292] Meanwhile, the Pico workers union filed a suit in a U.S. court alleging that the president of Pico Products in the U.S. interfered with the operation of Pico Korea and was responsible, by ordering the dissolution of the company, for the company not complying with its legal contract with the union. The suit also alleges that Pico Products failed to comply with the so-called "Plant Closures Act" (Worker Adjustment and Retraining Adjustment Act) requiring that notification of intent to close the plant be given to the workers 90 days in advance.

The role of U.S. companies in South Korea, despite the Chamber's claims, remains controversial. This is due to the mistreatment of workers by managers of U.S.-owned or U.S.-invested companies, as in the case of Orient Electronics cited in this report, coupled with the manner in which some U.S. companies have withdrawn from South Korea.

The American Chamber of Commerce should take a direct interest in the development and application of South Korean labor laws as they affect the work force and the country's business climate as a whole. To promote the protection of basic human rights for workers and the observance of international labor standards and principles, it should use its formal and informal channels with the government, its prestige and its substantial economic leverage.

The only sanction currently available for use against companies engaged in particularly egregious behavior would be a vote by the Chamber's board of governors to expel them. At the very least, the Chamber's labor committee should explore the establishment of an internal mechanism for monitoring the protection of basic human rights by its member companies. It should also take steps to more forcefully distance itself from U.S. invested companies like Pico and Orient Electronics which do not respect workers' rights. Finally, the Chamber does not have a code of conduct for member companies, which could be developed with strict guidelines for respecting workers' right to freedom of association, including the right to form trade unions and engage in collective action.

Role of the U.S. Labor Movement

Since 1971, the AFL-CIO has maintained an office in Seoul. The Asian-American Free Labor Institute (AAFLI) receives U.S. government funding as well as support from the AFL-CIO member unions.[293] It operates in South Korea at the invitation of the Federation of Korean Trade Unions

---

[292] On August 12, 1990, the Center for Constitutional Rights, representing the Pico workers union, filed a suit in Northern New York District Court under the Labor Relations Management Act (301). The union is seeking over $1 million in damages.

[293] AAFLI was established in 1968. It lists as funding sources: the AFL-CIO and its affiliates, labor groups in Asia and the Pacific, the U.S. Agency for International Development, the National Endowment for Democracy (which receives annual appropriations from the U.S. Congress), and the U.S. Information Agency. Its stated aims are "to

(FKTU), which is the South Korean member of the International Confederation of Free Trade Unions (ICFTU). With the permission of the Seoul government, AAFLI provides labor education and training to FKTU affiliates. It is therefore not viewed legally as a "third party" under the South Korean labor laws. AAFLI sees its role as contributing to the development of long-term trade union institutions, within a legal framework and provisions of the South Korean constitution guaranteeing workers rights of free association and collective bargaining. AAFLI is in a strategic position to be a positive force and catalyst for change in official policies and practices, both within the FKTU and with the South Korean government. It can do this, for example, by encouraging reforms in the labor laws, as well as taking up cases of independent trade union educators or organizers who are arrested or detained for peaceful union activities. Within the U.S., the AAFLI can assist in educating and mobilizing AFL-CIO affiliated unions to become actively involved in campaigns in support of repressed South Korean workers.

The AFL-CIO Executive Council has adopted public positions critical of the Korean government's crackdown on labor. In May 1990 it adopted a resolution condemning the repression of the Hyundai strikes and "attacks on freedom of expression as evidenced by the police breaking a strike at KBS." The council called on the Bush administration to show "as much concern and effort in the field of worker rights as it has shown in pressuring Korea on beef import quotas...."[294]

Within the ICFTU, the AFL-CIO has aligned itself with efforts at the international level to support trade union and human rights in South Korea. For example, at its executive board meeting in Brussels on May 9-11, the ICFTU adopted a resolution condemning the South Korean government's "restrictive and oppressive policies on industrial relations." The resolution praised the "determination and courage of the Korean workers and the spontaneous upsurge of their actions which led to the establishment of many new unions." At the same time, it expressed support for the FKTU and urged "the release of detained trade union activists, continuing dialogue between the trade unions and the authorities, and the revision of labor and trade union legislation in line with ILO standards and principles."

The International Metalworkers Federation (IMF), representing 13 million workers in North America, Europe and Asia, met in Seoul on June 7-8, 1990. At the conclusion of a meeting of its 150-member Central Committee, the IMF general secretary issued a statement condemning the South Korean government's "totalitarian attitudes towards individual trade unionists" and said that IMF affiliates in seventy countries would be given the names of arrested South Korean trade unionists and asked to launch local campaigns for their release. An IMF resolution adopted at the conference said trade unions rights were "lagging far behind the rapid economic development" of South Korea and criticized existing Korean labor laws which denied workers "any genuine right of association."[295]

Conclusions and Recommendations

Based on Asia Watch's ongoing research and on-site investigations, we believe that much more could be done, privately and publicly, by the U.S. government and by corporate and trade union representatives to promote human rights in South Korea.

---

cooperate with trade unions in the region in a wide range of educational, organization, and membership services activities." Pamphlet: AAFLI - Questions and Answers.
[294] *AAFLI News*, June 1990.
[295] Press statement by IMF, June 8, 1990

75

84 한국 인권문제 제 사안 2

The U.S. government should be more energetic on behalf of the right to freedom of expression. The Bush administration should publicly oppose the arrest and imprisonment of South Koreans for expressing opinions on reunification with the North or for making contact with the North. Steps toward opening a dialogue with the North and U.S. encouragement of such steps should not be allowed to obscure delays in the process of democratization in South Korea or blunt U.S. efforts to promote reforms there.

It is clear that Congressional concern and the active involvement of the American trade union movement--in conjunction with international trade union bodies--have a significant impact in South Korea which should be enhanced and expanded. Congress should challenge the State Department to provide an in-depth assessment of the state of human rights and labor rights and should consistently press U.S. officials in Seoul and Washington D.C. to speak out, privately and publicly, about specific human rights cases and concerns.

Finally, the insurance investment guarantees to U.S. investors in South Korea provided under the Overseas Investment Corporation should be ended, in compliance with U.S. legal conditions on the observance of internationally recognized worker rights. The South Korean government must not be allowed to view U.S. trade and investment as an endorsement of anti-union policies that violate workers' rights.

APPENDICES

I.   Statement of the Republic of Korea Ministry of Justice

II. Terms and Laws Cited in this Report

III. List of Jailed South Korean Unionists and Labor Activists

IV. List of Publishers and Others Jailed in Connection with Their Publishing Activities, 1989-90.

0080

APPENDIX 1. STATEMENT OF THE MINISTRY OF JUSTICE

Statement by the Minister of Justice Lee Jong-nam and read by Prosecutor Lee Sun-woo, Director of the Human Rights Division, to the Asia Watch Mission at the beginning of a discussion on June 15, 1990.

In launching the Sixth Republic the government has resolutely promoted policies of democratization, autonomy, and liberalization so that the authoritarianism of the old era could be liquidated and the true flower of democracy might bloom in this land. Thus in every segment of our society democratic systems and practices are being firmly established.

However, it is true that the process of promoting democratization has given us many trials and troubles. Before the new democratic order could completely send down its roots, the variegated demands of various sectors of the society which had been suppressed have exploded all at once and all the hidden problems have broken into the open.

In the midst of this, in order to achieve unreasonable objectives which are entirely their own, some people who lack discretion devoted themselves completely to illegal collective action. Moreover, left-wing violent revolutionary forces began to abuse the government's democratic measures and reveal machinations aimed at destroying the liberal democratic system.

Confronted with this situation the government patiently hoped that law and order would be obeyed and established through self-regulation. That is to say, recognizing that a truly democratic society maintains law and order through self-regulation, the government restrained itself from using public power in relation to repeated lawlessness and disorder which occurred in the early stages of democratization.

Nevertheless, some people lacking in discretion, starting with the left-wing violent revolutionary forces, have become more radical day by day. Thus, lawlessness and disorder which had not been seen in our society before became rampant and the worry and unease of the citizens increased daily.

Finally, it reached such an extreme situation that there was a worry that, if we continued to ignore their illegal collective actions and machinations to destroy the system, not only would it be impossible for democratization itself to progress but it also might endanger the very existence of the state.

In this kind of situation, the government, while, on the one hand, promoting democratization continuously, on the other hand was compelled to take stern legal action against the forces which were impeding democratization. No matter what sacrifice must be suffered, in the future the government must without fail have a policy -- based on the citizens' common feeling that the illegal collective action and the left-wing violent revolutionary forces must be eradicated -- of exerting its best effort to establish legal order in our society.

Nevertheless, this kind of effort to establish law and order is being distorted and propagandized by some at home and abroad as the suppression of democratic figures, and there are also even cases of

79

0081

한국 인권문제 관련 사안, 1990-91. 전2권 (V.1 1990-91.2월) 87

falsely conveying examples of human rights abuses in the judicial process as if they were common.[296] This is very regrettable and distressing.

By all means I earnestly hope that this pamphlet will help in the understanding of the government's effort to promote democratization and establish law and order and will help to some extent in achieving a truly democratic society.

Lee Jong-nam
Minister of Justice
July, 1990[297]

---

[296] The "and abroad" was written in by hand on the copy from which Mr. Lee read to us.

[297] Note that the reference to a pamphlet, the date, and the Minister of Justice's title and name were not read at the time. This statement was apparently prepared for publication by the Ministry, perhaps as the preface of a pamphlet.

80   0082

APPENDIX II. LAWS CITED IN THE REPORT

Frequently used terms about legal authority, and excerpts from the Constitution of the Republic of Korea, the Trade Union Law, and the Labor Dispute Adjustment Law. The terms and laws are cited from Labor Laws and Korea, *Ministry of Labor, Republic of Korea, 1989.*

TERMS

Administrative Authority: The governmental authority to which unions and employers must submit all required documents and notifications. The proper administrative authority depends upon the location of the union's membership. In case the union's membership is spread to more than one province, the Minister of Labor is the proper administrative authority. In other cases, the Mayor of Seoul Special City, Mayor of Pusan City, Taegu City or Governor of Provinces serve as the administrative authority to the unions within their geographical jurisdiction. (Art. 13(1), Trade Union Law) All these officials, except the mayor of Seoul, are appointed by the President.

Labor Relations Commission: There is a Central Labor Relations Commission established in the Ministry of Labor and Local Labor Relations Commissions established in each city and province. Each commission is composed of equal number of persons representing the workers, the employers, and the public. The appointments to and functions of the Labor Relations Commissions are governed by the Labor Relations Commission Law, which was promulgated in 1953 and most recently amended in 1984.

LAWS

The Constitution of the Republic of Korea (amended October 19, 1987)

Art. 21 (1) All citizens shall enjoy freedom of speech and the press, and freedom of assembly and association.

Art. 31 (6) Fundamental matters pertaining to the educational system, including...administration, finance, and the status of teachers, shall be determined by law.

Art. 33 (1) To enhance working conditions, workers shall have the right to independent association, collective bargaining and collective action.
(2) Only those public officials who are designated by law shall have the right to association, collective bargaining and collective action.
(3) The right to collective action of workers employed by important defense industries may be either restricted or denied as prescribed by law.

Trade Union Law (promulgated March 1953, amended most recently November 28, 1987)

Art. 3 (Definition of Trade Union): "The trade union" mentioned in this Law shall mean an organization or a federation of the organizations, which is voluntarily formed at the initiative of laborers for the purpose of maintaining and improving working conditions and enhancing welfare and socio-economic status of the workers.

However, in the cases falling under the category of the following items, the definition made in this Article shall not be applied:

(5) When the subject of the organization membership is the same as the already existing trade union, or the purpose of the organization is to hamper the normal operation of the already existing trade unions.

Art. 8 (Restriction on Formation and Membership of Trade Union): Workers may organize or join trade union at liberty. In case of public officials, however, the right shall be stipulated separately by Law.

Art. 12 (Prohibition of Political Activities):
    (1) A trade union shall not be allowed to conduct any act, in the election of any public office, in order to support a specific political party or have specific persons elected.
    (2) A trade union shall not be able to collect political funds from its members.
    (3) Fund for a trade union shall not be diverted to political funds.

Art.12-2 (Prohibition for Interference by a Third Party): Persons other than a worker who has actual employment relations with the employer, or concerned trade union, or other persons having legitimate authority under law shall not engage in an act of interference for the purpose of manipulating, instigation, obstructing, or any other act to influence the concerned parties in an establishment or dissolution of a trade union, joining or disjoining a trade union, or in collective bargaining with the employer.
    But the federation of unions or the industrial federations affiliated by concerned unions shall not be regarded as the Third Party.

Art. 13 (Establishment of a Trade Union):
    1. Any person who intends to establish a union, must submit a report including the statements specified hereunder, and the charter attached thereto, to the federation to which the union is affiliated....
        (1) Name of the union.
        (2) Address of the principal union office.
        (3) Number of membership ...
        (4) Names of the officers and their addresses.
        (5) Names of industrial federation to which a union is affiliated.
        (6) In case of a federation of unions, names of member unions, number of membership, address of the principal office and names of officers and their addresses.
    2. "The federation to which union is affiliated" mentioned in Paragraph 1 shall mean, the federation of unions by industry whose membership consists of unit trade union of the same kind, or a national federation whose membership consists of unit trade union by industry on a national scale.

Art. 14. (Charter):
    1. In order to secure democratic and autonomous operation of the organization, a trade union shall specify in its charter the following contents.
        (1) Name;
        (2) Purpose and undertakings;
        (3) Address of main office;
        (4) Matters concerning union members;
        (5) Name of the federation to which the union is affiliated;
        (6) In case there is a council of delegates, matters concerning thereof;
        (7) In the case of a trade union which is a federate organization, matters concerning its constituent organizations;

82

0084

(8) Matters concerning conferences;

(9) Matters concerning its representative and executive members;

(10) Matters concerning union fees and accounting;

(11) Matters concerning changes of charter;

(12) Matters concerning dissolution;

(13) Matters concerning representatives of labor-management councils;

(14) Matters concerning labor disputes;

(15) Matters concerning impeachment of representatives and executive members for violation of the charter;

(16) Matters concerning election procedures of executive members and convention delegates; and

(17) Matters concerning rules and regulations.

Art. 15. (Certificate of Report):

1. Upon receipt of a report of establishment prescribed in paragraph 1, Article 13, the Administrative Authority shall issue a certificate of report in accordance with the provisions of the Presidential Decree within 3 days.

Art. 16. (Amendment of, or Supplementation to, the Charter): In case any provision of the union charter conflicts with labor-related law and decree, the Administrative Authority may, with the approval of the Labor Relations Commission, order the amendment, or supplementation to the charter.

Art. 30 (Submission of the Documents): When it deemed necessary, the Administrative Authority may have the accounting status or other necessary documents of the trade union be submitted for investigation.

Art. 34 (Drawing Up of a Collective Agreement):

3. Administrative Authority may order change or nullification of a term in collective agreement when the term is improper in violation of laws, after obtaining resolution of the Labor Relations Commission.

Art. 38. (Regional Binding Force):

1. In case two-thirds or more of the laborers of the same kind who are engaged in a business in an area come under the application of a collective agreement, the pertinent administrative authority may, through the decision of the Labor Relations Commission, at the request of one party or both parties to the collective agreement or ex officio, decide that the same collective agreement shall be applied to the other laborers and employers of the same kind engaged in the same area.

Art. 47 (Penal Provision): Any person who, in violation of the provisions of Article 30, failed to submit the required documents or filed false report, or who refuses, obstructs or obviates investigation, shall be subjected to an imprisonment for the term not exceeding three months or a fine for the amount not exceeding 200 thousand *won*.

Labor Dispute Adjustment Law (promulgated March 1953, amended most recently November 1987)

Art. 4 (Definition of Business of Public Interest): The terms "business of public interest" as used in this Law shall mean a business indispensable for daily public life, or the suspension or termination of which has severe impact upon national economy, and which falls under one of the following categories.

(1) Public transportation business

0085

83

(2) Water, electricity, gas supply, and petroleum refinery business.
(3) Public hygiene and medical business
(4) Banking business
(5) Broadcasting and communication business

Art. 13-2. (Prohibition for Interference by a Third Party): Persons other than an employee who has actual employment relations with the employer, or concerned trade union and employer, or persons other than having legitimate authority under law shall not engage in an act of interference, in a dispute, for the purpose of manipulating, instigating, or any other act to influence the parties concerned.

Art. 14. (Cooling-off Period): No acts of dispute shall be conducted unless 10 days have elapsed in the case of ordinary enterprise and 15 days in the case of public utility after receipt of the report prescribed in the paragraph 2 of Article 16, by the Labor Relations Commission, has been rendered.

Art. 16 (Notice on a Labor Dispute):
    1. In case a labor dispute has occurred, the one of the parties concerned shall notice it thereof to the Administrative Authority and the Labor Relations Commission concerned and notify the fact to the other.

Art. 40 (Decision of Emergency Adjustment):
    1. The Minister of the Ministry of Labor may render a decision for an emergency adjustment, in case an act of dispute is related to public interests, or it is of large scale or of specific character, and that, because of such act of dispute there exist the same danger which might impair the national economy or endanger the daily life of the general public.

Art. 41 (Suspension of an Act of Dispute at the Time of Emergency Adjustment): The parties concerned shall immediately suspend any act of dispute when a decision for an emergency adjustment under paragraph 3 of Article 40 is announced, and no act of dispute shall be commenced again unless 20 days has elapsed from the date of announcement.

0086

84

APPENDIX III. JAILED SOUTH KOREAN UNIONISTS AND LABOR ACTIVISTS

This list was compiled by the Korea Research and Information Center, a Seoul-based labor research institute as of October 1, 1990. We have also included information from Minkahyup's June 16, 1990 list of political prisoners, which are noted in brackets, and other sources as noted.

Some of the persons included on this list have been charged with violent offenses, such as physical assault and throwing firebombs. Their mention in the report should not be taken as Asia Watch's endorsement of such actions. Asia Watch calls for the release of only those who have neither engaged in or advocated the use of violence.

SEOUL

KO Min-taek: Choongwon Electronics, union's education officer, [arrested March 16, 1989], charged with "third-party interference" provision of the Labor Dispute Adjustment Law [and obstruction of business].

KIM Jum-soon: Choongwon Electronics, union president, charged with "third-party interference" provision of the Labor Dispute Adjustment Law [and obstruction of business].

HAN Sook-woong: Chunji Industry Company, union vice-president, arrested on May 18, 1990, charged with obstructing business.

KANG Keum-joo: Chunji Industry Company, union president, arrested on May 18, 1990, charged with obstructing business.

NAM Bae-hong: Daerim Plastics Company, union's cultural officer, arrested on May 4, 1990, charged under the Special Law against Firebombs and the Law on Assembly and Demonstration.

DAN Byung-ho: Dong-a Construction Company, chairman of Chonnohyop (Korean Council of Trade Unions), arrested on February 28, 1990, charged with violating the Law on Assembly and Demonstration. [On July 13, 1990, he was sentenced to a one-and-a-half years' imprisonment. *Korea Herald*.]

CHOI Bong-young: Dong-a Construction, union's general secretary, charged with violating the Law on Assembly and Demonstration.

LEE Tae-hyung: Dongbu Metal Company, rank-and-file worker, arrested on May 4, 1990, charged under the Special Law against Firebombs and the Law on Assembly and Demonstration.

YOON Kyu-hyun: Dongbu Metal Company, union's dispute officer, arrested on May 4, 1990, charged under the Special Law against Firebombs and the Law on Assembly and Demonstration.

KIM Il-sook: Dongsuh Culture Co., general secretary, arrested on May 17, 1990, charged with obstructing business and committing physical violence.

LEE Eon-joo: Dongsuh Culture Co., president, arrested on May 17, 1990, charged with obstructing business and committing physical violence.

LEE Tae-wan: Dongsuh Culture Co., vice-president, arrested on May 17, 1990, charged with obstructing business and committing physical violence.

BAEK Wan-ki: Education Insurance Company, planning director, arrested on June 1, 1990, charged with obstructing business (Criminal Code) and committing physical violence (Criminal Code).

HONG Eon-sook: Education Insurance Company, information officer, arrested on August 1, 1990, charged with obstructing business.

KIM Joo-sam: Education Insurance Company, general manager, arrested on June 1, 1990, charged with obstructing business (Criminal Code) and committing physical violence (Criminal Code).

LEE Sang-hak: Education Insurance Company, president, arrested in September 1990 (?), charged with "obstructing business."

YANG Dal-hwi: Education Insurance Company, union executive, arrested on June 1, 1990, charged with obstructing business (Criminal Code) and committing physical violence (Criminal Code).

YU Jin-bee: Hanjoo Electronics, arrested on June 20, 1990, charged with obstructing business.

CHOI Seung-nyul: Kwangrim Electronics Company, president, arrested on June 1, 1990, charged with obstructing business.

KIM Chae-bok: Kwangrim Electronics Company, convention delegate, arrested on June 1, 1990, charged with obstructing business.

KO Eun-jeong: Kwangrim Electronics Company, former general secretary, arrested on June 1, 1990, charged with obstructing business.

OH Eun-sook: Minsung Electricity Company, president, arrested on May 31, 1990, charged with violating the Law on Assembly and Demonstration.

85

0087

CHOI Yoon-cheol. Minsung Electricity Company, rank-and-file worker, arrested on May 4, 1990, charged with violating the Law on Assembly and Demonstration and Special Law against Firebombs.

JI Dong-hwan. Minsung Electricity Company, general secretary, arrested on May 4, 1990, charged with violating the Law on Assembly and Demonstration and Special Law against Firebombs. [Arrest date given as May 6.]

KIM Hyung-tae: Minsung Electricity Company, deputy president, arrested on May 4, 1990, charged with violating the Law on Assembly and Demonstration and Special Law against Firebombs.

BANG Seung-kwan: Nambu Mechanical and Metalworkers Union, organizer, arrested on April 6, 1990, charged with obstructing business and physical violence.

CHO Won-bong: Nambu Mechanical and Metalworkers Union, statistics officer, arrested on April 6, 1990, charged with obstructing business and physical violence.

CHOI Do-hyun: Nambu Mechanical and Metalworkers Union, director, arrested on April 10, 1990, charged with obstructing business and physical violence.

CHOI Ki-tae: Nambu Mechanical and Metalworkers Union, officer at the Sang-won branch, arrested on May 10, 1990, charged with obstructing business and physical violence. [Arrest date given as April 10, 1990.]

KIM Ho-kyum: Nambu Mechanical and Metalworkers Union, general secretary, arrested on April 6, 1990, charged with obstructing business and physical violence.

KIM Yong-koo: Nambu Mechanical and Metalworkers Union, officer at the Shin-pyung branch, arrested on May 3, 1990, charged with obstructing business and physical violence.

LEE Jung-il: Nambu Mechanical and Metalworkers Union, dispute officer, arrested on April 6, 1990, charged with obstructing business and physical violence.

WOO Il-do: Nambu Mechanical and Metalworkers Union, rank-and-file worker, arrested on April 6, 1990, charged with obstructing business and physical violence.

YOON Tae-kyung: [noted as Mae-kyung] Nambu Mechanical and Metalworkers Union, research officer, arrested on April 6, 1990, charged with obstructing business and physical violence.

LEE Eon-soon: Naewoo Precision, president, arrested on June 14, 1990, charged with violating the Labor Dispute Adjustment Law.

CHUNG Yoon-kwang: Seoul Subway, president, arrested on March 16, 1989, and charged with violating the Labor Dispute Adjustment Law.

DO Il-hee: Shinhan Valve Company, president, arrested on April 16, 1990, charged with physical violence and violating the Labor Dispute Adjustment Law.

PARK Kwang-kook: Shinhan Valve Company, education officer, arrested on May 9, 1990, charged with obstructing business and "third-party interference" ban in the Labor Dispute Adjustment Law.

YOON Myung-sun: Taepyungyang Chemical Company, director of the union's Seoul branch, [arrested in 1989], charged under the National Security Law.

EUN Hi-yul: Union of Booth Shops, education director, arrested on May 10, 1990, charged with interference of police operation (Criminal Code).

KIM Nam-soo: Yakurt Co., president, arrested on June 12, 1990, charged with obstructing business.

CHO Seon-kyung: labor movement activist, charged with violating the National Security Law.

CHOI Eun-seok: labor movement activist, charged with violating the National Security Law.

CHOI Jong-myung: [Bukbu Noryon], labor movement activist, arrested on February 15, 1990, charged with violating the National Security Law.

IM Jong-myung: [Bukbu Noryon], labor movement activist, arrested on February 15, 1990, charged with violating the National Security Law.

IM Young-hwan: labor movement activist, charged with violating the National Security Law.

JANG Myung-guk: labor movement activist, director of the Suktap Labor Center, arrested on June 19, 1990, charged with violating the National Security Law and "third-party interference" ban in the Labor Dispute Adjustment Law. [Information from *Dong-a Ilbo*, other sources.]

KIM Hyung-cheol: labor movement activist, arrested on July 20, 1990, charged with violating the National Security Law.

KIM Keon-Joo: labor movement activist, charged with violating the National Security Law.

KIM Seon-hee: labor movement activist, charged with violating the National Security Law.

KIM Seon-mi: labor movement activist, charged with violating the National Security Law.

LEE Byung-kil: [Bukbu Noryon], labor movement activist, charged with violating the National Security Law.

LEE Deok-Joo: labor movement activist, charged with violating the National Security Law.

LEE Deok-Joon: labor movement activist, charged with violating the National Security Law.

LEE Kyung-sook: [Bukbu Noryon], labor movement activist, arrested on February 15, 1990, charged with violating the National Security Law.

86

0088

LEE Seong-jae: labor movement activist, charged with violating the National Security Law.
LEE Seong-yong: [Bukbu Noryon], labor movement activist, arrested on February 15, 1990, charged with violating the National Security Law.
MIN Byung-kon: labor movement activist, charged with violating the National Security Law.
PARK Hyun-hee: labor movement activist, charged with violating the National Security Law.
PARK Moon-jae: labor movement activist, charged with violating the National Security Law.
PARK Nam-il: [Bukbu Noryon], labor movement activist, arrested on February 15, 1990, charged with violating the National Security Law.
WANG Hae-jeon: [Bukbu Noryon], labor movement activist, arrested on February 15, 1990, charged with violating the National Security Law.

INCHON

AHN Jae-hwan, [Inchon Puchon Workers' Center], labor movement activist, charged with violating the National Security Law, [being held in Anyang].
CHOI Byung-guk: labor movement activist, charged with violating the National Security Law, [being held in Seoul].
CHOI Keon-seop: labor movement activist, charged with violating the National Security Law, [being held in Seoul].
CHOI Kwi-sung: labor movement activist, charged with violating the National Security Law, [associated with "Inchon Workers' College," arrested on March 17, 1990, being held in Inchon].
CHOI Nam-ki: labor movement activist, charged with violating the National Security Law, [being held in Seoul].
HA Seong-chang: labor movement activist, arrested on April 28, 1990, charged with violating the National Security Law.
HWANG Soon-hyun: labor movement activist, arrested on April 28, 1990, charged with violating the National Security Law.
IM Jung-hwa: labor movement activist, charged with violating the National Security Law, [associated with "Inchon Workers' College," arrested on March 17, 1990, being held in Inchon].
JUNG Jong-joo: labor movement activist, charged with violating the National Security Law, [being held in Seoul].
KIM Hyung-su: labor movement activist, arrested on July 31, 1990, charged with violating the National Security Law.
KIM In-seon: labor movement activist, arrested on April 28, 1990, charged with violating the National Security Law.
KIM Jin-hee: labor movement activist, charged with violating the National Security Law, [being held in Seoul].
KIM Jin-guk: labor movement activist, arrested on April 28, 1990, charged with violating the National Security Law.
KIM Joong-sung: labor movement activist, arrested on April 28, 1990, charged with violating the National Security Law.
KIM Neong-koo: labor movement activist, charged with violating the National Security Law.
KIM Seong-kyun: labor movement activist, charged with violating the National Security Law, [associated with "Inchon Workers' College," arrested on March 17, 1990, being held in Inchon].
KIM So-young: labor movement activist, arrested on April 28, 1990, charged with violating the National Security Law.
KIM Tae-jin: labor movement activist, arrested on April 28, 1990, charged with violating the National Security Law.
KIM Yong-ki: labor movement activist, arrested on April 28, 1990, charged with violating the National Security Law.
KIM Yong-sook: labor movement activist, charged with violating the National Security Law, [being held in Seoul].
KIM Young-min: labor movement activist, charged with violating the National Security Law, [associated with the Inchon Workers' Group].
KWON Sang-man: labor movement activist, charged with violating the National Security Law, [associated with "Inchon Workers' College," arrested on March 17, 1990, being held in Inchon].
KWON Woo-cheol: labor movement activist, charged with violating the National Security Law, [being held in Seoul].
LEE Hyun-young: labor movement activist, charged with violating the National Security Law.
LEE Kang-seok: labor movement activist, arrested on April 28, 1990, charged with violating the National Security Law.
LEE Myun-jae: labor movement activist, charged with violating the National Security Law, [being held in Seoul].
LEE Myung-bak: labor movement activist, arrested on April 28, 1990, charged with violating the National Security Law.
LEE Sang-joon: labor movement activist, charged with violating the National Security Law, [associated with "Inchon Workers' College," arrested on March 17, 1990, being held in Inchon].
LEE Se-ran: labor movement activist, charged with violating the National Security Law, [associated with "Inchon Workers' College," arrested on March 17, 1990, being held in Inchon].
LEE Tae-joo: labor movement activist, charged with violating the National Security Law.
MIN Cheol-hong: labor movement activist, charged with violating the National Security Law, [associated with "Inchon Workers' College," arrested on March 17, 1990, being held in Inchon].
NHO Byung-jik: labor movement activist, charged with violating the National Security Law, [being held in Seoul].
NHO Hui-chan: labor movement activist, charged with violating the National Security Law, [being held in Seoul].
OH Dong-ryul: labor movement activist, charged with violating the National Security Law, [being held in Seoul].

PARK Jae-young: labor movement activist, charged with violating the National Security Law, [associated with "Inchon Workers' College," arrested on March 17, 1990, being held in Inchon].

PARK Yoon-bae. labor movement activist, arrested on April 28, 1990, charged with violating the National Security Law.

SUH Jae-seok: labor movement activist, arrested on April 28, 1990, charged with violating the National Security Law.

SUH Kyung-seon: labor movement activist, charged with violating the National Security Law, [associated with the Inchon Workers' Group].

SHIN Dong-soo: labor movement activist, charged with violating the National Security Law, [being held in Seoul].

SHIN Hyun-jik: labor movement activist, charged with violating the National Security Law, [associated with "Inchon Workers' College," arrested on March 17, 1990, being held in Inchon].

SHIN Joon-soo: labor movement activist, arrested on April 28, 1990, charged with violating the National Security Law.

SHIN Jung-kil: [Inchon Puchon Workers' Center], labor movement activist, charged with violating the National Security Law, [being held in Chonju].

SHIN Nam-hee: labor movement activist, arrested on April 28, 1990, charged with violating the National Security Law.

SON Hyung-min: [Inchon Puchon Workers' Center], labor movement activist, charged with violating the National Security Law, [being held in Kongju].

YOON Cheol-ho: labor movement activist, charged with violating the National Security Law, [being held in Seoul].

LEE Seong-yong: Colt Musical Instruments Company, charged with violating the Law on Assembly and Demonstration.

HWANG In-beom: Daedong Chemical, acting president, arrested on July 5, 1990, charged with obstructing business and violating the Labor Dispute Adjustment Law.

IM Hye-ran: Daehan Trans. Company, organization director, charged with obstructing business, [arrested on April 26, 1990, also charged with physical violence].

IM Joon-shik: Daehan Trans. Company, cultural activities director, charged with obstructing business, [arrested on April 26, 1990, also charged with physical violence].

KIM Eon-hee: Daehan Trans. Company, general secretary, arrested on March 1, 1990, charged with obstructing business, [arrested on April 26, 1990, also charged with physical violence].

CHOI Joo-nam: Daewoo Precision Company, organization director

CHOI Seong-bok: Daewoo Precision Company, general secretary, arrested on June 4, 1990, charged with obstructing business and committing physical violence.

HWANG In-cheol: Daewoo Precision Company, president, arrested on June 4, 1990.

JUNG Kwang-hoon: Daewoo Precision Company, convention delegate, arrested on May 17, 1990, charged with obstructing business.

LEE Mi-ja: Daewoo Precision Company, vice-president.

IM Myung-seon: Daewon Steel Company

JUNG Chan: Dongsung Enterprises Company, president, arrested on December 24, 1989, charged with violating the National Security Law, [associated with Inchon Workers' Group].

KIM Yoon-mi: Handok Watches Company, convention delegate, arrested on June 4, 1990, charged with obstructing business.

LEE In-ja: Handok Watches Company, convention delegate, arrested on June 4, 1990, charged with obstructing business.

LEE Seong-sook: Handok Watches Company, convention delegate, arrested on June 4, 1990, charged with obstructing business.

PARK Mi-ae: Handok Watches Company, dismissed worker, arrested on April 28, 1990.

PARK Oh-soon: Handok Watches Company, convention delegate, arrested on June 4, 1990, charged with obstructing business.

LEE Jae-koo: Ilkoon Counseling Center, charged with violating the National Security Law.

MOON Jin-hyun: Ilkoon Counseling Center, charged with violating the National Security Law.

PARK Kwi-young: Ilkoon Counseling Center, charged with violating the National Security Law.

JUNG Chang-kyo: Incheon Trade Union Council, statistics officer, arrested on January 31, 1990, charged with violating the Law on Assembly and Demonstration and "third-party interference" ban in the Labor Dispute Adjustment Law. [Law on Assembly and Demonstration, not the Labor Dispute Adjustment Law.]

CHO Tae-cheon: Incheon Trade Union Council, vice-president, arrested on May 19, 1990, charged with violating the Law on Assembly and Demonstration.

LEE Sang-mok: Inchon Labor Counseling Center, [arrested April 13, 1989], charged with violating the National Security Law.

YANG Jae-deok: Inchon Labor Counseling Center, president, [arrested April 13, 1990], charged with violating the National Security Law.

CHANG Il-su: Jindo Co. (Metal), convention delegate, arrested on July 20, 1990, charged with violating the National Security Law.

OH Hye-ran: Jinsung Electronics Company, educational director, arrested on May 13, 1990, charged with obstructing business.

YOON Hwa-sim: Jinsung Electronics Company, president, arrested on May 13, 1990, charged with obstructing business.

CHAE Joong-young: Kyungdong Industry (Metal)

88

0090

96   한국 인권문제 제 사안 2

CHAE Sung-choon [noted as Sung-Joon]: Kyungdong Industry (Metal), [charged with obstructing business and "third-party interference," sentenced to three years' imprisonment, being held at Youngdungpo].

CHOI Yong-Jin: Kyungdong Industry (Metal)

CHOI Un-kyu: Kyungdong Industry (Metal), [charged with abetting suicide, obstructing business and committing physical violence, sentenced to two years' imprisonment, being held at Youngdungpo].

KIM Nam-pil: Kyungdong Industry (Metal)

KIM Sang-yong: Kyungdong Industry (Metal)

LEE Jae-kwon: Kyungdong Industry (Metal)

LEE Jae-min: Kyungdong Industry (Metal)

LEE Kun-tak: Kyungdong Industry (Metal) Union, charged with obstructing business. [Also charged with "third-party interference," sentenced to one-and-a-half years' imprisonment, being held at Youngdungpo.]

LEE Young-hwan: Kyungdong Industry (Metal), [charged with obstructing business and "third-party interference," sentenced to two years' imprisonment, being held at Youngdungpo].

LEE Young-sik: Kyungdong Industry (Metal)

OH Dong-jin: Kyungdong Industry (Metal)

PARK Ji-boon: Kyungdong Industry (Metal)

PARK Sun-tae: Kyungdong Industry (Metal), [charged with obstructing business and "third-party interference," sentenced to four years' imprisonment, being held at Youngdungpo].

PARK Young-oh: Kyungdong Industry (Metal)

SUH Kwang-il: Kyungdong Industry (Metal)

WON Hong-sik: Kyungdong Industry (Metal), [charged with obstructing business and "third-party interference," sentenced to two years' imprisonment, being held at Youngdungpo].

YOON Pil-koo: Kochang Industry Company, president, charged with violating the Law on Assembly and Demonstration.

AHN Joong-joon: Kyungdong Industry Company, charged with abetting suicide (Criminal Code) and committing physical violence. [Kyungdong Industrial Union, arrested on February 21, 1990, charged with obstructing business and "third-party interference," being held in Inchon.]

CHOI Sung-choon: Kyungdong Industry Company, charged with abetting suicide (Criminal Code) and committing physical violence.

AHN Sun-ha: Myungsung Electronics (Metal), education officer.

KIM Ki-ja: Myungsung Electronics (Metal), president.

PARK Sun-sook: Myungsung Electronics (Metal), general secretary.

CHOI Dong-sik: Namil Metal Co., president.

IM Nak-bin: Samwon Plastic Company

SEOK Jung-nam: Sunmi Industry Company, female affairs director.

LEE Eon-young: Union of Construction, president, arrested on June 30, 1990, charged with obstructing business.

LEE Hyung-Jin: Workers' Center, manager, [arrested on April 13, 1990], charged with violating the National Security Law.

SEONGNAM CITY

YANG Hee-soo: Rank-and-file worker, charged with technical interference with police operations.

KANG Kwan-bol: Changsung Precision Company, rank-and-file worker, charged with technical interference with police operations.

KIM Hyun-Joong: Hanyang Rubber, education director, [charged with obstructing business and forging private documents, being held in Sungdong].

YOON Yong-joo: Kookdong Company, deputy president, charged with falsification of private document (regarding his educational background) [Criminal Code].

LEE Joo-wan: Nassau, education director, [charged with forging private documents].

LEE Yong-keun: Nassau, dismissed worker.

SON Kil-soo: OPC (Metal), president [and chairman of the Sungnam Noryon, charged with "third-party interference," being held in Suwon].

JUNG Doo-wan: Pongkook Company, former dispute officer, charged with obstructing business and technical interference with police operations. [Charges listed as obstructing business, violating Law on Assembly and Demonstration, and forging private documents, being held in Sungdong.]

OH Haeng-seon: Pongkook Company, former general secretary, charged with obstructing business and violation of the Law on Assembly and Demonstration, [being held in Sungdong].

89

0091

BAE Dae-yul: Shani Cake Bakery (Chemical), arrested on May 1, 1989, charged with deprivation of arms, [being held in Anyang].

HAN Kang-sik: Sung Ji Precision, president.

JUN Dong-woon: Samho Company, president, arrested on May 9, 1990, charged with obstructing business.

SEO Hee-young: Samho Company, convention delegate, arrested on May 12, 1990, charged with obstructing business.

SOH Jae-bong: Samho Company, arrested on June 5, 1990, charged with obstructing business.

YOON Sang-son: Samho Company, arrested on June 5, 1990, charged with obstructing business.

MYUNG Sung-kyu: Sungnam Bags Workshop Area Trade Union, rank-and-file worker, charged with technical interference with police operations.

PARK Jin-koo: Sungnam Bags Workshop Area Trade Union, president, charged with committing physical violence and technical interference with police operations.

PARK Jin-hyun: Sungnam Workers' House, education director, arrested on February 27, 1990, charged under the National Security Law.

YOO Hwan-rae: Sungnam Workers' House, education director, arrested on March 1, 1990, charged under the National Security Law.

KYUNGKI-NAMBU

PARK Chul-min: labor movement activist, arrested on September 14, 1990, charged with technical interference with police operation, Law on Assembly and Demonstration, and deprivation of arms.

KIM Jong-wan: Ansan Workers' House, charged with violating the "third-party interference" ban in the Labor Dispute Adjustment Law.

KIM Jong-kwan: Ansan Workers' House, arrested on November 23, 1989, charged with violating the "third-party interference" ban in the Labor Dispute Adjustment Law.

LEE Phan-doll: Ansan Workers' House, officer.

LEE Si-jung: Anyang Electronics, [charged with "third-party interference"].

BAEK Da-rye: Anyang Electronics, president, [charged with obstructing business].

LEE Hee-jung: Anyang Trade Union Center, general secretary, arrested on November 23, 1989, charged with "third-party interference."

OH Byung-chan: Baejoo Industry Co., rank-and-file worker, arrested on September 14, 1990, charged with technical interference with police operation, Law on Assembly and Demonstration, and deprivation of arms.

KIM Tae-yeon: Baemyung Metal Co., president, arrested on September 14, 1990, charged with technical interference with police operation, Law on Assembly and Demonstration, and abetting suicide.

CHOI Sook-joo: Chonnohyop, officer for the Ansan District, arrested on September 14, 1990, charged with technical interference with police operation, Law on Assembly and Demonstration, and deprivation of arms.

KIM Ki-whan: Chonnohyop, officer for the Ansan District, arrested on September 14, 1990, charged with technical interference with police operation, Law on Assembly and Demonstration, and deprivation of arms.

KANG Yun-hee: Daesin Electronics, rank-and-file worker, [charged with obstructing business].

LEE Young-hee: Daewoo Electronics, président, arrested on January 23, 1990, charged with obstructing business.

CHUN Kyel-ryong: Dukboo Jinheong Co., president, arrested on September 14, 1990, charged with technical interference with police operation, Law on Assembly and Demonstration, and abetting suicide.

YOO Mi-kyung: Haetae Dye Works, president, charged with obstructing business.

JOO Sel-lak: Hanchang Co.

LEE Jae-hee: Hanchang Co.

KIM Hee-sung: Kyungwon, arrested on October 17, 1989, charged with technical interference with police operations.

CHOI Yoon-bong: Kongyoung Engineering Company, president, charged with obstructing business.

KANG Woo-pil: Kongyoung Engineering Company, arrested on April 5, 1990, charged with obstructing business, [and committing physical violence, arrested on April 25, 1990].

KIM Ho-joong: Kongyoung Engineering Company, arrested on April 5, 1990, charged with obstructing business, [and committing physical violence, arrested on April 25, 1990].

KIM Man-il: Korea-Seakrit Co.

LEE Si-jeong: Kyungki Province Union Center, general secretary, charged with violating the "third-party interference" ban in the Labor Dispute Adjustment Law.

LEE Doh-kil: Kyungwoo Leather Co., president, arrested on September 14, 1990, charged with technical interference with police duties, Law on Assembly and Demonstration, and abetting suicide.

90

0092

KIM Mi-sook: Oslo Electronics Company, dispute officer, arrested on May 2, 1990, charged with obstructing business and committing physical violence. [Arrest date listed as May 4.]

KIM Ok-soon: Oslo Electronics Company, president, arrested on May 2, 1990, charged with obstructing business and committing physical violence. [Arrest date listed as May 4.]

SHIN Hyang-kyung: Oslo Electronics Company, rank-and-file worker, arrested on May 2, 1990, charged with obstructing business and committing physical violence. [Arrest date listed as May 4.]

WHANG Dae-hyun: Samjung Pulp Co., president, arrested in June 1990 (?), charged with obstructing business.

Name unknown: Samjung Pulp Co., organizing officer, charged with obstructing business.

CHOI Young-soo: Samryuk Machinery, president, [charged with violating the Labor Dispute Adjustment Law, being held in Suwon].

PARK Kong-woo: Samsung Electronics (Metal), dismissed worker, [charged with "third-party interference"].

LEE Mi-sook: Sankyo Precision (Metal), president, arrested on December 21, 1989, charged with violating the "third-party interference" ban in the Labor Dispute Adjustment Law.

LEE Seong-ok: Shinho Paper Mill, vice-president, arrested in June 1990 (?), charged with violating the Law on Assembly and Demonstration and obstructing business.

KIM Boon-jong: TND Company (Metal), president, [charged with obstructing business].

KANG Young-Joo: Won Electronics, organization director.

CHUN Sam-soo: Won Electronics, president, charged with obstructing business. [Also on the list as JUN Sam-soo, additionally charged with committing physical violence.]

BAEK Sung-hwa: Won Electronics (Metal).

KWON Yong-ho: Yoosin Heavy Electrical, general secretary, arrested in November 23, 1989, charged with violating the "third-party interference" ban in the Labor Dispute Adjustment Law.

PARK Jong-won: Yakun Company, director of the Pyungtaek branch, charged with obstructing business.

PUCHON

CHOI Mi-ja: Bosung Electronics, information officer, arrested on July 27, 1990, charged with obstructing business.

KIM Soo-wah: Bosung Electronics, dispute officer, arrested on July 27, 1990, charged with obstructing business.

LEE Mi-ja: Bosung Electronics, inspector, arrested on July 27, 1990, charged with obstructing business.

PARK Young-mi: Bosung Electronics, vanguard director, arrested on July 27, 1990, charged with obstructing business.

SUH Soon-lim: Bosung Electronics, information officer, arrested on July 27, 1990, charged with obstructing business.

CHO Sung-wook: Cerart Company, education director, arrested on June 7, 1990, charged with obstructing business.

HAN Hoo-ja: Cerart Company, vice-president, arrested on June 7, 1990, charged with obstructing business.

JEON Mal-jin: Cerart Company, president, arrested on June 7, 1990, charged with obstructing business.

CHA Kyu-keon: Cerite Company, general secretary, arrested on May 1, 1990, charged with violating the Law on Assembly and Demonstration.

LEE Jang-han: Cerite Company, general secretary, arrested on May 1, 1990, charged with violating the Law on Assembly and Demonstration.

WON Young-han: Cerite Company, cultural activities officer, arrested on May 1, 1990, charged with violating the Law on Assembly and Demonstration.

HAN Kyung-suk: Chonnohyop, president, arrested on June 14, 1990, charged with violating the Labor Dispute Adjustment Law and Law on Assembly and Demonstration and committing physical violence.

LEE Byung-chul: Doosung Industry Company (Metal), rank-and-file worker, [charged with committing physical violence, obstructing business].

YOON Ki-soo: Doosung Industry Company (Metal), auditor, [charged with committing physical violence, obstructing business].

SON Eun-hyun: Doosung Industry Company (Metal), president, [charged with committing physical violence, obstructing business].

OH Hyun-Jin: Dukchang Industry Company

CHA Nam-hong: Dukchang Industry Company, director.

LEE Soo-chan: Dongyang Elevator Company, general secretary, arrested on May 9, 1990, charged with Special Law against Firebombs.

PARK Seong-kyu: Dongyang Elevator Company, convention delegate, arrested on May 1, 1990, charged with violating the Law on Assembly and Demonstration.

PARK Seong-ryong: Dongyang Elevator Company, education director, charged with violating the "third-party interference" ban in the Labor Dispute Adjustment Law.

91

0093

SO Soon-hong: Dongyang Elevator Company, rank-and-file worker, arrested on May 9, 1990, charged with violating the Law on Assembly and Demonstration.

PARK Jong-moon: Hanyang Precision Company, general secretary, arrested on May 1, 1990, charged with violating the Law on Assembly and Demonstration.

CHEON Young-sin: Heungyang Company, dispute director, arrested on May 24, 1990, charged with obstructing business.

JUNG Kyung-hwa: Heungyang Company, vice-president, arrested on May 24, 1990, charged with obstructing business.

IM Mi-ran: Heungyang Company, general secretary, arrested on May 24, 1990, charged with obstructing business.

PARK Mi-kyung: Heungyang Company, president, arrested on May 24, 1990, charged with obstructing business.

LEE Yong-keon: Puchon Dismissed Workers' Association, president, arrested on May 24, 1990, charged with violating the "third-party interference" ban in the Labor Dispute Adjustment Law.

LEE Sang-bin: Puchon Labor Institute, arrested on May 9, 1990, charged with violating Special Law against Firebombs.

CHOI Deok-hee: Poongwon Electronics Company, education officer, arrested on May 10, 1990, charged with obstructing business.

KIM Cheol-young: Sejin Communication Company, president, arrested on June 7, 1990, charged with falsification of public documents (Criminal Code).

HONG Kyung-ho: Yoosung Company, general secretary, arrested on May 21, 1990, charged with obstructing business.

KIM Dong-am: Yoosung Company, president, arrested on May 21, 1990, charged with obstructing business.

TAEJON

LEE Dong-ho: Daesung Traffic Service Company, arrested on March 28, 1990, charged with committing physical violence.

MIN Byung-soo: Daesung Traffic Service Company, arrested on March 28, 1990, charged with committing physical violence.

CHEONAN

SONG Nam-ki: Cheonan Dye., vice-president.

CHUNGJU

PARK Mi-soon: AMK Company, union activist, arrested on June 3, 1990, charged with obstructing business and violation of the Labor Dispute Adjustment Law.

PARK Pil-soon: AMK Company, vice-president, arrested on June 3, 1990, charged with obstructing business and violation of the Labor Dispute Adjustment Law.

JEONPUK

LEE Seon-Jae: labor movement activist [Jeonpuk Labor Association Preparation Committee], arrested on February 1, 1990, charged with violating the National Security Law.

CHO Sung-hoon: Hyundai Motor Service, president. [Also listed as Jo Seong-ho, arrested on February 1, 1990, charged with violating the National Security Law.]

JIN Doo-hwan: Plant Company, vanguard team member, arrested on January 23, 1990, charged with violating the Law on Assembly and Demonstration and committing physical violence.

BAEK Nam-soo: Sun Electronics, [charged with obstructing business].

CHOI Ki-hwa: Sungil Manufacturing Company, president, arrested on May 23, 1990, charged with obstructing business.

KWANGJU

KIM Doo-hwan: Daewoo Carrier Company (Metal), president [Chunbok Noryon, plant].

LEE Sang-hoe: Daewoo Carrier Company (Metal), president.

LEE Seung-hui: Daewoo Carrier Company (Metal), president.

PARK Jong-hyun: Daewoo Carrier Company (Metal), president, arrested on December 27, 1989, charged with obstructing business and violation of the Labor Dispute Adjustment Law. [Minkahyup lists charges as obstructing business and physical violence, being held in Kwangju.]

JUNG Soon-mi: [also listed as Soon-im], Kemsung Alps Company, vice-president, arrested on April 12, 1990, charged with obstructing business and violation of Law on Assembly and Demonstration.

KIM Cheon: Kemsung Alps Company, general secretary, charged with obstructing business.

92

0094

KIM Soon-lm: Kemsung Alps Company, president, arrested on December 27, 1989, charged with obstructing business, violation of Law on Assembly and Demonstration, and "third-party interference" ban in the Labor Dispute Adjustment Law.
OH Yeo-ok: Kemsung Alps Company, education officer, arrested in April 27, 1990, charged with obstructing business and violation of Law on Assembly and Demonstration.

TAEGU

SHIN Ki-bok: Daedong Industry Company (Metal), president.
LEE Beom-kyu: Daeha Dyeing Company, vice-president,
PARK Soon-deok: Daeha Dyeing Company, general secretary, arrested on May 14, 1990, charged with obstructing business.
PARK Young-bae: Daeha Dyeing Company, president, arrested on May 14, 1990, charged with obstructing business.
HONG Seong-koo: Daesung Precision Company, president, arrested on May 14, 1990, charged with obstructing business.
SEOL Tae-koo: Dongsan Bearings Company, president, arrested on May 7, 1990, charged with violating the Labor Dispute Adjustment Law and obstructing business.
KIM Hyun-cheol: Dongwon Metal Company, president, arrested on April 10, 1990, charged with violation of Law on Assembly and Demonstration and Special Law against Firebombs. [Minkahyup lists his charges as violation of the Law on Assembly and Demonstration and committing physical violence and his arrest date as April 14.]
LEE Yu-whung: Kangjin Manufacturing Co.
YOO Young-yong: Korea M.B.I. (Textile), president, arrested on February 26, 1990, charged with violating the Law on Assembly and Demonstration and the Labor Dispute Adjustment Law. [Mingahyup identifies the company as L.B.I., the arrest as February 8, 1989, and the charge as committing physical violence.]
PARK Min-ho: Namyoung Textile, president.
CHOI Byung-won: Namseon Manufacturing Company, vice-president, arrested on May 30, 1990, charged with obstructing business.
CHOI Han-soo: Namseon Manufacturing Company, acting president, arrested on August 31, 1990, charged with obstructing business and violating the Labor Dispute Adjustment Law.
CHUN Sung-tae: Namseon Manufacturing Company, dispute director, arrested on August 31, 1990, charged with obstructing business and violating the Labor Dispute Adjustment Law.
HONG Hoo-ki: Namseon Manufacturing Company, director, arrested on May 30, 1990, charged with obstructing business.
KOH Tae-kwon: Namseon Manufacturing Company, president, arrested on July 17, 1990, charged with obstructing business, and sentenced to 18 months' imprisonment.
LEE Jae-yeol: Namseon Manufacturing Company, director of branch, arrested on July 17, 1990, charged with obstructing business, and sentenced to 18 months' imprisonment.
LEE Jung-rim: Namseon Manufacturing Company, director, arrested on May 30, 1990, charged with obstructing business.
LEE Sung-hae: Namseon Manufacturing Company, education director, arrested on August 31, 1990, charged with obstructing business and violating the Labor Dispute Adjustment Law.
LEE Wol-nyeo: Sangkong Electronics Company, organization director, arrested on April 25, 1990, charged with obstructing business. [Arrest date given as April 28, being held in Taegu.]
AHN Byung-man: Taehwa Dyeing Company, general secretary, arrested on May 25, 1990, charged with obstructing business and "third-party interference" ban in the Labor Dispute Adjustment Law.
KIM Joo-kap: Taehwa Dyeing Company, dispute officer, arrested on May 12, 1990, charged with obstructing business.
KIM Joon-tae: Taehwa Dyeing Company, auditor, arrested on May 14, 1990, charged with obstructing business.
KIM Tae-ki: Taehwa Dyeing Company, convention delegate, arrested on May 14, 1990, charged with obstructing business.
KWON Seok-ho: Taehwa Dyeing Company, vice-president, arrested on June 1, charged with obstructing business and "third-party interference" ban in the Labor Dispute Adjustment Law.
LEE Myung-hwa: Taehwa Dyeing Company, female affairs director, arrested on May 25, 1990, charged with obstructing business and physical violence.
LEE Myung-jae: Taehwa Dyeing Company, vice-president, arrested on May 12, 1990, charged with obstructing business.
SEO Choong-jin: Taegu Workers Association, director, arrested on May 19, 1990, charged with violation of the Law on Assembly and Demonstration.

KUMI

KIM Jung-won: Pohang Dongjin Manufacturing Company, former president, charged with obstructing business [and "third-party interference, arrested in April 1990].

93

0095

JANG Mi-jung: Hankook Sinix Company, arrested on May 8, 1990, charged with falsification of private documents (educational background).

CHO Myung-rae: Pohang Saehan Electronics Company, statistics director, arrested on May 8, 1990, charged with falsification of private documents (educational background).

POHANG, KYUNGJU

HUH Young: labor movement activist, charged with interference with police operations.

LEE Hee-chang: Chosun Ceramics Company, dismissed labor, charged with violation of Special Law against Firebombs.

BAE Young-Jin: Daedong Steel Company, education officer, charged with technical interference with police operations, [arrested on April 9, 1990, being held in Taegu].

KIM Chan-soo: Hyosung Textile, auditor.

KIM Kyo-jung: Hyosung Textile, auditor.

LEE Byung-soo: Hyosung Textile, auditor, ["third-party interference," being held in Taegu].

PARK Joo-chul: Hyosung Textile, auditor.

JOO Sang-Joon: Heunghwa Manufacturing Company, rank-and-file worker, arrested on November 1, 1989, charged with falsification of public documents, [being held in Taegu].

HAN Eu-keun: Hyundai Metal Complex Company, charged with falsification of public documents, [arrested in March 1990, being held in Taegu].

JANG Young-tae: Jecheol Facilities Company, president, charged with violation of the Law on Assembly and Demonstration, obstructing business and "third-party interference" ban in the Labor Dispute Adjustment Law, [arrested on June 5, 1989, being held in Kangteung].

KWON Oh-man: Kangwon Industry (Metal), president, charged with obstructing business and violation of the Labor Dispute Adjustment Law.

CHOI Young-min: Kangwon Industry (Metal), acting president, charged with obstructing business.

JUNG Kwang-soo: Kangwon Industry (Metal), education director, charged with obstructing business and violation of the Labor Dispute Adjustment Law.

LEE Yoo-hyung: Kwangjin Enterprise Company, president, charged with violation of the Law on Assembly and Demonstration, [arrested on April 9, 1990, being held in Taegu].

JUNG Tae-young: Kyungjoo Daeha Taxi Company, former president, arrested on May 28, 1990, charged with interference with police operation and violation of the Law on Assembly and Demonstration.

KIM Chang-Joo: Poongsan, welfare officer.

KWON Young-kook: Poongsan, education director, charged with committing physical violence and violation of the Labor Dispute Adjustment Law. [Arrested on January 2, 1989, being held in Jangheung, charges listed as obstructing business and violation of the Labor Dispute Adjustment Law.]

CHUNG Jong-kil: Poongsan Metal Industry, president, charged with committing physical violence and violation of the Labor Dispute Adjustment Law. [Arrested on January 2, 1989, being held in Andong, charges listed as obstructing business and violation of the Labor Dispute Adjustment Law.]

KIM Doo-seong: Pohang Boiler Company, president, arrested on June 4, 1990, charged with committing physical violence and obstructing business.

PARK Chang-ho: Pohang Workers' House, director, charged with interference with police operations.

JO Myung-lae: Sanhan Electronics

CHANG Young-tae: Sujin.

CHOI Jin-shik: Sujin, president.

CHOO Yun-man: Sujin.

KIM Byung-koo: Sujin.

LEE Sang-mo: Sujin.

LEE Sun-hee: Sujin.

PUSAN

LEE Sung-do: Chonnohyop, chairman, arrested on June 12, 1990, charged with "third-party interference."

CHOI Nak-yoon: Copart Company, acting president, arrested on August 3, 1990, charged with obstructing business.

CHOI Sang-kook: Copart Company, arrested on August 3, 1990, charged with obstructing business.

IM Chul-Jin: Copart Company, director of the vanguard team, arrested on August 3, 1990, charged with obstructing business.

JOO U-jong: Copart Company, officer of the vanguard team, arrested on August 3, 1990, charged with obstructing business.

94

JUNG Dae-shik: Copart Company, general secretary, arrested on August 3, 1990, charged with obstructing business.
KANG Sun-Jin: Copart Company, president, arrested on August 3, 1990, charged with obstructing business.
LEE Sung-tae: Copart Company, arrested on August 3, 1990, charged with obstructing business.
SONG Wang-joon: Copart Company, dispute director, arrested on August 3, 1990, charged with obstructing business.
YU Choong-ki: Copart Company, arrested on August 3, 1990, charged with obstructing business.
PARK Tae-chun: Copart Company, arrested on August 3, 1990, charged with obstructing business.
YU Choong-ki: Copart Company, arrested on August 3, 1990, charged with obstructing business.
CHA Sang-keun: Dongsin Chemical Company, president.
IM Yo-taek: Dongsin Chemical Company
LEE Sang-kyu: Haehan Shipbuilding Company, arrested on May 1, 1990, charged with violating the Special Law against Firebombs. [Charge listed as violating the Labor Disputes Adjustment Law.]
LEE Mi-kyung: Hwasung (Textile), president, arrested on January 29, 1990, charged with violating the National Security Law. [Arrest date noted as February 1990, charged with committing physical violence, being held in Pusan.]
KIM Dae-keon: Hyosung Taxi Company, president, arrested on June 5, 1990, charged with obstructing business.
LEE Sung-bee: Ilkook Workers' Library, arrested on January 29, 1990, charged with violating the National Security Law.
PARK Hyun-yul: Ilsong Precision Company, arrested on April 28, 1990, charged with violating the Special Law against Firebombs. [Charge listed as violation the Labor Dispute Adjustment Law.]
KIM Young-joon: Manho Steel Mill, president, [charged with committing physical violence].
KIM In-kyu: Poongsan Metal Industry, delegate, arrested on September 11, 1990, charged with obstructing business.
KIM Jin-hak: Poongsan Metal Industry, organizing director, arrested on September 11, 1990, charged with obstructing business.
KIM Kook-kyung: Poongsan Metal Industry, arrested on September 11, 1990, charged with obstructing business.
KIM Myung-sil: Poongsan Metal Industry, delegate, arrested on September 11, 1990, charged with obstructing business.
KIM Young-il: Poongsan Metal Industry, vice-president, arrested on September 11, 1990, charged with obstructing business.
KWAK Sung-il: Poongsan Metal Industry, culture director, arrested on September 11, 1990, charged with obstructing business.
LEE Ho-woo: Poongsan Metal Industry, delegate, arrested on September 11, 1990, charged with obstructing business.
LEE Jin-soo: Poongsan Metal Industry, delegate, arrested on September 11, 1990, charged with obstructing business.
LEE Sang-woon: Poongsan Metal Industry, delegate, arrested on September 11, 1990, charged with obstructing business.
LEE Yang-soo: Poongsan Metal Industry, communication director, arrested on September 11, 1990, charged with obstructing business.
SHIN Gil-whu: Poongsan Metal Industry, athletic director, arrested on September 11, 1990, charged with obstructing business.
SONG Woon-Jin: Poongsan Metal Industry, arrested on September 11, 1990, charged with obstructing business.
KIM Jin-sook: Pusan Workers' Association, president, arrested on June 1, 1990, charged with violating the "third-party interference" ban in the Labor Dispute Adjustment Law.
NHO Chang-kyu: Samsung Industry Company, president, arrested on May 31, 1990, charged with obstructing business and violating the "third-party interference" ban in the Labor Dispute Adjustment Law.

ULSAN (excluding Hyundai Workers, who are listed separately below)

CHO Yoo-shik: labor movement activist, charged with violation of the National Security Law, arrested in January 1990 and sentenced in September to two years' imprisonment.
CHUNG Dae-hwa: labor movement activist, charged with violation of the National Security Law, [arrested in January 1990]. Sentenced (date unknown) to 24 months' imprisonment.
KIM Jong-seop: labor movement activist, charged with violation of the National Security Law.
KANG Bong-jin: Daesung Development Company, arrested on May 2, 1990, charged with technical interference with police operation.
JUNG Ho-young: Dongyang Nylon Company, former education director, [arrested in August 1989, charged with obstructing business and being held in Pusan].
LEE Yong-ryul: Dongyang Nylon Company, former president, [arrested in August 1989, charged with obstructing business and being held in Pusan].
KWAK Tak-sung: Sejong Industry, rank-and-file worker, charged with falsification of private documents (educational background), [arrested in February 1990].
YANG Dong-joo: Yooil Manufacturing Company, former president, charged with falsification of private documents (educational background).

MASAN-CHANGWON CITY

KIM Seon-joong: charged with falsification of private documents (educational background), [arrested in March 1990].

0097

95

IM Chae-Jung: labor movement activist, arrested in January 1990, charged with violating the National Security Law, [arrested on March 8, 1990, affiliated with the Kyungnohyop].

PARK Chang-seok: Association of day laborers, president, arrested on July 26, 1990, charged with technical interference with police operations.

KIM Ki-chul: Booyoung Engineering.

PARK Eun-tae: Booyoung Engineering.

YOO Byung-tae: Booyoung Engineering.

SEONG Myung-heon: Bong-am Company, arrested on March 3, 1990, charged with violating the National Security Law.

SON Taek-man: Bong-am Company, arrested on March 5, 1990, charged with committing physical violence, [being held in Masan].

LEE Bong-Joo: Carbreaker Company, president, arrested in July 1990 (?), charged with obstructing business.

SHIN Yong-jung: Carburetor Company, dispute officer, charged with violating the Special Law against Firebombs, [arrested on May 3, 1990, in connection with the Lee Yong-il funeral rally].

HUH Tae-kwan: Changwon Air Conditioner Company, arrested on March 5, 1990, charged with committing physical violence, [being held in Masan].

CHOI Je-woo: Daelim Automobile Company, arrested in June 1990 (?), charged with committing physical violence and violating the Labor Dispute Adjustment Law.

HONG Ji-wook: Daelim Automobile Company, arrested in August 1990, charged with violating the Labor Dispute Adjustment Law.

JO Hyun-Joon: Daelim Automobile Company, organization officer, charged with violating the Labor Dispute Adjustment Law.

KIM Yoon-soo: Daelim Automobile Company, communication director, arrested on March 16, 1990, charged with violating the National Security Law.

KO Young-tae: Daelim Automobile Company, education director, arrested on August (?) 1990, charged with violating the National Security Law.

LEE Seung-pil: Daelim Automobile Company, president, arrested on March 8, 1990, charged with violating the Law on Assembly and Demonstration. [Mingahyup listed his charge as the National Security Law.]

SHIN Duk-woo: Daewon Company (Metal), president, [arrested on May 26, 1989 and being held in Andong].

JOO Yun-ok: Dongkyung Electronics Company, president, arrested on March 13, 1990, [being held in Masan].

KIM Jung-Ja: Dongkyung Electronics Company, vice-president, arrested on March 13, 1990, [being held in Masan].

CHOI Mi-yang: Dongyang Metal Company, arrested on March 12, 1990, charged with violating the National Security Law.

KIM Pil-hyun: Dukyang Industry Company

BYUN Hwa-seok: Goldstar (Metal), branch director, arrested on June 8, 1989, charged with violating the Labor Dispute Adjustment Law and committing physical violence, [sentenced to a one-and-a-half year prison term, being held in Andong].

HA Tae-wook: Goldstar (Metal), [arrested on June 8, 1989, sentenced to a two year prison term, being held in Mokpo].

KIM Hyun-shik: Goldstar (Metal), rank-and-file worker, charged with violating the National Security Law.

LEE Kyun-ha: Goldstar (Metal). [Arrested on May 26, 1989, sentenced to a two year prison term, being held in Soonchun].

PARK Won-Joo: Goldstar Industrial Elec. Company, dismissed worker, arrested on February 5, 1990.

KIM Heong-suk: Hankook Hotcoil Company, convention delegate, charged with violating the National Security Law.

HONG Yeo-po: Hyosung Heavy Industry, branch director, arrested on July 5, 1989, charged with violating the Labor Dispute Adjustment Law and committing physical violence, [being held in Pusan].

PARK Sang-oh: Hyosung Heavy Industry, [arrested June 30, 1989, being held in Pusan].

SUH Woo-keun: Hyosung Heavy Industry, arrested on June 30, 1989, charged with violating the National Security Law, [being held in Pusan].

LEE Chang-sub: Hyosung Machinery, [arrested in September 26, 1989, being held in Mokpo].

JOO Jin-sung: Hyundai Precision Company, arrested on August 30, 1990, charged with committing physical violence.

KIM Je-kab: Hyundai Precision Company, arrested on August 30, 1990, charged with committing physical violence.

KIM Jung-myung: Hyundai Precision (Metal) Company, organizing director, arrested on August 30, 1990, charged with "third party" interference.

KIM Kook-han: Hyundai Precision Company, arrested on September 21, 1990, charged with "third-party" interference.

KIM Sang-hap: Hyundai Precision (Metal), arrested on June 2, 1989, charged with violating the "third-party interference" ban in the Labor Dispute Adjustment Law and committing physical violence, [sentenced to a two year jail term, being held in Mokpo].

LEE Jung-ho: Hyundai Precision (Metal).

LEE Jae-koo: Ilkook Labor Center, director, arrested on March 5, 1990, charged with violating the National Security Law [and committing physical violence, being held in Masan].

MOON Jin-hun: Ilkook Labor Center, director, arrested on March 5, 1990, charged with violating the National Security Law, [arrest date as April 4].

PARK Ki-young: Ilkook Labor Center, director, arrested on March 5, 1990, charged with violating the National Security Law, [and committing physical violence, being held in Masan].

KIM Hong-joon: Ilsun Industry Company, convention delegate, arrested on May 3, 1990, [in connection with the Lee Yong-il funeral rally].

KIM Yong-sook: Ilsun Industry Company, convention delegate, arrested on May 10, 1990, charged with violating the National Security Law.

PARK Young-soon: Joongchun Company, general secretary, arrested on December 18, 1989, charged with obstructing business, [sentenced to a one-and-a-half year prison term].

JUNG Kwang-sik: Kia Manufacturing Company, rank-and-file worker, charged with violating the Law on Assembly and Demonstration.

CHUN Doll-ja: Korea Star (Electronics, Japanese-owned), arrested on August 29, 1990, charged with obstructing business.

CHUN Yoon-hee: Korea Star (Electronics, Japanese-owned), ex-president, arrested on August 29, 1990, charged with obstructing business and committing violence.

MIN Jung-sook: Korea Star (Electronics, Japanese-owned), general secretary, arrested on August 31, 1990, charged with obstructing business and committing violence.

SON Sung-ran: Korea Star (Electronics, Japanese-owned), president, arrested on August 29, 1990, charged with obstructing business and committing violence.

CHOI Dae-won: Korea Takoma (Shipbuilding), president.

LEE Chang-hoon: Korea Takoma (Shipbuilding), rank-and-file worker, charged with violating the Special Law against Firebombs.

LEE Heung-suk: Korea Takoma (Shipbuilding), president, Ma-chang, arrested on April 27, 1989, charged with violating the Law on Assembly and Demonstration and the "third-party interference" ban in the Labor Dispute Adjustment Law, [being held in Hongsung].

CHUNG Min-soo: Korex Sports Company, arrested on July 26, 1990, charged with technical interference with police operations.

JUN Chang-hyun: Korex Sports Company, dismissed worker, arrested on April 1, 1990, charged with violating the Law on Assembly and Demonstration.

SON Soon-do: Korex Sports Company, disputes director, arrested on August 16, 1990, charged with obstructing business and "third-party" interference.

JUNG Sang-cheol: Machang Council of Trade Unions, acting president, arrested on May 22, 1990, charged with violating the "third-party interference" ban in the Labor Dispute Adjustment Law.

LEE Jong-yup: Machang Council of Trade Unions, acting president, arrested on March 31, 1990, charged with violating the Labor Dispute Adjustment Law and obstructing business. [Mingahyup lists his charge as violation of the National Security Law.]

BAEK Seung-man: Pusan Industry Machine.

CHO Kwang-hyun: Pusan Industry Machine.

KIM Sung-bae: Poongsung Electricity Company, arrested on June 8, 1990, charged with falsification of private documents (educational background).

PARK Hee-keun: Sammi Metal Company

SUH Il-bum: Sebang Electronics.

YOO Eun-soon: Soyo Enterprise, president.

KIM Jung-im: TC Company, president, arrested on December 1, 1989, charged with committing physical violence, [being held in Masan].

LEE Yon-sil: TC Company, vice-president, arrested on December 1, 1989, charged with committing physical violence, [being held in Masan].

CHUNG Ki-ho: Tong-il Company (Unification Church-invested), dismissed worker, arrested on October 31, 1989, charged with obstructing business, [sentenced to a one-and-a-half year prison term, being held in Masan].

IM Jong-ho: Tong-il Company (Unification Church-invested), convention delegate, arrested on April 24, 1989, charged with arson, [sentenced to a one-and-a-half-years prison term, being held in Andong].

IM Soo-kwan: Tong-il Company (Unification Church-invested), arrested on August 22, 1990, charged with violating the National Security Law and obstructing business.

JIN Soon-chan: Tong-il Company (Unification Church-invested).

JIN Young-kyu: Tong-il Company (Unification Church-invested), acting president, arrested on October 18, 1989, charged with committing physical violence and violating the "third-party interference" ban in the Labor Dispute Adjustment Law, [sentenced to two-and-a-half-years prison term, being held in Masan].

LEE Bong-woo: Tong-il Company (Unification Church-invested).

97

LEE Ho-sung: Tong-il Company (Unification Church-invested), arrested August 22, 1990.

LYU Hae-choon: Tong-il Company (Unification Church-invested), dismissed worker, arrested on September 21, 1989, charged with violating the Labor Dispute Adjustment Law, [sentenced to a two year prison term, being held in Masan].

MOON Sung-hyun: Tong-il Company (Unification Church-invested), dismissed worker and former president, arrested on April 22, 1989, charged with violating the "third-party interference" ban in the Labor Dispute Adjustment Law, [sentenced to one-and-a-half-year prison term].

PARK Choon-yul: Tong-il Company (Unification Church-invested), dismissed worker, arrested on September 21, 1989, charged with violating the Labor Dispute Adjustment Law, [sentenced to a two year prison term, being held in Masan].

SHIN Chun-sub: Tong-il Company (Unification Church-invested), dismissed worker, arrested on October 31, 1989, charged with obstructing business, [sentenced to a one-and-a-half-year prison term, being held in Masan].

SHIN Sang-hwan: Tong-il Company (Unification Church-invested), organization director, arrested on October 31, 1989, charged with obstructing business, [sentenced to a one-and-a-half-year prison term, being held in Masan].

SONG Min-seok: Tong-il Company (Unification Church-invested), organizational director, arrested on September 21, 1989, charged with violating the Labor Dispute Adjustment Law, [sentenced to a two year prison term].

YANG Eon-cheol: Tong-il Company (Unification Church-invested), organization officer, charged with violating the Special Law against Firebombs.

YEO Young-guk: Tong-il Company (Unification Church-invested), dismissed worker, arrested on November 1, 1989, charged with violating the "third-party interference" ban in the Labor Dispute Adjustment Law, [sentenced to a one-and-a-half-year prison term, being held in Masan].

YOO Soo-Jong: Tong-il Company (Unification Church-invested), general secretary, arrested on October 31, 1989, charged with violating the Labor Dispute Adjustment Law, [sentenced to a one-year prison term, being held in Masan].

JANG Suk-kyo: Wooyoung Industry Company, [arrested in March 1990, charged with violating the National Security Law, associated with the Nodong Danche Shilmuja (Workers' Group Affairs), may have been released in June].

KEOJE ISLAND

IM Bok-je: Daewoo Shipbuilding Company, union activist, charged with violating the Labor Dispute Adjustment Law.

LEE Myung-ha: Daewoo Shipbuilding Company, union activist, charged with violating the Labor Dispute Adjustment Law.

SHIN Yoo-sik: Daewoo Shipbuilding Company, union activist, charged with violating the Labor Dispute Adjustment Law.

SOH Soon-sam: Daewoo Shipbuilding Company, union activist, charged with violating the Labor Dispute Adjustment Law.

BYUN Sung-Joon: Samsung Shipbuilding Company, arrested on June 21, 1990, charged with violating the National Security Law.

KO Jae-kwun: Samsung Shipbuilding Company, arrested on June 22, 1990, charged with violating the Labor Dispute Adjustment Law.

LEE Kyo-woo: Samsung Shipbuilding Company, president, arrested on June 21, 1990, charged with violating the National Security Law.

TAEBAEK

KIM Chang-wan: Dongwon Coal Mine, [charged with violating the Kuangsan Security Law and the Law on Assembly and Demonstration and obstructing business].

YOO Sang-yul: Dongwon Coal Mine, [charged with violating the Kuangsan Security Law and the Law on Assembly and Demonstration and obstructing business].

BAEK Hyung-keon: Hanbo Mine, arrested on July 25, 1990, charged with obstructing business and committing physical violence.

CHANG Sung-ku: Hanbo Mine, dismissed worker, arrested on July 25, 1990, charged with obstructing business and committing physical violence.

CHO Sung-koon: Hanbo Mine, arrested on July 25, 1990, charged with obstructing business and committing physical violence.

CHOI Heong-kyung: Hanbo Mine, arrested on July 25, 1990, charged with obstructing business and committing physical violence.

LEE Mok: Hanbo Mine, arrested on July 25, 1990, charged with obstructing business and committing physical violence.

BAE Jin: Miners' Association, president, arrested on August 13, 1990, charged with violating the National Security Law, obstructing business, and committing physical violence.

CHUNG Moon-ho: Miners' Association, member, arrested on August 6, 1990, charged with violating the Law on Assembly and Demonstration, obstructing business, and committing physical violence.

KIM Hong-dae: Miners' Association, member, arrested on August 8, 1990, charged with violating the Law on Assembly and Demonstration, obstructing business, and committing physical violence.

CHO Yong-il: Miners' Association, charged with violating the National Security Law.

JUN Mi-young: Kuangsan Miners' Association, charged with violating the National Security Law.

CHANG Dong-chul: Kyungdong Mine, arrested on July 24, 1990, charged with obstructing business.

CHUNG Woon-hwan: Samchuk Coal Mine.

WON Ki-joon: Samchuk Coal Mine, [charged with violating the National Security Law and the ban on "third-party interference"].

KOREAN NATIONAL TEACHERS AND EDUCATIONAL WORKERS UNION (CHUNKYOJO)

AHN Jong-bok: Masan Vocational High School, arrested on March 27, 1990, charged with obstructing business.

CHOI Yun-ho: Taegu Shimin Middle School, arrested on April 27, 1990, charged with violating the Law on Assembly and Demonstration and committing physical violence.

KANG Sin-oh: Incheon Myungsin Female High School, arrested on April 12, 1990, charged with obstructing business and committing physical violence.

KIM Bang-sik: Incheon Myungsin Female High School, arrested on April 12, 1990, charged with obstructing business.

KIM In-kyo: Suhsan Seopo Middle School, arrested on July 15, 1990, charged with interference with police operation.

KO Heung-deok: Incheon Myungsin Female High School, arrested on April 12, 1990, charged with obstructing business.

KWON Bok-kyung: Pusan Branch, arrested on May 11, 1990, charged with violating the Law on Assembly and Demonstration.

KWON Kyung-bok: Pusan Sungdo High School, arrested on May 12, 1990, charged with violating the Law on Assembly and Demonstration.

LEE Young-Joo: Sachun Seopo Middle School, arrested on March 27, 1990, charged with obstructing business.

LIM Il-taek: Masan branch, arrested on May 11, 1990.

PARK Jung-keon: Kyungki Province Branch, director, arrested on May 11, 1990, charged with violating the Law on Assembly and Demonstration.

SHIN Hyen-kyung: arrested May 11, 1990.

KOREAN BROADCASTING SYSTEM (KBS) UNION

AHN Deok-sang: emergency committee member, charged with obstructing business.

AHN Dong-soo: former president, charged with obstructing business.

CHA Hyung-hoon: planning officer, emergency committee, arrested on August 14, 1990, charged with interference with police operation and physical violence.

CHOI Chang-hoon: dispute director, charged with obstructing business, [arrested May 7, 1990].

JUN Young-il: director, charged with obstructing business.

JUNG Hee-chun

KIM Cheol-soo: president, charged with obstructing business.

KIM Jung-yuk

KIM Man-seok: reporter, charged with obstructing business, [arrested May 2, 1990].

KIM Young-dal: organization director, charged with obstructing business.

KIM Yu-young

KO Peom-joon: general secretary, charged with obstructing business, [arrested May 7, 1990].

LEE Hyung-mo: emergency committee director, charged with obstructing business.

LEE Im-ho: director of the fair broadcast committee director, charged with obstructing business, [arrested May 2, 1990].

LEE Kyung-hee: director of female affairs, charged with obstructing business, [arrested May 2, 1990].

LEE Yang-hoon

OH San-keon

PARK Chan-uk

PARK Myung-chul

WHUN Chun-gun

KOREAN FEDERATION OF HOSPITAL WORKERS' UNIONS

CHA Soo-ryun: Hanyang University Hospital, president, charged with "third-party interference".

99

KIM Jin-han: Pohang Seonlin Hospital, director on industrial disputes, charged with violating the Labor Dispute Adjustment Law, charged with violating the Labor Dispute Adjustment Law and obstructing business.

KIM Yoo-mee: Seoul National University Hospital, president, arrested on October 4, 1990, charged with obstructing business.

HYUNDAI WORKERS (ULSAN)

BAE Man-soo: Hyundai Automobile Company, convention delegate, arrested on June 3, 1990, charged with interference with police operations and arson. Currently on trial.

JUNG Kap-deuk: Hyundai Automobile Company, vanguard team member, arrested on June 3, 1990, charged with interference with police operations and arson. On trial.

KIM Jong-jin: Hyundai Automobile Company, president, democratic association, arrested on June 3, 1990 and charged with interference with police operation and arson. On trial.

KIM Kang-hee: Hyundai Automobile Company, management committee member, arrested on May 3, 1990, charged with obstructing business. On trial.

KIM Sung-eon. Hyundai Automobile Company, convention delegate, arrested on June 3, 1990, charged with interference with police operations. On trial.

LEE Soo-won: Hyundai Automobile Company, union specialist, arrested on May 18, 1990, charged with committing physical violence. Sentenced in September to six months' imprisonment.

KANG Seong-cheol: Hyundai Heavy Equipment Company, organization director, arrested on May 23, 1990. Charged with obstructing business.

KIM Hak-doo. Hyundai Heavy Equipment Company, president, arrested on May 15, 1990. Charged with obstructing business. On trial.

CHOI Jung-bo: Hyundai Heavy Industry, convention delegate, arrested on April 28, 1990, charged with technical interference with police operations. On trial.

CHOI Kap-yong: Hyundai Heavy Industry, rank-and-file worker, charged with technical interference with police operations. On trial.

CHUNG Young-min: Hyundai Heavy Industry (also listed as Young-bin), charged with obstructing business and violating the Labor Dispute Adjustment Law.

JANG Moon-ho: Hyundai Heavy Industry, convention delegate, charged with obstructing business. On trial.

JO Don-hwul: Hyundai Heavy Industry, cultural activities officer, charged with obstructing business. On trial.

JO Joo-nam: Hyundai Heavy Industry, convention delegate, charged with obstructing business. On trial.

JUNG Young-bin: Hyundai Heavy Industry, female affairs officer, charged with committing violence and obstructing business.

KANG Seong-man: Hyundai Heavy Industry, arrested on May 7, 1990, charged with obstructing business. On trial.

KIM Nam-suk: Hyundai Heavy Industry, convention delegate, charged with violation of the National Security Law. Sentenced to one years' imprisonment.

KIM Sang-hoon: Hyundai Heavy Industry, planning officer, charged with obstructing business. On trial.

KIM Won-pil: Hyundai Heavy Industry, dispute officer, charged with obstructing business. On trial.

KOO Young-sik: Hyundai Heavy Industry, convention delegate, charged with obstructing business. On trial.

KWON Yong-mok: Hyundai Heavy Industry, chairman of Council of Hyundai Unions, arrested on March 1, 1990, charged with violating the "third-party interference" ban in the Labor Dispute Adjustment Law. In September, sentenced to two years' imprisonment.

LEE Bong-soo: Hyundai Heavy Industry, convention delegate, charged with obstructing business. On trial.

LEE Jae-kwan: Hyundai Heavy Industry, convention delegate, arrested on May 16, 1990, charged with obstructing business. Sentenced to 18 months' imprisonment.

LEE Jung-seop: Hyundai Heavy Industry, rank-and-file worker, charged with technical interference with police operations. On trial.

LEE Kap-yong: Hyundai Heavy Industry, general secretary, charged with obstructing business. On trial.

LEE Won-kap: Hyundai Heavy Industry, former dispute director, charged with obstructing business.

LEE Won-keon: Hyundai Heavy Industry, strike leader, charged with committing physical violence and obstructing business, arrested in April 1989, charged with violating the Labor Dispute Adjustment Law, sentenced to 18 months' imprisonment.

LEE Young-hyun: Hyundai Heavy Industry. President, arrested in February 1990, charged with obstructing business. Sentenced to 12 months' imprisonment.

PARK Dae-yong: Hyundai Heavy Industry, planning officer, charged with obstructing business. On trial.

PARK Seong-woo: Hyundai Heavy Industry, convention delegate, charged with obstructing business. On trial.

SEO Pil-woo: Hyundai Heavy Industry, convention delegate, charged with obstructing business. On trial.

100

0102

SEOL Nam-jong: Hyundai Heavy Industry, planning director, arrested in March 1990, charged with obstructing business, sentenced in September to one year's imprisonment.

WOO Ki-ha: Hyundai Heavy Industry, vice-president. On trial.

YOON Jae-keon: Hyundai Heavy Industry, organization director, charged with obstructing business, sentenced in September to one year's imprisonment.

KOO Ja-choon: Hyundai Wood Complex, former statistics director, arrested in February 1990, charged with violating the National Security Law, sentenced to 18 months' imprisonment.

LEE Young-do: Hyundai Wood Complex, president, arrested in March 1990, charged with obstructing business, and sentenced in September to one year's imprisonment.

APPENDIX IV: LIST OF PUBLISHERS AND OTHERS JAILED IN CONNECTION WITH PUBLISHING ACTIVITIES, 1989-90.

This information was compiled in Korean by the Korea Publishing Culture Movement, a Seoul-based organization of publishers, for their May 1990 list and June 1990 report on the state of publishing in South Korea during President Roh's tenure. Additional names have been noted and the source is as cited. Unless otherwise specified, all persons named on the list were arrested or charged under the National Security Law.

1989

January 19:
CHOI Pil-seung: A representative of the Han Madang Publishing Company, he was sentenced on April 3, 1989 to one year's imprisonment and one year's deprivation of civil rights. The sentence was suspended for two years, and Choi was released.
BAEK Yong: A representative of the Shinhak Munsa (Modern Sciences) Publishing Company, he was sentenced on April 6, 1989 to one year's imprisonment and one year's deprivation of civil rights. The sentence was suspended for two years and Baek was released.
BAE Jung-kyu: Representative of the Daedong (Korea) Publishing Company, he was sentenced on April 6, 1989 to one year's imprisonment and one year's deprivation of civil rights. The sentence was suspended for two years, and Bae was released.

February 9:
KIM Sung-jae: Head of the Hyungsungsa Publishing Company, which published *Biography of Kim Il-sung*, he was sentenced on May 24, 1989, to a one-year jail term and one year's deprivation of civil rights. The sentence was suspended for two years and he was released.

February 18:
KOH Kyu-tae: 30, a poet and representative of the Indong Publishing Company, he was sentenced on May 23, 1989, to one-and-a-half years' imprisonment and one year's deprivation of civil rights. The sentence was suspended for three years, and he was released.

March 3:
KIM Yon-in: A representative of the Him (Power) Publishing Company, he was sentenced on June 22, 1989, to a one year prison term; on October 19, his sentence was suspended, and he was released.

March 29:
JUNG Ji-suk: A representative of the Baekdu Publishing Company, he was sentenced on June 16, 1989, to a one-year prison term and one year's deprivation of civil rights. The sentence was suspended for three years, and he was released..
KANG Byung-sun: A representative of the Pulenseup Publishing Company, released on June 29, 1989 after he was given a suspended sentence.

April 7:
LEE Choon-ho: The police raided the Noon (Snow) Publishing Company's offices and confiscated 4,000 copies of books. The authorities took Lee, a representative, and SO Jung-chul and KIM Eun-kyo, editors of the publishing company, for questioning. The next day, So and Kim were released, but Lee was formally arrested. The confiscated copies of the "Tong-il Shisunjib" were returned. Lee was released on June 22, 1989 after being given a suspended sentence.

May 2
PARK Kang-hui: Investigators of the Agency for National Security Planning raided the Nonjang Publishing Company's offices, confiscating nearly 2,000 copies of books. Park was apprehended as he was leaving his home for work; he was formally arrested on the next day. On July 10, the publishing company's offices were searched, and 3,000 copies of a book on Marx and Engel were seized. The next day, the police searched Park's home. On October 30, 1989, he was released on bail.

0104

103

May 4:
CHOI Kwang-ryul: Investigators of the Agency for National Security Planning apprehended Choi, a representative of the Galmuji Publishing Company, as he was leaving his home to go to work. The investigators raided the publishing company's offices and confiscated nearly 1,000 copies of books. Choi was indicted on September 27, 1989. On October 24, Choi was sentenced to two years' imprisonment and two years' deprivation of civil rights; the sentence was suspended for three years, and Choi was released.

May 26:
KIM Sa-in and IM Kyu-chan: An editor and a representative (respectively) of the Labor Literature Company were taken in for questioning. Investigators attached to the Agency for National Security Planning raided the publishing company's offices and conficated the June issues of the *Labor Liberation Literature* magazine and documents. Kim and Im were formally arrested on May 29. On September 18, they were each sentenced to two years' imprisonment and two years' deprivation of civil rights. Their sentences were suspended for three years and they were released.

May 30:
PARK Jong-kyu, YU Hwan-ok, and LEE Sang-dong, representative, business manager and editor, respectively, of the Baek Book Publishing Company were taken in for questioning after police raided the company's offices. On June 1, the three men were booked on charges without physical detention.

June 7:
KIM Jae-wan: A representative of the Ohweol (May) Book Publishing Company, Kim was taken in for questioning after police raided the company's offices. The authorities confiscated publications and documents belonging to the company. Kim was formally arrested the next day. On September 22, he was released on a suspended sentence.

June 22:
KIM Sun-ho: A representative of the Yul Salam Publishing Company, he was taken in for questioning along with ten other employees of the publishing company. Kim was formally arrested the next day; the rest were released. The publishing company's offices were also raided and books confiscated. Kim was released on October 6, 1989 on a suspended sentence.

June 23:
NOH Seung-il: A representative of the Geunal (Some Day) Publishing Company, Noh was arrested for publishing the books, *Reform and Reunification* and *Present Society and New Understanding*. On June 23, there had been police raids at nine Seoul bookstores and 196 copies of books were confiscated. Noh was found guilty.

June 26:
KIM Joon-ki: Publisher of the *Together with Farmers* magazine, was arrested for alleged violation of the National Security Law because the magazine contained articles on North Korea's agricultural policy. He was convicted in late 1989 to two years' imprisonment and was jailed.

LEE Sam-haeng: a writer for the *Together with Farmers* magazine, Lee was arrested along with Kim Joon-ki and later released on a suspended sentence.

YU Si-keun: A representative of the Arirang Publishing Company, Yu was taken in for questioning and formally arrested two days later. The publishing company's offices were raided and 1,700 copies of two books were confiscated. On October 12, 1989, he was given a suspended sentence and released.

July 4:
IM Seung-nam: A representative of the Dolbaegae (Stone Pillow) Publishing Company, Im was taken in for questioning. On October 11, he was sentenced to one year's imprisonment and one year's deprivation of civil rights; his sentence was suspended for two years, and he was released.

KIM Yong-hang: A representative of the Onnuri Book Publishing Company, Kim was taken in for questioning. In the afternoon the publishing company's offices were raided and 623 copies of *Bukhan Tongil Jungchaek Byunchunsa* were confiscated. Kim was formally arrested on October 5. On October 17, he was sentenced to a one-year prison term and one year's deprivation of civil rights; the sentence was suspended for two years, and he was released.

July 5:
JUNG Dong-ik: A representative of the Achim (Morning) Book Publishing Company, Jung was taken in for questioning following police raids of Achim and other publishing companies' offices which resulted in the confiscation of over 4,000 copies of North Korean books. Jung was formally arrested on July 7. On October 25,

104

Jung was sentenced to one year's imprisonment and one year's deprivation of civil rights; the sentence was suspended for three years, and Jung was released.

July 7:

LEE Seung-chul: The authorities had raided the Hwangto Publishing Company's offices on July 5, and confiscated copies of the *Flower Selling Maiden* a North Korean book. Lee was formally arrested on July 7. On October 20, 1989, he was sentenced to a three-year jail term, which was suspended for three years.

August 1:

KIM Yong-hwan: A representative of the Manduri bookstore in Inchon, Kim was arrested for allegedly continuing to sell North Korean books. On November 9, 1989, Kim was sentenced to one year's imprisonment and one year's deprivation of civil rights; the sentence was suspended for two years, and he was released.

August 4:

CHO Nam-il: A representative of the Juksan Publishing Company, Cho had been wanted for arrest in connection with his role in publishing the *Celebration of Pyongyang* (*Pyongyang Chukjun*). On August 6, Cho was formally arrested. On November 1, Cho was sentenced to one-and-a-half years' imprisonment and two years' deprivation of civil rights; the sentence was suspended for two years, and Cho was released.

August 9:

KIM Hong-jo, a representative, and LEE Sang-woo, an editor, of the Han Book Publishing Company were arrested for publishing *For New Life* (*Saesamul Wuihayul*) and *Essay on National Liberation, the Masses, Democracy and Revolution* (*Minjok haebang minjung minjujui hyukmyungnyon*). On November 9, they were each sentenced to one year's imprisonment and one year's deprivation of civil rights. Their sentences were suspended for two years, and they were released.

August 25:

CHO Sung-il, a representative, and LEE Byung-hoon, an editor, of the Namnyuk Book Publishing Company, were taken in for questioning following an August 21 raid of the company's offices. Cho and Lee were formally arrested the next day. They were released on suspended sentences. [No additional details given.]

August 29:

PARK Jong-kyu, a representative, and LEE Sang-don, an editor, of the Baek Book Publishing Company were apprehended at the home of the publishing company business manager's home by the investigators of the Agency for National Security Planning. Park and Lee were held for questioning and formally arrested the next day. The publishing company's offices were raided and nearly 3,000 copies of books were confiscated. KWAK Myung-dan, an editor of the same company had also been taken in for questioning on August 29 but was released the next day. Park was sentenced on December 1 to one year's imprisonment and one year's deprivation of civil rights; his sentence was suspended for two years, and he was released. Lee was sentenced on the same day to eight months' imprisonment and one year's deprivation of civil rights.

September 25:

CHOI Hae-sung: A representative of the Hamsung Book Publishing Company, Choi was taken in for questioning following a police raid of the publishing company's offices in which the authorities confiscated copies of *From Leningrad to Pyongyang* and company documents. Park Sang-sun, an editor at Hamsung, was also taken in for questioning but released shortly thereafter. Choi was formally arrested the next day; he was released on December 29 on a suspended sentence.

October 4:

HONG Sa-yong: A representative of the Korean-American Culture Institute (Hanyoung Munhwasa), Hong was arrested for violation of the law on construction and buildings. He was released later [date not given].

October 7:

KANG Young-kil: A representative of the Taebaek Book Publishing Company and SHIN Ha-seop, a business manager of the Danggerae Book Publishing Company, were apprehended in front of their homes and taken in for questioning. Shin was released. Kang was formally arrested for his publishing activities. On February 2, 1990, Kang was sentenced to two years' imprisonment and two years' deprivation of civil rights; his sentence was suspended for two years, and he was released.

105

October 16:
LEE Jae-yeun: A representative of the Saenal (New Day) Book Publishing Company, Lee was arrested for alleged violation of the National Security Law following a police raid of the publishing company's offices. The authorities confiscated copies of books on Marxism and the labor movement. On February 2, 1990, Lee was sentenced to one year's imprisonment and one year's deprivation of civil rights. The sentence was suspended for two years, and he was released.

October 23:
NAM Eun-kyung: An editor of the Daedong Book Publishing Company, Nam was taken in for questioning. On October 24, the police raided the company's offices and Nam's home and confiscated several books on reunification and people's revolution and formally arrested Nam. On February 1, 1990, Nam was sentenced to one year's imprisonment and one year's deprivation of civil rights. His sentence was suspended for two years, and he was released.

October 25:
KIM Young-jeung: A representative of the Sagaesul Book Publishing Company, Kim was arrested for alleged violation of the National Security Law after a police raid of the publishing company's offices. He was apprehended in front of his home. On January 25, 1990, he was sentenced to one-and-a-half years' imprisonment and deprivation of civil rights. The sentence was suspended for two years, and he was released.

October 31:
LEE Ho-ung: A representative of the Hyungsungsa, was taken in for questioning by the Inchon police. He was released on November 4, 1989.

November 17:
KWON Hyung-woo: A representative of the Maga Bookstore in Taegu, Kwon was arrested for alleged violation of the National Security Law. He was released in February 1990 on a suspended sentence.

November 20:
LEE Wui-won: A representative of the Fiction Bookstore in Taejon, was taken in for questioning after the police raided the bookstore and confiscated issues 3 and 4 of the *Working Class*. On March 3, 1990, he was sentenced to imprisonment. [No additional details available.]

November 23:
LEE Shi-young: Editor of the *Creation and Criticism* magazine, Lee was formally arrested on November 25 for his role in publishing a travelogue on North Korea. On February 3, 1990, he was released on bail.

November 29:
HA Tae-wan: A representative of Chungnyun Saedae (Young Generation), Ha was taken in for questioning after the police raided the company's office and confiscated 2000 copies of the *Morning Sun* sixth issue. On December 2, Ha was formally arrested for alleged violation of the National Security Law.

December 1:
LEE Jae-hwa: The penname of Lee Seung-hwan, the chairman of the South Seoul Munchungnyon, was arrested for various essays that he had written on Kim Il-sung and other topics. On May 14, 1990, he was sentenced to a one-year jail term and deprivation of his civil rights for one year.

December 10:
KIM Sung-jae: editor at Hyungsungsa, was taken in for questioning by the police. He was released on December 12 after a police search of the company's offices failed to turn up evidence against Kim.

PARK Sang-ryul, the business manager of Hyungsungsa, was apprehened on December 17 in front of his home and taken in for questioning. He was released after being investigated about the company's finances.

1990

January 6:
KWAK Han-wang: A representative of the Kwangya bookstore, he was arrested for alleged violation of the National Security Law. On February 22, Kwak was released on a suspended sentence.

January 10:
PARK In-hae: A representative of the Hyungsungsa, Park was arrested. On April 6, Park was released on a suspended sentence.

106

0107

January 11:
IM Kyu-chan: An editor of the *Labor Liberation Literature* magazine, he was taken in for questioning after a police search of his and the magazine's other staff members' homes and offices. On June 13, he was formally arrested for alleged violation of the National Security Law. May 1, he was sentenced to two years' imprisonment and two years' deprivation of civil rights. The sentence was suspended for two years, and he was released. On December 18, 1989, the authorities had ordered a six-month suspension against the *Labor Liberation Literature*.
January 16:
Jun Yong-ho: An editor of the Kwangju Book Publishing Company, he was taken in for questioning by the police. On April 30, he was sentenced to a one-and-a-half years' imprisonment; his sentence was suspended for two years, and he was released.
January 17:
LEE Jin-kyung: Whose real name is PARK Tae-ho, was arrested for alleged violation of the National Security Law for various essays he contributed to magazines.
January 22:
KIM Sun-ho: A representative of the Him Publishing Company The police raided the company's offices and seized 3,000 copies of the *Flower Selling Maiden* Kim was arrested for alleged violation of the National Security Law. On May 22, he was sentenced to two years' imprisonment and two-and-a-half years' deprivation of civil rights.
February 9:
KIM Tae-jong: Founder of the Labor Literature Company, Kim was arrested for alleged violation of the National Security Law for the May-December issues of the *Labor Liberation Literature* magazine.
February 17:
JUNG Min: A planning committee member of the *Society and Life*, a monthly magazine, was arrested for various articles he contributed on North Korea and reunification and democracy movement. On May 28, he was sentenced to a one-year prison term and one year's deprivation of civil rights. The sentence was suspended for two years and Jung was released.
YI Tae-hak: A representative of the Him Publishing Company, Lee was arrested and later released on a suspended sentence. [No additional information.]
February 22:
SEUNG Ki-won: Representative of the Silchon Munhak Publishing Company, he was arrested for alleged violation of the National Security Law. The police raided his office and home and confiscated 73 copies of the *Red Mountain, Black Blood* and copies of *Shilchun Munhak*'s fall 1988 issue. LEE Mun-ku, also a representative of the publishing company was taken in for questioning. OH Bong-ok: A poet, was also arrested for alleged violation of the National Security Law.
February 27:
JUNG Sung-hyun: Representative of Chungnyunsa, Jung was apprehended in front of his house and taken in for questioning. He was later formally arrested for alleged violation of the National Security Law. The Chungnyunsa offices were raided and books confiscated.
February 28:
CHOI Pil-seung: Representative of the Han Madang Publishing Company, was taken in for questioning; the authorities raided the publishing company's offices and confiscated 3,000 copies of *Sea of Masses*. KIM Hong-bum, business manager of Inkansa Publishing Company and CHOI Seung-bok, business manager for the Silchon Munhak Publishing Company were also taken in for questioning. The authorities released the three men that evening.
March 6:
JUN Young-shik: Representative of the Han Madang bookstore, Jun was taken in for questioning. The bookstore was searched by the police, who confiscated copies of books and pamphlets. Jun was released the next day. On March 1, the authorities had raided the offices of the Daedong Publishing Company, and confiscated, among other items, Hanmadang's magazine.

0108

March 9:
JUNG Soo-ung: Ilsongjung Book Publishing House representative, Jung was taken in for questioning. Over 2,000 copies of books were confiscated from the offices of the publishing company. On March 10, Jung was formally arrested for alleged violation of the National Security Law.

March 13:
YU Chang-sun: Representative of the Dulee Book Publishing Company, Yu was apprehended in front of his home on March 12, and taken in for questioning. The publishing company's offices were also raided that day and 45 books and the business ledger were confiscated. Yu was formally arrested the next day.

March 21:
LEE Sang-ho: An editor at the Daedong Book Publishing Company, Lee was taken in for questioning by the authorities who raided the publishing company's offices and seized thousands of copies of several books on reunification, including *Flower of Reunification*. Lee was released later that afternoon.

March 23:
IM Sung-an: Business manager of the Hamsung Publishing Company, was taken in for questioning and his office was searched. The police confiscated 900 copies of *From Leningrad to Pyongyang*, 100 copies of *Current Situation in North Korea* and documents.

YU Hwan-ok: Business manager for the Baek Book Publishing Company, was taken in by the authorities for questioning. He may have been released.

April 3:
KIM Yon-in: Representative of the Him (Power) Publishing House, arrested on charges of violating the National Security Law. The authorities had raided the offices of the publishing company on March 23, confiscating a number of books published by Him. He was previously arrested on March 3, 1989.

April 14 or 15:
SHIN Hyung-shik: Representative of the Nokdu Publishing Company, was arrested for alleged violation of the National Security Law. On April 13, the police raided the offices of the Nokdu Publishing Company and confiscated over 100 copies of the *Nokdu Suhpyung (Nokdu Book Review)*. The day before the raid, it was suspected that Shin had been taken in for questioning.

April 26:
KIM Jong-hyun: Representative of the Jipyung book publishing company was arrested for alleged violation of the National Security Law for his writings, among which are *Yungdo System* and *Yungdo Art*.

May 9:
Kim Su-kil: penname Kim No-bak, was apprehended in front of his house by the authorities who arrested him for questioning for alleged violation of the National Security Law. He had written an essay entitled "What is Marxism?"

May 23:
Park Il-tae: The authorities raided the offices of the *Nala Salang* (Love of Land) Publishing Company and confiscated 247 copies of *Marxist-Leninist Nationalism Theories* and 22 copies of *The Sino-Soviet Antagonism and North Korea*. Park was taken in for questioning.

June 11 (information from AI Urgent Action, July 13, 1990, #298-90):
KIM Myong-shik: A well-known poet and director of the Asia Africa Latin America Research Institute (AALARI) was being held for interrogation in connection with a book by the AALARI. Also being held were: PUH Sah-hyon, 34, a former philosophy student and the secretary general of the AALARI; LEE Jae-ho, 26, a former history student and a researcher with the Institute; and YUH Jae-hyon, 37, president of the Sonamu (Pine tree) Publishing Company, which is believed to have published the books of the Asia Africa Latin America Research Institute. Yuh is accused of violating the National Security Law.

August 6:
NOH Jong-sang: Noh was apprehended near his house by investigators of the Agency for National Security Planning in connection with his article that appeared in the *Sisa Journal*, a weekly newsmagazine. The article, entitled "Kim Bok-dong Angles for Power in Rebellion against President Roh," alleged that Kim Bok-dong, President Roh's brother-in-law, was planning an opposition party to counter the newly-formed Democratic Liberal Party. Noh had reportedly been hiding in a nearby inn for three days to evade arrest. He was released after hours of questioning. (*Korea Herald*, August 7, 1990.)

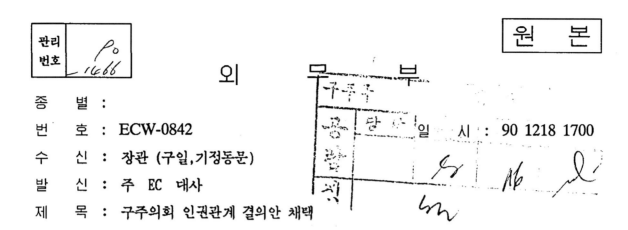

외 무 부

관리번호 : 1666

종 별 :

번 호 : ECW-0842

수 신 : 장관 (구일,기정동문)

발 신 : 주 EC 대사

제 목 : 구주의회 인권관계 결의안 채택

일 시 : 90 1218 1700

1. 구주의회는 12.13. 오후 본회의에서 한국을 포함한 세계각국 (중국, 과테말라, 이란, 시리아, 소련, 필리핀, 남아공등)의 인권존중 결의안을 채택한바, 그중 아국관련 내용은 아래와같음 (결의안 전문 파편송부 예정)

0 최근 남북총리회담 개최를 환영하고 동 회담에서 자유로운 인적왕래등 남북한 신뢰회복 조치가 합의될수 있기를 희망

0 북한에는 다원적 민주제와 기본적 인권보장이 전혀 확립되어 있지 않음을 지적하고, 북한당국에 정치적 자유화조치 촉구

0 한국정부의 방북인사 처벌은 남북한 신뢰회복에 저해될 것임을 언급하고, 임수경, 문규현, 홍성담, 조용설(베를린 범민련회의 관계), 유원호, 김진엽등의 최근 불법방북 또는 북한인사 접촉이유로 구속된 인사의 석방을 촉구

2. QUITIN 구주의회 사무국 한국담당관에 의하면 녹색당및 공산당등 구주의회내 좌익그룹이 금번회기중 방북인사 석방을 요구하는 결의안을 긴급제출 (기민당, 구라파 민주동맹그룹, 우익그룹등 반대)하였으나, 여타 정치그룹에서 북한측의 정치적 자유화를 요구하는 수정안을 제출하여 타협안으로서 상기 결의안이 채택되었다 함

3. 또한 동담당관은 상기 결의안이 금번회기 (12.14. 까지)의 종반기에 접어들어 대부분 의원이 귀국한 가운데에 12.13. 재적 518 명중 100 여명만이 출석, 여타 결의안과 함께 특별한 토의없이 채택되었음을 언급하고, 이는 <u>사실상 구주의회 대다수의원의 견해를 반영한것으로</u> 보기에는 어려운점이 있음을 설명하면서, 구주의회측은 과거 회기종료에 임박하여 대다수의원이 귀국한후 일부 소수의원의 의사에따라 구주의회 전체의 명의를 앞세워 국제문제를 포함한 각종 결의안을 채택하는 폐단이 있어 최근 이와같은 결의안 채택 절차상의 문제점을 시정하는 방안을 검토중이라고 말함

구주국	장관	차관	1차보	2차보	청와대	안기부

90.12.19 06:33

외신 2과 통제관 CF

0110

4. 당관은 공산당, 녹색당등 구주의회내 좌익정치그룹 지도자들과 가능한 가까운 시일내에 접촉, 한국정치, 인권사항에 관하여 올바른 인식을 갖도록 노력하겠음. 끝
(대사 권동만-국장)
예고: 91.6.30. 까지

관리
번호 90
    -1426

외 무 부

종 별 :

번 호 : ECW-0844

일 시 : 90 1219 1800

수 신 : 장관 (구일,기정동문)

발 신 : 주 EC 대사

제 목 : 구주의회 인권관계 결의

연: ECW-0842

1. 본직은 작 12.18. JAMES FORD 구주의회의원 면담시 연호 구주의회의 아국관계 인권결의안 채택에대해 최근 한국의 정치발전과 민주화과정에 비추어 납득할수 없는 조치임을 지적하고 이에 유감을 표시함. 본직은 보도한 동결의에 언급된 구속인사들은 정부의 사전허가를 득하지않고 밀입북내지 북한측과 접촉함으로써 우리의 구체적 실정법을 위반한 자들로서 현재 한국에서는 정치범이 없음을 설명하고 앞으로 구주의회 내에서 여사한 문제가 제기될 경우 사회당그룹에서우리측 입장을 적극 대변토록 협조요청함

2. FORD 의원은 자신도 12 월 스트라스부르그 본회의에 참석하였지만 상기 결의안 채택사실은 몰랐다고 말하고, 인권문제를 담당하는 정치위원장에게 동 결의안 제의 배경등을 확인해 보겠다고 함. 이어 동의원은 구주의회 의원들이 세계도처, 특히 정보접근이 용이한 자유우방국의 인권상황에 대하여 정확한 사실의 뒷받침없이 편파적인 결의안을 남발함으로써 구주의회의 대외적 공신력을 실추하는 경우가 많았다고 자인하면서, 앞으로 구주의회측은 북한, 쿠바, 알바니아등 기본적 인권이 보장되지 않고 있는 공산권 국가에 관심을 경주해야 할것으로 본다고 말함. 끝

(대사 권동만-국장)

예고: 91.6.30. 까지

예고문에 의거 일반문서 19...
재 위   3

구주국   차관   1차보   2차보   국기국   정문국   청와대   안기부

PAGE 1

90.12.20   06:14

외신 2과 통제관 CW

0112

발 신 전 보

번 호 : WGV-1691   901221 1806 CG   종별 :

수 신 : 주 제네바   대사 . 총영사//   (사본 : 주유엔대사)

발 신 : 장 관 (국연)

제 목 : 구주의회 인권관계 결의 채택

　　　1.　구주의회는 12.13. 본회의에서 한국을 포함한 세계각국 (중동,
과테말라, 이란, 시리아, 소련, 필리핀, 남아공등)의 인권존중 결의를 채택한
바, 그중 아국관련 내용은 아래와 같음. (결의 전문 추후 파편 송부예정)

　　　　　o　최근 남북총리회담 개최를 환영하고 동 회담에서 자유로운
　　　　　　인적왕래등 남북한 신뢰회복 조치가 합의될 수 있기를 희망

　　　　　o　북한에는 다원적 민주제와 기본적 인권보장이 전혀 확립되어
　　　　　　있지 않음을 지적하고, 북한당국에 정치적 자유화 조치 촉구

　　　　　o　한국정부의 방북인사 처벌은 남북한 신뢰회복에 저해될 것임을
　　　　　　언급하고, 임수경, 문규현, 홍성담, 조용설 (베를린 범민련회의
　　　　　　관계), 유원호, 김진엽등의 최근 불법방북 또는 북한인사 접촉
　　　　　　이유로 구속된 인사의 석방을 촉구

　　　2.　주 EC 대표부가 QUITIN 구주의회 사무국 한국담당관을 접촉, 보고한
바에 의하면, 녹색당 및 공산당등 구주의회내 좌익그룹이 금번 회기중 방북인사
석방을 요구하는 결의안을 제출 (기민당, 구라파 민주동맹그룹, 우익그룹등
반대)하였으나, 여타 정치그룹에서 북한측의 정치적 자유화를 요구하는 수정안을
제출하여 타협안으로서 상기 결의안이 채택되었다 함.

　　　　　　　　　　　　　　　／ 계속 ／

서구1과장 : 웅

앙 고 재	90 년 12 월 21 일	기안자	과 장	국 장	차 관	장 관
		정영욱		강영희		

보안통제	외신과통지

0113

3. 또한 동 담당관은 상기 결의안이 금번 회기(12.14.까지)의 종반기에 접어들어 대부분 의원이 귀국한 가운데에 12.13. 재적 518명중 100여명만이 출석, 여타 결의안과 함께 특별한 토의없이 채택되었음을 언급하고, 이는 사실상 구주의회 대다수의원의 견해를 반영한 것으로 보기에는 어려운 점이 있음을 설명하면서, 구주의회측은 과거 회기종료에 임박하여 대다수의원이 귀국한 후 일부 소수의원의 의사에 따라 구주의회 전체의 명의를 앞세워 국제문제를 포함한 각종 결의안을 채택하는 폐단이 있어 최근 이와 같은 결의안 채택 절차상의 문제점을 시정하는 방안을 검토중이라고 언급하였다 함.

4. 주 EC대사는 공산당, 녹색당등 구주의회내 좌익 정치그룹 지도자들과 조속한 시일내 접촉하여 한국정치, 인권상황에 대한 올바른 인식을 갖도록 조치 예정이며, 본부는 주EC 대표부로부터 상기 결의문안 접수후 관계부처와의 협의 하에 구체적 대응방안을 강구할 예정인 바, 동 대응방안 확정시 귀관에도 통보 예정임. 끝.

(국제기구조약국장 문동석)

1991. 6. 30에 예고문에 의거 일반문서로 재분류 됨

주 E C 대 표 부

이씨정 20524- 447

수신 : 외무부 장관

참조 : 구주국장

제목 : 구주의회 아국 인권관계 결의채택

　　　연 : ECW-0842

　　1. 연호, 12.13. 구주의회 본회의에서 채택된 한국관계 인권 결의내용을
별첨 송부합니다.

　　2. 참고로 구주의회 의사규칙(제89조)에 의하면, 본회의 의사 정족수는
재적의원 ⅓이지만 최소 13명 이상의 의원이 표결전 의장에게 의사 정족수
충원여부 확인을 특별히 요청하지 않는한, 참석 의원수와 관계없이 모든 투표는
다수결로 유효한 것으로 되어있음을 첨언합니다.
(단, EC 집행위원 전원에 대한 불신임결의시 총의원 과반수 출석에 출석의원
⅔ 이상의 찬성 필요)

첨부 : 구주의회 한국인권관계 결의 사본 1부.　　끝.

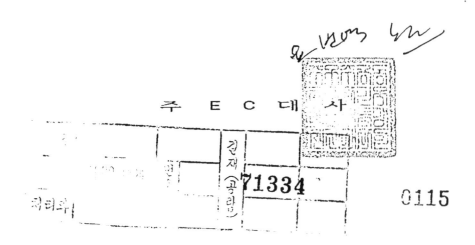

주 E C 대 사

71334　　　　0115

관리 번호	90 - 1501				

분류기호 문서번호	구일 202- **3089**	기 안 용 지	시 행 상 특별취급	
보존기간	영구.준영구 10. 5. 3. 1	장 관		
수 신 처 보존기간				
시행일자	1990. 12. 29.			

보조 기관	국 장	전 결	협조기관		문 서 통 제 1990.12.31
	심 의 관				
	과 장				
기안책임자		설 경 훈			발 송 인

경 유		발신명의	
수 신	법무부장관		
참 조			

제 목	구주의회 아국 인권관계 결의채택

1. 구주의회는 12.13. 본회의에서 한국을 포함한 세계각국

(중동, 과테말라, 이란, 시리아, 소련, 필리핀, 남아공등)의 인권존중에

관한 결의를 채택한 바, 그중 아국관련 내용(결의문 전문 및 번역문 별첨)

은 아래와 같습니다.

- 최근 남북총리회담 개최를 환영하고 동 회담에서 자유로운

인적왕래 등 남북한 신뢰회복 조치가 합의되기를 희망

- 북한에는 다원적 민주주의와 기본적 인권보장이 전혀

확립되어 있지 않음을 지적하고 북한 당국에 정치적 자유화 조치 촉구

0116 / 계속..

- 한국정부의 방북인사 처벌은 남북한 신뢰회복에 저해될

것임을 언급하고, 임수경, 문규현, 홍성담, 조용설(베를린 범민련회의

관계), 유원호, 김진엽 등의 최근 불법 방북 또한 북한인사 접촉 이유로

구속된 인사의 석방을 촉구

2. 구주의회는 동 결의문을 EC 집행위, 구주이사회(EC 정상

회담), 구주정치협력(EPC) 및 한국정부에 전달키로 하고, 특히 구주정치

협력(EPC)에 대해서는 조용설, 홍성담, 임수경, 문규현, 김진협, 유원호의

석방을 위한 압력을 행사토록 촉구하고 있습니다.

3. 구주의회는 구주공동체(EC) 회원국 시민전체의 정치적

대변기관으로서 각 회원국에서 직접.보통선거로 선출된 518명의 의원으로

구성된 범유럽적인 기구이며, 또한, 동 결의문이 구주이사회(EC 정상회담)

에 전달되는 경우의 파급효과를 감안, 이에 대해 반박등 적절한 대응

필요성이 큰 바, 다음사항에 대한 자료 및 귀부 입장을 당부로 조속

회보하여 주시기 바랍니다.

가. 결의문에서 거명하고 있는 인사들의 구속여부, 범죄사실,

확정 판결내용(근거법 포함) 및 기타 참고사항

- 특히 홍성담의 경우 고문여부에 대한 자료

/ 계 속...

0117

　　　　나. 아국의 전반적인 인권상황에 대한 설명자료

　　　　다. 동건 관련 귀부가 포함시키고자 하는 사항

　첨부: 　1. 구주의회 채택 결의문 및 번역문 사본 1부.

　　　　　2. 관련전문(ECW-842,844) 사본 각 1부.

　　　　　3. 관련 공문(이씨정 20524-457) 사본 1부. 끝.

0118

대한민국에서의 인권위반에 관한 결의

구주의회는

A. 베를린에서 북한의원과 회동하고 한국에 돌아간 후 11.30. 두 동료와
   함께 구속된 조용술 목사건에 대해 심히 우려하며,

B. 국제청년학생축제에 전대협 대표자격으로 참석한 22세의 여학생
   임수경과 또한 동행한 문규현 신부, 그리고 북한의 국제청년학생
   축제에 자신의 정치적인 벽보잡지 음화를 송부하였다는 이유로 투옥된
   홍성담처럼 북한을 불법적으로 방문했다는 죄목하에 또는 단순히 북한사람과
   접촉했다는 이유로 몇몇의 죄수가 이미 오랫동안 감옥에 있다는 것을
   인식하며,

C. 12월초에 재판이 재개될 것이라고 알고 있는 홍성담의 경우, 고문이
   이루어졌다는 증언에 매우 주의하며,

D. 남북총리간에 현재 진행중인 일련의 협상이 상호관계와 통일전망에
   관계되고, 모든 한국인에게 한반도내에서 자유롭게 이동할 수 있도록
   하는 것을 목표로 하는 토론이 기본요소라는 것을 고려하며,

E. 북한에 다원주의적 민주주의도 기본적 인권도 존재하지 않는다는 것을
   고려하며,
   1. 모든 범죄자 특히 조용술, 홍성담, 임수경, 문규현, 김진엽과
      유원호등의 즉각적인 석방을 위해 즉시 구주정치협력(EPC)이
      압력을 행사할 수 있는 조치를 취할 것을 요구하며;

0119

2. 대한민국 정부에게 표현의 자유에 관련되는 UN의 인권선언 제9조
   또한 모든 형태의 고문을 금지하는 대한민국 헌법 제12조 2항과
   UN 인권선언 제5조를 존중할 것을 요구하며,

3. 남북한 정부간의 협상을 환영하며, 이것이 이동의 자유부여 등
   신뢰를 회복하기 위한 조치들에 신속히 다다르기를 기대하며;

4. 한국전쟁후 40년동안 많은 한국가족들이 헤어져 있음을 인지하고;

5. 북한인과 선량한 의도로 접촉을 시도하는 한국인들을 체포, 구금하고
   있는 한국당국의 정책이 신뢰회복을 위한 여러 조치들에 장애가 되며
   기본적인 인권을 침해할 뿐이라고 평가하며,

6. 북한정부가 남북대화의 성공을 보장하기 위한 정치적 자유화를 축으로
   하는 조치들을 실행해야 한다고 평가하며,

7. 의장으로 하여금 본 결의안을 집행위, 이사회, 정치협력체제(EPC) 및
   대한민국 정부에 전달케한다.

0120

<u>RESOLUTION</u>

sur les violations des droits de l'homme en République de Corée
(Corée du Sud)

<u>Le Parlement européen</u>,

A. vivement inquiet à la suite de l'arrestation du Révérend Cho-Yong-Sul et de
   ses deux compagnons, le 30 novembre, à leur retour en Corée du Sud et à
   l'issue d'une rencontre avec des parlementaires de Corée du Nord à Berlin,

B. conscient que certains prisonniers sont déjà détenus depuis longtemps en
   Corée du Sud, sous l'inculpation de s'être rendus illégalement en Corée du
   Nord, ou simplement d'avoir eu des contacts avec des Coréens du Nord, comme
   Im Su Kyong, une étudiante de 22 ans, qui a assisté au Festival
   international de la jeunesse et des étudiants en qualité de représentante
   du Conseil national des représentants des étudiants (Chondaehyop), ainsi
   que le Père Moon Kyu-Hyun qui l'accompagnait, et Hong Song-Dam, qui est
   emprisonné pour avoir envoyé des diapositives de ses magazines muraux et
   politiques au Festival international de la jeunesse et des étudiants en
   Corée du Nord,

C. vivement préoccupé à la suite des témoignages faisant état de tortures dans
   le cas de Hong Song-Dam, dont il sait que le procès va être réouvert au
   début du mois de décembre,

D. considérant la série de négociations en cours entre les Premiers ministres
   de Corée du Nord et de Corée du Sud, relatives aux relations mutuelles et
   aux perspectives de réunification et dont les discussions visant à
   autoriser tous les Coréens à se déplacer librement dans la péninsule
   constituent un aspect essentiel,

E. considérant qu'il n'existe ni démocratie pluraliste ni droits de l'homme
   fondamentaux en Corée du Nord,

1. invite instamment la Coopération politique européenne à prendre des mesures
   en vue de faire pression pour la libération immédiate de tous ces
   prisonniers, notamment Cho Yong-Sul, Hong Song-Dam, Im Su-Kyong,
   Moon Kyu-Hyun, Kim Chin-Yop et Yu Won-Ho;

2. demande au gouvernement de la République de Corée de respecter l'article 19
   de la Déclaration des droits de l'homme des Nations unies, relatif à la
   liberté d'expression, ainsi que l'article 12 paragraphe 2 de la
   Constitution de la République de Corée et l'article 5 de la Déclaration des
   droits de l'homme des Nations unies interdisant toute sorte de torture;

3. se félicite des discussions entre les gouvernements de Corée du Nord et de
   Corée du Sud et espère qu'elles déboucheront rapidement sur des mesures
   destinées à restaurer la confiance, tel que l'octroi de la liberté de se
   déplacer;

4. fait observer que quarante ans après la guerre de Corée, de nombreuses
   familles coréennes restent divisées;

5. estime que la politique menée en permanence par les autorités sud-coréennes, qui consiste à arrêter et à emprisonner des Coréens du Sud essayant d'établir des contacts de bonne foi avec des gens de la Corée du Nord, ne peut que contribuer à entraver de telles mesures pour la restauration de la confiance et constitue une violation des droits de l'homme fondamentaux;

6. estime que le gouvernement de Corée du Nord doit mettre en oeuvre des mesures axées sur une libéralisation politique en vue de garantir le succès de ce dialogue entre le Nord et le Sud;

7. charge son Président de transmettre la présente résolution à la Commission, au Conseil, à la Coopération politique européenne et au gouvernement de la République de Corée.

0122

주 영 대 사 관

영국(정) 723- *0001*   1991.1.3.

수신 : 장관

참조 : 국제기구조약국장

제목 : 인권서한

　　　　　　　연 : 영국(정) 723-1460 (90.11.29)

1. 당지소재 Electrical Electronic Telecommunication &
   plumbing Union 이 연호 2개의 서한과 같은 취지(첨부물은동일)의
   서한을 당관에　보내온 바, 별첨 송부합니다.

2. 상기 총 3개의 서한에 대하여 본직은 우선 별첨과 같이 회신하였는 바,
   본부 설명자료 작성시 참고해 주시기 바랍니다.

첨부 : EEPTU측 서한사본 및 본직회신(3부) 사본.　　　끝.

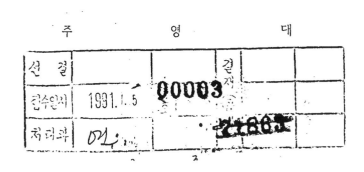

0123

ELECTRICAL ELECTRONIC TELECOMMUNICATION & PLUMBING UNION

Hayes Court, West Common Road, Bromley, Kent. BR2 7AU.
Tel: 081-462 7755 Fax: 081-462 4959

General Secretary
E A B Hammond O.B.E.

Our Ref: EAH/RF/CP/RES

SUBJECT: Imprisoned Trade Unionists

Your Ref:

Date 17th December 1990

The Ambassador
Korean Embassy
4 Palace Gate
London
W8 5NF

Dear Ambassador,

Please find enclosed a list of trade unionists currently held in prison in your country for their trade union activities.

I would respectfully ask that you convey to your government my Union's deep concern about the record number of trade unionists currently imprisoned in your country.

Furthermore I would request that your police and security authorities cease to harass and imprison trade unionists going about their duties in comformity with international conventions on trade union activity.

Yours faithfully

E.A.B. Hammond
General Secretary

Enc.

0124

EMBASSY OF THE REPUBLIC OF KOREA

4 PALACE GATE

LONDON W8 5NF

21st December, 1990

Dear Mr Jordan,

Thank you for your letter of 23rd November.

I have conveyed your concern to the relevant authorities of my government and will forward to you any further information in this regard.

I would like to point out that, as you indicated in your letter, the trade unionists in question have violated laws some of which were, in fact, passed or amended during the period between April 1988 and January 1990 when the opposition parties held a majority in the Korean National Assembly.

Yours sincerely,

Jay Hee Oh
Ambassador

Mr Bill Jordan,
President,
Amalgamated Engineering Union,
110 Peckham Road,
London SE15 5EL.

0125

EMBASSY OF THE REPUBLIC OF KOREA

4 PALACE GATE

LONDON W8 5NF

21st December, 1990

Dear Mr Hammond,

Thank you for your letter of 17th December.

I have conveyed your concern to the relevant
authorities of my government and will forward to you
any further information in this regard.

I would like to point out that, as you indicated
in your letter, the trade unionists in question have
violated laws some of which were, in fact, passed
or amended during the period between April 1988 and
January 1990 when the opposition parties held a
majority in the Korean National Assembly.

Yours sincerely,

Jay Hee Oh
Ambassador

Mr E.A. B. Hammond,
General Secretary,
Electrical Electronic Telecommunication
        & Plumbing Union,
Hayes Court,
West Common Road,
Bromley,
Kent,
BR2 7AU.

0126

EMBASSY OF THE REPUBLIC OF KOREA

4 PALACE GATE

LONDON W8 5NF

21st December, 1990

Dear Mr Evans,

Thank you for your letter of 26th November.

I have conveyed your concern to the relevant authorities of my government and will forward to you any further information in this regard.

I would like to point out that, as you indicated in your letter, the trade unionists in question have violated laws some of which were, in fact, passed or amended during the period between April 1988 and January 1990 when the opposition parties held a majority in the Korean National Assembly.

Yours sincerely,

Jay Hee Oh
Ambassador

Mr R.L. Evans,
General Secretary,
Iron & Steel Trades Confederation,
Swinton House,
324 Gray's Inn Road,
London WC1X 8DD.

0127

공　　　란

공   란

공   란

공 란

" 노사관계 안정 "

노   동   부

노정   32220-153   (503-9730)   91. 1. 7.
수신   외무부장관
참조   국제기구조약국장
제목   인권관련 자료 송부

    1. 관련 : 외무부 국연 2031-59788   ('90.12.5.)

    2. 관련호로 요청한 영국노조 The Amalgamated Engineering Union 과
Iron & Steel Trade Confederation 의 아국 노동권 현실 비난에 대한 설명자료
를 별첨과 같이 송부하오니 업무에 참고하시기 바랍니다.

    첨부   인권 관련 설명자료 1부.   끝.

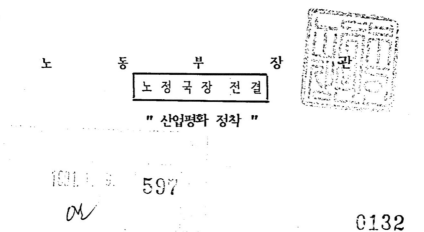

노   동   부   장

노 정 국 장 전 결

" 산업평화 정착 "

597

0132

인권 관련 설명 자료

1. 세계 각국이 나름대로의 법률과 규범, 관습을 가지고 국가를 통치하듯이 우리나라 또한 법치국가로서 모든국민이 법률앞에 평등하며 법률이 허용하는 범위내에서 자유롭게 생활하고 있읍니다. 이러한 국가질서의 기본적 바탕위에서 근로자들의 노동운동의 기본이되는 노동조합 활동에 대하여는 헌법을 비롯 노동관계 법령에서 노동 3권이 확고히 보장되고 있을 뿐 아니라 특히 노동조합 활동에 대하여는 노동조합법에서 특별히 규정하여 보장하고 있읍니다. 따라서 정당한 노동조합 활동에 대하여는 국가의 공권력으로 탄압할 수 가 없으며, 사용자에 의하여 부당하게 침해되지 아니하도록 보호하고 있읍니다.

법령으로 근로자의 단결권, 단체교섭권 및 단체행동권을 보장한 기본취지는 근로자가 노동조합을 결성하여 사용자와 대등한 입장에서 근로조건을 집단적으로 결정할 수 있도록 하기 위한 것입니다. 우리나라의 경우 근로자 2인 이상이면 노동조합을 결성할 수 있으며, 일단 정당하게 설립된 노동조합의 대표자는 사용자에게 단체협약의 체결을 요구할 수 있고, 사용자가 이를 거부시 부당노동 행위로 제재를 받게 되어 있읍니다. 아울러 단체교섭이 결렬되었을 경우 노동조합은 단체행동을 통하여 그들의 요구사항을 관철시킬 수도 있읍니다.

2. 이렇듯 근로자는 헌법 및 노동관계 법령으로 노동 3권을 보장받고 있지만 이를 무제한으로 행사할 수는 없는 것이며, 노동권 보장의 기본취지에 적합하게 행사되어야 하는 것입니다. 더구나 노동조합 활동을 보장한다고 하더라도 국민으로서 지켜야 할 권리와 의무가 있는 것이며, 그 권리와 의무를 무시하고 국가의 근본인 법 질서를 파괴하는 행위에 대하여 개별적 인권을 침해

0133

하지 않는한 법위내에서 엄정한 법 적용은 불가피한 것입니다. 이러한 차원에서 우리나라 노동현장에서 발생되는 노사간의 갈등문제 해결을 위한 정당한 활동에 대하여는 노사를 막론하고 구속을 하거나 국가권력으로 탄압하는 예는 없으며, 다만 반국가적인 행동(사상적 행동)이나 불법적인 파괴, 폭력등 지나친 과격 행동을 하는 일부 근로자들에 대하여는 국가의 존립과 법 질서 확립의 차원에서 엄격하게 처벌하고 있으며 이는 앞으로도 그러할 것입니다.

　　　　　3. 따라서 노동권을 정당하게 행사하는 노동조합이나 조합원 개인의 인권을 탄압한다는 비판은 전혀 현실과 다르며, 그러한 자료를 어떠한 경로를 통하여 입수하였는지 알수는 없으나 이는 허위과장된 내용일 것으로 사료됩니다. 노동부로서도 구체적이고 정확한 구속 근로자수를 파악할 수는 없지만, 예를 들어 IMF 측 명단에 포함되어 있는 「정운광」(서울지하철공사 전 노조위원장)의 경우 법 절차를 무시한 불법파업,사무실 점거 및 파괴, 폭력행사 (폭력 및 업무 방해죄) 로 구속된 바 있으며 현대 앤진 노조위원장 「권용묵」의 경우에도 88.12, 89.4 2차에 걸쳐 같은 그룹의 타회사인 현대중공업의 불법파업을 선동하고 공권력 격퇴 를위한 노동지 출정식을 주도한 (폭력 및 업무방해죄 등) 이유로 구속된 바 있 읍니다.

　　요컨대 그들 스스로는 정당한 노동운동을 하다가 구속되었다고 주장하지만, 사실을 살펴보면 야당 주도하에 개정된 현행 노동관계법에 규정되어 있는 정당한 절차를 무시하였거나, 노동관계법과는 관계없는 기타 법을 위반하였기 때문에 구속된 것에 불과한 것이며, 이를 두고 노동운동을 탄압하였다고 주장하는 것은 잘못된 것이라고 아니할 수 없으며 사실확인 없이 일방적으로 우리나라를 비판한 귀측의 태도에 유감을 표명하지 않을 수 없습니다.

　　앞으로는 어느 일방의 그릇된 목적으로 선전하는 자료를 인용하기 보다는 좀더 사실내용 확인을 통한 올바른 이해가 있었으면 합니다.

0134

분류기호 문서번호	정흥 20501- /2	협조문용지 (720-2339)	결 재	담 당	과 장	국 장
						분석관
시행일자	1991. 1. 19					
수 신	수신처참조	발 신 정보문화국장 (서명)				
제 목	인권문제 관련 대책회의 개최					

최근 외국정부 및 인권단체 (Amnesty Int'l 포합) 가 거론

하고 있는 아국의 소위 "인권문제" 에 관한 대책 수립을 위해 아래와

같이 관계부처 회의를 개최코저 하오니 귀국도 인권관련 소관사항에

관한 대책방안을 마련하여 동 회의에 참석하여 주시기 바랍니다.

- 아 래 -

가. 회의일시 : 1991.1.22 (화) 오후 4시

나. 장 소 : 외무부 제1차관보실 (제1종합청사 806호)

다. 참석대상자: 외무부 제1차관보 (회의 주재)

대통령 비서관

행정조정실 조정관

외무부 관계국장

국가안전기획부 담당국장

법무부 담당국장

라. 준비사항 : 인권문제로 거론되고 있는 내국민 및 외국인

/ 계 속 /

0135

(국내 거주자 포함) 들의 명단, 법법

사실, 재판 진행 상황 및 수형 현황

(국가안전기획부, 법무부 소관)과

대책 방안.   끝.

수신처 : 아주국장, 미주국장, 구주국장, 국제기구조약국장

人權關聯 懸案問題 檢討

1991. 1.

法務部 人權課

0137

1. 背 景

o 6共和國 出帆이후 대폭적인 拘束者 釋放, 關聯制度의 改善, 國際人權規約 加入등을 통해 人權伸張에 적극 노력 하여 왔음에도 불구하고

o 그동안 國際赦免委員會, 아시아워치등 일부 國際人權團體가 우리 人權狀況이 惡化된 것으로 왜곡 주장하고, 言論이 이를 報道

o 이러한 일부의 잘못된 주장은 우리 人權狀況에 대하여 國內外的으로 誤解素地를 제공하고 있으므로 이를 올바로 弘報할 필요성을 인식, 그간 青瓦台, 總理室, 安企部, 公報處 등 關係部處와 협조, 體系的, 積極的, 持續的인 對處努力을 傾注함

2. 主要報道事項 및 對應實績

가. 人權關聯 主要報道事項 (90. ‑91. 1. 현재)

(1) 人權報告書

o 國際赦免委員會 韓國人權報告書 (90. 1. 16. 發刊)

o 美國務部 90年度 年例人權報告書
(90. 2. 21. 發刊)

1

0138

ㅇ 大韓辯協　人權報告書 (90. 2. 23. 發刊)

ㅇ 아시아워치　年例報告書 (90. 11. 9. 發刊)

ㅇ 휴먼라이트워치　年例報告書 (91. 1. 11. 發刊)

(2) 主要書信

ㅇ 英國 Joan Battle　議員등　3名 (90. 4. 26)

ㅇ 케네디議員등　10名의　美上院議員 (90. 6. 18)

ㅇ 英國　Micheal　Latham　下院議員 (90. 8. 28)

ㅇ 美下院議員 (46人, 美下院　人權모임) (90. 10. 30)

ㅇ 美國　John　Kerry　上院議員등　3名 (90. 12. 5)

＊國際赦免委員會會員　個人書信　22,451件

(3) 主要擧論事項

ㅇ 政治. 勞使關聯　拘束者들은　暴力행사등　實定法　違反者
　들임에도　마치　　政治犯　또는　　良心囚인양　記述하고
　釋放　要求

ㅇ 國家保安法, 集會및示威에관한法律, 勞動組合法, 勞動爭議
　調整法등의　改正要求

2

0139

나. 對應實績

(1) 人權團體報告書 등에 대하여

　o 反駁文 작성, 內.外信에 배포

　o 關聯部處別로 해당부분을 분석, 政府 입장을 정리
　　하여 해당團體에 外交經路를 통하여 설명

(2) 人權狀況 설명책자 "法과 秩序 그리고 人權" 발간 배포

　o 國內版— 6,000부 발간 배포

　o 英文版— 2,000부 발간 배포 (公報處)

(3) 關係部處間 긴밀한 협조체제 구축

　o 人權擁護政策協議會

　　. 構成— 政策調査補佐官 (主管), 外務.內務.法務.
　　　　公報處次官, 安企部 3 特補

　　. 任務— 人權問題관련 各種對策 및 弘報에 따른
　　　　基本方向 수립

　o 人權問題實務協議會

　　. 構成— 政策調査補佐官 (主管), 外務.內務.法務.
　　　　公報處.安企部등의 實務 局.課長級

　　. 任務— 問題發生時 會議開催, 對應方案 신속 강구

3

0140

(4) 人權擔當機構　補強

　　ㅇ人權關聯問題　효율적　對應　및　國際人權規約加入등에
　　따른　　業務增大에　對處하기　위해　　法務部　人權課
　　職員　增員（檢事２名，　　一般職３名）

　　　　＊日本：　法務省　人權擁護局ー　總１４０名（對內．外
　　　　　　　　　人權問題에　　有機的　협조．활동으로　문제
　　　　　　　　　극소화　처리）

3. 向後對策

　(1) 汎政府的　차원의　體系的　對應　적극　전개
　　ㅇ各　部處別로　　人權問題의　重要事案에　대해　　사전에
　　필요한　資料를　綜合，　　說明資料를　體系的으로　작성

　　ㅇ問題提起時　言論등에　즉각　배포，설명　및　是正要求

　(2) 효율적이고　적극적인　對應方案　講究
　　ㅇ人權狀況　설명책자″法과　秩序　그리고　人權″을　基本
　　指針書로　활용，　수시．적기　弘報對應

4

0141

- 國内 : 言論機關, 辯協등 人權團體, 韓國駐在 外國
公舘, 外國人權團體 韓國支部등을 對象으로
접촉 및 媒體弘報 병행

- 國外 : 人權問題에 관심있는 主要外國政府, 유엔등
國際機構, 國際赦免委를 비롯한 人權團體
등에 대한 수시접촉, 資料에 의한 사전
說明등 적극적 對應

ㅇ 統一院등과 협조, 北韓의 人權實狀을 기회있는대로
弘報, 人權問題에 관한 우리 國民의 올바른 시각
정립

(3) 國際人權規約報告書 작성. 제출

ㅇ 國際人權規約 B規約 第40條에 따라 作成, UN人權
理事會에 提出 (시한 7. 9)

ㅇ 關係部處와 협조, 우리 政府의 입장을 說得力있게
弘報할 수 있도록 작성

5

0142

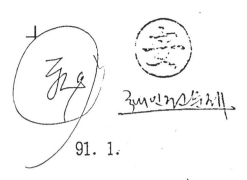

人權問題 關聯 動向

91. 1.

1. 第 47次 유엔人權委 開催

o 제 47차 유엔人權委가 91.1.28 ~3.8 간 스위스 제네바에서 開催
중인 바 이락의 쿠웨이트 侵攻에 따른 人權違反問題가 중점적
으로 擧論될 것으로 예상됨

〈 主要暫定 議題 〉

- 팔레스타인을 포함, 아랍점령 지역에서의 人權侵害問題

- 모든형태의 拘留와 投獄의 대상이 된 모든 인물들의 人權問題

- "宗敎나 信念에 근거한 差別과 모든 형태의 宗敎的 偏見
　除去에 대한 宣言" 問題

- "어린이의 權利에 관한 協約" 問題등

o 금번 제 47차 유엔人權委에서는 韓國 人權問題와 관련하여
임수경, 백림 3자會談代表, 國家保安法 改正, 全勞協拘束者 등의
문제거론이 예상되나 蘇聯, 中國, 소말리아, 라이베리아 등의 잇슈에
밀려 크게 문제시되지는 않을 것으로 전망됨

1

0143

※ 外務部는 90.2 제 46차 유엔人權委에서 北韓代表 (이철
駐제나바 代表部大使) 에 의해 문익환, 임수경등 구속자 문제가
거론된 바 있어 금번에도 北韓에 의해 국내문제가 거론 될
시에는 北韓의 人權問題를 강력히 거론, 對應하는 한편 차제에
북한인권 비판여론이 조성될 수 있도록 적극 대처키로 하였음

2. KNCC, 世界敎會協議會에 韓國人權報告書 提出

o 최근 韓國基督敎敎會協議會 (KNCC, 總務 : 權皓景) 는 제네바 소재
世界敎會協議會(WCC) 에 韓國 人權實態에 관한 報告書를 提出
하였음 → 처벌은?

〈 報告書 內容 要旨 〉

- 90.11.30 현재 한국내 수감되어 있는 良心囚는 총 1,746명으로
  하루평균 5.2명이 拘禁되고 있음

  : 학생 686명   : 근로자 334명   : 간첩죄 및 장기수 147명

  : 재야인사 71명 : 언론출판 24명 : 군인 및 경찰 37명

  : 농민 29명   : 어부 4명

- 한국내 一般罪囚(5만여명) 는 13〜15평방미터 (약 4평) 감방에
  10〜20명씩 수감되 있고, 醫師 54명이 배치되어 있으나 醫師
  및 醫院施設 不足으로 년 20명씩 死亡하고 있음

2

- 동린어한 병에 수한 -

0144

- 韓國軍은 일반인 1,000명당 20명 정도로 총 90여만명이며, 1980.1.1~1988.7.31 간 軍服務期間中 9,060명이 死亡하였음

    : 안전사고 3,723명   : 무기취급부주의 2,670명

    : 자살 2,254명   : 기타 413명

- "犯罪와 戰爭宣布" 는 경찰의 權力濫用을 조장시켜 무고한 국민을 위협하고 拷問하는데 惡用되고 있음

o 동 報告書는 KNCC가 「第 47次 유엔 人權委員會」(91.1.28~3.8 제네바 개최) 를 앞두고 參考資料로 작성, WCC에 提供한 것으로 보임

3. KNCC, 駐韓外交使節 對象 國內人權에 대한 關心 促求

o KNCC는 1.17 신라호텔로 오지리·벨기에등 13개국 大使와 美國 (부대사)·濠洲·카나다·蘇聯을 비롯한 8個國 公館員등 21명을 招請, 晩餐宴을 베풀고 韓國人權問題 등에 대한 各國의 支援을 要請하였음

3

< 支援要請 內容 >

- 韓國人權狀況은 정부 발표와는 달리 惡化되어 있다며 각국의
  支援을 要望

- 1995년 "統一禧年" 사업을 실현하기 위해 추진중인 北韓 및
  海外 教會와의 交流에 적극 協助해 줄 것을 當付

- 世界敎會協議會(WCC) 「에밀리오 카스트로」總務가 「걸프」戰爭과
  관련하여 美國・이락政府에 보낸 平和維持 促求內容의 호소문을
  배포

4

비록 (오편의2너)
-정랑고동 참고.
/3거

법　　　무　.　　　부

인권　2031-0846　　　503-7045　　　　1991. 1. 21

수신　외무부장관

참조　미주국장

제목　아시아워치 인권보고서 및 휴먼라이트워치 연례보고서에 대한

　　　대응자료 송부

　　　우리부는 인권문제관련 관계기관대책회의 ('90.11.23) 결과에
따라 아시아워치 인권보고서에 대하여 각 부서별로 분석검토한 자료의
종합결과 및 '91.1.11에 발간한 휴먼라이트워치 연례보고서에 대한
당부업장을 별첨과 같이 송부하오니 상기 단체에 설명될 수 있도록 적의
조치하여 주시기 바랍니다.

첨부 :　관련자료 1부.　끝.

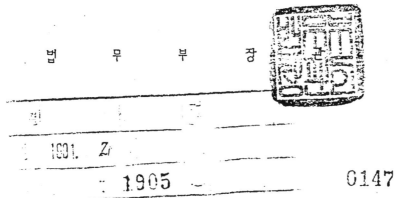

법　무　부　장

1991. 2.

1905　　　　　　　0147

공   란

공 란

공   란

공 란

공 란

공 란

공   란

공   란

공 란

공 란

공   란

공 란

공   란

공 란

공   란

공　　　란

공   란

공   란

공 란

공   란

공 란

공   란

공   란

공   란

공   란

공   란

공 란

공   란

공   란

공 란

공　　　　란

공   란

공   란

공   란

공 란

공   란

공 란

공   란

공 란

공   란

공 란

공   란

공 란

공   란

공　　　　란

공 란

공   란

공 란

공   란

공　　　　란

공   란

공   란

공　　　　란

공 란

공 란

공   란

공　　　　란

공   란

공　　　란

공　　　란

공 란

공 란

공 란

공   란

공 란

공   란

공 란

공 란

공 란

공 란

공   란

공　　　　란

공 란

공 란

공 란

공   란

발 신 전 보

번   호 : WEC-0044   910123 1717 DP   종별 :

수   신 : 주   EC   대사. 총영사

발   신 : 장 관   (구일)

제   목 : 구주의회 아국 인권관계 결의 채택

대 : ECW-842,844

대호, 구주의회의 아국 인권관련 결의 채택관련, 결의문에서 언급하고있는 인사들에 대한 개인별 관련자료 및 아국 인권에 관한 영문책자(Human Rights in Korea : Facts and Fiction)를 차파편 송부 예정이니 동 자료를 참고, 구주의회측이 아국의 인권상황에 관하여 올바른 인식을 갖도록 적절히 대처 바람. 끝.

(구주국장 라원찬)

예고 : 1991.12.31. 일반

앙고재	91년 1월 23일	부1과	기안자 성명 설경훈	과장	심의반	국장	차관	장관	
									외신과통제

0224

분류기호 문서번호	구일 202- 3723	기안용지		시 행 상 특별취급	
보존기간	영구·준영구 10. 5. 3. 1	장 관			
수 신 처 보존기간					
시행일자	1991. 1. 23.				

보조기관	국 장	전 결	협조기관		문 서 통 제
	심의관				1991. 1. 24
	과 장				
기안책임자		설 경 훈			발 송 인

경 유		발신명의	
수 신	주EC 대사		
참 조			1991. 1. 24

제 목	구주의회 아국 인권 관계 결의

구주의회의 아국 인권관련 결의 채택과 관련, 동 결의문에서

언급하고 있는 아래 인사들에 대한 개인별 관련자료와 아국 인권 상황에

관한 영문책자를 별첨 송부하오니, 구주의회측에 대한 아국 인권상황

설명등에 활용하시기 바랍니다.

- 아 래 -

1. 개인별 자료

   임수경, 문규현, 홍성담, 조용술, 유원호, 김진엽

2. 아국 인권 상황에 관한 영문책자

   - Human Rights in Korea : Facts and Fiction.

첨부 : 상기자료 각 1부. 끝.

0225

주 스 위 스 대 사 관

스위스(정) 790-60   1991.2.4.

수신: 장관

참조: 국제기구조약국장

제목: 인권관련 진정서

　　　주재국 민간단체인 ACAT (Action of Christians for the Abolition of
Torture)측은 90.9 구속되어 현재 형 집행중에 있는 현연덕외 6명에 관한 진정서를
당관에 송부하여 왔는 바, 이를 이송하오니 참고 바랍니다.

첨부: 상기 진정서. 끝.

주 　 스 　 위 　 스 　 대

08319

0226

```
Hanspeter Wasmer                  6003 Luzern, 30. Januar 1991
Spannortstrasse 1
6003 Luzern


KOPIE !                           S.Exc. M. Won Ho LEE
**********                        Ambassadeur de la République
                                  de Corée
                                  Kalcheggweg 38

                                  3006   BERN
```

Exzellenz,

Als Mitglieder und Freunde von ACAT (Action of Christians for the Abolition of Torture) sind wir äusserst besorgt über Nachrichten betreffend die Verletzung der Menschenrechte in den Gefängnissen von Seoul und Mokpo. Aus sicherer Quelle wissen wir, dass Häftlinge gefoltert werden und durch Entzug von Wasser, Nahrung und Schlaf zur Unterzeichnung bestimmter Erklärungen gezwungen werden. Hungerstreikende werden zwangsernährt. Ärztliche Hilfe und auch der Besuch sogenannt politisch engagierter >Personen wird ihnen verweigert. Es handelt sich insbesondere um folgende sechs Personen, die im September 1990 verhaftet worden sind:

   Hyeun Yeun Deuk, Ri Soung Sou, Nam Bo Hyeun, Djeun Mi Hwa,
   Ri Myeung, Ri Seung Ou

Die letzten zwei wurden durch Misshandlungen lebensgefährlich verletzt.

Wir wenden uns an Sie, Exzellenz, als Staatsoberhaupt, mit der dringenden Bitte die Haftbedingungen in den koreanischen Gefängnissen untersuchen zu lassen. Gesundheitlich gefährdeten Personden ist sofort medizinische Hilfe zu gewähren. Alle Gefangenen sind einem ordentlichen Gericht zuzuführen. Sofern ihnen kein kriminelles Vergehen nachgewiesen werden kann, müssen sie unverzüglich freigelassen werden.

Alle Gefangenen sind menschlich zu behandeln. Misshandlungen von Menschen sind eines Rechtsstaates unwürdig.

Exzellenz, wir hoffen, dass Sie unserem Schreiben Ihre volle Aufmerksamkeit schenken werden, und danken Ihnen im voraus.

                                  Mit vorzüglicher Hochachtung
                                  Hanspeter Wasmer

Excellence,

ci-joint vous trouvez la copie de la lettre, que j'ai envoyé au gouvernement de votre pays. Je vous serais très reconnaissant si vous pouviez soutenier mon engagement en faveur de ces personnes.

Recevez, Excellence, l'expression de mes sentments distingués.

0227

H.Exc. Roh Tae-woo
President of the Republic of Korea
The Blue House
1 Sejong-no Chongno-gu
SEOUL
Republic of Korea

Exzellenz,

Als Mitglieder und Freunde von ACAT (Action of Christians for the abolition of
torture) sind wir äusserst besorgt über Nachrichten betreffend die Verletzung
der Menschenrechte in den Gefnägnissen von Seoul und Mokpo. Aus sicherer Quelle
wissen wir, dass Häftlinge gefoltert werden und durch Entzug von Wasser, Nahrung
und Schlaf zur Unterzeichnung bestimmter Erklärungen gezwungen werden. Hunger-
streikende werden zwangsernährt. Aerztliche Hilfe und auch der Besuch sogenannt
politisch engagierter Personen wird ihnen verweigert. Es handelt sich insbesondere
um folgende sechs Personen, die im September 1990 verhaftet worden sind:

    Hyeun Yeun Deuk, Ri Soung Sou, Nam Bo Hyeun, Djeun Mi Hwa
    Ri Myeung, Ri Seung Ou

Die letzten zwei wurden durch Misshandlungen lebensgefährlich verletzt.

Wir wenden uns an Sie, Exzellenz, als Staatsoberhaupt, mit der dringenden Bitte,
die Haftbedingungen in den koreanischen Gefängnissen untersuchen zu lassen. Gesundheitlich gefährdeten Personen ist sofort medizinische Hilfe zu gewähren.
Alle Gefangenen sind einem ordentlichen Gericht zuzuführen. Sofern ihnen kein
kriminelles Vergehen nachgewiesen werden kann, sollten sie unverzüglich frei-
gelassen werden.

Alle Gefangenen sind menschlich zu behandeln. Misshandlungen von Menschen sind
eines Rechtsstaates unwürdig.

Exzellenz, wir hoffen, dass Sie unserem Schreiben Ihre volle Aufmerksamkeit
schenken werden, und danken Ihnen im voraus.

                        Mit vorzüglicher Hochachtung

0228

Kopie zur Kenntnis an:
S.Exc. M. Won Ho LEE
Ambassadeur de la République de Corée
38, Kalcheggweg
3006 Berne

H.Exc. Roh Tae-woo
President of the Republic of Korea
The Blue House
1 Sejong-no Chongno-gu
SEOUL
Republic of Korea

Exzellenz,

Als Mitglieder und Freunde von ACAT (Action of Christians for the abolition of torture) sind wir äusserst besorgt über Nachrichten betreffend die Verletzung der Menschenrechte in den Gefnägnissen von Seoul und Mokpo. Aus sicherer Quelle wissen wir, dass Häftlinge gefoltert werden und durch Entzug von Wasser, Nahrung und Schlaf zur Unterzeichnung bestimmter Erklärungen gezwungen werden. Hunger-streikende werden zwangsernährt. Aerztliche Hilfe und auch der Besuch sogenannt politisch engagierter Personen wird ihnen verweigert. Es handelt sich insbesondere um folgende sechs Personen, die im September 1990 verhaftet worden sind:

Hyeun Yeun Deuk, Ri Soung Sou, Nam Bo Hyeun, Djeun Mi Hwa
Ri Myeung, Ri Seung Ou

Die letzten zwei wurden durch Misshandlungen lebensgefährlich verletzt.

Wir wenden uns an Sie, Exzellenz, als Staatsoberhaupt, mit der dringenden Bitte, die Haftbedingungen in den koreanischen Gefängnissen untersuchen zu lassen. Ge-sundheitlich gefährdeten Personen ist sofort medizinische Hilfe zu gewähren. Alle Gefangenen sind einem ordentlichen Gericht zuzuführen. Sofern ihnen kein kriminelles Vergehen nachgewiesen werden kann, sollten sie unverzüglich frei-gelassen werden.

Alle Gefangenen sind menschlich zu behandeln. Misshandlungen von Menschen sind eines Rechtsstaates unwürdig.

Exzellenz, wir hoffen, dass Sie unserem Schreiben Ihre volle Aufmerksamkeit schenken werden, und danken Ihnen im voraus.

Mit vorzüglicher Hochachtung

Babini Elisabeth

0229

Peter Kirchebner
Tittwiesenstr. 80
Ø 081 - 24 60 79
CH-7000 CHUR

H.Exc. Roh Tae-woo
President of the Republic of Korea
The Blue House
1 Sejong-no Chongno-gu
SEOUL
Republic of Korea

Copie

Exzellenz,

Als Mitglieder und Freunde von ACAT (Action of Christians for the abolition of torture) sind wir äusserst besorgt über Nachrichten betreffend die Verletzung der Menschenrechte in den Gefnägnissen von Seoul und Mokpo. Aus sicherer Quelle wissen wir, dass Häftlinge gefoltert werden und durch Entzug von Wasser, Nahrung und Schlaf zur Unterzeichnung bestimmter Erklärungen gezwungen werden. Hunger-streikende werden zwangsernährt. Aerztliche Hilfe und auch der Besuch sogenannt politisch engagierter Personen wird ihnen verweigert. Es handelt sich insbesondere um folgende sechs Personen, die im September 1990 verhaftet worden sind:

Hyeun Yeun Deuk, Ri Soung Sou, Nam Bo Hyeun, Djeun Mi Hwa
Ri Myeung, Ri Seung Ou

Die letzten zwei wurden durch Misshandlungen lebensgefährlich verletzt.

Wir wenden uns an Sie, Exzellenz, als Staatsoberhaupt, mit der dringenden Bitte, die Haftbedingungen in den koreanischen Gefängnissen untersuchen zu lassen. Gesundheitlich gefährdeten Personen ist sofort medizinische Hilfe zu gewähren. Alle Gefangenen sind einem ordentlichen Gericht zuzuführen. Sofern ihnen kein kriminelles Vergehen nachgewiesen werden kann, sollten sie unverzüglich frei-gelassen werden.

Alle Gefangenen sind menschlich zu behandeln. Misshandlungen von Menschen sind eines Rechtsstaates unwürdig.

Exzellenz, wir hoffen, dass Sie unserem Schreiben Ihre volle Aufmerksamkeit schenken werden, und danken Ihnen im voraus.

Mit vorzüglicher Hochachtung

0230

Copie

H.Exc. Roh Tae-woo
President of the Republic of Korea
The Blue House
1 Sejong-no Chongno-gu
SEOUL
Republic of Korea

Exzellenz,

Als Mitglieder und Freunde von ACAT (Action of Christians for the abolition of torture) sind wir äusserst besorgt über Nachrichten betreffend die Verletzung der Menschenrechte in den Gefnägnissen von Seoul und Mokpo. Aus sicherer Quelle wissen wir, dass Häftlinge gefoltert werden und durch Entzug von Wasser, Nahrung und Schlaf zur Unterzeichnung bestimmter Erklärungen gezwungen werden. Hunger- streikende werden zwangsernährt. Aerztliche Hilfe und auch der Besuch sogenannt politisch engagierter Personen wird ihnen verweigert. Es handelt sich insbesondere um folgende sechs Personen, die im September 1990 verhaftet worden sind:

Hyeun Yeun Deuk, Ri Soung Sou, Nam Bo Hyeun, Djeun Mi Hwa
Ri Myeung, Ri Seung Ou

Die letzten zwei wurden durch Misshandlungen lebensgefährlich verletzt.

Wir wenden uns an Sie, Exzellenz, als Staatsoberhaupt, mit der dringenden Bitte, die Haftbedingungen in den koreanischen Gefängnissen untersuchen zu lassen. Ge- sundheitlich gefährdeten Personen ist sofort medizinische Hilfe zu gewähren. Alle Gefangenen sind einem ordentlichen Gericht zuzuführen. Sofern ihnen kein kriminelles Vergehen nachgewiesen werden kann, sollten sie unverzüglich frei- gelassen werden.

Alle Gefangenen sind menschlich zu behandeln. Misshandlungen von Menschen sind eines Rechtsstaates unwürdig.

Exzellenz, wir hoffen, dass Sie unserem Schreiben Ihre volle Aufmerksamkeit schenken werden, und danken Ihnen im voraus.

Mit vorzüglicher Hochachtung

Elsbeth Hungerbühler
Aeulistr. 5
Weinfelden

0231

Ruth Eberhard
Paradiesweg 3
CH4102 Binningen

H.Exc. Roh Tae-woo
President of the Republic of Korea
The Blue House
1 Sejong-no Chongno-gu
SEOUL
Republic of Korea

Exzellenz,

Als Mitglieder und Freunde von ACAT (Action of Christians for the abolition of torture) sind wir äusserst besorgt über Nachrichten betreffend die Verletzung der Menschenrechte in den Gefnägnissen von Seoul und Mokpo. Aus sicherer Quelle wissen wir, dass Häftlinge gefoltert werden und durch Entzug von Wasser, Nahrung und Schlaf zur Unterzeichnung bestimmter Erklärungen gezwungen werden. Hungerstreikende werden zwangsernährt. Aerztliche Hilfe und auch der Besuch sogenannt politisch engagierter Personen wird ihnen verweigert. Es handelt sich insbesondere um folgende sechs Personen, die im September 1990 verhaftet worden sind:

Hyeun Yeun Deuk, Ri Soung Sou, Nam Bo Hyeun, Djeun Mi Hwa
Ri Myeung, Ri Seung Ou

Die letzten zwei wurden durch Misshandlungen lebensgefährlich verletzt.

Wir wenden uns an Sie, Exzellenz, als Staatsoberhaupt, mit der dringenden Bitte, die Haftbedingungen in den koreanischen Gefängnissen untersuchen zu lassen. Gesundheitlich gefährdeten Personen ist sofort medizinische Hilfe zu gewähren. Alle Gefangenen sind einem ordentlichen Gericht zuzuführen. Sofern ihnen kein kriminelles Vergehen nachgewiesen werden kann, sollten sie unverzüglich freigelassen werden.

Alle Gefangenen sind menschlich zu behandeln. Misshandlungen von Menschen sind eines Rechtsstaates unwürdig.

Exzellenz, wir hoffen, dass Sie unserem Schreiben Ihre volle Aufmerksamkeit schenken werden, und danken Ihnen im voraus.

Mit vorzüglicher Hochachtung

R. Choce

0232

H.Exc. Roh Tae-woo
President of the Republic of Korea
The Blue House
1 Sejong-no Chongno-gu
SEOUL
Republic of Korea

Exzellenz,

Als Mitglieder und Freunde von ACAT (Action of Christians for the abolition of torture) sind wir äusserst besorgt über Nachrichten betreffend die Verletzung der Menschenrechte in den Gefnägnissen von Seoul und Mokpo. Aus sicherer Quelle wissen wir, dass Häftlinge gefoltert werden und durch Entzug von Wasser, Nahrung und Schlaf zur Unterzeichnung bestimmter Erklärungen gezwungen werden. Hunger-streikende werden zwangsernährt. Aerztliche Hilfe und auch der Besuch sogenannt politisch engagierter Personen wird ihnen verweigert. Es handelt sich insbesondere um folgende sechs Personen, die im September 1990 verhaftet worden sind:

Hyeun Yeun Deuk, Ri Soung Sou, Nam Bo Hyeun, Djeun Mi Hwa
Ri Myeung, Ri Seung Ou

Die letzten zwei wurden durch Misshandlungen lebensgefährlich verletzt.

Wir wenden uns an Sie, Exzellenz, als Staatsoberhaupt, mit der dringenden Bitte, die Haftbedingungen in den koreanischen Gefängnissen untersuchen zu lassen. Ge-sundheitlich gefährdeten Personen ist sofort medizinische Hilfe zu gewähren. Alle Gefangenen sind einem ordentlichen Gericht zuzuführen. Sofern ihnen kein kriminelles Vergehen nachgewiesen werden kann, sollten sie unverzüglich frei-gelassen werden.

Alle Gefangenen sind menschlich zu behandeln. Misshandlungen von Menschen sind eines Rechtsstaates unwürdig.

Exzellenz, wir hoffen, dass Sie unserem Schreiben Ihre volle Aufmerksamkeit schenken werden, und danken Ihnen im voraus.

Mit vorzüglicher Hochachtung

Liselotte Haller
12, Niesenblickstreet
CH-3600 THUN

0233

Sr. Renate Killinger
Friedbühlweg 26
CH-3653 Oberhofen
Tel. 033 / 43 20 39

Oberhofen, den 30. Januar 1991

H.Exc. Roh Tae-woo
President of the Republic of Korea
The Blue House
1 Sejong-no Chongno-gu
SEOUL
Republic of Korea

Exzellenz,

Als Mitglieder und Freunde von ACAT (Action of Christians for the abolition of torture) sind wir äusserst besorgt über Nachrichten betreffend die Verletzung der Menschenrechte in den Gefnägnissen von Seoul und Mokpo. Aus sicherer Quelle wissen wir, dass Häftlinge gefoltert werden und durch Entzug von Wasser, Nahrung und Schlaf zur Unterzeichnung bestimmter Erklärungen gezwungen werden. Hunger- streikende werden zwangsernährt. Aerztliche Hilfe und auch der Besuch sogenannt politisch engagierter Personen wird ihnen verweigert. Es handelt sich insbesondere um folgende sechs Personen, die im September 1990 verhaftet worden sind:

Hyeun Yeun Deuk, Ri Soung Sou, Nam Bo Hyeun, Djeun Mi Hwa
Ri Myeung, Ri Seung Ou

Die letzten zwei wurden durch Misshandlungen lebensgefährlich verletzt.

Wir wenden uns an Sie, Exzellenz, als Staatsoberhaupt, mit der dringenden Bitte, die Haftbedingungen in den koreanischen Gefängnissen untersuchen zu lassen. Ge- sundheitlich gefährdeten Personen ist sofort medizinische Hilfe zu gewähren. Alle Gefangenen sind einem ordentlichen Gericht zuzuführen. Sofern ihnen kein kriminelles Vergehen nachgewiesen werden kann, sollten sie unverzüglich frei- gelassen werden.

Alle Gefangenen sind menschlich zu behandeln. Misshandlungen von Menschen sind eines Rechtsstaates unwürdig.

Exzellenz, wir hoffen, dass Sie unserem Schreiben Ihre volle Aufmerksamkeit schenken werden, und danken Ihnen im voraus.

Mit vorzüglicher Hochachtung

Sr. Renate Killinger

Kopie an:

S. Exc. M. Won Ho LEE
Ambassadeur de la République de Corée
38, Kalcheggweg

3006 Berne

0234

H.Exc. Roh Tae-woo
President of the Republic of Korea
The Blue House
1 Sejong-no Chongno-gu
SEOUL
· Republic of Korea

Exzellenz,

Als Mitglieder und Freunde von ACAT (Action of Christians for the abolition of torture) sind wir äusserst besorgt über Nachrichten betreffend die Verletzung der Menschenrechte in den Gefnägnissen von Seoul und Mokpo. Aus sicherer Quelle wissen wir, dass Häftlinge gefoltert werden und durch Entzug von Wasser, Nahrung und Schlaf zur Unterzeichnung bestimmter Erklärungen gezwungen werden. Hunger- streikende werden zwangsernährt. Aerztliche Hilfe und auch der Besuch sogenannt politisch engagierter Personen wird ihnen verweigert. Es handelt sich insbesondere um folgende sechs Personen, die im September 1990 verhaftet worden sind:

    Hyeun Yeun Deuk, Ri Soung Sou, Nam Bo Hyeun, Djeun Mi Hwa
    Ri Myeung, Ri Seung Ou

Die letzten zwei wurden durch Misshandlungen lebensgefährlich verletzt.

Wir wenden uns an Sie, Exzellenz, als Staatsoberhaupt, mit der dringenden Bitte, die Haftbedingungen in den koreanischen Gefängnissen untersuchen zu lassen. Gesundheitlich gefährdeten Personen ist sofort medizinische Hilfe zu gewähren. Alle Gefangenen sind einem ordentlichen Gericht zuzuführen. Sofern ihnen kein kriminelles Vergehen nachgewiesen werden kann, sollten sie unverzüglich freigelassen werden.

Alle Gefangenen sind menschlich zu behandeln. Misshandlungen von Menschen sind eines Rechtsstaates unwürdig.

Exzellenz, wir hoffen, dass Sie unserem Schreiben Ihre volle Aufmerksamkeit schenken werden, und danken Ihnen im voraus.

               Mit vorzüglicher Hochachtung

                  H. Vidal

0235

Dr. Xaver Pfister
Mörsbergerstrasse 34
4057 BASEL
Tel. 061/692 71 71

H.Exc. Roh Tae-woo
President of the Republic of Korea
The Blue House
1 Sejong-no Chongno-gu
SEOUL
Republic of Korea

Exzellenz,

Als Mitglieder und Freunde von ACAT (Action of Christians for the abolition of torture) sind wir äusserst besorgt über Nachrichten betreffend die Verletzung der Menschenrechte in den Gefnägnissen von Seoul und Mokpo. Aus sicherer Quelle wissen wir, dass Häftlinge gefoltert werden und durch Entzug von Wasser, Nahrung und Schlaf zur Unterzeichnung bestimmter Erklärungen gezwungen werden. Hungerstreikende werden zwangsernährt. Aerztliche Hilfe und auch der Besuch sogenannt politisch engagierter Personen wird ihnen verweigert. Es handelt sich insbesondere um folgende sechs Personen, die im September 1990 verhaftet worden sind:

Hyeun Yeun Deuk, Ri Soung Sou, Nam Bo Hyeun, Djeun Mi Hwa
Ri Myeung, Ri Seung Ou

Die letzten zwei wurden durch Misshandlungen lebensgefährlich verletzt.

Wir wenden uns an Sie, Exzellenz, als Staatsoberhaupt, mit der dringenden Bitte, die Haftbedingungen in den koreanischen Gefängnissen untersuchen zu lassen. Gesundheitlich gefährdeten Personen ist sofort medizinische Hilfe zu gewähren. Alle Gefangenen sind einem ordentlichen Gericht zuzuführen. Sofern ihnen kein kriminelles Vergehen nachgewiesen werden kann, sollten sie unverzüglich freigelassen werden.

Alle Gefangenen sind menschlich zu behandeln. Misshandlungen von Menschen sind eines Rechtsstaates unwürdig.

Exzellenz, wir hoffen, dass Sie unserem Schreiben Ihre volle Aufmerksamkeit schenken werden, und danken Ihnen im voraus.

Mit vorzüglicher Hochachtung

0236

H.Exc. Roh Tae-woo
President of the Republic of Korea
The Blue House
1 Sejong-no Chongno-gu
SEOUL
Republic of Korea

Exzellenz,

Als Mitglieder und Freunde von ACAT (Action of Christians for the abolition of torture) sind wir äusserst besorgt über Nachrichten betreffend die Verletzung der Menschenrechte in den Gefnägnissen von Seoul und Mokpo. Aus sicherer Quelle wissen wir, dass Häftlinge gefoltert werden und durch Entzug von Wasser, Nahrung und Schlaf zur Unterzeichnung bestimmter Erklärungen gezwungen werden. Hunger-streikende werden zwangsernährt. Aerztliche Hilfe und auch der Besuch sogenannt politisch engagierter Personen wird ihnen verweigert. Es handelt sich insbesondere um folgende sechs Personen, die im September 1990 verhaftet worden sind:

Hyeun Yeun Deuk, Ri Soung Sou, Nam Bo Hyeun, Djeun Mi Hwa
Ri Myeung, Ri Seung Ou

Die letzten zwei wurden durch Misshandlungen lebensgefährlich verletzt.

Wir wenden uns an Sie, Exzellenz, als Staatsoberhaupt, mit der dringenden Bitte, die Haftbedingungen in den koreanischen Gefängnissen untersuchen zu lassen. Gesundheitlich gefährdeten Personen ist sofort medizinische Hilfe zu gewähren. Alle Gefangenen sind einem ordentlichen Gericht zuzuführen. Sofern ihnen kein kriminelles Vergehen nachgewiesen werden kann, sollten sie unverzüglich freigelassen werden.

Alle Gefangenen sind menschlich zu behandeln. Misshandlungen von Menschen sind eines Rechtsstaates unwürdig.

Exzellenz, wir hoffen, dass Sie unserem Schreiben Ihre volle Aufmerksamkeit schenken werden, und danken Ihnen im voraus.

Mit vorzüglicher Hochachtung

M. Neithauer-Weber
Lerchenhuschesse 9
0000 Chur

0237

관리
번호 91 -128

외 무 부

종 별 :

번 호 : DEW-0068

일 시 : 91 0206 1400

수 신 : 장관(국연)

발 신 : 주 덴마크 대사

제 목 : 국가보안법 위반사범 처리결과

　　　연: 덴막 2031-243(90.11.7)

　　　당관 업무에 참고코자하니 연호 요청한 함주명 관련사항을 당관에 조속 회시바람.

끝.

　　　(대사 장선섭-국장)

　　　예고:91.6.30 까지

국기국

91.02.06　22:09
외신 2과　통제관 BW

0238

분류기호 문서번호	국연 2031- 138 ( )	협조문용지	결 재	담당	과장	국장
시행일자	1991. 2. 8.					
수 신	수신처 참조	발 신	국제기구조약국장 (서명)			
제 목	인권문제 대책회의 개최결과					

91.2.5. 대통령비서실 김학준 정책조사보좌관 주재로 개최된

인권문제 대책회의 토의개요를 별첨 송부하니 업무에 참고하시기

바랍니다.

첨 부 : 상기 자료 1부.   끝.

수신처 : 미주국장, 구주국장, 정보문화국장

검 토 필(1991. 6. 30.)

일반문서로 재분류(1991. 12. 31.)

0239

인권문제 대책회의 개최결과

91. 2. 6.
국제연합과

1. 일시 및 장소 : 1991.2.5(화), 청와대

2. 참 석 자 : 김학준 정책조사보좌관 (회의주재)

　　　　　　　　　외무부, 법무부, 대통령비서실(외고안보), 안기부,

　　　　　　　　　치안본부, 해외공보관 관계관 참석

3. 토의요지

　가. 제 47차 유연인권위원회 대책

　　　o 외무부 국기국장 : 유연인권위 주요의제, 남북한 인권문제 거론

　　　　　　　　　　　　　　사례 및 금차 회의 토의전망, 아국 인권상황

　　　　　　　　　　　　　　거론시 대책 및 북한인권문제 거론 방안등 설명

　　　　　　　　　　　　　　(북한인권문제 거론을 위해서는 민간인권단체

　　　　　　　　　　　　　　육성 긴요)

　나. 인권규약 가입에 따른 인권보고서 작성

　　　o 법무부 인권과장 : 인권규약(B규약) 가입에 따른 아국 인권보고서를

　　　　　　　　　　　　　　91.7.9.한 유연인권사무국에 제출해야 하는 바,

　　　　　　　　　　　　　　동 보고서 작성요령, 작성시 유의사항 및 보고서

　　　　　　　　　　　　　　작성을 위한 각부처 작업 일정등 설명

　　　o 외무부 국기국장 : 인권보고서가 포괄적이고 체계적으로 작성되기

　　　　　　　　　　　　　　위해서는 각부처의 긴밀한 협조가 필수적임.

　　　　　　　　　　　　　　제출시한 관련, 가급적 시한내(91.7.9한) 제출을

　　　　　　　　　　　　　　목표로 하되 현재 검토중인 개혁입법이 충분히

　　　　　　　　　　　　　　반영될 수 있도록 신축적으로 대처함이 바람직함.

0240

다. 국무부 인권보고서 분석 및 대응

　ㅇ 법무부 인권과장 　: 2.6.중 정부입장을 설명하는 내용의 반박논평
　　　　　　　　　　　　발표 예정

　ㅇ 외무부 국기국장 　: 법무부 반박논평(안)중 " 북한의 인권과 자유가
　　　　　　　　　　　　세계 최악수준으로 더이상 방치할 수 없는
　　　　　　　　　　　　상황에 이르렀음에 우려 " 부분에서 "더이상
　　　　　　　　　　　　방치할 수 없는 상황 " 삭제함이 바람직함.

라. 독일 바이체커 대통령 방한시 인권거론 대책

　ㅇ 외무부 국기국장 　: 독일 대통령 방한에 대비하여 외무부가 취한
　　　　　　　　　　　　조치설명. 그러나 바이체커 대통령이 공개석상
　　　　　　　　　　　　에서 아국인권문제를 거론할 가능성을 완전
　　　　　　　　　　　　배제할 수 없으므로 우리의 대응 방안 강구 필요

마. KNCC의 한국인권보고서 대책

　ㅇ 안 기 부 　: 최근 한국기독교교회 협의회(KNCC)는 세계고회협의회
　　　　　　　　　(WCC)에 한국인권실태에 대한 보고서를 제출함.

　- 보고서요지 　: 90.11월 현재 한국내 양심수는 1,746명임. 한국
　　　　　　　　군인중 1980.1-1988.7간 복무중 사망자는 9,060명에 달함. 범죄
　　　　　　　　와의 전쟁으로 인하여 경찰에 의한 인권침해 사례가 증대되고 있음.

　ㅇ 동건관련, 김학준 보좌관 주재로 별도 회의를 개최하여 대책을 논의
　　키로 함.

바. KNCC, 주한외교사절 대상 국내 인권에 대한 관심 촉구

　ㅇ 안 기 부 　: KNCC는 1.17. 신라호텔에서 오지리, 벨기에등 13개국
　　　　　　　　　대사, 미국공사등 21명의 주한외교사절을 초청하여
　　　　　　　　　한국 인권문제거론 및 인권상황 개선을 위한 각국의
　　　　　　　　　지원을 요청함.

　ㅇ 외무부에서 적절히 대처토록 논의

0241

발 신 전 보

번 호 : WDE-0062   910208 1841 AO   종별 : 지급

수 신 : 주 덴마크   대사.총영사////

발 신 : 장 관   (국연)

제 목 : 국가보안법 위반사범 처리 결과

대 : 덴박 2031-243, DEW-0068

대호, 법무부 회보내용 하기 통보함.

1. 범죄사실 (국보법 위반, 간첩)
   o 54.2.1. 간첩으로 남파, 학원 및 관공서에 침투하여 지하당 조직
     등을 하라는 지령 수행
   o 54.8.23. 간첩으로 침투후 2차에 걸쳐 남파공작원과 접선, 공작금
     20만원을 수수하고 무전지령에 의거 동해안, 서울근고 등지의
     군사기밀을 탐지 수집

2. 처리상황
   o 83.4.4. 구속
   o 83.9.29. 1심 선고 (무기)
   o 84.1.30. 2심 선고 (항소기각)
   o 84.5.29. 3심 선고 (상고기각).   끝.

1991. 6. 30 ~~고문에~~
의거 ~~인민문서로~~ ~~재분류~~ 용

(국제기구조약국장 문동석)

앙 고 재	91 년 2 월 8 일	사 과	기안자	과 장	국 장	차 관	장 관	보안통제	외신과통제
			홍성화						

0242

원 본

외 무 부

종 별 :

번 호 : ECW-0191   일 시 : 91 0222 1800

수 신 : 장관 (구일,국회,기정동문)

발 신 : 주 EC 대사

제 목 : 구주의회 인권관계 결의

대: WEC-44

연: ECW-189

1. 본직은 연호 구주의회 한국친선협회 소속 의원들과의 간담회및 VANDEMEUL
EBROUCKE 레인보우 그룹 의장과의 면담 (한국 인권관계 결의 제안자중 한사람)시,
대호 본부 송부자료에 의거, 제 6 공화국 출범이후 한국정부의 인권상황 개선을위한
각종 노력을 설명하고, 약국에서 인권문제는 더이상 제기되지 않고 있음을 지적, EC
12 개국을 대표한 구주의회에서 구체적 사실확인이 없이 우방국인 한국의 인권상황에
대한 편파적 결의를 채택한데 대해 유감을 표시함

2. 특히 본직은 임수경등은 정부의 사전승인 없이 방북 또는 북한측과 비밀접촉,
북한에의해 대남공작 차원에서 악용되었으며 이는 인권문제와는 별개의 실정법
위반사항임을 지적하고, 현재 북한내에는 15 만명의 정치범이 10 여개의 수용소에
강제 수용되어 있는 사실을 상기시키고 앞으로 구주의회측에서는 이와같은 북한의
심각한 인권위반 사례에대해 각별히 주의를 경주해야 할것이라고 언급하였음

3. 이에대하여 동의원은 구주의회 인권소위에서 세계도처의 인권상황 검토시
정확하고 객관적 정보수집을 위한 독자적인 채널이 없기 때문에 AMNESTY
INTERNATIONAL 보고서에 주로 의존하며, 이과정에서 사실착오 또는 편파적 시각이
개채될 소지가 있다고 솔직히 시인하고, 금번 구주의회의 한국 인권관계 결의내용에
사실과 다른 부분이 있었다면 심심한 사과를 표시한다고 답변함. 이어 동의원은
구라파거주 일부 한국인들이 한국 인권상황에 대하여 비판적 발언을 하고 있어
진의파악에 어려움이 있음을 언급하고, 자신으로서는 추후 한국관계 결의안 검토시
보다 신중한 자세로 임하겠으며, 특히 당관과 사전 긴밀한 협의를 하겠다 함

4. 한편, RINSCHE 구주의회 한국친선협회 회장과 BEAZLEY 부회장도 본직과의

구주국   장관   차관   1차보   2차보   정와대   안기부   국회

오찬시, 대호 결의안이 지난 12월 본회의 종료직전에 일부 의원들에 의해 사전 예고없이 긴급의제로 상정되어 충분한 토의과정 없이 근소한 표결차로 채택된데 대해 유감을 표시하고, 구주의회내에서 한국과같은 우방국의 민감한 문제에 대하여 구체적 사실 확인없이 편파적 결의를 채택한것은 구주의회의 권위와 이미지를 실추시키며, 제 3 국과의 관계를 저해할 것이라는 자성의 분위기가 있었다고 전함. 특히 BAEZLEY 부회장은 금번 사례에서 보듯이 구주의회의 의사규칙 (긴급의제 상정, 표결방식등) 에 심각한 문제점이 있음을 지적하고, 자신이 조만간 동 의사규칙 개정을위한 활동을 개시하겠다고 언급하였음. 끝

(대사 권동만-국장)

예고: 91.12.31 까지

0244

'90년 인권현황

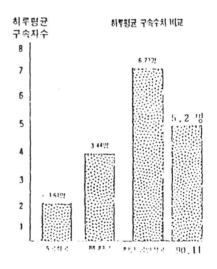

국가보안법, 집시법, 노동관계법 등 각종 악법으로 구속된
양심수가 하루 평균 5명, 전국교도소에 수감된 양심수만도
1300여명, 세계 최장기복역수(?)로 일컬어지는 만델라의
27년형보다 더많은 형량을 선고받고 수감중인 147명의
진기복역 양심수, 이들은 바로 독재와 분단의 죄책을 대신
쥐어진 분들입니다. 우리는 이분들의 석방을 바랍니다.

한국기독교교회협의회 인권위원회

서울특별시 종로구 연지동 136 - 46 / 한국기독교회관 708호 ☎ 764-0203

0245

'90년 인권현황

1. 1990년 양심수 현황

노태우대통령은 취임이후 줄곧 국내외 공식석상에서 "한국에는 양심수가 한명도 없다."라고 공인했습니다. 그러나 90년 11월말 현재 본회에서 파악한 구속자의 누계만해도 1746명에 이르고 있으며, 이를 하루평균 구속자 수로 환산하면 5.2명입니다.

이는 5공과 같은 철저한 독재정권때의 하루평균 구속자 1.6명의 3배를 넘는 수치입니다. 90년 11월말까지 석방된 사람을 제외하고 현재 구속된 사람의 수는 1332명으로 작년 900여명에 비해 50%가 늘어났습니다. 직업별 구속자 수로 분류하면 학생 686명, 노동자 334명, 재야인사 71명, 출판인 24명, 군인, 전경 38명, 농어민 29명, 교사 4명, 장기수 147명입니다. 이와 같은 통계는 인권상황이 날로 개선되고 있다는 현정권의 선전이 거짓임을 증명하는 것입니다. 뿐만 아니라 국가보안법으로 구속된 수가 전체 구속자 40%에 이르고 있다는 사실은, 현정권이 떠들어 대는 통일이 얼마나 허구적인가를 잘 말해주고 있습니다.

2. 장기복역 양심수 실태

장기복역 양심수는 7년이상의 형기를 선고 받은 사람들입니다. 이들 대부분은 20년에서 40년까지의 옥고를 치루고 있습니다. 이들에게는 현재 대체로 간첩혐의가 걸려 있습니다. 11월말 현재 대전, 대구 교도소등에는 147명의 장기양심수가 복역하고 있으며, 작년 사회안전법폐지로 보안감호소에서 출소한 장기양심수는 52명입니다.

지난달 21일 장기복역양심수였던 고 정대철씨는 35년여의 옥살이 후 자유의 몸이 된지 1년만에 사회의 냉대속에 자살하였습니다.

정대철씨는 1951년 빨치산활동혐의로 21년의 옥살이를 한후 1973년 출소했으나 다시 1975년 비전향자라는 이유로 14년동안의 보안감호생활을 하다가 작년 10월에 출감하였습니다. 출감후에는 막노동으로 근근히 생계를 유지하였습니다. 그러나 돌보아줄 가족과 친지도 없을 뿐더러 오랜 옥살이로 인해 사회적응능력을 상실하였고, 설상가상으로 장기간의 옥로로 말미암아 병마에 시달리다가 끝내는 자살로 한 많은 인생의 막을 내렸습니다.

우리나라에서 간첩개념은 분명 조국분단으로 말미암은 개념이며, 따라서 간첩들은 분명 조국분단의 희생양들입니다. 이들의 인권문제는 곧 분단상황의 극복내지는 조국 통일의 문제에 직결되어 있습니다. 또한 세계 어느나라에서도 사상과 양심의 문제 때문에 20년이상 장기구금을 시키는데가 없음을 볼때 이들의 석방은 인도주의적 견지에서도 조속히 이루어져야 합니다. 결론적으로 장기복역수들의 석방과 사회복귀를 위해 일하는 것은 곧 통일운동에 일조하는 것이요, 인권신장에 기여하는 것입니다.

0246

3. 재소자의 인권문제

지난 8월 27일 서울구치소 폭력사태는 재소자들의 인권이 얼마나 심각하게 유린당하는가를 잘 보여주었습니다. 법으로도 보장되어있는 재소자들의 권리인 도서차입을 불허한 데 대해 항의했다는 이유로 70여명을 구타하여 장명국씨등 수십명의 부상자가 발생하였습니다. 뿐만 아니라 7월의 마산교도소, 8월의 목포교도소 폭력사건은 이제 온 국민이 재소자들의 인권문제를 중대하게 받아들여야 함을 시사해 주고 있습니다.

지금 전국교도소에는 양심수 1300여명외에 5만여의 일반수들이 수감되어 있습니다. 그러나 수용시설을 비롯한 기타 재소자들의 처우는 매우 열악합니다. 일반 재소자들이 수감되어 있는 시설의 크기는 보통 4~5평인데 보통 10~20명이 수용되어 1인당 0.2~0.4평을 차지합니다. 이런 과다한 수용의 원인은 마구잡이 구속수사의 남용에 있습니다. 또한 의료 상태를 살펴보면 전국 5만여명의 재소자들을 상대로 54명의 의사가 근무하고 있으나 이들 진부는 개인병원을 운영하고 있어 재소자들에 대한 진료는 거의 형식적으로 이루어 집니다.

이로 인해 해마다 20명이상이 의료혜택을 받지 못해 사망하고 있습니다.

여기에 그치지 않고 재소자들은 수사로 교도관들의 폭언과 폭행에 시달리고 있습니다. 그러나 이러한 인권유린은 사회로부터 차단되어 있다는 교도소의 특수성으로 인해 외부로 알려지지 않고 있습니다.

양심수들이 폭행을 당하면 외부로 알려지지만 일반수들은 맞아 죽지않은 이상 외부로 알려지지 않습니다. 89년 법부부 국정감사에서 밝혀진 교도소내 인권침해 관련 고소, 고발 총 127건중 121건이 교도관에 의한 폭행과 가혹행위에 관한 것이었습니다. 재소자들도 그 범죄여부를 떠나 국가권력에 의해 침해되어서는 안될 인간으로서의 존엄성과 기본권을 향유해야 할 것입니다.

4. 군대인권

우리나라의 군인수는 90만 정도로 국민 1000명당 20명 꼴입니다.

군에서의 안전사고 군기사고로 인한 수많은 병영내 사망자 수는 인권상황의 열악함을 단적으로 드러냅니다. 공식적인 금지에도 불구하고 획일적인 조직을 유지하기 위하여 구타·기합등이 공공연히 일어나고 있음이 그 엄청난 숫자로도 알수 있습니다. 80.1.1.부터 88.7.31일까지의 병영내 사망자수는 총 9.060여명으로 이중 안전사고로 3.723명, 군기사고로 2.670명이 목숨을 잃었으며 특히 자살로 보고된 사가 2천 2백 54명이나 돼 군대내 자살률은 사회의 25배에 이르고 있습니다. 한편 군민주화운동 구속자 숫자는 90년 12월 현재 38명으로 학생, 노동자 다음으로 많은 구속자를 보이고 있으며 구속유형은 양심선언, 군대의식화, 유인물, 사회활동의 보부등입니다. 이들은 수사도중 변호사 접견도 이루어지지 않았는데 정광민 일병의 경우 구속 된 지 25일 후에야 접견이 가능하여 심한 가혹행위 고문등이 이루어졌고 무거운 형을 선고 받았습니

0247

다. 사단영창에서는 비인간적인 성추행 및 모독 등이 이루어지고(31사단) 군교도소내에서 노역조건과 환경이 아주 열악해 안전사고 위험이 높다고 할 수 있습니다.

끊이지 않는 군대내 의문사는 84년 강제 징집을 통한 녹화사업으로 6명이 발생하면서 현재까지 접수된것만 해도 22건이됩니다. 특히 윤석양 이병 양심선언에서 밝혀진 것처럼 어느곳에도 피할 곳 없는 병사들에게 프락치 강요등 반인륜적 행위들이 지금 현재에도 진행되고 있다는 것입니다.

이러한 죽음들은 자식을 잃은 부모들의 가정파탄과 지난달 12일 의문사한 아들 이이동군의 진상규명을 외치며 자살한 이춘원씨의 예처럼 부모를 자살케하는 상황으로까지 내몰고 있는 실정입니다. 이제는 군대의 인권문제에 대한 관심을 더이상 미룰 수 없습니다.

5. 민간인사찰과 '범죄와의 전쟁'등으로 인한 인권문제

지난 10월 4일 윤석양 이병의 양심선언으로 현정권의 부도덕성이 만천하에 드러났습니다. 정권유지를 위해 1700여명에 이르는 사람들의 일거수 일투족을 감시하고, 위기시에는 제거라도 하겠다는 현정권의 사악한 의도가 폭로되었습니다.

보안사의 사찰 뿐만아니라 안기부, 치안본부등도 막대한 자금을 동원해 국익과 민생 치안과는 하등의 관계가 없는 정치사찰을 하고 있음이 증명되었습니다.

위정당국이 국민의 사생활을 침해하는 명백한 범법행위를 저질렀음에도 불구하고 이를 방지하기 위한 단호한 조치가 취해지지 않았음을 볼때 현정권이 인권을 존중하고 민주화를 정착시킬 의지가 없다는 것이 증명되었습니다.

보안사 사찰파동으로 실추된 정권의 도덕성을 회복하기 위해 '범죄와의 전쟁'을 선포했지만, 오히려 그전보다 끔찍한 사회범죄가 늘어가는 현상을 보여주고 있습니다. 뿐만 아니라 실적을 강요하는 치안풍토로 무고한 시민들을 협박하고 고문하는 공권력 침해사건도 빈빈하게 발생하고 있습니다. 비근한 예로 지난 11월 서울 청량리 경찰서는 강도피의자 3명을 검거했다고 발표하면서 범행에 사용한 증거품이라며 공기총을 인근총포사에서 급히 빌려오는 조작수사까지도 자행했었습니다. 현직 여당의원, 판검사와 깡패조직과의 결탁사건은 범죄와의 전쟁의 허구성을 드러내 주었습니다. 이러한 부도덕한 정권이 범죄와의 전쟁을 선포하겠다는 것은 곧 인권과의 전쟁을 하겠다는 의미로 밖에 볼 수 없습니다.

이밖에도 노동자, 농민, 빈민들의 생존권등 우리가 해결해야 만 할 인권문제는 산적해 있습니다. 온 국민이 단결하여 인권침해를 감시하고 그 방지를 위해 헌신할 때만 우리사회의 인권상황이 개선될 것입니다.

0248

○ 한국 NCC에서 WCC 로 한국인권보고서를 발송 하였음

그 내용중

1. 한국의 재소자가 5만명이 넘음

   재소자 수는 맞는 것임. 5만명 수용시설은 충분함

2. 4평되는 방에 14-20명을 수용하고 있음

   사실과 다름. 4평방에 8-10명을 수용하고 있는데 겨울에는

   재소자들의 요구에 따라 몇몇씩 더 수용하는 경우가 있음

3. 교정시설에 의사가 50명 뿐임.

   의사가 50명이며 공중보건의사가 56명, 또 의료기사, 보건기사

   등이 57명 있어 모두 167명의 의료요원이 있으므로 아무런 문제점이

   없음. 교도소 인근병원 107개를 전국에 지정 계약병원으로 운영하고

   있음. 급한 환자의 외부의사, 외부병원 진료등에 아무런 지장이 없음

4. 교도소내에서 연 평균 20명이 사망하고 있음

   사망인원은 거의 맞음

   수용인원에 비하여 0.04%에 해당하나 한국의 사회 일반인

   이는

   사망률은 인구 대비 0.58%임.

0249

정 리 보 존 문 서 목 록					
기록물종류	일반공문서철	등록번호	2020020065	등록일자	2020-02-11
분류번호	701	국가코드		보존기간	영구
명 칭	한국 인권문제 관련 사안, 1990-91. 전2권				
생 산 과	서구1과/국제연합과	생산년도	1990~1991	담당그룹	
권 차 명	V.2 1991.3-12월				
내용목차	* 인권관련 진정서 및 서한, 구주의회 인권문제 동향				

0001

기 안 용 지

분류기호 문서번호	국연 2031-ᄂᄀ3	(전화:)	시 행 상 특별취급	
보존기간	영구·준영구. 10.5.3.1.	장 관		
수 신 처 보존기간				
시행일자	1991. 3. 14.			
보 조 기 관	국장 전결	협 조 기 관		문 서 통 제
	과장			기안 1991.3.14
기안책임자	송영완			발 송 인
경 유 수 신 참 조	법무부장관 법무실장	발신명의		발송 1991.3.14
제 목	인권문제 탄원 (홍성담)			

1. 국제사면위 영국지부가 주영대사관에 보내온 홍성담

탄원 서명록을 별첨 송부합니다.

2. 상기관련, 주영대사관 인권담당관은 A.I. 영국지부장 앞

별첨 공한 및 A.I. 본부의 F. Vandale 한국담당연구원 면담을 통하여

홍성담에 대한 우리정부의 입장을 기전달하였음을 재차 상기시켰는 바,

Vandale 연구원은 한국정부가 기제공한 홍성담 설명자료를 검토하였으나

동인이 양심수라는 A.I.의 입장에는 변함이 없다고 언급하였음을 참고

하시기 바랍니다.   / 계속 /   0002

첨 부 : 1. 주영국대사관 공한

2. 홍성담 석방탄원 서명록.   끝.

검 토 필(1991. 6. 30.)

일반문서로 재분류 (1991. 12. 31.)

0003

1505－25(2－2) 일(1)을
85. 9. 9. 승인   "내가아낀 종이 한장 늘어나는 나라살림"   190㎜×268㎜ 인쇄용지 2 급 60g/㎡
가 40－41 1989. 12. 7.

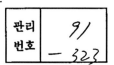

외 무 부

원 본

종 별 :

번 호 : ECW-0260

수 신 : 장관 (구일, 기정동문)

발 신 : 주 EC 대사

제 목 : 구주의회 인권관계 결의

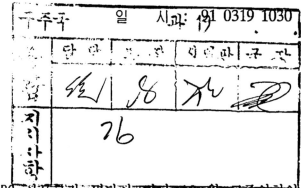

대: WEC-0044

연: ECW-0259

1. 연호, 본직의 3.18. JANNUZZI EPC 사무국장 면담시 지난 12 월 구주의회의 한국 인권관계 결의안 채택에 유감을 표시하고, 제 6 공화국 출범이후 한국정부의 인권상황 개선을위한 각종 노력을 설명하고, 앞으로 EC 측에서 북한의 심각한 인권침해 상황에 대하여 보다 깊은 관심을 경주하여야 할것으로 본다고 언급함

2. 이에 대하여 JANNUZZI 사무국장은 상기 결의는 구주의회내 소수의원이 긴급의제로 발의하여, 구주의회 의사절차상의 문제점으로 회기말에 일방적으로 통과된 것으로 518 명 구주의회 의원 다수의 의사표시가 아님을 해명하면서, 구주의회측은 이와같은 문제점 시정을위해 1988 년 부터 의사절차 개정방안을 논의하였으나, 구주의회의 비효율성으로 아직까지 실현되지 못하고 있다고 답변함

3. 동 국장은 또한 EC 대외관계 정책의 기본입장을 결정하는 것은 구주의회나 EC 집행위가 아니라 EC 12 개 회원국 정부임을 강조하면서 구주의회 결의에 너무 유념할 필요가 없다고 언급함. 끝

(대사 권동만-국장)

예고: 91.12.31. 까지

검토필(19   .   .   .)

구주국	차관	1차보	2차보	청와대	안기부

PAGE 1

91.03.20   07:24

외신 2과 통제관 FE

0004

→ 서리과

```
┌─────────────────────────────────────┐
│                                       │
│   유럽의회 의원 (Dr. Gordon Adam)      │
│                                       │
│      인권과장 면담내용                  │
│                                       │
└─────────────────────────────────────┘
```

1991. 3. 21

인 권 과

0005

1. 개 요

  ○ 일 시 : 1991. 3. 21(목) 16:10-17:20

  ○ 장 소 : 인권과장실

  ○ 면담자 : Dr. Gordon Adam (유럽의회의원 : 영국)

  ○ 배석자

    . 인권과 권 영 석 검사

    . "   김 웅 기 검사

    . 검찰제3과 신 종 대 검사

    . 주영대사관 서기관 Guy A. Harrison

.1

2. 대화요지

o 의 원

최근 유럽의회는 한국의 인권상황에 대하여 비판적 시각에
입각한 결의를 채택한 사실이 있다.
우리는 한국 외무부측과(대사를 지칭) 인권상황에 관하여 의견을
교환한 사실이 있고 오늘 오전에는 국회의사당에서 국회의원과
한국의 인권상황에 관하여 토론을 했다.
유럽의회는 한국과 보다 긴밀한 협조관계를 유지하기를 희망
하며, 한국내의 인권상황이 장애가 되는 것을 피하고 싶다.
한국에 있어서 형사피의자의 체포, 구속수사절차는 어떠한가

o 인권과장

최근 유럽의회에서 채택한 한국내 인권상황에 관한 결의서를
접하고 나서 유럽의회 의원과 이에 관하여 의견교환을 하고
싶었다. 마침 기회가 되었으니 아무런 제한없이 모든 문제에
관하여 대화하고자 한다
우리는 아국내 인권사항에 관하여 어느 누구와도 진지하고
솔직하게 공개적으로 논의를 할 준비가 되어 있다.

2

0007

우선 질문에 답하고자 한다.

아국의 법체계는 civil law 체계이고, 형사소송법의
경우도 마찬가지이다.

형사사건의 수사는 검찰, 사법경찰이 주도하며 수사단서에
의하여 증거를 수집한 후 수집된 증거자료에 대하여 판사
에게 구속영장을 청구하면 판사가 이를 심사하여 구속영장을
발부한다.

구속영장 없이는 어느 피의자도 구속되지 아니하나 현행범인
경우 구속영장 없이 구속할 수 있다. 인신구속절차에 관한
형사소송법의 영문번역이 있으니 복사하여 제공하고자 한다
(관계조문 영역문 복사본 수교)

o 의 원

재판전 구금기간은 얼마나 허용되는가
제한없이 구금할 수 있는가

o 인권과장

형사소송법상 구속영장을 발부받아 사법경찰이 10일간에
한하여 수사할 수 있고, 검찰은 사법경찰관으로부터 사건을
송치받아 1차적으로 10일간 수사한 후 부득이 보강수사가

3

0008

필요한 경우에 한하여 판사의 허가를 받아 최대한 10일간 수사기간을 연장할 수 있다.

단, 국가보안법의 경우에는 수사상 사법경찰이 1회에 한하여 구속기간을 연장할 수 있고, 검찰이 2회에 한하여 구속기간을 연장하여 최대한 50일간 구속수사할 수 있도록 규정되어 있다

o 의 원

국가보안법 이외에 다른 예외규정이 있는가

o 인권과장

재판전 구금기간에 대한 예외는 국가보안법 뿐이다

o 의 원

왜 국가보안법은 위와 같이 구금기간을 연장하는가

o 인권과장

국가보안법 위반사건은 성질상 그 혐의내용이 간첩죄 등 전문적이고 장기간의 수사와 정보수집 및 공작을 필요로 하는 사건이므로 일반 형사사건보다 수사기간을 연장한 것이며, 귀하도 그 필요성은 당연히 이해할 것이다

4

0009

o 의 원

그점은 물론 이해를 하고 있다

법원에서의 구속재판기간은 어떠한가

o 인권과장

1심법원에서는 구속재판기간이 6개월이고, 그 기간내에

재판심리가 종결, 선고되지 아니하면 피고인을 석방한 후

불구속 상태로 재판을 진행해야 한다.

항소된 경우에는 항소심에서 1회에 한하여 6개월간 구속

기간을 연장하여 재판할 수 있고, 그 기간내에 재판이 종료

되지 아니하면 그 처리절차는 1심재판의 경우와 같다

o 의 원

국가보안법은 한국의 인권문제에 장애가 된다고 생각한다.

동법의 개정이 계획되고 있는가

o 인권과장

국가보안법과 관련하여 우리들이 보는 시각과 유럽인들이

보는 시각에는 차이가 있는 것으로 알고 있다.

그러나 유럽인들은 이 문제를 접근함에 있어 한국의 분단

상황이라는 기초적이고도 실질적인 측면을 간과하거나

5

0010

이 부분을 경시하는 점이 없지 않다고 생각된다.

우리의 역사적, 문화적 설명이나 분단의 과정 및 우리

국민의 성향에 대하여는 굳이 언급을 하지 않겠다.

많은 자료가 있으니 읽어 볼 기회를 갖기 기대한다.

다만, 몇가지만 이야기하면 우선 한국을 독일과 같은

상황에 있는 나라로 평가하여서는 안된다.

독일은 서로 총을 맞대고 피를 흘리며 전쟁을 치른 경험이

없다. 피를 흘리고 좌절을 경험한 국민은 누구나 자신이

보호되지 아니할 경우 맞아야 하는 위험성을 피부로 느끼며

살고 있음을 지적하고 싶다.

전세계가 알다시피 북한은 3년간 피비린내나는 동족상잔의

비극을 야기하였다.

이들은 정권수립시부터 현재까지 일관되게 남한적화전략을

추진하고 있으며, 최근까지도 미얀마 랭구운 폭파사건,

KAL기 폭파사건 등 상식적으로는 도저히 상상할 수 없는

파괴적, 극렬테러를 자행하고 있다.

국가보안법이 제정.시행되는 가장 큰 이유는 이와 같은

우리의 경험과 우리가 처해 있는 상황하에서 우리 스스로의

존립을 지켜내기 위한 것임을 이해하여야 한다.

일부 불순분자들의 주장만을 액면 그대로 원용하여 국가보안법

을 공격하는 것은 공정한 접근이 아니라고 생각한다.

대다수의 한국국민이 느끼고 있는 공산주의와 북한의 위험성도

함께 확인되어야 할 것이다.

6

0011

동법에 대하여 많은 논쟁이 있는 것은 사실이다. 이러한
논쟁이 발전적인 방향으로 결실을 거두길 바라고 있다.
현재 여당·야당이 각각 국회에 개정안을 제출하여 협상을
벌이고 있으므로 금명간 개정방향의 윤곽이 드러날 것이다.

o 의 원

이해에 크게 도움이 되었다. 의문점이 또 있는데,
국가보안법 사범중 장기복역수들은 남한 거주자들인가
북한으로부터 이주해 온 자들인가

o 인권과장

장기복역수들은 대부분 간첩죄로 복역중인 자들이며,
북한 거주자들이 대부분이나 남한거주자중 월북자,
납치된 어부들도 있다. 이들은 모두 북한당국의 세뇌
교육을 받은 뒤 간첩활동의 지령을 받고 남한으로 잠입한
자들이다.

o 의 원

학생의 신분으로 장기복역하는 경우도 있는가

7   0012

o 인권과장

    재미.재일교포 학생이나 외국에 유학중인 학생이 북한
    당국에 포섭되어 북한에 가서 간첩교육을 받은 후 남한에
    잠입하여 간첩행위를 하다가 적발되어 복역중인 사례가
    몇 건 있다.
    이들은 간단히 이야기해서 "스파이" 일 뿐이다.
    왜 한국만 이들이 인권과 관련하여 문제가 되는지 선뜻
    이해가 안간다.
    쟁점이 좀 더 명확히 되어야 할 것이다.

o 의 원

    이 부분은 이해가 되었다.
    방향을 바꾸어서 노동운동문제와 관련하여 노조지도자가 구속
    되는 이유는 무엇인지.
    국가보안법 사건의 경우에는 국가안보라는 이유에 의해 구속
    하는 것이라고 이해되나 노동운동에 있어서는 어떤 근거가
    제시되는지 궁금하다

o 인권과장

    아국에 있어서 헌법상 근로자의 단결권, 단체교섭권, 단체
    행동권을 보장하고 있고 원칙적으로 노조활동은 자유이나

8

0013

이와 관련하여 순수한 노조활동의 차원을 넘어 공공기관에
방화를 하거나 화염병을 부척하는 등 폭력을 행사하거나
이를 선동하는 등 실정법 질서를 어긴 경우에 구속수사의
대상이 되는 것이다

o 의 원

대우조선 파업의 경우를 보면, 노조지도자가 구속되었는 데
구체적으로 어떤 행위를 했기 때문에 구속되었는지에 관한
자료를 구할 수 있겠는가

o 인권과장

위 사건의 경우에는 아국의 노동쟁의조정법상 금지된 제3자
개입혐의로 노조지도자가 구속된 것이며, 그 구체적 자료를
제공할 수 있다. 가급적 체한기간내에 영국대사관에 자료를
제공하도록 노력하겠다.

o 의 원

유럽의회에서 금년 가을 회기에 논의될 가능성이 있는 한국내
인권문제에 관한 자료를 제공하겠으니 참고하길 바란다.
(유럽의회측 자료접수 - 첨부자료 참조)

9

0014

o 인권과장

유럽의회에 대한 우리의 입장은 특히 아국내 인권문제에
대한 결의안을 접하고 느낀 점은 아국과 유럽의회간에
한국내의 정치, 경제, 사회적 상황이나 전통적 관습 등에
관한 충분한 의견교환이 이루어지지 않고 있고, 인권문제를
보는 시각에 대해서도 상호 의견교환이 부족하다는 점이다.
위 결의안은 아국내의 급진세력에 의해 제공된 정보에
기초를 두고 있는 것으로 보인다.
아국 정부는 언제든지 누구에게나 문호를 개방하고
솔직하고 진지하게 인권문제 등 모든 상호관심사에 관하여
대화를 나눌 용의가 있다.
유럽의회와도 아국주재 대사관이나 여타 가능한 모든
채널을 봉하여 의견을 교환할 용의가 있음을 첨언한다

o 의 원

오늘 방문은 매우 유익하였으며, 한국의 인권상황에
관한 많은 정보를 제공해 주어서 감사하다

o 인권과장

이러한 대화가 상호간 이해를 증진시키는 데 도움이
된다면 언제든지 기꺼이 응하겠다.
좋은 여행이 되기를 빈다

10

0015

〈 참고사항 〉

1. '90.12 유럽의회가 채택한 아국 인권관계 결의문 요지

  ○ 최근 남북총리회담 개최를 환영하고, 동 회담에서 자유로운
     인적왕래 등 남북한 신뢰회복 조치가 합의되기를 희망

  ○ 북한에는 다원적 민주주의와 기본적 인권보장이 전혀 확립
     되어 있지 않음을 지적하고 북한 당국에 정치적 자유화
     조치 촉구

  ○ 불법방북 또는 북한인사 접촉이유로 구속된 임수경, 문규현,
     홍성담, 조용설, 유원호 등의 석방촉구

2. 금년 가을회기에 유럽의회에서 거론될 가능성이 있는 한국내
   인권문제에 관한 자료첨부

  ○ 요지
     유럽의회 정치위원회내 인권위원회에서 한국내의 인권문제
     (특히 1,300명에 이르는 양심수 문제)에 관한 청문회를 열어
     심의한다는 것으로 KNCC측에서 배포한 자료를 근거로 하고
     있으며,

  ○ 재유럽 반한운동권인 유럽민협 측에서 유럽의회에 심의
     요청한 것임

11

0016

기 안 용 지

분류기호 문서번호	국연 2031-365	(전화 :)	시 행 상 특별취급	

보존기간	영구·준영구. 10. 5. 3. 1.	장 관

수 신 처 보존기간	

시행일자	1991. 4. 1.

보 조 기 관	국 장	전 결
	과 장	*uy*

협 조 기 관	

문 서 통 제	
1991. 4. 02	

기안책임자	송 영 완

발 송 인

경 수 참	유 신 조	법무부장관 법무실장

발신명의

제 목	인권문제 구주의회 제기

유럽민협의 구주의회 접촉경위 및 한국 인권문제 청문회를

구주의회가 개최토록 추진하는 문서의 작성 및 배포와 관련, 주 EC

대사 보고 전문사본을 별첨 송부하니 업무에 참고하시기 바랍니다.

일반문서로재분류 (1991 .12. 31.

    첨 부 : ECW-0290 사본 1부.   끝.

예고 : 1991. 12. 31. 없음.

검 토 필 (1991. 6. 30.)

0017

외 무 부

종   별 :

번   호 : ECW-0290   일   시 : 91 0328 1600

수   신 : 장관 (구일,국회) 사본: 주독대사-직송필

발   신 : 주 EC 대사

제   목 : 인권문제

대: WECM-0017,18

1. 대호관련, 본직은 3.26. 구주의회 브랏셀 사무소에서 GORDON ADAM 의원을 면담, 유럽민협측의 구주의회 접촉경위와 청문회 개최 가능성등을 타진한바, 동 의원은 한국 인권문제를 다루는 청문회를 구주의회가 개최토록 추진하는 문서를 유럽민협측이 작성 배포한바 있으나 작성자나 수신인이 명기되어 있는것도 아니며 구주의회측에도 정식으로 제출된것이 아닌것으로 안다고 말하고, 금번 방한시 주한 영국대사 주선으로 한국 기독교 교회협의회 김영주 (KIM KYOUG-JU) 목사를 면담하였으며, 동인의 알선으로 법무부 인권과장을 면담하게 된것이라고 그 경위를 설명함

2. 이에대하여 본직은 제 6 공화국 정부의 민주화및 인권정책을 설명하고 일부 방북 구속인사들은 소정의 절차를 거치지 않고 밀입북함으로써 실정법을 위반한 것임을 지적하고, 유럽 민협측의 청문회 요청이 있을 경우, 이를 적절히 DISCOURAGE 해 줄것을 부탁한바, 동 의원으로서는 이에 유념하겠다고 하면서 다만유럽 민협측의 접촉요청이 있을경우 구주의회측 인사가 이를 전적으로 거절할수는 없다고 답변함

3. 상기와 별도로 당관 윤서기관은 구주의회 사무국의 QUITIN 한국 친선협회 담당관, STAHLSCHMIDT 정치위원회 담당과장, WATERS 인권소위 담당관및 사회당 그룹의 VALLIN 사무차장과 접촉한바, 이들은 모두 유럽민협측의 청문회 개최 요청에대해 아는바 없다고 답변함. 특히 WATERS 담당관은 동 요청이 아직 구주의회에 정식으로 제출된바 없으며, 구주의회내에서 인권문제를 담당하는 인권소위 KENNETH COATES 위원장 (영국, 사회당 그룹) 도 동내용을 알지 못하고 있는것 같다고 언급함

4. 당관은 유럽민협측의 청문회 개최 요청 가능성에 대비, 4 월 구주의회 본회의 기간중인 4.15-17 간 강신성공사와 김광동 참사관을 스트라스부르그에 출장, 구주의회

구주국   1차보   국회   국기국

PAGE 1

인권소위 위원장, 구주의회 사무국위원회 담당 총국장및 각 정치그룹소속 주요의원들과의 접촉등 적극 대처 계획임

5. GORDON 의원과 QUITIN 한국담당관은 구주의회 한국친선협회 의원단의 금번 방한결과에 대해 RINSCHE 회장을 위시한 대부분의 소속의원들이 만족을 표명하고 있다고 전하고, 이와관련 한국국회와 정부측의 협조에 사의를 표시하고, 이와같은 한. 구주의회간 정기적 인사교류가 앞으로도 계속 활성화 될것을 희망함.끝

(대사 권동만-국장)

예고: 91.12.31. 일반

일반문서로재분류(1991.12.3).

검토필(1991. 6. 30.)

PAGE 2

0019

분류기호 문서번호	국연 2031- 124	협조문용지 ( )	결 재	담당	과장	국장
시행일자	1991. 4. 6.			(서명)		
수 신	미주국장, 구주국장	발 신	국제기구조약국장			
제 목	아국 인권문제					

　　　1. 제 6공화국 출범이래 정부가 인권신장을 위하여 적극 노력

하고 있고 특히 아국이 90.7.10. 국제인권규약에 가입함에 따라 국제

사회에서의 아국 인권현황에 대한 인식과 관심이 한층 제고되고

있습니다.

　　　2. 당국은 유엔내 인권관련회의 대책수립과 이행, 국제인권

규약 가입에 따른 의무이행에 관련된 인권업무 및 A.I. 관련업무를

담당하고 있으나 간혹 재외공관으로부터 상기 유엔차원의 인권논의

와는 무관한 주재국 정부, 의회 또는 민간단체, 인사들로 부터의

질의.청원 관련 문건을 당국에 송부하여 오는 경우가 있습니다.

　　　3. 상기 각국정부 또는 단체등이 제기하는 아국 인권관련 문건

등은 접수즉시 귀국으로 이첩할 예정이며 사안에 따라 법무부로부터

당국이 기접수한 설명자료가 있는 경우는 첨송할 예정임을 알려드립니다.

끝. 0020

1505 - 8 일 (1)
85. 9. 9 승인 "내가아낀 종이 한장 늘어나는 나라살림"
190㎜×268㎜ (인쇄용지 2 급 60g / ㎡)
가 40-41 1990. 7. 9.

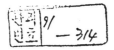

분류기호 문서번호	국연 2031- 129 ( )	협조문용지	결 재	담당	과장	국장
시행일자	1991. 4. 8.					(서명)
수 신	구주국장	발 신		국제기구조약국장		
제 목	아국 인권문제					

연 : 국연 2031-124 (91.4.6)

주영대사는 영국 하원의원 2인이 제기한 아국인권문제 관련

문서를 송부하여 온 바, 동 문서를 이첩하오니 필요한 조치를 취하여

주시기 바랍니다.

첨 부 : 영국(정) 723-25 (91.3.25) 사본 1부.   끝.

0021

1505 - 8 일 (1)
85. 9. 9 승인 "내가아낀 종이 한장 늘어나는 나라살림"
190mm×268mm (인쇄용지 2급 60g / ㎡)
가 40-41 1990. 7. 9.

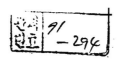

주 영 대 사 관

영국(정) 723- 25   1991. 3. 25.

수신 : 장관

참조 : 국제기구조약국장

제목 : 인권서한

    연 : 영국(정) 723-185

1. 주재국 Michael Shaw 하원의원(보수)은 자신의 선거구민이 90.8.8. 체포된
   이상필의 조속한 석방 또는 재판을 요청하여 왔음을 별첨(1) 서한으로 당관에
   알려 왔는 바, 이에 대한 답변자료를 송부하여 주시기 바랍니다.

2. 연호 노조관계자 7명의 체포에 대하여, 주재국 Harry Barnes 하원의원(노동)이
   별첨(2) 서한을 송부해 왔으니 참고하시기 바랍니다.

첨부 : 1. Shaw 의원 및 선거구민 서한사본 각 1부.
        2. Barnes 의원 서한 사본 1부.   끝.

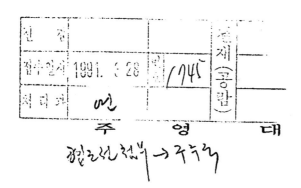

일반문서로 재분류 (1991. 12. 31.)

0022

6 Belgrave Terrace
Scarborough
North Yorkshire
YO11 1UA

17 February 1991

Sir Michael Shaw JP DL MP
House of Commons
London SW1A 0AA

Dear Sir Michael

We would be very grateful if you could help us obtain the release or
early trial of a South Korean citizen who has been held in prison
without trial or charge since his arrest six months ago.

His name is Lee Sang-pil and he is an Amnesty International 'prisoner
of conscience', imprisoned purely for his political beliefs, expressed
without violence. As you are probably aware, central Amnesty allocates
one or more prisoners of conscience to individual branches around the
world. We would particularly like you to approach the South Korean
government as Lee Sang-pil is one of two prisoners of conscience
'adopted' by the Scarborough branch of Amnesty.

Lee Sang-pil, a student of Japanese at Seoul University, was arrested
on 8 August 1990 in Seoul after publishing a 'pro-North Korea' article
in the student magazine he edits.

Scarborough Amnesty's other prisoner of conscience is the Syrian, Yasir
Makhluf, about whom we have also written to you. Thank you for your
reply, saying that you had initiated enquiries about our prisoner, and
that you would contact us again in due course.

With thanks, in anticipation of your help.

Yours sincerely

David Barry
Scarborough branch
Amnesty International

0023

HARRY BARNES MP
House of Commons, London SW1A OAA

3년 3월

Mr Choe Byung-yul
Minister of Labour
Ministry of Labour
1 Chungang-dong
Kwachon-myon
Shihung-gun
Kyonggi Province
Republic Of Korea

February 28th 1991

Dear Choe Byung-yul

I have received strong representations from the respected
and non-partisan human rights organisation, Amnesty
International concerning the fate of the following citizens;

LEE Eun-ku, CHUNG Yoon-kwang, LEE Chul-kyu, SON Jong-kyu,
YOON Myung-won, PARK Chang-soo, HONG Young-pyo.

I understand that these seven trade union leaders were
arrested by police on 9th February and charged under article
13-2 of the Trade Union Law, which prohibits third part
interference in labour disputes.

I share the concern of Amnesty International that these
seven trade union leaders may have been detained for the
non-violent exercise of their right to freedom of
association.

I am therefore writing to urge you to support their
immediate release.

I look forward to hearing from you.

Yours sincerely

Harry Barnes MP
North East Derbyshire

cc Ambassador
Embassy of Korea (South)
4 Palace Gate
London W8 5NX

0024

SIR MICHAEL SHAW, J.P., D.L., M.P.

HOUSE OF COMMONS
LONDON SW1A 0AA

21st February, 1991

Excellency

I enclose herewith a copy of a letter
that I have received from my constituent
David Barry, with regard to a South Korean
citizen, Lee Sang-pil.

I would be most grateful if you could
let me have your comments on it.

Michael Shaw

His Excellency Jay Hee Oh,
Korean Embassy,
4 Palace Gate,
London. W8 5NF

0025

관리 번호	9 1 - 4 2 2				

분류기호 문서번호	구일 202- 824	기 안 용 지	시 행 상 특별취급	
보존기간	영구;준영구 10. 5. 3. 1	장 관		
수 신 처 보존기간				
시행일자	1991. 4. 9.			

보 조 기 관	국 장	전 결	협 조 기 관		문 서 통 제	
	심의관				1991. 4. 10	
	과 장	✓				
기안책임자	김 영 준			발 송 인	

경 유		발 신 명 의		발송송 1991. 4. 외무부
수 신	법무부장관			
참 조				
제 목	아국 인권문제			

Michael Shaw 영국 하원의원은 자신의 선거구민으로부터

90.8.8. 체포된 이상필의 석방 또는 조속한 재판을 요구하는 별첨(1)

서한을 받고, 이에 대한 코멘트를 주영대사에게 요청하여 왔는 바,

이와 관련한 적절한 설명자료를 당부로 송부하여 주시기 바랍니다.

첨부: 상기 서한 및 상기의원의 요청 서한 각 1부. 끝.

0026

점 도 필 (1991. 6. 30)

분류기호 문서번호	구일 202- _825_		기 안 용 지		시 행 상 특 별 취 급	
보 존 기 간	영구.준영구 10. 5. 3. 1		장		관	
수 신 처 보 존 기 간						
시 행 일 자	1991. 4. 10.					
보조 기관	국 장	전 결	협조기관		문 서 통 제	
	심 의 관				1991. 4. 10	
	과 장				발 송 인	
기안책임자	김 영 준					
경 유				발신명의		
수 신	노동부 장관					
참 조						
제 목	노조원 인권 문제					

Harry Barnes 영국 하원의원은 노조관계자 7명의 석방을 요청

하는 별첨 내용의 서한을 귀부 장관에게 발송하였는 바, 동 서한에 대한

귀부의 조치 결과를 당부로 알려 주시기 바랍니다.

첨부: 상기 의원 서한 사본 1부. 끝.

검토필(1991. 6. 30)

0027

법 무 부

인권 202- 85   503-7045   1991. 4. 19

수신 외무부장관

참조 구주국장

제목 인권관련자료 송부

1. 구일 202-824 ('91.4.10)와 관련입니다.

2. Michael Shaw 의원 서한에서 언급된 이상필이라는 이름으로
구속된 사람은 없으며, 우리부에서 파악한 바에 의하면 이상필 (▮▮▮▮▮
▮▮▮▮) 이라는 학생이 현재 외대 용인캠퍼스 일어과 4학년에 재학
중이며, '90년에 외대신문 편집장으로 활동한 사실이 있으나 동인에
대해 구속 등 사법조치가 취해진 사실은 없습니다.   끝.

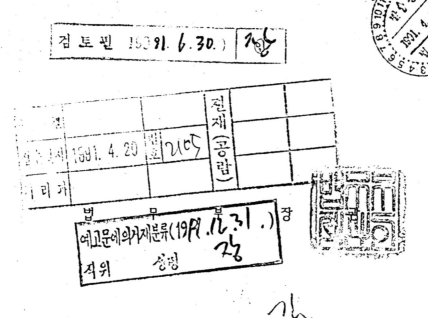

관리 번호	9 1 - 4r5				

분류기호 문서번호	구일 202- 973	기 안 용 지		시 행 상 특별취급	
보존기간	영구.준영구 10. 5. 3. 1		장 관		
수 신 처 보존기간					
시행일자	1991. 4. 22.				
보조 기관	국 장	전 결	협조기관		문 서 통 제 1991. 4. 26
	심의관				
	과 장				
기안책임자	김 영 준			발 송 인	
경 유 수 신 참 조	주영대사		발신명의		
제 목	인권 서한				

대: 영국(정) 723-25

　　1. 법무부는 대호 Michael Shaw 의원 서한에서 언급된 이상필

이라는 이름으로 구속된 사람은 없다고 하니, 동 사실을 동 의원에게

알려 주시기 바랍니다.

　　2. 법무부에서 파악한 바에 의하면, 이상필(주민등록번호:

███████)이라는 학생은 현재 외대 용인캠퍼스 일어과 4학년에

재학중이며, 1990년에 외대신문 편집장으로 활동한 사실이 있으나,

동인에 대해 구속 등 사법조치를 취한 사실은 없다고 하니 참고하시기

바랍니다. 끝.

　　　　　　　　　　　　　　　　관으로 재분류(1991 6.3비)
　　　　　　　　　　　　　　　　위 5 　상밀 김명간

0029

BRITISH EMBASSY

4 Chung-dong Chung-Ku Seoul Republic of Korea

Telephone 735-7341/3 735-7471/3
Facsimile (02) 733-8368
Telex K27320 PRODROM

To: Prosecutor Yoo Kook-hyun
Director, Human Rights Div
Ministry of Justice

Mr Kim Young-joon
Western European Div. MFA

Fax No: 503 7046 & 720 2686

No of pages, including this one: 1

From: G A Harrison

Date: 25 April 1991

Dear Prosecutor Yoo,

KIM YANG-GI

1. The Foreign and Commonwealth Office in London have asked our Embassy for some information on Kim Yang-gi in order to reply to a letter from a British Member of Parliament. I should be grateful for any information on Kim's case which your Ministry could provide, particularly:

a) the exact charges against Kim;

b) any information on allegations that Kim was tortured under interrogation;

c) information on allegations that Kim is currently suffering from arthritis and neuralgia as a result of his alleged torture.

2. I am approaching your Ministry directly because the Foreign and Commonwealth Office have asked for a reply by 30 April. However, a copy of this fax goes to Western European Division 1 at the Ministry of Foreign Affairs.

3. Thanking you for your cooperation,

Yours sincerely,

Guy Harrison

G A Harrison

0030

공   란

공　　　　란

공 란

공　　　란

외 무 부

종 별 : 지 급

번 호 : USW-2057

일 시 : 91 0430 1817

수 신 : 장관(미북,정이,기정)

발 신 : 주 미 대사

제 목 : 조승형 의원 방미활동

　　　연:USW-2018

　　　대:WUS-1794

1. 금 4.30 당관 박흥신 서기관이 미하원 인권 코커스 ARRIAGA 전문위원 및HELFAND 전문위원을 오찬 접촉, 표제관련 탐문한바, 특기사항 아래 보고함.

　　　가. 인권 코커스 회합

O 금 4.30 오전 상기 두 전문위원을 포함 8 명의 인권 관련 의원 보좌관이 참석한 가운데 하원 사무실에서 조의원과의 간담회가 예정대로 개최된바, 동간담회는 조 의원이 한국 인권상황에 관한 준비된 영문 원고를 낭독, 배포한데 이어 질의 응답순(질의응답시는 동행인이 통역)으로 약 1 시간동안 진행되었음.

O 모두 연설 (원고 전문 별전 FAX 송부)에서 조의원은 한국의 인권상황이 앞서의 정권들과 비교하여 개선되기는 커녕 오히려 점점 악화되고 있으며, 4.26. 경찰에 의한 데모학생 치사사건은 억압적이고 어두운 한국의 정치 상황을 그대로반영하는 것이라고 말하면서 현재 5 공시절 정치범 최대치 보다 세배나 많은 1,400 여명의 정치범이 수감되어 있다고 주장하였음.

이어 동의원은 국가보안법 문제와 관련, 방북인사 구속, 서경원 의원 구속 및 이와 관련한 김대중 총재 기소, 김근태 수감등의 예를 들어 동법이 반체제 인사 및 야당 탄압에 악용되고 있다고 말하고, 신민당이 동법 철폐를 위해 진력하고 있으나 정부 여당에서는 동법의 개정이나 철폐에 반대 (AGAINST REWRITING ORREPEALING IT)하고 있다고 주장하였음.

동인은 이외에 김대중 총재가 한국내 반미감정의 해소에 매우 중요한 역할을 하였다고 주장하는 한편, 정부의 봉일정책,3 당 봉합, 내각제 개헌 시도등을 비난하면서 미국이 한국의 인권상황에 대해 좀더 능동적으로 관심을 표명해줄것을

미주국　　차관　　1차보　　2차보　　정문국　　청와대　　안기부　국기국

요청하였음.

0 이어 진행된 질의응답에서는 주로 국가 보안법 개정문제, 남북한 교류, 방북 수감인사 (문익환, 임수경등)및 기타 김근태등 국가 보안법 위반 수감자 관련 문제들이 논의되었다 함.

　　나. 미의원 접촉 활동

0 조 의원은 5.1. 중 아국의 인권문제에 비판성향을 보여온 EDWARD F.FEIGHAN (D-OHIO)하원의원 및 THOMAS M.FOGLIETTA(D-PA) 하원의원과 면담 예정임.

0 인권코커스 공동의장인 LANTOS 하원의원 및 PORTER 하원의원과의 면담요청은 동의원들의 분주한 일정관계로 성사되지 않았다 함.

　　2. 한편 조의원은 5.1. 09:00 N.P.C. MORNING NEWS MAKER 에 출연, 한국의 정치 상황, 특히 인권문제에 관해 간담회를 가질예정이며, 당지 소재 한국 인권연구소에서 조의원 활동을 지원하고 있는 것으로 알려지고 있는바, 북이활동사항추보 예정임.

　　(대사 현홍주-국장)

　　예고:91.12.31 일반

일반문서로재분류 (1991 .12.31 .)

검토필(1991. 6.30.)

공   란

공 란

공 란

공   란

공　　　란

주 영 대 사 관

영국(정) 723-488   1991. 5. 13.

수신 : 장관

참조 : 국제기구조약국장

제목 : 인권서한

        연 : 영국(정) 723-282 (91.3.19)

        Korea Ecumenical Education Program (KEEP)는 연호 홍근수 목사와
이삼열 교수의 채포에 대하여 문의하는 별첨서한을 당관에 보내왔는 바, 동건
회신에 필요한 자료를 송부하여 주시기 바랍니다.

        첨부 : KEEP측 서한 사본 1부.   끝.

        주   영   대

KEEP

Korea Ecumenical Education Programme

Co-ordinator: Patricia Hamilton

KEEP

C/O PWM
Partnership House
157 Waterloo Road
London SE1 8XA

Tel: (Fridays Only)
071 928 8681 Ext 555
(Home) 071 790 0535

30th April 1991

The Ambassador
Embassy of the Republic of Korea
4 Palace Gate
Kensington
London W8

Your Excellency,

As you are aware, the Korea Ecumenical Education Programme is an association of people and organisations within the British and Irish Churches who share a common interest in Korea. I enclose a copy of our leaflet.

As a concerned body, we feel that once again the National Security Law has been used out of proportion with regard to two particular cases which have been brought to our attention. These are notably:

(1)   Rev. Hong Keun Soo, minister of Hyang Lin Church appears to have been arrested on three accounts "(1) benefitting an anti-State organization by way of praising, encouraging, or siding with the activities of an anti-State organisation or communist organisations abroad; (2) anyone who produces, imports, duplicates, possesses, transports, disseminates, sells or acquires documents, drawings and any other similar means of expression which benefit an anti-State organization; and (3) organizing or participating in an anti-State organization.

    The first charge evidently refers to various comments, sermons, writings in newspapers etc. in which he asserted "there are some positive aspects to north Korea...in order to bring about national reunification, we must get to know the society the people in north Korea have built, and what they are saying....."

    The second charge apparently refers to the publication of "Now Is the Time To Realize National Reunification" which is a collection of texts of Sunday worship sermons and various other articles written for newspapers, magazines, periodicals, etc., on the themes of national issues and reunification issues.

/continued.....

KEEP operates under the general supervision of the Asia Committee of the Conference for World Mission of the Council of Churches for Britain and Ireland.

0043

The third charge seems to refer to Rev. Hong's participation in the Pan-Korean Alliance for Reunification, which was organized as an umbrella body of Koreans in south Korea, north Korea, and Koreans living aboroad for national reunification.

(2)   Professor Lee Sam Yol, Professor of Philosophy at Soongsil University, Seoul. We understand he was arrested on 6 March 1991 and has been charged with contacting North Korean pastors at an international meeting of Protestant preachers which was held in July 1990 in Japan. He is also accused of passing documents from the Rev. Hong Dong Keun, a lecturer in Christianity at Kim Il Sung University, North Korea, to the Rev Hong Keun Soo in South Korea.

These men seem to be being held for the peaceful exercise of their right of freedom of expression and association. We would be very grateful if you would convey our concern in the appropriate direction.

In addition, would you please explain to us the reasons for the detention of these men and why they are considered a threat to National Security.

I look forward to hearing from you.

Yours sincerely,

Patricia Hamilton.

Patricia Hamilton

0044

법 무 부 인 권 과

1991. *6. 15.*

아래 문건을 수신자에게 전달하여 주시기 바랍니다.

제 목 : _____

수 신 : _____

(수신처 FAX NO: _____)

발 신 : _____법무부　인권과_____

표지포함　총 ____매

0045

배부처	법 무 부						대검	청와대	기 타 기 관						
	⊘	⊘	⊘	⊘	⊘	⊘	⊘	⊘	⊘	⊘	⊘	⊘	○	○	○
	장	차	법검교		검	교	공	경정학보화	제안외공법						
			무	찰청정			안	사정	1						
			실	국국			부	조사	행	기무보제					
	판	관	장장		장		장	보좌관	조부부처처						

정 보 보 고

1. 제 목
영국 외무성 한국담당관 등 당부 방문 결과

2. 출 처
인 권 과

('91. 5. 15)

3. 내 용

영국 외무성 한국담당관 Ian Davies 등

2명이 5. 14, 15:00 당부를 방문하여 인권과장

등과 아국 인권상황에 관하여 면담하였는 바,

면담결과는 별첨과 같음

첨 부 : 면담결과 1부. 끝.

0046

영국 외무성 한국담당관 (Ian Davies)

인권과장 면담내용

1991. 5. 14

인 권 과

1. 개 요

o 일   시 : 1991. 5. 14 (화), 15:00 - 16:40

o 장   소 : 인권과장실

o 면담자   : Ian Davies (영국 외무성 한국담당관)

o 배석자

  . 인권과   권 영 석 검사

  . "   김 웅 기 검사

  . 검찰제3과 차 몽 민 검사

  . 주영대사관 서기관 Guy A. Harrison

1

0048

2. 대화요지

O 한국담당관

우리는 한국의 인권상황에 관하여 깊은 관심을 가지고 있고
많은 질문사항이 있다.
그리고 특별히 영국 국회로부터 현재 구속중인 김양기에 관해서
동인이 어떤 혐의를 받고 있는지, 그리고 동인이 조사를 받는
중에 고문을 당하였다는 주장에 관한 정보를 제공해 달라는 요청
을 받고 주한 영국대사관을 통해서 법무부에 자료제공 협조의뢰
를 하였는데, 그 결과를 알고 싶다.

O 인권과장

김양기 사건에 관하여는 주한 영국대사관으로부터 자료제공 협조
의뢰를 받아 그에 상응하는 자료를 지난 5.11. 아국 외무부에
송부하였기 때문에 2-3일 내로 귀 대사관에서 이 자료를 받을
것이라고 본다.
그리고 한국 인권상황에 관하여 많은 질문사항이 있다고 했는데
우리는 누구와도 아국의 인권상황에 관하여 공개적으로 진지하게
논의할 의사가 있으며 그 준비가 되어 있다.
어떠한 질문이라도 서슴없이 해 주면 좋겠다.

2

0049

o 한국담당관

한국은 민주화 과정에 있는 것으로 알고 있으나, 북한을 알고
싶어하는 사람이 북한을 방문하고 귀국하면 여행의 자유가 있는
데도 국가보안법에 의해 구속된다.
최근에 이와 같은 국가보안법이 개정된 것을 알고 있는데 그
내용이 무엇인지 설명해 주면 좋겠다.

o 인권과장

귀하는 국가보안법 개정에 때맞추어 매우 적절한 시기에 한국을
방문한 것 같다.
동법은 비난의 표적이었고 많은 오해를 받아 왔었다.
이번 법개정에서는 기본적으로 국가안보를 해칠 목적이 있는
경우에만 처벌을 할 수 있도록 제한하였다.
그리고 순전한 간첩활동 외의 동법 위반행위에 대한 불고지죄를
삭제하였다.
동법 개정안이 지난 5.10. 통과된 관계로 이에 관한 영문자료가
없으나 향후 준비되는대로 제공하겠다.

그리고 최근의 인권상황에 관한 우리 정부의 입장을 정리한
영문책자(Facts and Fiction of human rights in Korea)를
재공하겠다.

위 책자에는 소위 정치범 문제, 국가보안법 문제 등에 관한
공식적 견해가 기술되어 있으니 우리의 인권상황을 이해하는
데 도움이 되었으면 좋겠다.

우리 정부는 아국의 인권상황에 관하여 어느 누구와도 공개적
으로 논의할 입장을 취하고 있으나, 단 한가지 우려되는 점은
아국의 인권상황에 관하여 비판적인 국제인권기구에 의해 수집
되는 정보가 왜곡된 정보일 수 있다는 점이다.

O 한국담당관

본인은 기본적으로 엠네스티의 입장을 지지한다.
귀하가 준 이 영문책자(Facts and Fiction of human rights
in Korea)를 엠네스티에 전해 주어 한국 인권상황에 관하여
참고가 되도록 하겠다.

4

0051

o 인권과장

고맙다.

귀하가 귀국하면 엠네스티 한국담당자에게 동인이 한국의
인권상황에 관하여 알고 싶은 점이 있으면 본인에게 직접
편지를 하거나 아니면 서로 만나서 의견교환을 할 수도
있다는 점을 전해주면 좋겠다.

o 한국담당관

매우 좋은 제안이다. 틀림없이 귀하의 제안을 전해 주겠다.
국가보안법에 의하여 판결을 선고받아 수감중인 자들이
개정된 동법에 의하여 재심을 청구할 수 있는가.

o 인권과장

개정된 동법 부칙에 의하여 구법에 의해 판결이 선고되어 확정
된 경우에는 재심이 허용되지 않는다.
그러나 법개정의 근본취지와 정신을 살리고 국민화합의 계기를
마련하기 위해 온전을 검보중이다.

5   0052

o 한국담당관

    김양기는 수사과정에서 고문을 받았다고 주장하고 있고, 또한
    일반적으로도 교도소 당국이 어떤 북정한 수형자에 대하여
    악감정을 가지고 고문을 가하는 경우도 있다고 본다.
    이에 관하여 답변해 주었으면 좋겠다.

o 인권과장

    물론 어떤 공무원 개인적으로 어느 조사대상자 또는 수형자에
    관하여 좋지 못한 감정을 가지고 고문이나 가혹한 행위를 가하
    는 경우는 충분히 있을 수 있다. 이는 명백히 범죄행위이며,
    그 공무원은 가중처벌된다.
    그러나 이러한 잘못은 그 공무원의 인격과 자질에서 비롯된
    문제이지 정부의 정책이나 제도가 잘못되었기 때문은 아니다.
    중요한 것은 고문이나 가혹행위를 저지르는 공무원이 있을
    경우 이를 찾아 내어 엄벌함으로써 정부의 확고한 고문근절
    의지를 밝히는 것이다. 최근에 나온 가혹행위를 한 공무원에
    대한 실형판결 등은 바로 정부의 의지를 나타내는 하나의 예가
    될 수 있을 것이다.
    김양기 사건의 경우에는 변호사가 진술의 임의성을 부인하는
    근거로 그가 고문당하였다고 주장하였으나 최종심인 대법원은
    동인의 진술이 임의성이 없다고 의심할만한 사유를 인정할
    증거가 없다고 판시하였다.

6   0053

또한 덧붙여 말하고 싶은 점은 자칭 정치범이라고 주장하는
공안사범은 한결같이 첫 공판에서 고문을 받았다고 주장하여
모든 증거의 증거능력을 배척하려고 시도하나 본인이 알고
있는 한 그런 주장을 한 자가 실제로 고문을 받은 경우는 없고
이는 어디까지나 그들의 전술전략이다.
만약 귀하가 이들에 대한 재판 진행상황을 방청할 기회가
있다면 그들이 얼마나 고의적이고 치밀하게 재판진행을 방해
하는지를 확인할 수 있을 것이다.   이들은 재판받는 것도 투쟁
의 일환으로 여기고 있다.

ㅇ 한국담당관

엠네스티 직원이 김양기를 만나 동인이 실제로 고문을 당했는지
여부를 조사할 수 있도록 허용할 수 있는가

ㅇ 인권과장

재소자의 접견에 관한 교도소 규칙에 의하면 재소자와 아무런
연관이 없는 제3자의 접견은 원칙적으로 허용되지 아니한다.
더구나 공정성의 담보가 전혀 없는 민간인이 조사를 위하여
재소자 접견을 신청하는 경우에는 이를 허용할 수 없다.
이는 다른 나라의 경우도 마찬가지라고 본다.

7

0054

o 한국답방관

국가보안법을 개정하게 된 원인은 무엇인가.

국민의 압력인가, 아니면 엠네스티의 압력인가.

o 인권과장

정부가 동법을 개정하게 된 것은 엠네스티의 압력에 의한

것은 명백히 아니다. 우리는 기본적으로 엠네스티가 한국의

인권상황에 대하여는 매우 편향적이고 일방적인 시각을 갖고

있음을 지적하여 왔다. 귀하가 알다시피 남북교류가 활발해

짐에 따라 정부는 남북교류에 관한 법률을 제정하였고, 동법

내용과 국가보안법이 상충되는 부분에 관하여 원활한 남북교류

를 위한 정책적 목적으로 동법 일부를 개정하였고, 또한 동법에

의한 인권침해에 관하여 많은 논쟁이 있었는 바, 그러한 인권

침해 논쟁을 종식시키기 위한 측면에서 동법 일부를 개정하게

된 것이다.

특히 최근에 헌법재판소는 동법 위반행위가 국가의 존립·안전

이나 자유민주적 기본질서를 위태롭게 한다는 정을 알면서 행해

진 경우에만 처벌할 수 있다는 해석을 하였는 바, 이와 같은

해석을 그대로 수용하여 인권침해를 방지하도록 제도화한

것이다.

8

0055

o 한국담당관

한국은 작년에 국제인권규약에 가입한 것으로 알고 있는데
이는 인권문제에 관한 적극적인 자세로 보인다.
동 규약에 기하여 보고서를 제출하도록 되어 있는 것으로
알고 있는데 이에 관하여 어떻게 진전되고 있는지 궁금하다.

o 인권과장

우리 인권과에서 시민적 및 정치적 권리에 관한 국제인권규약
보고서를 이미 작성하여 현재 영역작업이 진행중에 있다.
위 보고서 제출시한은 금년 7.9.인바, 그 시한내에 UN에
보고서를 제출할 예정이다.
귀하는 한국의 인권상황을 어떻게 보고 있는가.

o 한국담당관

많이 개선되고 있다고 본다.
그러나 거리 한 모퉁이에서 어떤 사람이 나는 김일성을 찬양
한다라고 주장하지 못하거나. 제3국을 통해서 입북하지 못하는
이유가 무엇인지 궁금하다.

9

0056

o 인권과장

이러한 질문에 관하여 수없이 답변한 경험이 있다.

거리 한 모퉁이에서 어떤 사람이 나는 김일성을 찬양한다
라고 소리치더라도 그 행위 자체만으로 처벌받는 것은 아니며,
동인이 북한을 이롭게 하려는 이적의사를 가지고 있어야만
처벌되는 것이다.

서구 각국은 한국의 분단상황에 관하여 좀더 깊은 이해를
가져야 할 필요가 있다고 본다.

전통적.유교적.윤리적 사고방식을 가진 단일혈통민족이 외세
에 의해 남북으로 분단되면서 이데올로기적으로 대립하게
되었고, 그 과정에서 북한이 도발한 6.25전쟁으로 3년간 피
비린내나는 동족상잔의 비극을 겪었다.

이러한 비극적 경험으로 인하여 대다수 국민은 아직도 남한
적화정책을 최우선 목표로 하고 있는 북한의 위협성을 피부로
느끼고 있으며, 정부를 중심으로 일치단결하여 대처해 나가야
함을 깊이 인식하고 있다.

이와 같은 대다수 국민의 지지하에 정부는 우리의 자유민주
주의체제를 수호하기 위하여 대북한 개인접촉을 불허하고
정부를 유일한 대북한 접촉창구로 하는 국가정책을 수립.시행
하고 있는 것이다.

위 정책에 대하여 일부 급진세력에 의하여 한국의 특수한 분단
상황을 도외시한 채 서구적 분단개념에 관한 논리로 포장된 비판
이 있으나 이러한 비판은 국민 대다수의 지지를 얻고 있지는
못하다.

이러한 극소수의 급진세력 (급진학생운동세력 등)은 아마도
지구상에서 유일하게 시위현장에서 화염병을 던지는 등 폭력
시위를 자행하며 매우 과격한 행동을 취하고 있다.

사회개혁을 요구하면서도 화염병을 던지거나 공공건물에 방화
한 자를 과연 정치범이라고 할 수 있는가.

예를들면 미문화원 방화사건에 관계된 김현장을 엠네스티에서
는 대표적인 정치범으로 분류하고 있는데, 이와 같이 엠네스티
에서 채택된 정치범의 개념을 그대로 인정할 수는 없다.

ㅇ 한국담당관

김현장이 미문화원에 방화한 것이 사실인가. 놀랍다.

본인도 이 사실을 반드시 확인해 볼 필요가 있다고 느낀다.

엠네스티 직원이 최근에 북한 평양에서 개최된 국제의원연맹
(IPU)총회에 참석하여 북한의 인권상황을 조사하였는데
귀하가 이에 관심이 있다면 그 결과를 알려주겠다.

ㅇ 인권과장

물론 많은 관심이 있다. 그 결과를 알려주면 좋겠다.

사실 북한은 워낙 폐쇄적인 사회이기 때문에 우리도 그곳의
인권상황에 관하여 자세히 알고 있지는 못하다.

11

0058

o 한국담당관

사실 엠네스티의 최대 관심사는 북한의 인권문제에 있다.

o 인권과장

그런 움직임이 폐쇄된 북한사회의 개방을 유도하였으면 좋겠다.

o 한국담당관

남한에서 북한 TV방송을 시청할 수 있는가.

o 인권과장

남한과 북한의 TV 방송방식이 다르기 때문에 남한에서는 북한
TV방송을 시청할 수는 없으며 우리 정부에서 북한에 TV 방송
방식을 봉일하여 서로 자유롭게 상대방 TV 방송을 시청하도록
하자고 수차에 걸쳐 촉구하였으나 거절되었다. 그러나 라디오
방송은 청취할 수 있다.

o 한국담당관

오늘 방문은 매우 유익하였으며, 귀중한 시간을 내 주어서
고맙게 생각한다. 귀하가 제네바의 UN인권사무국에 올 기회가
있다고 했는데, 그런 기회에 다시 만나서 진지한 의견교환을
할 수 있기를 바란다.

12

o 인권과장

한국 정부의 정책.노력 등에 대한 활발한 논의는 인권증진에
많은 기여를 할 것이라고 본다.
오늘과 같은 대화가 상호간 이해를 증진시키는데 도움이 된다면
언제든지 기꺼이 응하겠다.
좋은 여행이 되기를 빈다.

13

0060

분류기호 문서번호	국연 2031- 199 ( )	협조문용지	결 재	담당	과장	국장
시행일자	1991. 5. 18.					(서명)
수 신	미주국장, 구주국장	발 신	국제기구조약국장			
제 목	국가보안법개정 보도자료 송부					

　　　　1991.5.10. 국회에서 의결된 국가보안법 개정 내용에 관한

　　법무부의 보도자료(국.영문)를 별첨 송부하니 업무에 참고하시기

　　바랍니다.

　　　첨 부 : 표제자료(국.영문) 각 1부.　　끝.

0061

1505 - 8 일 (1)
85. 9. 9 승인 "내가아낀 종이 한장 늘어나는 나라살림"

190mm×268mm(인쇄용지 2급 60g / ㎡)
가 40-41 1990. 7. 9.

기 안 용 지

분류기호 문서번호	국연 2031- **17938** (전화:)	시 행 상 특별취급	
보존기간	영구·준영구. 10.5.3.1.	장	관
수 신 처 보존기간			
시행일자	1991. 5. 18.		

보 조 기 관	국 장	전 결	협 조 기 관		문 서 통 제
	과 장				
기안책임자		송 영 완			발 송 인

경 유 수 신 참 조	수신처 참조	발 신 명 의	
제 목	국가보안법개정 보도자료 송부		

1991.5.10. 국회에서 의결된 국가보안법 개정 내용에 관한

법무부의 보도자료(국.영문)를 별첨 송부하니 업무에 참고하시기

바랍니다.

첨 부 : 표제자료(국.영문) 각 1부. 끝.

수신처 : 주영, 미, 스웨덴, 화란, 노르웨이, 덴마크, 유엔,

제네바, EC,UNESCO 대사

0062

1505-25(2-1) 일(1)갑
85. 9. 9. 승인   "내가아낀 종이 한장 늘어나는 나라살림"

190mm×268mm 인쇄용지 2급 60g/㎡
가 40-41 1989. 6. 8

국가보안법 개정 보도자료

0063

개정방향

o "민족자존과 통일번영을 위한 대통령 특별선언" (7.7선언)과 북방정책의
   효율적 추진을 적극 뒷받침하는 동시에 국가의 존립·안전이나 자유민주적기본
   질서를 위태롭게 하는 경우에만 이 법을 적용하도록 함으로써 국민의 기본적
   인권이 최대한 보장되도록 한다는 원칙아래

o 개정의 기본방향을

   - 안보의 여건에 근본적인 변화가 없는 한 현행법의 기본골격을 유지
      하도록 하되

   - 남북관계의 진전과 시대상황의 변화에 상응하는 진향적개정으로
      균형을 유지하도록 하고

   - 현행법에 대한 그동안의 각계의 주장과 비판을 겸허히 받아들여
      인권침해의 소지를 철저히 방지하는데 두었음

0064

구체적 개정방침

o 헌법재판소 결정을 법전반에 대폭 반영함

   - 헌법재판소 결정대상인 찬양고무동조죄에 헌재결정을 반영함은 물론,

   - 금품수수죄, 잠입탈출죄, 회합통신등 죄에도 헌법재판소의 결정정신을

     전폭 수용하여 규제대상을 안보침해행위로 제한하고 남북교류협력에

     관한법률과의 적용한계를 명백히 함으로써 기본적인권 보장과 통일

     정책 수행에 최대한 기여함

o 국가안보에 필요불가결하지 않은 조항은 과감히 삭제 또는 제한함

   - 반국가단체의 개념과 불고지죄의 대상범죄범위 및 예비음모죄 조항을

     대폭 삭제.축소하고,

   - 찬양고무죄의 구성요건을 엄격하고 명확하게 하여 남용될 소지를

     완전히 제거하였으며

0065

- 간첩이 탐지수집한 기밀의 경중을 구분하여 법정형을 조정하는등 국민의

  민주화요구를 최대한 반영하고 자유의 영역을 일층 확대함

o 북방정책 수행의 장애조항을 전면 삭제함

- 국외공산계열과 관련된 처벌조항을 전부 폐지하여 공산권국가들과의

  교류협력에 있어서의 장애요인을 완전히 제거함

o 민자당개정안 원안중 여야협상과정에서 제기된 문제점을 최대한 수렴함

- 민자당개정안 제출후 선고된 헌법재판소 결정을 전폭 수용하고

- 불고지죄 대상범죄에서 잠입탈출죄를 추가로 제외하며

- 구속기간 1회 추가연장을 허용하도록 한 종전 개정안을 철회함

0066

o 국가보안법을 해석 적용함에 있어 국민의 기본적 인권을 최대한 보장하여야 한다는 규정을 신설함으로써 기본적인권의 보장을 위하여 법집행의 신중성을 제고하도록 함

o 반국가단체의 개념을 축소하여 '지휘통솔체제'를 갖춘 단체에만 엄격히 한정 처벌범위를 제한함으로써 남용될 소지를 제도적으로 방지함

o 반국가단체 및 그 구성원등과의 회합통신, 잠입·탈출, 찬양·고무,금품수수 행위의 경우에 종전에는 단순한 잠입·탈출과 찬양·고무등이가 할지라도 무조건 처벌토록 하였으나, 헌법재판소의 결정과 남북교류협력에관한법률의 취지를 살려 앞으로는 그러한 행위들이 '국가의 존립·안전이나 자유민주적 기본질서를 위태롭게 한다는 정을 알면서' 행해진 경우에만 처벌토록 처벌 범위를 대폭 축소함으로써 지금까지의 국가보안법을 둘러싼 인권침해 시비에 종지부를 찍음

0067

o 국외공산계열과 관련한 잠입·탈출, 찬양·고무, 회합·통신 등은 처벌대상
   에서 제외함

o 국가기밀의 범위를 '국가의 안전에 중대한 불이익을 회피하기 위하여
   한정된 사람만이 접근할 수 있는 지식' 등과 그밖의 것으로 세분하여
   법정형을 조정함

o 불고지죄에 있어서 목적수행등 간첩관련범죄에 대한 불고지만 처벌하도록
   하고 금품수수, 잠입탈출, 찬양·고무, 회합·통신, 편의제공죄에 대한
   불고지는 처벌대상에서 제외하며, 반국가사범과 친족관계에 있는 자가
   불고지죄를 범한 경우 종래에는 임의적으로 형을 감면할 수 있도록 하였던
   것을 형을 반드시 경감 또는 면제하도록 함

o 반국가단체가입 권유, 금품수수, 찬양·고무·허위사실 날조·유포, 이적
   표현물 소지, 회합·통신, 편의제공의 죄에 대한 예비음모는 처벌대상에서
   제외함

0068

o   반국가사범에 대하여 유죄판결을 하는 경우에는 반드시 자격정지형을 병과

하도록   하던 것을 판사의 재량으로 이를 병과하지 아니할 수 있도록 함

o   개정국가보안법은 현재의 우리시대상황에 비추어 볼때 가장 적합한 내용을

집약하고 있으나 우리가 지향하는 영구불변의 최종목표는 아님

o   시대여건이 변화하면 여에 따라 더욱 전향적인 입법을 고려할 수

있음

0069

신·구 국가보안법 대비표

항 목	현 행 법 률	개 정 법 률
1. 기본적인권보장 규정 신설		○ 이 법을 해석적용함에 있어 목적달성을 위하여 필요한 최소한도에 그쳐야 하며 이를 확대해석하거나 국민의 기본적 인권을 부당하게 제한하는 일이 있어서는 아니된다는 조항 신설 (제1조 제2항)
2. 반국가단체의 개념제한으로 반국가단체구성죄 등의 처벌범위 축소	○ 반국가단체를 정부를 참칭하거나 국가를 변란할 것을 목적으로 하는 국내외의 결사 또는 집단으로 규정 (제2조 제1항)	○ 반국가단체를 정부를 참칭하거나 국가를 변란할 것을 목적으로 하는 국내외의 결사 또는 집단으로서 지휘통솔체제를 갖춘 단체로 제한 (제2조제1항)
3. 국외공산계열관련 반국가단체개념 및 관련처벌조항 삭제로 북방정책 수행 뒷받침	○ 정부를 참칭하거나 국가를 변란할 것을 목적으로 공산계열의 노선에 따라 활동하는 국내외의 결사 또는 집단도 반국가단체로 봄 (제2조 제2항)	○ 삭 제
	○ 국외공산계열과 관련한 잠입 탈출, 찬양고무, 회합통신에 대해 처벌 (제6조제3항, 제7조제2항, 제8조제2항)	○ 삭 제

0070

항 목	현 행 법 률	개 정 법 률
4. 국가기밀 또는 군사기밀의 경중을 구분하여 법정형 세분화	○ 형법제98조에 규정된 행위를 하거나 국가기밀을 탐지, 수집, 누설, 전달, 중개한 때에는 사형 또는 무기징역에 처함 (제4조제1항 제2호)	○ 형법제98조에 규정된 행위를 하거나 국가기밀을 탐지수집, 누설, 전달, 중개한 때에 이를 구별하여 기밀이 국가안전에 대한 중대한 불이익을 회피하기 위하여 한정된 사람에게만 지득이 허용되는 사실, 물건 또는 지식인 경우에는 사형 또는 무기징역에 처하고, 그 외의 기밀인 경우에는 사형, 무기 또는 7년이상의 징역에 처함 (제4조제1항제2호 가.나목)
5. 남북왕래, 접촉 등 남북교류협력관련 행위는 안보위해한 경우만 처벌	○ 동기나 목적에 관계없이 잠입·탈출, 회합통신, 금품수수 행위를 처벌 (제5조제2항, 제6조, 제8조)	○ 국가존립·안전과 자유민주적기본질서에 위태로운 경우에 한하여 처벌 (제5조제2항, 제6조, 제8조) ○ 헌법개정 결정정신 전폭 수용

0071

항 목	현 행 법 률	개 정 법 률
6. 찬양고무죄의 구성요건 명확화로 남용소지 제거	○ 찬양·고무·동조행위는 물론 기타 행위도 반국가단체를 이롭게 하는 경우 모두 처벌 (제7조)	○ 찬양고무, 동조행위중 국가존립안전이나 자유민주적기본질서를 위태롭게 한다는 정을 안 경우만 처벌 ○ 기타 반국가단체를 이롭게 하는 행위 삭제로 처벌범위 축소
7. 헌법재판소 결정취지 전면 수용	○ 반국가단체 및 그 구성원등과의 금품수수, 잠입탈출, 찬양고무, 회합통신행위 처벌 (제5조제2항, 제6조제1항, 제7조제1항, 제8조제1항)	○ "국가의 존립·안전이나 자유민주적기본질서를 위태롭게 한다는 정을 알면서" 행해진 경우에만 처벌토록 처벌범위를 대폭 축소 (제5조제2항, 제6조제1항, 제7조제1항, 제8조제1항)
8. 불고지죄의 신고대상범죄를 대폭 축소하고 친족간 개서 필요적 감면으로 변경	○ 제3조 내지 제9조의 죄에 대한 불고지를 처벌 (제10조 본문)	○ 반국가단체의 구성등 (제3조) 목적수행(제4조), 가진지원 (제5조제1항)등 간첩관련 범죄에 대한 불고지만 처벌하고 금품수수 (제5조제2항), 잠입탈출 (제6조), 찬양고무 (제7조), 회합통신 (제8조), 편의제공 (제9조)에 대한 불고지는 처벌대상에서 제외

0072

개정내용	현 행 법 률	개 정 법 률
	○ 본법과 친족관계에 있는때 형을 감경 또는 면제할 수 있음 (제10조 단서)	○ 본법과 친족관계에 있는때 형을 필요적으로 감경 또는 면제하게 함 (제10조단서)
9. 필요적 자격정 지 병과규정을 임의적규정으로 변경	○ 유기징역형을 선고할 때에는 그 형의 장기이하의 자격정 지를 필요적으로 병과함 (제14조)	○ 자격정지를 임의적으로 병과 할 수 있게 함 (제14조)
10. 예비음모죄를 대폭 축소	○ 제3조 내지 제9조의 죄에 대하여 예비음모 처벌	○ 반국가단체 가입권유, 금품수 수, 찬양고무, 이적단체구성 원의 허위사실 날조유포, 이 적표현물 소지, 회합통신,편 의제공의 예비음모를 처벌대 상에서 삭제

협조문용지				결	담 당	과 장	국 장
분류기호 문서번호	국연 2031- 208	(2179-80)		재			
시행일자	1991. 5. 24.					(서명)	
수 신	구주국장		발 신	국제기구조약국장			
제 목	인권서한						

1. 영국소재 Korea Ecumenical Education Program(KEEP)는

홍근수 목사와 이삼열 교수의 체포에 대하여 문의하는 서한을 주영

대사관에 송부하여 온 바, 동 문건을 이첩하니 적의 처리하여

주시기 바랍니다.

2. KEEP 제기한 2인중 홍근수목사 자료는 당국이 법무부로

부터 기수령한 바 있어 별첨 송부하며, 이삼렬교수 관련 자료는

안기부에 요청하여야 할 것으로 판단됨을 참고하시기 바랍니다.

첨 부 : 1. KEEP 서한 사본 1부.

2. 홍근수 목사 설명자료 1부. 끝.

0074

24167

기 안 용 지

분류기호 문서번호	국연 2031 -	(전화:)	시 행 상 특별취급	
보존기간	영구·준영구· 10. 5. 3. 1	장		관
수 신 처 보존기간				
시행일자	1991. 5. 24.		ㄴ	

보조기관	국 장	전결	협조기관		문서통제 검열 91. 5. 27
	과 장	*uy*			
기안책임자		송영완			발 송 인

경 유			발신명의	반송 1991. 5. 27
수 신	법무부장관	
참 조	법무실장	

| 제 목 | 국보법 위반사범에 대한 특별관용조치 |

91.5.25자 국가보안법 위반사범 총 258명에 대한 석방,

감형, 기소유예등 특별관용조치와 관련, 당부는 동조치를

인권관련 국제회의에서는 물론, 국제기구 및 A.I.등 주요 민간

인권기구에 대하여 적극 홍보함으로써 아국정부의 인권신장을

위한 확고한 의지를 재인식시키는 계기로 활용코자 하오니

금번 특별관용조치의 대상자 명단, 조치내역등 설명자료를

당부로 송부하여 주시기 바랍니다. 끝.

0075

보 도 자 료

국가보안법 전면개정에 따른
국가보안법위반사범에 대한 특별관용조치

1991. 5.

법 무 부

1. 개 요

ㅇ 정부는 1991.5.25.자로 국가보안법위반사범 총258 명에 대하여 석방, 감형, 기소유예등 특별관용조치를 단행하기로 하였음

ㅇ 대상자에 대하여는 사법처리단계에 맞추어 특별감형, 특별가석방, 형집행정지, 공소취소, 기소유예등을 실시하게 되는 바, 그 내용은 특별가석방.구속취소등 석방이 74명, 특별감형이 30명, 공소취소가 3명, 기소유예가 151명임

2. 조치배경

ㅇ 제6공화국 출범이후 지금까지 3년여동안 추진해 온 개혁 입법논의를 마무리 짓고 6.29민주화 선언을 법적.제도적으로 완결하는 의미를 가지는 국가보안법이 지난 제154회 임시국회에서 전면 개정되었음

ㅇ 개정된 국가보안법은 변화하는 시대상황과 주변정세에 능동적으로 대처하면서 작년 4.2.선고된 헌법재판소의 결정을 포함하여 그동안 제기되었던 각계의 건설적 주장을 전폭적으로 수용한 것임

1

0077

ㅇ 특히 "민족자존과 통일번영을 위한 대통령 특별선언"
(7.7선언)과 북방정책의 효율적 추진을 적극 뒷받침하여
남북관계 개선을 도모하고 평화통일을 능동적으로 준비하기
위하여 전향적으로 개정하였음

ㅇ 또한 개정된 국가보안법은 국가의 존립과 국민의 생존권을
지키기 위한 최소한의 법적장치에 국한함으로써 인권침해의
소지를 근원적으로 불식시킴과 동시에 아직도 낡은 이데올로
기를 고집하면서 적화통일야욕을 버리지 않고 있는 북한
공산집단의 대남 전복전략에도 대처할 수 있도록 하였음

ㅇ 정부는 이와 같이 뜻깊고 대표적 개혁입법인 국가보안법
개정의 취지와 정신을 최대한 살리고 그 바탕위에서 굳건한
사회안정과 국민 대화합을 이루어야 한다는 우리사회 각계의
의견을 적극 수렴하여 구 국가보안법 규정에 따라 재판을
받고 복역중이거나 수사 또는 재판이 진행중인 자에 대하여
획기적 관용조치를 단행하게 된 것임

3. 기본방침

ㅇ 이번 조치를 함에 있어 자유민주주의 체제수호와 형사사법 운용에 지장을 주어서는 안된다는 기본명제를 전제로 하여 그 범위안에서 국가보안법 개정취지에 따라 최대한 관용을 베풀 수 있도록 대상자를 선정하였음

ㅇ 선정기준은 이번에 개정된 국가보안법 조항 해당여부를 우선적으로 고려하되, 사안의 경중, 죄질, 개전의 정 유무를 참작하고 특히 기결수의 경우에는 복역기간, 행형성적, 건강상태등 인도적 사유 유무에 중점을 두었음

ㅇ 이번 조치는 전례없이 파격적인 내용으로서 법집행기관으로서도 결단을 내리기 어려웠으나 국가보안법 개정을 계기로 가급적 많은 사람이 민주발전과 통일번영에 동참할 수 있도록 한다는 취지에서 지금까지의 사법처리기준에 구애받지 아니하였음

3

0079

4. 대상 및 범위

가. 간첩 (관련) 사범

ㅇ 국가기밀 수집·누설 (간첩) 죄에 대하여 구 국가보안법은
   사형 또는 무기징역에 처하였으나 새 국가보안법은
   기밀의 경중에 따라 사형, 무기징역 또는 7년이상의
   유기징역에 처할 수 있도록 법정형을 하향조정하였는 바
   법개정 정신을 감안하여 형기의 1／2이상을 복역한
   전향좌익수 36명에 대하여 특별가석방을 실시하고

ㅇ 10년이상 복역한 전향무기수로서 죄질이 비교적 중하지
   아니한 1명과 19년을 복역한 전향 좌익수 1명에
   대하여 특별감형을 실시하며

ㅇ 미전향 간첩 무기수중 60세이상 고령이고 25년이상
   복역한 질병자 2명에 대하여 인도적 차원에서 형집행
   정지를 실시함

4

0080

나. 찬양. 고무. 동조등 기타사법

ㅇ 새 국가보안법은 찬양. 고무등죄의 경우 국가 존립. 안전 이나 자유민주적기본질서를 위태롭게 한다는 정을 알면서 한 행위만 처벌할 수 있도록 개정되었는 바 법 개정 취지를 감안하여 다른 법률위반죄와 경합되지 않은 국가 보안법 제7조 위반사범중 형기의 2／3가 경과한 기결수 2 7명에 대하여 특별가석방을 실시하고

ㅇ 형기의 2／3가 경과하지 아니한 기결수 2 8명에 대하 여는 특별감형을 실시하며

ㅇ 구속 수사중인 이적표현물 소지등 사안이 다소 가볍고 개전의 정이 있는 9명에 대하여는 구속을 취소하여 석방하고

ㅇ 불구속 수사중인 찬양. 고무등 사안이 가볍고 개전의 정이 있는 1 5 1명에 대하여는 불기소 (기소유예) 처분을 하여 관용을 베풀며

ㅇ 또 이번 개정에 의하여 대상법위가 축소된 불고지죄로 기소되어 불구속 재판중인 3명에 대하여 공소를 취소 하고

5

0081

ㅇ 재판 진행중인 국가보안법위반사범에 대하여는 공소유지
  과정에서 법개정의 정신과 취지를 구형등에 적절히 반영
  해 나갈 것임

6. 효 과

  ㅇ 특별감형된 사람은

    ─ 무기수 1명의 경우 징역 15년으로 형이 변경되고

    ─ 유기수의 경우 나머지 형기의 1/2 또는 1/3이
      감경되며

  ㅇ 특별가석방된 사람은

    ─ 가석방이 취소됨이 없이 잔형기가 경과되면 형집행을
      종료한 것으로 간주되고

  ㅇ 형집행정지된 사람은

    ─ 일시 석방되어 신병등을 치료하게 됨

6

0082

7. 주요대상자

  ο 공소취소

    - 김대중, 김원기, 이철용

8. 특 징

  ο 자유민주주의 체제를 인정하고 대한민국의 법을 지키며 민주
    시민으로서 생활하기를 원하는 전향좌익수 3 6 명에 대하여
    대폭 석방의 관용을 베풀었고

  ο 왕영안등 2 명은 전향하지 않는 남파간첩들이지만 2 5 년이상
    복역하였고 질병자임을 감안하여 인도적 차원에서 형집행
    정지를 결정하여 질병을 치료하면서 그들 스스로 자유세계를
    직접 체험할 수 있도록 석방하였으며

  ο 특히 이번에 개정된 국가보안법 제7조 찬양.고무등 죄로
    수사 또는 형확정 복역중인 6 4 명에 대하여 과감하게 석방
    (3 6 명) 과 감형 (2 8 명) 의 은전을 베풀었으며, 공공기관
    점거, 방화, 공무집행방해, 화염병투척등 타법률위반죄와 경합
    되어 처벌을 받은 폭력사범은 제외하였음

7

0083

9. 맺는 말

ㅇ 이번 조치가 우리 사회가 겪고 있는 전환기적 상황을 조속히 매듭짓고 국민 모두가 국가발전 대열에 동참하는 뜻깊은 시발점이 되기를 기대함

ㅇ 정부는 국민여망에 따라 새 국가보안법의 개정취지와 정신을 살린다는 차원에서 이번의 경우 예외적으로 대폭적인 관용조치를 실시하였으나, 앞으로 개정 국가보안법에 충실하게 "국가의 존립안전과 자유민주적기본질서를 위태롭게 하는" 반국가활동에 대하여는 엄격히 법집행을 해 나갈 방침임

ㅇ 국민 여러분들께서는 민주시민으로서의 긍지를 가지고 정부의 법질서 유지 노력에 적극 협조해 주시기를 당부드림

8

＊국가보안법위반사법에 대한 특별관용조치 내역

구 분		인 원	비 고
총 계		2 5 8	
석방	소 계	7 4	
	특별가석방	6 3	좌익수 3 6 명 찬양·고무사법 2 7 명
	구속취소	9	구속 수사중
	형집행정지	2	고령·질병
특 별 감 형		3 0	무기수 1 명 포함
공 소 취 소		3	
기 소 유 예		1 5 1	불구속 수사중

9   0085

Highlights of Amendments to the National Security Law
As Passed by the National Assembly on May 10, 1991

The amendments are designed to eliminate overly stringent aspects of the past National Security Law and to ensure that it provides for only minimal restrictions needed to defend freedom and democracy against external and internal subversion and sabotage. To that end, 14 of the 25 articles of the law have been rewritten to abolish 20 punitive clauses, which pertain, among other things, to meeting or communicating with or contacting foreign Communists or Communist organizations, misprision of clandestine travel to or from the territory controlled by an antistate organization and various forms of preparations and conspiracies to undermine national security.

A new paragraph (Paragraph 2, Article 1) has been created. It provides that in interpreting and implementing the National Security Law, only minimum necessary legal steps shall be taken to achieve its intrinsic purposes of preserving national security and survival and protecting freedom of the people and that there shall be no extended interpretation of the law. This provision is intended to prevent any abuse of the law, and thus end past controversies over its enforcement.

Special care has been taken to make sure that human rights abuses will not be perpetrated under the law. In particular, the amended statute much more narrowly defines an "antistate organization" as a group equipped with a "command and control system" so that there will be no room for arbitrary applications of the "antistate organization" clause.

In the past, the law prescribed unconditional punishment for the giving or receiving of money or goods to or from an antistate organization or its member (Para. 2, Article 5); clandestine travel to or from the territory controlled by an antistate organization (Article 6); the praising, encouraging or siding with an antistate organization

1

or its members (Article 7); and meeting or communicating with or contacting a member of an antistate organization (Article 8). The just-revised National Security Law, however, punishes such acts only when they are committed "with the knowledge that this will imperil national survival and security or the basic free and democratic order." This revision is in keeping with the April 2, 1990 ruling of the Constitution Court that the National Security Law is "constitutional with certain reservations." The narrowing of the scope of punishment will end human rights controversies in connection with the enforcement of the law.

Furthermore, the just-passed amendments have deleted the vague phrase, "otherwise gives aid and comfort to an antistate organization" from Article 7, which is intended to punish anyone who "praises, encourages and sides with" an enemy. This has eliminated a lattitude for arbitrary enforcement of that article.

The revised National Security Law is aimed at actively promoting and guaranteeing peaceful inter-Korean exchanges with a view to advancing the goal of national reconciliation leading to unification. This is the revised statute punishes such acts as the giving or receiving of money or goods to or from an antistate organization or its member, clandestine travel to or from the territory controlled by an antistate organization, the praising, encouraging or siding with an antistate organization or its member only when such acts endanger national security and survival. In that way, all legal obstacles to genuine peaceful inter-Korean exchanges have been eliminated.

In addition, the revised law exempts from punishment the above-mentioned acts in regard to foreign Communist organizations and their members with the aim of providing institutional guarantees for active exchanges and cooperation with all former or present Communist countries, except North Korea, in the political, economic, social and all other fields.

2

0087.

The amended National Security Law has other revised provisions also designed to reflect the people's desire for full democratization to the maximum possible extent with a view to helping build a truly free and democratic nation advancing into the 21st century.

In the provisions against espionage (Items 2 and 3, Para. 1, Article 4), the revised law much more narrowly and clearly defines "state secrets" as "knowledge access to which is limited to authorized persons only in order to prevent serious disadvantages to national security" that will stem from its leakage or disclosure and other specific types of information. This will promote freedom of information to the maximum extent.

Whereas Article 14 of the old National Security Law provided that anyone sentenced to imprisonment for a definite term for treason should mandatorily be subjected to post-imprisonment suspension of civil rights, the amended version provides that such suspension of rights may be waived in consideration of extenuating circumstances. This change aims to more effectively protect the civil rights of citizens.

Article 10, which punishes misprision, has been amended to limit its application only to failures to report acts (including espionage) committed to serve the purposes of an antistate organization by its member or any other person following its instructions. To elaborate, the amended version of Article 10 does not punish failures to report the giving or receiving of money or goods, clandestine travel, praising, encouraging or siding with the enemy, and meeting or communicating with the enemy, as defined earlier. In other words, misprision is now punishable only when unreported acts imperil national survival. The scope of misprision has thus been minimized.

Furthermore, the revised version requires a lightening or waiver of punishment for misprision when such an offense is committed by a relative of the person found guilty of treason. The old law provided that such leniency might be granted at the discretion of the judge. This revision is designed to protect freedom of conscience and thought to the maximum extent.

3

0088

It should be noted that the governing Democratic Liberal Party
accepted most of the demands raised by the opposition in the course
of negotiations with it over amendments to the National Security Law.
The DLP thus revised its draft bill to extensively reflect the spirit
of the ruling by the Constitution Court regarding the constitutionality
of the old law. In particular, unauthorized travel to or from enemy
territory has been excluded from the list of offenses to which
misprision is applicable. Furthermore, the DLP withdrew a proposed
clause for permitting an additional extension of the pretrial detention
of suspects charged with grave violations of the National Security Law.

In sum, the just-passed amendments represent the maximum relaxation
of the law permissible under the prevailing security situation of the
nation.

4

Comparison between the Old and
Revised National Security Law

On May 10, 1991, the National Assembly of the Republic of Korea
passed a series of amendments to the National Security Law to moderate
the scope of its application as far as possible without basically
affecting its intrinsic purpose of "safeguarding the nation's security,
survival and freedom by controlling antistate activities endangering
national security." The law was first enacted in December 1980,
superseding previous security-related laws in keeping with changing
times and had not undergone a major revision until the recent passage of
amendments to it. Principal differences between the amended and old
National Security Law are described below.

1. Creation of a Clause to Better Protect Human Rights

Under the just-passed amendments, Paragraph 2 has been added to
Article 1, providing, "The interpretation and application of this Law
shall be confined to the minimum extent necessary to achieve its purpose:
the Law shall not be loosely interpreted or otherwise misapplied to
unreasonably restrict the basic human rights of citizens."

2. Narrower Definition of Antistate Organizations

Para. 1, Article 2 of the old Law defined "an antistate organization"
merely as "a domestic or foreign association or group whose purpose is
to usurp the government or to subvert the State."

The revised Law adds a qualifier, "equipped with a command and control
system," to that definition so that only well-organized subversive groups

1

0090

will be subject to this Article, the most prominent example being the
North Korean Communist regime.

This distinction is important because the top leader of an antistate
organization is punishable by death or life imprisonment, other leaders
by death, life imprisonment or imprisonment for not less than five years
and other members by imprisonment for not less than two years.

3. Exclusion of Foreign Communist Organizations from the Concept of Antistate Organizations

The amendments have deleted Para. 2, Article 2 of the old law, which
read, "Any domestic or foreign association or group operating along the
Communist lines for the purposes described in the foregoing paragraph
(namely, to usurp the government or to subvert the State) shall also be
deemed an antistate organization." The principal effect of this is to
leave foreign Communist parties and associated groups out of the scope
of the Law.

Also repealed are Para. 3 of Article 6, Para. 2 of Article 7 and Para.
2 of Article 8--clauses intended to punish anyone who praises, encourages
or shows sympathy with a foreign Communist party or government, meets or
communicates with such an organization or escapes to or sneaks in from the
territory under its control. Thus the National Security Law no longer
restricts exchanges with Communist countries except North Korea.

4. Gradation of Penalties for Espionage Depending on the Importance of State Secrets Involved

The old Law provided in Item 2, Para. 1, Article 4, that if and when a
member of an antistate organization or any other person following its
instructions commits offenses (of espionage) described in Article 98 of the
Criminal Law or seeks, collects, leaks, transmits or relays State secrets...
shall be subject to the death penalty or life imprisonment."

2

0091

The amended Law applies such severe punishment to only cases of espionage involving "facts, objects or knowledge access to which are allowed to a limited number of people only in order to prevent grave disadvantages" that their disclosure would "inflict on national security." For acts of espionage involving lesser secrets, the revised Law prescribes death, life imprisonment or imprisonment for not less than seven years.

5. <u>A Stricter Delineation of Punishment for the Giving or Receipt of Money or Goods to or from the Enemy, Unauthorized Travel to or from Enemy Territory, or Meeting or Communicating with the Enemy</u>

In Paragraph 2 of Article 2 and in Articles 6 and 8, the old Law provided for unconditional punishment of anyone who "gives to or receives from a member of an antistate organization money or goods, escapes to or sneaks in from the territory controlled by an antistate organization or meets or communicates with or otherwise contacts a member of an antistate organization or any other person acting under its instructions."

Under the revised Law, however, such an act is punishable only when committed with "the knowledge that it will endanger national security and survival and the free and democratic basic order." This change is part of efforts to fully accommodate the spirit of the ruling by the Constitution Court about the reservations concerning the constitutionality of the National Security Law.

6. <u>A Clearer Definition of Punishable Acts of Praising or Encouraging the Enemy</u>

The old Law provided in Para. 1, Article 7 that "Whoever praises, encourages or shows sympathy with the activities of a member of an antistate organization or of any other person following its instructions or otherwise gives aid and comfort to such an organization shall be subject

3

0092

to imprisonment for not more than seven years."

The amended Law, however, stipulates punishment for such an act only when committed "with the knowledge that it will endanger national security and survival and the free and democratic basic order." The amendment also is designed to punish anyone who agitates for or incites subversion of the State with the same kind of knowledge. The vague phrase, "otherwise gives aid and comfort to an antistate organization" has been deleted to make the scope of punishable acts clearer and more specific, also in keeping with the above-mentioned ruling by the Constitution Court.

7. A Drastically Reduced Range of Offenses of Misprision

The old Law prescribed punishment for misprision (failure to report a crime to the proper authorities) of violations of practically all its provisions.

However, the amended Law limits the application of misprision only to violations of Article 3 (formation of or affiliation with an antistate organization), Article 4 (acts of treason, espionage or sabotage committed by a member of an antistate organization or any other person following its instructions) and Para. 1 of Article 5 (willing provision of material and other assistance to anyone violating Article 4).

Thus, the amended version will not punish misprision of the giving to or receiving from an antistate organization money or goods as defined in Para. 2 of Article 5; of clandestine travel to or from enemy territory as defined in Article 6; of acts of praising, encouraging or showing sympathy with the enemy as defined in Article 7; acts of meeting or communicating with the enemy as defined in Article 8 and of the provision of convenience to anyone violating this Law as defined in Article 9.

The old Law provided, in the proviso to Article 10, that if and when an offense of misprision is committed by a relative of a violator of the Law, punishment for him may be lessened or waived. The revised version

4

stipulates that punishment shall be lessened or waived in such a case.

8. The Requirement for Suspension of Civil Rights of Convicts Eased

The old Law provided in Article 14 that if and when anyone is sentenced to imprisonment for a definite term for violating this Law, he shall be subject to (post-imprisonment) suspension of civil rights for a period not exceeding the maximum length of the sentence.

The amended Law, however, empowers the judge to decide at his discretion whether or not to impose such suspension of civil rights.

9. A Sharply Reduced Range of Punishable Preparations or Conspiracies to Violate the Law

The old Law prescribed punishment for preparations or conspiracies to commit offenses violating Articles 3 through 9.

However, the revised Law does not call for punishing preparations or conspiracies to commit such offenses as attempts to recruit members for an antistate organization; the praising or encouraging of such an organization or its members; the concoction and dissemination of groundless rumors by a member of an antistate organization with the aim of creating social unrest; the possession of written or audio-visual materials benefiting the enemy; meeting or communicating with the enemy; and the provision of convenience to the enemy.

5

공 란

공 란

공   란

공　　　란

공　　　　란

공   란

공 란

공 란

공 란

공 란

한국 인권문제 제 사안 2

공   란

공 란

공　　　란

공   란

공 란

공 란

공　　　란

발 신 전 보

번   호 : WGV-0777   910614 1636 FO   종별 :

수   신 : 주   제네바 (국연)대사. 총영사 (사본 주 ~~번기끼랜치~~) WBB-0304

발   신 : 장 관

제   목 : 인권문제

1. 제네바발 AFP 보도(6.14. 조선일보 전재)에 의하면 제네바국제 자유노조연맹(ICFTU)은 6.13. 공개한 ~~외사의 중동국가에서의~~ 노조활동에 관한 보고서에서 중국과 한국, 필리핀등을 노조활동 탄압국으로 지적하고 한국의 노동운동가들은 수시로 국가보안법의 희생자들이 되고 있다고 지적했다 함.

2. 상기 관련, ~~제네바에 본부를 두고 있는~~ 자유노조연맹~~은~~ 부~~렷셀에 본부를 두고 있다하는바~~ ~~개요를 파악, 보고바라며~~ 상기 보고서를 가급적 입수 (불가시 아국관련사항 상세내용)하여   송부바람.   끝.

일반문서로 재분류 (1991.12.31.)

(국제기구조약국장   문동석)

검 토 필(1991. 6. 30.)

국제기구과장: (서명)

앙고재	91년 6월 14일		기안자 성명	홍영우과	과장	국장	전결	차관	장관	보안 통제	(서명)
										외신과통제	

국제자유노조연맹 보고서

한국 등 노조운동 탄압국으로 지목

　　(제네바 AFP.로이터=聯合) 국제자유노조연맹(ICFTU)은 14일 전 세계 72개국에서 노조운동이 탄압받고 있으며 지난해 1월부터 올해 3월까지 15개월 동안 최소한 2백64명의 노동운동가가 살해되고 2천4백22명이 투옥됐다고 밝혔다.

　　이 단체는 제네바에서 열릴 국제노동기구(ILO) 연례 정기총회에 맞춰 발표한 58페이지 분량의 각국 노조활동에 관한 보고서에서 라틴 아메리카가 노조운동가들에게는 가장 위험한 지역이라고 지적하고 한국, 중국, 필리핀, 터키 등에서 노동운동을 탄압하고 폭력이 자행되고 있다고 보고했다.

　　이 보고서는 북한, 아프가니스탄, 캄보디아, 중국, 라오스, 및 베트남등 공산국에서는 공산당이 단일노조운동을 완벽하게 통제하고 있다고 지적했다.

　　보고서는 또 콜롬비아에서만 이 기간 중 1백38명이 살해됐으며 이 가운데 상당수 사건에 지주나 마약단체의 사주를 받은 보안군이 "직접 가담"했다고 비난했다.

　　과테말라에서도 33명이 살해됐으며 엘살바도르에서는 軍과 정부가 노조운동가를 좌익게릴라들의 동맹세력으로 몰아부쳐 암살대의 목표로 만들었다고 주장했다.

　　보고서는 이어 중국에서는 천안문사태 이후 노조활동에 대한 탄압이 계속되고 있으며 노동자자치연맹(WAF)이 불법화되고 그 지도자들이 구금상태에 있다고 공개하고 필리핀의 경우 지난 15개월간 10명의 노조활동가들이 살해됐다고 말했다.

　　보고서는 또 공산당이 완전장악한 유일 노조운동만이 인정되는 국가로 北韓, 베트남, 중국, 캄보디아등을 들고 부탄과 카타르, 오만, 사우디아라비아, 아랍에미리트연합 등 20여개국은 노조결성 자체가 금지되고 있다고 공개하면서 태국에서는 지난 2월 쿠데타이후 공공부문 노조가 해체됐다고 밝혔다.

　　ICFTU는 한편 전세계적으로 보세 수출자유지역내에서 일하는 수백만 노동자들이 착취당하고 있다고 비난했다.

　　ICFTU는 브뤼셀에 본부를 두고 있으며 세계 1백1개 국가의 1백만 노동자들로 구성된 단체이다.(끝)

0113

(YONHAP)　910614　0205　KST

관리	91
번호	—620

외 무 부

종 별 :

번 호 : GVW-1105

일 시 : 91 0614 1900

수 신 : 장관(국연,국기,노동부)

발 신 : 주 제네바 대사

제 목 : ICFTU 노조권리 침해 보고서

대: WGV-0777

연: GVW-11(462)5

1. 대호 보도는 국제 자유노조 연맹(ICFTU) 이 발간한 각국의 노조권리 침해에 관한 91 년도 연차 보고서(ANNUAL SURVEY ON VIOLATIONS OF TRADE UNION RIGHTS 1991) 를 인용한 것인바, 아국관련 부분 별첨 팩스 송부함

2. 상기 보고서는 금파편 송부 예정임.

첨부: 상기 아국관련 부분(GVW(F)-0207). 끝

(대사 박수길-국장)

예고:1991.12.31. 까지

일반문서로 재분류(1991 .12.31.)

검 토 필(1991. 6.30.)

국기국   1차보   2차보   국기국   분석관   노동부

PAGE 1

91.06.15   05:35

외신 2과 통제관 DO

0114

370 한국 인권문제 제 사안 2

A further anti-union tactic, notably by the National Cash Register Company, has been the illegal conversion of permanent employment relationships into short, fixed-term contracts. This has the intent and effect of intimidating workers, and discouraging trade union activity.

Police repression followed a strike by 350,000 public workers on 17 February 1991, against planned privatisation of public enterprises. Large numbers of trade unionists were arrested as a result of their participation in the strike.

Philippines

Trade unionists were again victims of violence from both sides of the civil conflict that continued to afflict Philippine society. The government did not act effectively to curb serious abuses by its own security forces or by the Citizens Armed Forces Geographical Units during their counter-insurgency operations, and the New People's Army also targetted trade union leaders in their military operations.

Among those killed were Mariano Caspe, an activist in the KMU-affiliated United Workers of the Philippines, who was shot after a trade union rally on 18 March; KMU National Council member David Borja, killed on 29 April; three striking TUCP members, Ariel de la Torre, Ernesto Grepal, and Nestor Apolonio were killed on 28 September when security guards opened fire on a picketline at Goldilocks Bakeshop, twenty others were injured; Ferdinand Pelaro, Reynaldo de la Fuente and Aguinaldo Marfil of the National Federation of Sugar workers, shot dead on 22 November, allegedly by a CAFGU member; Eddie Frederico, President of the Democratic and Independent Workers' Association, and Ernesto Gonzalez, murdered during the Convention of the independent Lakas Manggagawa Labour Centre (LMCC) on 10 December in an incident in which Norvic Bacalao was also wounded; and Warlito Lisondra, a union organiser, shot dead on 18 December.

Violence by employer-controlled vigilante groups or as a result of police intervention was also reported to have resulted in a number of deaths during industrial conflicts. The right to strike in the public sector was further limited by the constant threat of dismissal of those taking part in stoppages. This threat was acted upon in the dismissal of over 800 and suspension of some 1,500 teachers in the last four months of 1990, of 550 employees of the national oil company who were later reinstated, and of 17 cement workers.

Republic of Korea

The sharp interruption in 1990 of the process of democratisation of South Korean society which began in 1987 was reflected in an intensification of the repression of the country's trade union movement.

Labour legislation prohibits the right to organise of civil servants, employees of state enterprises and those engaged in defence-related industries, and severely restricts the right to strike, particularly of workers in sectors designated as being of public interest where disputes are subject to compulsory arbitration.

Legislation further provides that only one union may be established at any workplace. Similar restrictions on registration of industrial federations and national centres place many newly established unions outside the law. There is a ban on political activities by trade unions and on third party intervention by unregistered trade union federations on behalf of workers.

Trade unionists were frequent victims of South Korea's sweeping national security law which allows for the detention of those who «praise, encourage, or cooperate with anti-state organisations», and were subjected to close surveillance by security services. Violent police intervention against strikers occurred repeatedly and employers often used so-called «save-the-company squads» to intimidate trade unionists.

Violence was also used against trade unionists who were celebrating May Day for the first time in 32 years and against a peaceful workers' rally on 11 November when police arrested 1200 people.

The authorities gave tacit or active support to the widespread anti-union activities of companies operating in Korea. No action was taken on the previously recognised need for legislative reform to remove major trade union rights abuses. Instead, faced with the prospect of economic slowdown, the government promised in January a crackdown on illegal labour activities, and in a 16 November speech the Minister of Labour promised more stringent measures against labour activists who, he said, would be dealt with «strictly and sternly» if industrial peace was not established. The government also indicated that it would further tighten the control it presently exercises over collective bargaining through the wage guidelines issued by the Economic Groups Council.

In November, 561 people were known to be in detention because of their trade union activities, the figure remaining in excess of 200 at the end of the year. The government took highly repressive action against the Korean Trade Union Congress, Chonnohyop, which was declared illegal two days before its formal establishment on 22 January, 1990. The organisation's president, and over 350 of its leading activists were detained in the first four months of its existence, in which period more than 200 were also charged with offences.

A newly created teachers' union was also targetted under the general prohibition on public sector trade unionism. Some 1500 teachers were dismissed because of their union membership and two of the 93 arrested remained in detention at the end of the year.

Police intervention against strikers included action against Hyundai automobile workers who ended their stoppage in May. Industrial action in April by trade unionists at the Korean Broadcasting Service against measures to extend government control over the media was also broken up by riot police who maintained a presence at the company at the end of the year.

In September, management-promoted violence led to the hospitalisation of three trade union leaders in the course of a strike at the Australian-based multinational bank, Westpac, while 60 trade union leaders were arrested on 4 October when police intervened to end a strike at Seoul's university hospital.

A further 67 arrests were made on 9 February 1991, when police broke up a meeting to discuss solidarity with strikers at the Daewoo shipbuilding and heavy engineering company. Seven of those held, including leaders of the Conference of Large Factory Trade Unions formed in December, were subsequently charged for third party interference. Despite the peaceful settlement of the dispute, the president of the Daewoo shypyard workers' union, Baek Soon-hwan, was arrested on 27 March together with five other of the union's officials.

In addition to its longstanding campaign for reform of repressive labour legislation, the ICFTU-affiliate FKTU announced in January 1991 its intention to challenge the prohibition on trade unions' political activity by presenting candidates at local elections scheduled for later in the year.

Sri Lanka

Sri Lankan trade unionists were obliged to carry out their activities in conditions of acute civil conflict, which cost the lives of an estimated 2,600 people in the course of 1990. As many as 16,000 individuals were detained, many of them under emergency powers which also made it an offence for any person to engage in any activity that could adversely affect the functioning of a workplace; to enter any workplace without authorisation; or to hold any unauthorised workplace meeting.

Essential services legislation also gives the president full discretion to declare any strike action illegal, while the right to strike is denied to public servants.

Raymond Perera, a shop steward at Associated Batteries Manufacturers in Ratmalana, was abducted by unidentified gunmen on 14 September and reappeared on 21 September, only to hand himself over to the authorities once more on 4 October followed repeated police visits to his place of work. No reason has been given for the detention of Perera, who had been investigating the disappearance of a colleague earlier in the year.

Thailand

The National Peacekeeping Command, which took power in the military coup of 23 February 1991, announced in mid-March its intention to dissolve trade unions in public sector enterprises. This attack came in sharp contradiction to assurances given by military leaders at a meeting with trade unionists on 25 February when they had promised to respect basic union rights which were to be guaranteed in a new national constitution.

Army chief Suchenda Kraprayoon subsequently stated that the dissolution of trade unions in public sector enterprises and their replacement by State Enterprise Employee Associations was a principle objective of the coup and that martial law would be maintained until that aim had been achieved. He described the existing unions as an obstacle to national development. The right to organise was already denied to civil servants before the coup.

State enterprise unions, representing 200,000 of Thailand's 450,000 organised workers, had actively opposed government privatisation plans throughout 1990 in more than 60 enterprises. Illegal strike action taken included stoppages by portworkers in January and February, and by telecommunications employees in June after which two trade union leaders were removed from office.

A trade union research officer, Bhandit Thamtirat, was detained on security charges on 9 March and released on bail four days later.

Turkey

No progress was made by the government in amending labour legislation which restricts severely the basic rights of Turkish workers to organise, strike, and bargain collectively. Rather, the authorities introduced new measures which had the effect of intensifying longstanding rights violations.

While the authorities took the formal step of convening two tripartite summits in 1990 to review labour legislation issues they subsequently declared themselves dissatisfied with their outcome and said that early amendments appeared unlikely.

As a result, the ten year old legislative status quo is likely to continue, including as it does the denial of the right to organise of public servants and teachers and the prohibition of the right to strike in a wide range of designated sectors including public utilities and the petroleum industry. Strike action is further obstructed by the lengthy procedures that must precede the declaration of a legal stoppage and the possibility of imposing compulsory arbitration procedures.

Collective bargaining remains subject to the requirement that trade unions must have in membership 50% of the workers in a given bargaining unit and 10% of the workforce of the branch concerned before it may engage in negotiations. These provisions were invoked in July to remove the bargaining rights of the steelworkers' union, Celik-Is, at the Iskenderun and Karabük enterprise where half of its membership was employed.

In addition, Turkish legislation provides for extensive interference in the internal affairs of unions by imposing detailed qualification requirements on candidates for union office, prohibiting organisation at the enterprise level or along occupational lines, and requiring prior authorisation for international affiliation. Nor are trade unions allowed to undertake political activities.

The government added to these restrictions on trade union rights by issuing a decree in January which deprived public sector employees on fixed contracts of the right to organise or bargain collectively.

A further continuing cause for grave concern was the total absence of progress in the processing of the appeal by 584 leaders of the banned trade union centre, DISK, against sentences passed on them by military courts after the dissolution of DISK and its affiliates in 1986 for having adopted aims, principles and methods based entirely on Marxism-Leninism and for having abused constitutional rights. The penalties passed on the DISK activists include

29

기 안 용 지

분류기호 문서번호	국연 2031 - **22309**	(전화:)	시 행 상 특별취급	
보존기간	영구·준영구 10. 5. 3. 1		장 관	
수 신 처 보존기간				
시행일자	1991. 6. 15.		~	

보조기관	국 장	전 결	협조기관		문서통제
	과 장	/u/			접답 1991. 6. 17
기안책임자	송영완				발송인

경 유				
수 신	주영대사		발신명의	
참 조				
제 목	인권자료 송부			

대 : UKW-1168

1. 대호, 국가보안법 전면개정에 따른 국가보안법위반

사범에 대한 특별관용조치에 관한 보도자료 및 설명자료(각 1부)를

별첨 송부합니다.

2. 또한 법무부는 91년도 1/4분기중 아국이 접수한

석방탄원서를 검토한 결과, 오정균, 원기준, 박장균, 김종우,

이해학, 조용술, 조성우, 강용주, 배종열, 이대준(10명)이 주요

/ 계속 /

0117

석방요구 대상자였다 하며 동인들에 대한 설명자료를 송부하여

온 바, 동 설명자료를 별첨 송부하니 ( ) A.I.측에 적의

설명되도록 조치하여 주시기 바랍니다.

    3. 아울러 아국이 90.7.10. 국제인권규약에 가입함에

따라 국제인권규약(B규약) 제 40조에 의거, 시민적 및 정치적

권리에 관한 국제규약보고서를 91.7.9.한 제네바 인권사무국에

제출하여야 하는 바, 동 보고서(국문본)를 별첨 송부하니 업무에

참고하시기 바랍니다. (영문본은 91.7월초순경 번역이 완료되는

대로 추송할 예정임.)

첨 부 : 1. 국보법위반사범에 대한 특별관용조치 보도자료

        및 설명자료 각 1부.

    2. A.I.측의 주요 석방요구대상자(10명) 설명자료

    각 1부.

    3. 인권보고서 (국문본) 2부. 끝.

0118

인권문제 관련 외무부 조치사항(91.5.1-6.22)

-청와대 (민정, 외교안보)
- 법무부 담부.

1991.6.24.
외 무 부

1. 아국의 인권신장노력 홍보

양고재	91년 6월 24일	담 당	과 장	국 장
		송영완		

가. 국가보안법 개정

o 91.5.10. 국회에서 의결된 국가보안법 개정내용에 관한 법무부
보도자료(국.영문)를 미국, 영국, 유엔, 제네바등 주요공관에
송부, 아국의 인권보장을 위한 적극적 노력 홍보

나. 국보법 위반사범에 대한 특별관용조치

o 91.5.25. 국가보안법 위반사범 총 258명에 대한 특별관용조치에
대한 설명자료를 영국대사관에 송부, A.I.측에 설명

다. 국제자유노조연맹(ICFTU)의 연례보고서 대응

o ICFTU 개요
  - 브럿셀에 본부를 두고 있으며, 101개국의 100만 노동자를
    회원으로 두고 있음.

o 보고서 내용(91.6.13)
  - 북한, 중국, 캄보디아, 중국등을 노조활동이 완벽하게 통제되고
    있는 국가로 열거
  - 한국, 필리핀, 터키등에서는 노조운동이 탄압되고 있다고 지적

1

0119

o 대응방안

  - 아국이 노조활동을 탄압하고 있다고 비난하였으나, 북한의 경우
    노조활동이 완벽하게 국가에 의해 통제되고 있다고 언급하여
    남북한에 대해 일견 균형을 유지하려고 노력한 흔적이 있으므로
    단기적 대응보다는 장기적인 대아국 인권관 개선 및 북한의
    인권상황에 대한 주의를 환기시키는 방안 강구 필요

  - 현재 법무부와 중.장기 대응방안 협의중

라. 유네스코에서의 아국 인권문제 토의에 대한 대응활동

o 주유네스코 대표부를 통하여 유네스코 사무국 인권담당관을 접촉,
  아국 관련사항(임수경, 문규현 문제)이 유네스코 집행위에 회부
  되지 않도록 교섭한 결과, 6.11. 집행위 본회의에 아국문제 상정
  되지 않음.

  - 주유네스코 대표부는 과거수차 아국의 인권상황에 대하여
    유네스코 사무국측에 설명한 바 있음.

마. Freedom House의 아국 인권상황에 대한 평가오류 정정

o Freedom House 개요 : 1941년 창설된 민간 인권단체(본부 : 뉴욕)

o 아국 인권상황 평가 : Freedom House는 연례보고서에서 91년도
                       아국 인권상황을 본문에는 인권보장국
                       (Free)으로, 별도 목록표에는 부분 보장국
                       (Partly Free)으로 기재함.

o 정정조치 : 91.5.3. 주유엔대표부를 통하여 Freedom House 인권
            담당관을 접촉, 동 별도 목록표상의 오류를 정정토록
            조치. 91.5.16. Freedom House는 동 오류를 시정하고
            아측에 사과서한을 송부해옴. (사과서한 : 별첨)

2

바. A.I. 대응조치

　　o 주영대사관은 A.I. 회원들이 석방탄원서를 가장 많이 보내오는
　　　아국의 기결수등 대상자 20명에 대하여 A.I. 인권담당관을 접촉,
　　　동 석방탄원 대상자들의 범죄사실을 설명하고, 석방탄원편지 발송을
　　　자제토록 촉구(91.1.23 및 91.6.15)

　　o A.I.는 6월초 A.I. Newsletter를 통하여 홍성담, 장의균의 범죄
　　　사실 및 아국정부 입장을 게재함.

　　o 향후 지속적인 A.I. 대응활동 추진 예정

2. 북한의 인권문제 제기

가. A.I. Newsletter 방북활동 게재

　　o A.I.는 7월자 A.I. Newsletter를 통하여 제85차 IPU 총회
　　　(91.4.29-5.4)기간중 최초로 북한을 방문한 A.I. 대표단의 방북활동
　　　소개
　　　- 북한의 사법체계 조사활동 전개
　　　- 헌법, 형법(87년 개정), 민법(90년 개정), 형사소송법 법전입수
　　　- 북한 공안당국 접촉내용 게재

나. 방북활동 연구보고서 작성

　　o A.I.는 방북활동에 대한 상세한 분석 및 평가를 연구보고서에
　　　수록예정(배포는 금년 하반기중으로 예상)

3

0121

다. 당부 조치사항

o 주영대사관, A.I. Newsletter 7월호 기사를 파리주재 연합통신에
  제공(6.19자 국내순환 홍보)

o 6.25. KBS 특파원(정용석)이 A.I. 사무국 아.태지역 담당과장을
  인터뷰하여 상세한 방북내용 취재토록 조치

라. 향후 조치사항 검토

o A.I. 방북대표단으로부터 북한 법전사본 입수
  - 6.22. 주영대사관에 지시

o A.I. 방북대표단 연구보고서 입수
  - 연구보고서 발간시 입수, 국내 관련기관과 동 보고서 활용방안
    협의예정

o A.I. 방북활동 적극 추진토록 촉구
  - A.I. 대표단의 방북활동은 아측이 꾸준히 추진해온 북한 인권
    상황조사 촉구의 결실인 바, 향후 A.I.측에게 북한의 인권상황에
    더욱 관심을 갖고 정기적 방북조사활동을 전개토록 촉구

4

0122

Freedom House

ESTABLISHED 1941
48 East 21st Street
New York, New York 10010
212/473-9691
TELEX: 429439—FREEDOM
FAX: 212/477-4126

Mr. Jung Moo Choi
Counselor,
Korean Mission to the U.N.
866 U.N. Plaza
New York, N.Y. 10017

May 16, 1991

Dear Mr. Choi:

Thank you for contacting Freedom House about the error in our yearbook. The historical table in the back contains some misplaced freedom ratings, due to a computer problem. We regret the errors in the chart concerning South Korea and other countries. South Korea is indeed on the "Free" list for 1990-91, as one sees listed with the chart and report elsewhere in the book. I have enclosed a corrected version of the relevant page from the historical chart.

Thank you for your interest in our work.

Sincerely,

Dr. Joseph E. Ryan
Resident Scholar
Freedom House

0123

The Nineteen-Year Record of the Survey of Freedom

	1973	74	75	76	77	78	79	80	81	82	83	84	85	86	87	88	89	90	91
Dominican Republic	F	F	PF	PF	PF	PF	F	F	F	F	F	F	F	F	F	F	F	F	F
Ecuador	PF	PF	PF	PF	PF	PF	PF	F	F	F	F	F	F	F	F	F	F	F	F
Egypt	NF	NF	PF	PF	PF	PF	PF	PF	PF	PF	PF	PF	PF	PF	PF	PF	PF	PF	PF
El Salvador	F	F	F	F	PF	PF	PF	PF	PF	PF	PF	PF	PF	PF	PF	PF	PF	PF	PF
Equatorial Ginea	NF	NF	NF	NF	NF	NF	NF	NF	NF	NF	NF	NF	NF	NF	NF	NF	NF	NF	NF
Ethiopia	NF	PF	NF	NF	NF	NF	NF	NF	NF	NF	NF	NF	NF	NF	NF	NF	NF	NF	NF
Fiji	F	F	F	F	F	F	F	F	F	F	F	F	F	F	F	PF	PF	PF	PF
Finland	F	F	F	F	F	F	F	F	F	F	F	F	F	F	F	F	F	F	F
France	F	F	F	F	F	F	F	F	F	F	F	F	F	F	F	F	F	F	F
Gabon	NF	NF	NF	NF	NF	NF	NF	NF	NF	NF	NF	NF	NF	NF	NF	NF	NF	NF	PF
The Gambia	F	F	F	F	F	F	F	F	F	PF	PF	PF	PF	PF	PF	PF	PF	F	F
Germany East	NF	NF	NF	NF	NF	NF	NF	NF	NF	NF	NF	NF	NF	NF	NF	NF	NF	NF	F
Germany West	F	F	F	F	F	F	F	F	F	F	F	F	F	F	F	F	F	F	
Ghana	NF	NF	NF	NF	NF	PF	PF	PF	F	F	NF	NF	NF	NF	NF	NF	NF	NF	NF
Greece	NF	NF	F	F	F	F	F	F	F	F	F	F	F	F	F	F	F	F	F
Grenada	[U.K.]	PF	PF	PF	F	F	PF	PF	NF	NF	NF	PF	F	F	F	F	F	F	
Guatemala	F	F	PF	PF	PF	PF	PF	PF	PF	NF	NF	NF	PF	PF	PF	PF	PF	PF	PF
Guinea	NF	NF	NF	NF	NF	NF	NF	NF	NF	NF	NF	NF	NF	NF	NF	NF	NF	NF	NF
Guinea-Bissau	[PORTUGAL]	NF	NF	NF	NF	NF	NF	NF	NF	NF	NF	NF	NF	NF	NF	NF	NF	NF	NF
Guyana	F	PF	NF	PF	PF	PF	PF	PF	PF	PF	PF	PF	PF	PF	PF	PF	PF	PF	PF
Haiti	NF	NF	NF	NF	NF	NF	NF	NF	NF	NF	NF	NF	NF	NF	PF	PF	NF	NF	PF
Honduras	PF	PF	PF	PF	PF	PF	PF	PF	PF	PF	F	PF	F	F	F	F	F	F	F
Hungary	NF	NF	NF	NF	NF	NF	NF	NF	NF	NF	NF	NF	PF	PF	PF	PF	PF	PF	F
Iceland	F	F	F	F	F	F	F	F	F	F	F	F	F	F	F	F	F	F	F
India	F	F	F	PF	PF	F	F	F	F	F	F	F	F	F	F	F	F	F	F
Indonesia	PF	PF	PF	PF	PF	PF	PF	PF	PF	PF	PF	PF	PF	PF	PF	PF	PF	PF	PF
Iran	NF	NF	NF	NF	NF	NF	PF	PF	PF	NF	NF	NF	PF	PF	PF	PF	NF	NF	NF
Iraq	NF	NF	NF	NF	NF	NF	NF	NF	NF	NF	NF	NF	NF	NF	NF	NF	NF	NF	NF
Ireland	F	F	F	F	F	F	F	F	F	F	F	F	F	F	F	F	F	F	F
Israel	F	F	F	F	F	F	F	F	F	F	F	F	F	F	F	F	F	F	F
Italy	F	F	F	F	F	F	F	F	F	F	F	F	F	F	F	F	F	F	F
Ivory Coast	NF	NF	NF	NF	NF	NF	NF	PF	PF	PF	PF	PF	PF	PF	PF	PF	NF	PF	PF
Jamaica	F	F	F	F	F	F	F	F	F	F	F	F	F	F	F	F	F	F	F
Japan	F	F	F	F	F	F	F	F	F	F	F	F	F	F	F	F	F	F	F
Jordan	NF	NF	NF	NF	NF	NF	NF	NF	NF	NF	NF	NF	PF	PF	PF	PF	NF	PF	PF
Kenya	PF	PF	PF	PF	PF	PF	PF	PF	PF	PF	PF	PF	PF	PF	PF	NF	NF	NF	NF
Kiribati	[U.K.]							F	F	F	F	F	F	F	F	F	F	F	F
Korea, N	NF	NF	NF	NF	NF	NF	NF	NF	NF	NF	NF	NF	NF	NF	NF	NF	NF	NF	NF
Korea, S	PF	PF	PF	PF	PF	PF	PF	PF	PF	PF	PF	PF	PF	PF	PF	F	F	F	F
Kuwait	PF	PF	PF	NF	PF	PF	PF	PF	PF	PF	PF	PF	PF	PF	PF	NF	PF	NF	NF
Laos	PF	PF	NF	NF	NF	NF	NF	NF	NF	NF	NF	NF	NF	NF	NF	NF	NF	NF	NF
Lebanon	F	F	PF	PF	PF	PF	PF	PF	PF	PF	PF	PF	PF	PF	PF	NF	NF	NF	NF

463

정   보   보   고

1. 제 목	2. 출 처
인권문제 동향보고	인 권 과

3. 내 용

(1991. 7. 2)

　　　　최근 대한변호사협회에서 소속변호사들을

　　상대로 실시한 설문조사결과중 인권문제

　　관련부분이 별첨과 같이 연합통신, 중앙일보에

　　보도되었음

　　　　첨부 : 관련 기사사본 1부.

0125

변호사 절반이상 6共시 인권상황 호전 평가

"6共보다 오히려 나빠졌다"는 6.3%에 불과

(서울=聯合) 우리나라 변호사들중 과반수를 훨씬 넘는 57.9%가 6공화국의 인권상황이 5공시절보다 '약간 또는 많이 나아졌다'고 평가하고 있는 것으로 나타났다.

대한변협이 소속변호사 2천 2백여명(응답자 8백90명)를 상대로 지난 4월중순부터 5월중순까지 한달동안 설문조사를 실시, 그 결과를 취합해 1일 밝힌바에 따르면 6공화국의 인권상황이 5공때에 비해 개선됐는지 어부를 묻는 설문에 응답자의 38.2%(3백40명)와 19.7%(1백76명)가 '약간 개선됐다'또는 '많이 개선 됐다'고 각기 응답한 반면 34.9%(3백11명)는 '별로 개선된 바가 없다'고 답했고 6.3%(56명)는 '오히려 나빠졌다'고 응답했다.

또 인권용호와 관련한 변협의 활동내용을 묻는 데 대해서는 60.7%가 '별충분했다'고 지적한 반면 36%와 2.7%만이 각기 '대체로 적절했다' '적절하고 충분했다'고 답변, 변협의 인권용호 활동에 불만을 나타냈다.

사법시험의 주관을 현재의 총무처에서 대법원으로 바꾸어야하는 지 어부에 대해서는 응답자의 75.6%가 '대법원에서 주관해야한다'고 답변, 현행 체제를 바꾸기를 희망했으며 12.8%만이 현재대로 총무처에서 주관해야 한다고 답했다.

사법시험 합격자수를 현재와 같이 3백명선으로 하는 것과 관련, 72%는 인원수를 늘어야 한다고 했으며 '현수준을 유지해야 한다'는 23.4%에 불과했다.

이밖에 지방자치시대 개막에 때맞춰 변호사의 정계권을 포함한 자치권을 변협이 가져야 한다는 설문에 대해서는 84.5%의 응답자가 동의의 뜻을 나타낸 반면 나머지는 '현 체제 유지' 또는 '시기상조'라는 의견을 나타냈다.

변협내에 변호사의 윤리문제를 다룰 '변호사윤리위'를 설치하자는 의견에 대해서는 90.8%가 윤리위를 설치, 자체정화를 해야 한다는데 동의한다고 밝혔다.(끝)

(YONHAP) 910701 1938 KST

0126

6共늘어 「人權나아졌다」 58%

辯協 「변호사의식」 조사

변호사 징계 辯協서 해야 84%

同試 대법원서 주관 필요 76%

변호사들중 절반 이상 해 6공정부의 인권상황이 6공화국이 5共시절보다 나아졌다고 평가하고 있으며 대다수가 변호사 징계권을 협회가 행사해야 한다는 의견을 갖고 있는 것으로 나타났다.

2일 大韓辯協(회장 金洪梅)이 생정부 출범 계기로 전국 변호사를 상대로 실시한 「변호사의식」 조사결과 변호사들의 66.3%(368명)가 「어느정도 개선됐다」고 대답했으며 현재 법무부에 있는 변호사의 징계권을 협회가 가져야 한다는 의견이 84.5%(4백72명)가 되었으며 사법시험을 대법원이 주관해야 한다는 데 72%(6백4명)가 찬성했다.

<金石東기자>

大韓辯協會長 面談資料

1991. 7.

앙고재	담 당	과 장	국 장
91년 7월 2일	署	署	署

國 際 機 構 條 約 局

0128

I. 大韓辯協會長 人的事項

1. 姓　　名　: 김흥수 ████

2. 本　　籍　: 서울

3. 學　　歷　:

1947	서울大 法大卒
1950	서울大 大學院 法學科 修了
1958	美 아메리칸大 大學院 法學科 修了
1983	서울大 大學院 法學科 卒業(法學博士)

4. 資　　格　:

1949	辯護士 試驗 合格(3회)

5. 經　　歷　:

1950-	司法官(서울지법 및 지검)
1960-	서울高檢 檢事, 서울地檢 部長檢事
1961-	辯護士 開業(서울)
	東國大 法學科 敎授
1991.2.23-	大韓辯協 會長

6. 家族關係　:

既婚, 3男 3女

0129

Ⅱ. 말씀자료

1. 아국의 인권상황에 대한 올바른 인식 필요

  o 대한변협의 인권보고서는 아국내 민간단체가 발행하는 주요 인권
     보고서로서 국제민간 인권단체등에 의한 아국의 인권상황 판단시
     기초자료로서 참고되는 만큼 제6공화국의 인권상황 개선을 위한
     노력등을 보다 객관적이고 긍정적으로 평가해야 할것임.

     - 인권보고서 집필진이 운동권의 논리를 그대로 수용해서는
       안될것임.

     - 변협 명의로 발간되는 것인만큼 변협 임원진이 관심을 갖고
       보고서상의 문제점 지적 요망
       (변협회장 및 임원진은 인권보고서 집필진보다 긍정적 시각을
       갖고 있는 것으로 파악됨)

     - 특히 최근 인권상황이 악화되었다거나 단순히 정치범, 양심수가
       존재한다는 식의 논리전개는 곤란함.

0130

2. 인권문제 제기시에는 국익을 고려해야 함.

   O 대한변협의 인권보고서는 인권관련 주요국제회의에서 북한 및 친북한
     민간 인권단체에 의해 아국 인권상황을 비방하는 주요자료로서 악용
     되는 사례도 있음.

   O 아국의 인권보장제도가 완벽하다고는 할 수 없으나 인권침해시
     국내적으로 이를 시정할 수 있는 제도적 보장장치가 구비되어
     있으므로 아국의 국내 인권문제를 국제화하여 아국의 대외적 이미지
     및 국익을 저해하여서는 안될것임.

   O 특히 국제적으로 인권문제가 논의되고 있는 북한, 버마, 엘살바돌,
     과테말라, 이락등과 아국의 인권상황은 전혀 차원을 달리하는 바,
     변협의 보고서가 아국의 인권문제를 크게 부각시킴으로 인하여
     국제적으로 여타 인권침해국과 아국이 동일시되는 현상은 매우
     바람직하지 않음.

0131

3. 인권보고서 발간과 관련된 요망사항

  ○ 대한변협이 인권옹호적 차원에서 인권보고서를 작성하고 있으므로
    집필과정에서 다소 편향된 시각이 반영될 수 있는 바, 변협임원
    차원에서 이를 조정 또는 수정하기는 어려움이 있을 것이므로,

  ○ 향후 보고서의 내용을 인권침해사실 또는 구조적 문제점 지적에
    두기 보다는,
    - 인권신장을 위한 제도보완 또는 법령정비에 관한 제안
    - 국가 또는 시민에 의한 인권침해시 이를 시정하기 위한 구제책
      설명등 보다 미래지향적인 인권보장 지침서가 되는 것이 바람직
      하다고 봄.

0132

1. 인권관련 국제회의에서의 아국 인권문제 거론

가. 북한대표에 의한 아국 인권상황 비방

ㅇ 제46차 유엔인권위원회(90.1.26-3.9)에서 북한대표는 1989년도
대한변협 인권보고서를 그대로 인용하여 아국 인권상황(시국관련
사법구속자 관련) 비방발언 시행

나. 국제민간단체에 의한 아국 인권상황 거론

ㅇ 제42차 유엔인권 소위(90.8.6-8.31, 제네바)

- 국제인간정주위(Habitat International Coalition)이 11개국의
주민강제이주문제를 언급하면서 서울 재개발사업 거론

- 세계노조연맹(World Federation of Trade Union)이 전노련
결성관련 구속자문제 언급

ㅇ 제47차 유엔인권위(91.1.18-3.8, 제네바)

- 국제교회위원회(World Council of Churches)가 KNCC의 보고서를
인용, 90년도중 1,746명의 양심수가 체포되었다고 언급

- 국제법률가 협회(International Association of Democratic
Lawyers)는 정치적 사유의 구속자 현황 및 구금자 인권상황
거론

ㅇ 상기 인권관련 국제회의에서 국제민간단체에 의한 아국 인권상황
거론시 대한변협의 자료를 직접 인용하지는 않았으나 대한변협의
자료가 아국의 인권상황에 대한 주요 보고서로서 참조되었을
것으로 보임.

0133

2. 각국정부 및 민간인권단체가 발간하는 인권관련 주요보고서

가. 정부에 의한 인권보고서

   ○ 미국무부 세계인권상황 보고서(매년 2월 발간)

나. 민간인권단체에 의한 주요 인권보고서

   ○ 국제사면위원회(Amnesty International) 세계인권보고서
     (매년 7월 발간)

   ○ Asia Watch 인권보고서(매년 11월 발간)

   ○ Freedom House 인권보고서(매년 3월 발간) 등

다. 주요내용

   ○ 보안사범 증가

   ○ 양심수 문제

   ○ 장기 복역수 문제

   ○ 노조활동에 대한 아국정부 조치

   ○ 고문등 가혹 행위

   ○ 개별사건 관련사항

     - 임수경, 홍성담, 서경원등

3. 대한변협 인권보고서

가. 1989년도 인권보고서(90.2.23.발간) 요지

   ○ 88.12.28. 대통령의 "민생치안에 관한 특별지시"를 신호탄으로
     노동운동과 농민운동에 대하여 강경한 공권력 행사

   ○ 문익환 목사 방북사건을 계기로 공안정국이라는 극도의 정치적
     긴장상황 조성

0134

o 국가보안법이 무차별 남용됨으로써 제5공화국 시대보다 더 많은
  국가보안법 위반사건과 양심수를 만들어 냄.

o 안기부가 공안합수부를 주도하면서 국가보안법과 안기부가
  현 정부를 지탱하는 두 축임을 다시한번 천명

o 시국관련 구속자는 1,315명(88년 779명의 2배)

o 제6공화국 출범이래 시국관련 구속자의 숫자는 총 2,894명,
  1일평균 3.78명으로 제5공화국 시절의 하루평균 1.61명보다
  2배가 넘음.

o 긴급구속과 강제연행이 일반화됨.

o 수배자 가족에 대한 감시, 폭언, 세무조사, 위협등 인권침해 제기

o 서경원사건 관련자와 홍성담등 민족민중미술운동 전국연합 관련자에
  대한 가혹행위등 고문의 악습 재개

나. 1990년도 인권보고서(91.7-8월경 발간예정) 문제점
  (법무부측 사전입수 내용)

o 원고 집필진(13명) 모두가 급진적 성향을 갖고있는 민협소속 30대
  초반의 在朝 경력이 없는 변호사들로 구성

o 특히 "보안사(현 기무사)의 민간인 사찰" 부분과 "범죄와의 전쟁
  선포이후 인권침해사례"를 부각할 예정이며, 정치.경제상황의
  분석등에 있어서도 급진적이고 편향적인 시각에서 논리전개가
  예상됨.

o 1990년 인권보고서 분야별 집필진

  - 개 관   : 박승욱 변호사(31세)

  - 생명의 존엄과 신체의 자유 : 박찬운 변호사(28세)

  - 언론, 출판과 표현의 자유   : 박원순 변호사(37세)

  - 집회결사의 자유   : 유선호 변호사(38세)

0135

- 노동자의 권리   : 이오영 변호사(31세),
                    김진국 변호사(28세)

- 환경건강권   : 윤기원 변호사(31세)

- 농어민, 도시빈민, 노인, 장애자문제 : 박주현 변호사(28세)

- 사법, 헌재, 변호사와 민주화   : 박연철 변호사(40세)

- 재소자와 인권(양심수, 장기수등) : 백승헌 변호사(45세)

- 안기부, 군, 검찰, 경찰과 민주화 : 오양호 변호사(29세)

- 특집 "보안사의 민간인 사찰"   : 안상운 변호사(29세)

- 특집 "범죄와의 전쟁 분석"   : 이덕우 변호사(34세)

0136

정 보 보 고

1. 제 목

인권관련 언론보도

2. 출 처

인 권 과

(1991. 7. 5)

3. 내 용

o 보도요지

- 재야단체로 구성된 "학문과 사상의 자유탄압 및 학술연구자 불법
  연행 구속에 대한 궁동대책위 (상임공동대표 척장집, 고대교수)"는
  서울 사회과학연구소 연구원 6명의 구속과 관련, 유엔 인권위에
  제소하는 등 대응방안을 강구하겠다는 것임
- 연합통신 ('91.7.5)

o 전 망

- 국제인권규약상, 개인의 청원권 (B규약 선택의정서)을 인정하고
  있기는 하나 국내법상의 구제절차 (민사배상, 형사고발 등)를
  사전에 완료한 뒤 제소할 것을 요건으로 하므로 단기적으로는
  문제점이 없을 것으로 보임
- 기타 방법으로 "경제사회이사회 결의 1503호" 절차에 의해
  UN인권사무국에 청원할 수는 있으나, 동 절차는 개별적인 사건을
  다루는 것이 아니라 지속적 형태의 인권위반상황 죽, 장기간에
  걸쳐 다수의 사람들에게 영향을 미치는 상황을 다루는 절차이므로
  별다른 문제점이 없을 것으로 보임

o 대 책

- 향후 진전상황 주시
- 외무부와 긴밀 협조하여 유엔 인권사무국측의 동향 등 확인
- 정부차원의 대응자료 등 필요사항 철저 대비중

o 첨부 : 관련기사 사본 1부.

0137

* 연합통신 ('91.7.5)

연합 H1-390 S03 사회(537)

사회과학연구원 구속·유엔인권위 제소키로

　　(서울=聯合) 학술단체협의회, 민족예술인총연합등 재야 25개단체로 구성된 '학문과 사상의 자유탄압및 학술연구자 불법연행 구속에 대한 공동대책위(상임공동대표 崔章集·고대교수)'는 4일 서울사회과학연구소 연구원 6명을 당국이 국가보안법위반 혐의로 구속한 것과 관련, 다음주중으로 유엔인권위에 제소해 유엔의 조사를 촉구키로 했다고 밝혔다.

　　공대위는 이날 "연구자들의 학문적 연구·저술활동을 사법처리한 것은 헌법에 보장된 기본권인 학문과 사상의 자유에 대한 침해이며 군복무중인 연구자들의 입대이전 저술을 문제삼아 구속까지한 것은 국민의 기본권에 대한 중대한 탄압"이라고 규정하고 "다음주 초까지 정부의 반응을 지켜본뒤 사태 해결의 진전이 없으면 외신 기자회견을 통해 유엔인권위에의 제소를 정식발표할 계획"이라고 밝혔다.

　　한편 공대위는 오는 임시국회에서 이 문제를 다루어 주도록 이날 하오 신민당에 이 사건과 관련된 대정부 질문자료를 전달했다.

　　우리나라가 지난해 가입한·유엔인권규약의 B규약 선택의정서에 따르면 국가에서의 인권규약 위반사실에 대해 피해당사자가 직접 유엔인권위에 제소를 할 수 있으며 인권위는 이를 심의조사한뒤 해당국 정부에 결과를 통보, 시정을 권고할 수 있도록 되어 있다.(끝)

0138

관리
번호 91-
750

長 官 報 告 事 項

報 告 畢

1991. 7. 15.
美 洲 局
北 美 1 課 (63)

題 目: 我國의 勞動權 彈壓國 擧論 關聯 措置

最近 美 海外 民間投資 公社(Overseas Private Investment Corporation :
OPIC)에서 韓國을 勞動者 權利 彈壓國으로 지목코자하려는 움직임과 관련,
美國內 動向 및 措置事項等을 아래 報告 드립니다.

1. 我國의 勞動權 彈壓國 擧論 經緯 및 향후 展望

  ㅇ AFL/CIO 및 美 自動車 勞組인 UAW가 OPIC側에 대해 韓國을 勞動權 彈壓國
    으로 指定할 것을 청원함에 따라 問題 提起

  ㅇ OPIC側은 동사 정관규정에 따라 美 國務部, 勞動部에 자문을 要請中

  ㅇ OPIC側은 關係部處 자문 結果를 綜合, 內部 報告書를 作成하고, 關係機關
    會議 審議를 거쳐, OPIC의 <u>民間投資 支援 對象國</u> 名單에서 韓國을 削除할
    지 與否를 決定할 豫定

2. 美 關聯部處 意見

  가. 國務部(東亞·太局 韓國課 擔當官)

    ㅇ 國務部의 公式立場은 決定된 바 없으나, 韓國의 勞動權 保護가 改善
      趨勢에 있는 現狀況에서 韓國政府를 당혹케 하는 것은 <u>적절치 않음</u>.

0139

나. 勞動部(極東 擔當官)

ㅇ 勞動部의 公式立場도 아직 未定이나, 勞動部 意見은 參考意見에 불과하므로, OPIC自體가 決定할 事項임.

- OPIC이 韓國에 불리한 決定을 한다해도 <u>波及影響 微微할</u> 것으로 豫想

다. OPIC(Zeder 사장)

ㅇ 美 自動車 勞組, Asia Watch等 人權團體 및 同團體들의 壓力을 받는 <u>美 上.下院議員</u>들의 韓國의 勞動權 問題를 提起하고 있음.

ㅇ 韓國에 대한 새로운 事業支援을 對外發表없이 暫定中斷하는 것이 賢明한 方法으로 判斷된다고 言及

- 我側 希望時 韓國内 勞動 現況 把握을 위한 <u>OPIC 關係官 派韓</u> <u>檢討 用意 表明</u>

3. 措置 事項 및 計劃

ㅇ 駐美 大使館으로 하여금 美 關係 當局에 我國의 <u>勞動權 保護關聯 現況</u>을 説明토록 指示(勞動部 作成 説明 <u>資料 기송부</u>)

ㅇ 전문 홍보, 법률회사로 하여금 弘報論理 및 資料(영문)를 開發, 이를 지속 <u>弘報</u>하는 <u>方案을 推進</u>(駐美 大使建議-勞動部에 檢討 要請 公文 既發送)

ㅇ 駐美 大使로 하여금 OPIC의 對韓投資 支援事業現況(實積 및 計劃)과 勞動權 彈壓國으로 지정할 경우 對外發表問題 慣行등을 具體的으로 파악토록 指示

ㅇ OPIC 關係官의 訪韓問題는 狀況 파악후 關係部處 協議를 거쳐 決定　　끝.

일반문서로재분류(1991.12.31.)

검 토 필(1991. 6. 30.)

0140

법 무 부　인 권 과

1991.

수신 : 외무부 국제연합과　소년원사가장생

(수신처 FAX NO: 723-3505)

발 : _____ 법무부　인권과 _____

0141

배 부 처	법 무 부		대검	청와대	기 타 기 관
	⊘⊘⊘⊘⊘○		⊘○	⊘⊘	⊘⊘⊘○○○
	장차법검 무찰 실국 관관장장	김현선장	공 안 부 장	정책조사보좌관	제안외공법 1 행 조부부처처 기무보제

정 보 보 고

1. 제 목   2. 출 처

　　인권관련기사 진상보고   인 권 과

                                            (1991.9.12)

　ᄋ. 제 ᄋ

　　　1.　관련기사 요지

　　　　ᄆ　연합통신 9.12.자

　　　　ᄋ　우리나라가 유엔 인권규약에 가입한 이후 최초로
　　　　　동 규약에 따라 "유엔 인권이사회"는 사노맹 관련자
　　　　　등 17명이 수사과정에서 가혹행위를 당하였다는
　　　　　진정을 접수하고, 그에 대한 우리 정부의 의견을
　　　　　요청하는 질의서를 보냈다는 것이며, 그에 대하여
　　　　　법무부 관계자는 상기 규약에 따른 진정서는 국내적
　　　　　구제절차가 완료된 후에만 제기할 수 있는 것이므로
　　　　　정부의 답변의무는 없으나, 규약 가입정신을 살려
　　　　　자료수집 후 보낼 방침이라고 언급하였다는 것임

                                                        0142

2. 진 상

  ○ 본건은 9. 6경 연합통신 기자가 거론함에 따라 인권과장이
    답변한 바 있음.

  ○ 다만, 본건 진정서의 경우 우리가 보고서를 제출한 유엔 인권
    규약 (β규약)의 적용 대상이 아닐 뿐 아니라 질의서 발송
    기관도 "인권이사회"가 아닌 "인권위원회 고문문제특별보고관
    (1985 창설)"으로서, 동 보고관은 세계 각국의 고문문제에
    관한 진정서를 접수할 경우 사실상 협조의 차원에서 관례적
    으로 해당국에 의견을 질의하고 있음.
    우리나라의 경우도 상기 보고관의 협조 요청에 대해 1988년
    이후 매년 필요한 자료를 외무부를 통하여 보내준 바 있음.

3. 조치여부

  ○ 연합통신측과 상기 상위점을 재차 분명히 하였으며,
    그 외 별도 대처는 불요함

0143

UN,우리정부에 인권상황 질의서 보내와

사노맹등 17명 '가혹행위' 신상접수 따라

　　(서울=聯合) 우리나라가 유엔(UN) 인권규약에 가입한 지난해 7월 10일 이래 처음으로 유엔이 국내 인권문제에 대해 해명을 요구하는 질의서를 보내 그 처리결과가 주목되고 있다.

　　12일 법무부에 따르면 유엔 경제사회이사회 산하 「인권이사회」는 '사회주의노동자사동맹'(社勞盟)결성 사건과 관련, 국가보안법 위반 혐의로 구속기소돼 지난 9일 무기징역이 선고된 사노맹 중앙위원 朴노해씨(33.필명 박노해)등 모두 17명이 수사과정에서 삼안재우기.구타등 가혹행위를 당했다는 신상아 접수됐으니 이에대한 우리정부의 의견을 보내달라는 질의서를 지난 8월초 보내왔다.

　　유엔이 가혹행위 여부를 물어온 사람은 社勞盟 사건 관련자 7명외에 自民統 사건과 관련,구속기소된 崔元槇씨(26.외대 영어과졸.사민동 중앙위원).金配袜씨(24.경희대 경제학 4년)등 5명,일반 형사범 5명등 모두 17명이다.

　　유엔의 이번 인권관련 질의는 우리나라가 가입한 인권규약중 'B규약 선택의정서'에 따른 것이기는 하나 이들 사건에 대한 국내법 절차가 모두 마무리되지 않은 상태이기 때문에 우리정부가 반드시 의견서를 보내야할 규약상 의무는 없다.

　　법무부 관계자는 이와관련,'B규약 선택의정서'에 따른 진정서는 3審 재판등 모든 국내석 규제절차가 완료된 후 피해 당사자및 대리인만이 제기할 수 있도록 규정돼 있기 때문에 이번 질의에 우리가 반드시 답변해야할 필요는 없다"고 밝히고 "비록 이번 질의가 이에 해당되지는 않지만 일단 규약에 가입한 이상 성실히 시행할 수 십,오는 10월중에 답변을 보낼 방침"이라고 밝혔다.

　　이 관계자는 특히 'B규약 선택의정서'규정은 ▲악법이기나 ▲신청서 제출의 권리를 남용한 것 ▲해당문제가 다른 국제적 조사및 해결절차에 따라 검토되고 있는 사안에 대해서는 신청서 제출이 허용되지 않고 있다고 강조했다.

　　이에따라 법무부는 문의가 높아온 피의자들이 수감됐던 교도소,구시소내에서의 진료결과및 가혹행위와 관련한 재판자료등을 수집한 뒤 이를 취합해 다음달 중에 유엔에 제출키로 했다.

0144

한편 지난 79년이후 89년4월까지 인권이사회에 심수된 'B규약 선택의정서'에 의
한 신성서는 모두 3백52건이며, 인권이사회는 이중 94건에 대한 의견을 채택했었나,

인권이사회가 정부의 답변서및 냉사자의 의견서를 김토한 후 신청서에 관한 의
견(VIEW)을 재택하게되면 그 결과는 냉사자및 냉사북에 통보되는 것은 물론 경제사
회이사회를 거처 총회에 제출되는 「인권이사회 연자보고서」에 보함돼 해녕북기의
인신 위상에 대한 평가자료로 활용된나.(섭)

(YONHAP) 910912 0707 KST

0145

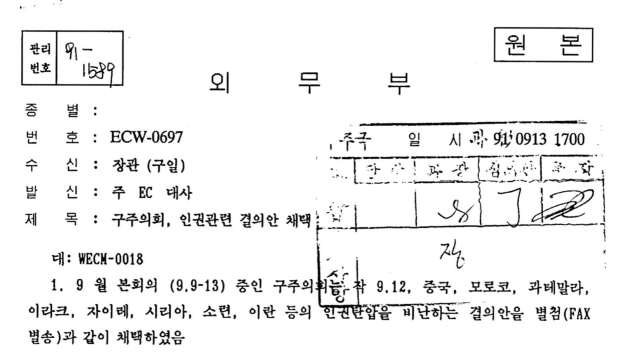

관리
번호 91-1589

원 본

외 무 부

종 별 :

번 호 : ECW-0697

수 신 : 장관 (구일)

발 신 : 주 EC 대사

제 목 : 구주의회, 인권관련 결의안 채택

주국 일 시 91 0913 1700

대: WECM-0018

1. 9월 본회의 (9.9-13) 중인 구주의회는 작 9.12, 중국, 모로코, 과테말라, 이라크, 자이레, 시리아, 소련, 이란 등의 인권탄압을 비난하는 결의안을 별첨(FAX 별송)과 같이 채택하였음

2. 대호관련 아국 인권문제 논의및 결의안은 없었음. 끝

(대사 권동만-국장)

예고: 91.12.31 일반

구주국	장관	차관	1차보	외정실	분석관	청와대	안기부

주 이 씨 대 표 부

종   번 :

번   호 : ECW(F)- 0047   임   시 : 0913 1700

수   신 : 장   관 (구미)

발   신 : 주이씨대사

제   목 : 구주의회 앤권앤건 결의안

(EU) HUMAN RIGHTS : THE EP CONDEMNS VIOLATIONS IN CHINA, MOROCCO, GUATEMALA, IRAQ, ZAIRE, SYRIA, EX-SOVIET UNION, IRAN

STRASBOURG, 12/09/1991 (AGENCE EUROPE) - On Thursday morning, the EP adopted a series of resolutions concerning human rights:

- China. With a resolution signed by the near totality of the groups, the EP calls on the Chinese Government to guarantee fair trials and humane conditions for political prisoners. The EP mentioned the cases of prisoners Wang and Chen, that the delegation for relations with China will raise on its visit to Beijing next week. During the debate, Mrs. Veil (Fr. Lib) invited her audience to fight to help those who still believe in the possibility of democracy in China. For the Commission, Mr. Schmidhuber said that the Dutch ambassador and the Commission's representative had recently done just that.

- Morocco. In a resolution signed by most groups, Parliament asked that Mrs. Serfaty should at least have the right to visit her husband.

- Guatemala. The EP adopted a resolution by the Socialist Group, the EPP and the Greens, who, concerned about a new murderous wave in the country, called on the Guatemalan Government to investigate the events. The paragraph calling on the Commission to suspend its aid, excluding humanitarian aid, was rejected. Mr. Schmidhuber considered that Guatemala needed aid.

- Iraq. The majority of the EP political groups subscribed to a resolution by which they deplored the situation of the situation of the refugees in the Gulf who are living in camps, demanding that the harassing operations by Iraqi helicopters to stopped and asking for an increase in aid for the population.

- Zaire. The majority of the EP political groups condemned the repression in Zaire, calling for the convening of a national conference on the participation of all opposition forces in political life.

- Syria. A resolution called on the EP delegation for relations with the Mashrek countries (to go to Syria this month) to raise with the authorities the case of Alois Brunner, Nazi criminal living in Damascus under the government's protection.

- Ex-Soviet Union. The EP adopted a resolution calling on the authorities to allow Olga Bondarenko, aged 16, to join her parents in The Netherlands.

- Iran. A resolution submitted by Mrs. Veil and Mr. Bertens for the Liberal group invites the French authorities to pursue the criminals who assassinated Chapour Bakhtiar, exile and opponent of the Iranian Government.

(총 / 매)

0147

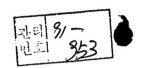

관리
번호 91-
853

분류기호 문서번호	구일 202- 2240	기 안 용 지		시 행 상 특별취급	
보존기간	영구·준영구 10. 5. 3. 1		장　　　　　관		
수 신 처 보존기간					
시행일자	1991. 9. 20.				

보 조 기 관	국 장	전결	협 조 기 관	
	심의관	署		
	과 장	署		
기안책임자		장시정		

경 유	
수 신	법무부장관
참 조	

발신명의

문서통제
검인
91.9.24
방
91. 9. 11
외무부

제 목　아국인권문제

　　　1. 9.16 주 EC대사 주최 만찬시, 91.3. 우리나라를 어∼ 방문

한바 있는 한·구주의회 의원 친선협회 소속 G.Adam 의원과 Randzio-

Plath 의원은 KNCC가 작성한 자료를 기초로 한국의 정치범이 91.5. 보안법

개정이후 오히려 증가하고 있음을 지적하면서 우리의 인권문제에 관심을

표명하여 왔습니다.

　　　2. 동 (KNCC) 자료에 의하면 양심수가 91.3.27 현재 1,149명에서

91.7.13. 현재 1,630명으로 증가되었다하는바, 이에 대한 대응 자료를

우리부로 송부하여 주시고 앞으로도 한·구주의회 친선협회 의원들의

한국내 인권문제에 대한 지속적 관심표명을 고려, 이에 효율적으로 대처

할 수 있도록 관련 자료를 수시로 우리부에 송부하여 주시기 바랍니다.

　　　　　　　　　　　　　　　　　　　　　　끝.

0148

인권문제관련 외무부 조치사항(91.7.1-9.25)

'91.9.25.
외 무 부

1. 우리의 인권신장노력 홍보

양 고 재	'91년 9월 26일	담 당 76명본	과 장	국 장

가 . 제43차 유엔 인권소위원회 참가활동

1) 회의일시 및 장소 : 91.8.5-30, 제네바

2) 아국대표단 구성 --- 박수길 주제네바 대사 및 대표부 직원 2인

3) 아국대표단 활동

○ 8.22. 의제 10항(법사행정) 토의시 반한 인권단체인 International
   League for the Rights and the Liberation of Peoples 대표의
   아국 인권상황 전반에 관한 왜곡발언에 대해 아국대표는 아래
   내용의 답변권을 행사, 강력히 대처함.

   - 상기 단체대표의 발언은 한국정부 및 한국의 민주화 발전
     이미지를 손상코자 하는 특정단체의 견해를 되풀이하면서
     허위와 왜곡으로 일관됨.

   - 동 대표가 제출한 정치범 리스트에는 7명의 경찰관을 살해한
     동의대 사건 관련자도 포함되어 있는등 폭력과 정치적 범죄를
     제대로 구분치 못하는 무지를 보임.

   - 동 대표가 한국의 인권상황에 관심이 있다면 직접 방한하여
     정확한 실상을 파악하기를 기대함.

   * 금번회의에서는 티벳트, 동티몰, 미얀마, 유고, 이라크, 터키,
     남아공, 이스라엘 점령지, 엘살바돌, 과테말라등 남미제국에서의
     인권위반문제와 토착민, 이주노동자 인권 문제등이 부각, 논의
     되었음.

0149

나. 시민적.정치적 권리에 관한 인권보고서 제출

  o 91.7.31. 시민적.정치적 권리에 관한 최초 인권보고서를 유엔
     인권국(제네바 소재)에 제출함으로써 우리나라의 인권보장을 위한
     사법적.행정적 제도를 포괄적으로 홍보함.

  o 시민적.정치적 권리에 관한 최초 인권보고서는 법무부, 내무부,
     노동부, 보건사회부등 11개 관련부처가 우리나라의 인권보장에
     관한 제반사항을 담당분야별로 작성(법무부 종합, 외무부 번역)한
     것임. 유엔 인권국에 제출한 영문 인권보고서에는 총 312개항,
     141페이지로 구성되어 전반부는 우리나라의 시민적.정치적 권리
     보장에 관한 일반적 법률체제를, 후반부는 시민적.정치적 권리에
     관한 국제규약(B규약)상의 각조항(27개 조항)의 권리를 보장하기
     위하여 우리나라에서 시행되고 있는 사법적.행정적 조치등이 기술
     되어 있음.

  * 우리나라는 90.7월 경제적.사회적 및 문화적 권리에 관한 국제규약
     (A규약), 시민적.정치적 권리에 관한 국제규약(B규약) 및 B규약
     선택의정서에 가입하였는 바, B규약 제40조에 따르면 B규약 가입국은
     가입후 1년이내에 시민적.정치적 권리에 관한 최초 인권보고서를
     제출하여야 하며, 최초 인권보고서 제출후 매 5년마다 정기적으로
     추가보고서를 제출토록 규정하고 있음.

다. 유엔 세계인권회의 준비회의

 1) 회의일시 및 장소 : 91.9.9-13, 제네바

 2) 회의목적 : 1993년 세계인권회의 개최 관련사항 협의

 3) 한국대표단 : 외무부 이동익 대사 및 주제네바 대표부 직원 2인

0150

4) 한국대표단 활동내용

가) 수석대표 발언요지

　　o 세계인권회의가 인권신장의 각별한 계기가 되기를 희망하고
　　　 우리의 협력 다짐

　　o 회의의 성과를 위하여 아래사항 제안

　　　- 각자 인권에 대한 사심없는 입장으로 돌아가 대립을
　　　　 지양하고 협조 정신으로 미래지향적인 토의 필요

　　　- 광범위한 참여와 협력확보를 위해 노력 경주 필요

　　　- 이념대립 완화에 따른 인권진전을 평가하고 이를 강화
　　　　 하는 노력에 유의 필요

　　　- 경제, 사회적 발전과 인권의 관계에도 적절한 배려 필요
　　　　 (한국의 사례 언급)

　　　- 인권에 대한 인식과 관심제고 노력 중요

　　　- 회의 개최지로 백림 지지

나) 각국 대표단 및 주요 인권단체 접촉활동

　　o 미국 인권담당대사 주최 리셉션등 참석을 통하여 각국 대표단
　　　 및 주요 인권단체에 대한 아국 인권신장노력 홍보활동 적극
　　　 전개

　　* 주한 미대사관 정무담당 서기관은 9.9. 외무부 유엔과에
　　　 상기 세계인권회의 준비회의 대책과 관련한 미측입장을
　　　 전달하고 우리의 협조를 요청하여 온 바 있음.
　　　 (동 미측 요청내용은 우리의 수석대표 연설문에 적절히 반영)

0151

라. 유엔 인권사무국에 접수된 우리나라 인권관련 진정서 대응활동

1) 우리나라 인권관련 진정서 접수(3건)
   ○ 사로맹사건 관련 가혹행위 주장(91.2월)
   ○ 임수경등 "정치법" 석방 및 국가보안법 철폐 요청(91.5월)
   ○ 홍성담 사건 관련 탄원(91.5월)

2) 대응활동
   ○ 외무부 본부 및 주제네바 대표부에서 상세한 답변자료를 작성하여
   유엔 인권사무국에 제출(91.5월 및 7월)하는 한편 유엔사무국
   인권담당관을 접촉하고 상기 3건의 진정서 내용의 허구성 적극
   설명

3) 진정서 처리결과
   ○ 91.8.2. 개최된 인권관련 진정서 실무소위 심의결과 우리나라
   인권관련 진정서는 모두 기각됨.

마. 국제사면위(A.I.) 대응활동

1) A.I. 91년도 연례보고서

가) 우리나라 인권관련 부분 : 별첨 1 참조

나) 평 가
   ○ 우리나라 관련부분의 일부가 수감자들의 주장 중심으로
   기술되어 있어 우리의 인권상황에 대한 균형잡힌 평가라고
   보기는 어려움.
   - 동 보고서는 90년도 상황만을 기술, 금년 국가보안법
   개정등 현상황을 반영한 것은 아님.

0152

ㅇ 특히 북한인과의 접촉, 북한을 이롭게하는 행위에 대한
   처벌사례들을 부각시킴으로써 국가보안법이 대북한 관계에
   있어 지나치게 엄격히 적용되고 있다는 인상 초래

ㅇ 그러나 90년중 우리나라의 세계인권규약 가입사실과
   양심수가 없다는 정부의 주장을 게재함으로써 어느정도
   우리당국의 입장을 기술한 것은 그동안 정부가 A.I측과
   긴밀한 협의를 지속한 성과로 평가됨.

   * 작년도에 비해 보고서 분량도 3페이지에서 2페이지로
     줄어듬.

다) 대응조치

   ㅇ 법무부와 협의, 동 보고서에 대한 정부입장을 정하여 이를
      주영대사관을 통해 A.I.측에 설명

   * A.I.는 국제민간기구로서 양심수 개개인의 석방을 주목표로
     하고 있는 바, 정부차원에서 민감하게 대응하는 것은 부적절

2) A.I. 회원들의 진정서 문제

   ㅇ A.I. 회원들이 '91년도 2/4분기중 우리정부에 보내온 석방탄원
      서한을 검토한 결과 주요 석방요구자 19명에 대한 설명자료(법무부
      작성)를 주영대사관에 송부, A.I.측에 동 석방탄원인들의 범법사실
      설명 및 무분별한 탄원서 발송 자제요청

바. 세계인권편람을 통한 우리나라 인권상황 홍보

   ㅇ 91.7. 영국의 유력주간지 Economist사에서 발간되는 세계인권편람
      (World Human Rights Guide)의 집필자(Mr. Charles Humana)는
      주영대사에게 우리나라의 인권상황에 대한 설명서 작성 의뢰

0153

o 세계인권편람 1985-86년도판의 우리나라 인권상황은 부정적인
측면도 반영되어 있음을 감안, 상기 설문서에 우리나라의 인권
신장노력과 민주적 인권보장제도가 충분히 반영되도록 작성후
91.9.7. 주영대사관측에 송부함.

* 세계인권편람 집필자인 Mr. Humana에 의하면 유엔개발계획(UNDP)의
인권지표가 동 세계인권편람에 기초하고 있다 함.

2. 국제사면위의 북한 인권문제 거론('91년도 A.I. 보고서 내용)

가. 보고서 요지 : 별첨 2 참조

나. 평 가

o 기초자료 부족으로 상세하지는 않으나 북한사회가 철저히 국가
통제하에 있다는 점을 부각함으로써 북한의 열악한 인권상황의
핵심 지적

- 동 보고서는 90년도 상황만을 기술, 금년 5월 A.I. 대표단의
방북(IPU 총회시) 결과등 최근상황은 게재되지 않음.

o 북한당국에 대한 A.I.의 협조요청 서한발송에도 불구하고 북한이
A.I.측에 계속 비협조적이라는 인상을 강하게 남김.

- A.I. 대표단의 90.10. 한국방문 활동과 대조

다. 외무부 조치사항

o 주요공관에 동 A.I. 보고서 내용 전파 및 각국 주요인사 및 주요
민간인권단체를 통한 북한 인권문제에 대한 관심 축구

o 향후 인권관련 주요 국제회의시 북한이 우리나라 인권상황 비방시
대응자료로 활용 예정

0154

국제사면위(A.I.) 91년도 연례 보고서중 아국관련 부분

(90.1.1-12.31.해당)

1. 개 요

- 약 150명의 양심수 또는 양심수 후보 상존

- 양심수 포함 30명이 사면으로 석방

- 국가보안법 위반 수감자 일부 학대행위 피해 주장

- 14명의 형사범 사형집행(89년보다 배증)

2. 내 용(요지)

- 국가보안법은 북한과의 접촉 및 반국가단체를 이롭게 하는 행위를
  계속 금지하고 있음.
  - 그러나 정부허가하에 북한방문, 북한인 초청 및 북한과의 교역,
    합작투자등 가능

- 시민.정치적 권리에 관한 국제인권규약 및 제1선택 의정서 가입(4월)
  및 경제.사회.문화적 권리에 관한 국제인권규약 가입(10월)

- 1,500명 이상이 정치적으로 기인된 행동과 관련 구금됨.
  - 이중 반이상이 불법 또는 폭력시위에 가담한 학생 및 노동자

- 국가보안법 위반 체포건수 증가
  - 89.9.-90.9간 758명 구속
  - 이중 250명이 북한동조 또는 간첩행위 관련

0155

o 25명 정도의 작가 및 출판인, 그리고 다수학생이 국가보안법 위반
　　혐의로 구속
　　- 대부분이 2년이하 집행유예로 석방
　　- 양심수인 시인 오봉옥 및 동국대 학생회장 김성규등 포함

o 현재 140명 이상이 간첩혐의로 복역중
　　- 1971년 이후 체포된 대부분은 북한방문 또는 북한요원 접촉 혐의
　　- 국가보안법에 의하면 북한에게 유용한 정보는 비록 자유롭게
　　　득할 수 있는 것이라도 국가기밀로 간주
　　- 간첩혐의로 체포된 많은 죄수들이 불공정한 재판을 받고, 또한
　　　재판전 구금상태에서 고문으로 자백을 강요당한 것으로 믿어짐.
　　- 박기래등 양심수도 "반공산주의"로의 전향의사를 서면으로 밝히기를
　　　거부하기 때문에 조기석방 대상에서 제외

o 허가받지않은 북한과의 접촉은 불법
　　- 양심수 홍성담 및 민자통.전민련 관계자들이 북한인과의 접촉 또는
　　　북한과 유사한 견해표명등으로 구속

o 반국가단체 조직 및 참여혐의로 90년 하반기에 약 200명 구속
　　- 혁노맹, 사노맹, 자민통, 전민학련등 지하혁명단체등과 연루

o 국가보안법 위반 30명이 2월 및 5월 대통령사면으로 석방
　　- 서승, 진두현, 최철교, 백옥광등 양심수 포함
　　- 양심수인 문익환 목사 10월에 건강상 이유로 석방

o 몇몇 수감자들은 구타, 잠안재우기등 가혹행위 피해주장
　　- 반국가단체 가담 협의자등
　　- 10월 "범죄에 대한 전쟁" 선포이후 체포된 형사범들
　　- 89.10-90.10간 고문관련 53건의 소송 접수
　　- 8월 서울구치소 사건관련 100명의 죄수들이 가혹행위 피해주장

0156

o 강력범 14명 사형집행

  - 2명 사형수는 감형(김현희 및 간첩 서순택)

o A.I.는 한국정부의 양심수석방 환영, 추가석방 요망

  - 간첩행위 수감자 관련 공정한 재판받았는지 재조사 희망

o A.I.는 국가보안법 개정, 고문방지, 사형제도 폐지 촉구

o 한국정부는 양심수 없음을 주장

  - 소위 "양심수"들은 국가존립 및 법질서를 위협하거나 자유민주체제를

  - 전복시키려는 과격분자들이라고 주장

  - 수감자에 대한 고문도 부인

o A.I. 대표단이 10월 방한, 법무부 관계자들과 인권상황 협의하였음.

0157

국제사면위(A.I.) 91년도 연례보고서중 북한관련 부분

(90.1.1-12.31. 해당)

1. 개 요

○ 양심수로 보이는 2명의 일본인 선원 석방

○ 수천명의 정치범이 있다고 하나 정보입수가 어려워 확인 불가

○ 모든 언론이 국가에 의해 통제상태

- 외국인이 접하는 뉴스에서는 정치적 구속, 재판등에 대해서는
  언급치 않음.

2. 내 용(요지)

○ 북한노동당, 일자민당, 일사회당간의 합의로 양심수로 보이는
  2명의 일본인 선원이 7년만에 석방됨. (10월)

- 그동안 북한당국은 이들이 정식 재판에서 15년간의 "노동을 통한
  개혁" 선고를 받았다고 말했으나, 석방된 일선원에 의하면 재판
  받은 적이 없다 함.

○ 수만명이 정치적 이유로 전국 각지에 있는 수용소에 감금되어 있다고
  하나 확인 불가함.

○ 89년말 동구에서 소환된 유학생들이 해외에서의 정부 비방혐의로
  구금되어 있다는 우려가 있으나 확인 불가

- 북한노동당이 최근 동구의 정치개혁에 대한 대응으로 사회주의
  사상교육을 강화하고 있다고 하며, 소식통들은 상기 유학생들이
  사상 "재교육" 과정에 들어가 있을 것으로 추측

0158

o A.I.는 2명 일본인 선원의 석방 환영

o A.I.는 구금자들 관련 북한당국으로부터 정보수집을 시도했으나
회신 미접수

- 북한당국과의 인권상황 협의를 위해 북한방문을 희망한다는
내용의 서한 발송 했으나 역시 회신 미접수

공   란

공 란

공　　　　란

공   란

공　　　란

공 란

공 란

공 란

공　　　　란

공 란

공　　　　　란

공   란

공   란

공   란

공 란

공   란

공 란

공   란

공 란

공 란

공　　　　란

공 란

공　　란

법 무 부 인 권 과

1991. . .

아래 문건을 수신자에게 전달하여 주시기 바랍니다.

제 목 :   정보보고

수 신 :   외무부 유엔2과

(수신처 FAX NO:)

발 신 :   법무부 인권과

표지포함 총 ___ 매

0183

배부처	법 무 부							대검	청와대	기 타 기 관						
	⊘	⊘	⊘	⊘	○	○	○	⊘○	⊘⊘	⊘	⊘	⊘	○	○	○	○
	장관	차관	법무실	검찰국				공안부장	정책조사보좌관(사정)	제안외	공법	기부보제				
				판	판	장	장			조부부처처			1행			

정 보 보 고

1. 제 목   2. 출 처

주한독일연방공화국 1등서기관 당부방문 결과   인 권 과

3. 내 용   (1991. 9. 27)

○ 주한독일연방공화국대사관 1등서기관 Viktor

   Elbling 이 9.25. 11:00, 당부를 방문하여

   인권과장과 아국의 인권상황 등 전반에 관하여

   면담하었는 바, 면담결과는 별첨과 같음

○ 첨부 :   면담결과 1부.

0184

주한독일연방공화국 대사관 1등서기관

(Viktor Elbling) 인권과장 면담내용

1991. 9.

인   권   과

0185

1. 개 요

o 일 시 : '91. 9. 25 (수), 11:00-14:00

o 장 소 : 인권과장실

o 면담자 : Viktor Elbling

(주한독일연방공화국대사관 1등서기관)

o 배석자 : 인권과 김 용 기 검사

          "   정 기 용 검사

1   0186

2. 대화요지

O 서기관

바쁜 업무 중에도 이와 같이 방문을 허락해 준 데 깊은 감사를
드린다.
특히, 한국의 인권문제를 전담하고 있는 귀 부서에 와서 인권
문제 전반에 관해 서로의 의견을 교환할 수 있게 된 것이
본인에게는 매우 귀중한 시간이 될 것 같다

O 과 장

방문을 환영한다. 이번 기회에 한국의 인권상황 등 관심있는
분야에 대해서 충분한 이해를 갖기 바란다

O 서기관

최근 귀하의 인권과에서 UN에 인권규약 최초보고서를 제출한
것으로 알고 있는 데, 이는 인권과에서 작성하여 UN에 직접
제출한 것인가

O 과 장

지난 7월에 UN에 제출한 인권규약 최초보고서는 시민적 및
정치적 권리에 관한 것으로, 광범위한 내용을 수록하고 있다.

2

0187

따라서, 내무, 노동, 보사부 등 관련부처들로부터 자료를 송부
받아 당부에서 이를 취합, 정리하여 외무부를 통해 UN에 제출한
것이다

o 서기관

지난 9.12. 연합통신발 기사내용에 따르면, 유엔 인권이사회는
사노맹 관련자 등 17명으로부터 수사과정에서 가혹행위를 당하
였다는 내용의 진정을 접수하였는 데, 이는 한국이 인권규약 가입후
최초로 접수된 것으로, 한국정부에 의견을 요청하는 질의서를
보냈다고 하는 데, 이와 관련해서 현재 인권과에서 준비하는게
있는가

o 과 장

귀하가 언급한 연합통신발 기사내용은 잘못된 것이다.
우선, 질의서 발송기관은 "인권이사회"가 아니고, "인권위원회
고문문제 특별보고관"으로, 보고관은 세계 각국의 고문문제에
관해서 진정서를 접수할 경우 사실상 협조의 차원에서 관례적
으로 해당국에 의견을 질의하고 있다.
따라서, 그와 같은 질의서는 비단 아국 뿐만이 아니라 독일을
포함하여 전세계 어느 나라에서도 접수하고 있는 것이다.
그리고, 진정서 내용도 아국이 보고서를 제출한 유엔 인권규약
(B규약)의 적용대상이 되지 않는 것이다.

0188

따라서, 위 기사내용은 인권규약 최초보고서 제출과는 전혀
관련이 없는 것이다.

그런데, 아국의 경우, 1988년부터 매년 보고관의 협조요청에
대하여 필요한 자료를 외무부를 봉해 보내주고 있다

O 서기관

잘 알겠다.
현재 한국의 전반적인 인권상황에 대한 귀하의 의견을 듣고 싶다

O 과 장

너무 광범위한 질문이어서 답변을 하기가 까다롭다.
근래 한국의 인권상황은 배우 향상되었다고 생각한다.
특히 지난 '88년 제6공화국 출범이후 정부는 헌법상의 기본권
조항을 대폭 강화하고 실제로 수사과정상 인권보장 등에 대해
강한 의지를 표명하는 등, 종래와 같이 인권시비가 재연되지
않도록 혼신의 노력을 기울여 왔다.
따라서, 현재 인권보장을 위한 각종 제도는 세계 어느 나라
에도 뒤지지 않을 정도의 수준에 도달해 있으므로, 제도상의
결함으로 인한 구조적인 인권유린은 존재하지 않는다.
물론, 어떤 공무원이 개인적으로 어느 조사대상자 또는 수형자
에 관하여 좋지 못한 감정을 가지고 고문이나 가혹행위를 가하
여 인권을 침해하는 경우는 충분히 있을 수 있다.

4

0189

이는 명백히 범죄행위이며, 그 공무원은 가중처벌된다.

그러나, 이러한 잘못은 그 공무원의 인격과 자질에서 비롯된 문제이지 정부의 정책이나 제도가 잘못되었기 때문은 아니다. 중요한 것은 고문이나 가혹행위 등 인권을 침해하는 공무원이 있을 경우, 이를 찾아내어 엄벌함으로써 정부의 확고한 고문 근절의지를 밝히는 것이다.

한국의 인권상황과 관련해서 한가지 첨언하고 싶은 점은, 소위 양심수, 정치범이라고 주장하는 자들은 한결같이 고문을 받았다고 주장하나, 본인이 알고 있는 한 그런 주장은 전혀 근거가 없는 것으로, 그들이 미리 준비하고 있는 고도의 전술 전략중 일환일 뿐이다.

나아가, 그들은 재판과정도 하나의 선전.선동장으로 간주하고 치밀한 계획하에 재판진행을 방해하고 있고, 또 국내외 인권 단체들까지도 동원하여 자신들의 거짓주장을 선전하고 있는 것이다.

귀하도 잘 아는 바와 같이 한국은 개방된 사회로 각 언론매체 들이 사회의 어두운 구석구석에서 활발하게 취재경쟁을 벌이고 있고, 재판절차 또한 엄격한 증거재판주의에 입각하여 모든 관련증거가 공개적으로 법정에 현출되고, 검증되고 있다. 이와 같은 상황에서 어떻게 정부차원의 고문이 이루어지거나 혹은 비호, 묵인이 가능하겠는가? 오히려 반문하고 싶다

5   0190

o 서기관

국가보안법에 대한 견해는 어떤가

o 과 장

국가보안법 문제에 관해 언급하기 위해서는 먼저 서구 각국은
한국의 분단상황에 관해 좀 더 깊은 이해를 가져야 할 필요가
있다고 본다.

단일혈통민족인 우리 민족이 1945년 해방후 외세에 의해 남북
으로 분단되면서 이데올로기적으로 대립하게 되고, 그 과정에서
북한이 도발한 6.25 전쟁으로 3년간 피비린내 나는 동족상잔
의 비극을 겪었다.

대다수 국민은 여전히 북한의 남침위협을 강하게 피부로 느끼고
있고, 이에 대항하기 위해 정부를 중심으로 일치단결하여 대처
해 나가야 할 필요성을 깊이 인식하고 있다.

이와 같은 대다수 국민의 지지하에 정부는 우리의 자유민주주의
체제를 수호할 목적으로 국가보안법을 제정, 시행하고 있는
것인데, 앞으로도 한국민의 북한남침위협에 대한 기본관념이
변하기 전까지는 국가보안법이 계속 유지되어야 한다고 생각한다

o 서기관

그러면, 국가보안법으로 말미암아 인간의 기본권인 표현 및
양심의 자유가 침해되는 것은 아닌가

6   0191

o 과 장

인간의 기본권이라 하더라도 자유라는 개념 자체에는 당연히
내재적인 한계가 포함되어 있는 것이다.

따라서, 단순한 의견개진이라는 외양을 가진다 하더라도
그 내용이 폭력혁명을 선동하고 현 자유민주주의체제의 전복을
옹호하는 것이라면, 이는 명백히 양심.표현의 자유에 내재된
본질적 한계를 일탈한 것이 된다.

이는 바로 AI에서 양심수를 개념정의하면서 "폭력을 사용하거나
또는 이를 옹호한 경우"에는 양심수에서 제외시킨 것에서도
볼 수 있는 바와 같다.

그러므로, 국가보안법 위반사범에 관한 재판은 공소제기된
범죄사실이 진정으로 양심의 자유 범주에 속하는 내용인지
혹은 실제적으로 폭력을 선동. 옹호하는 것인지 인정문제에
관해 심리가 집중되고, 또한 엄격한 증거자료의 제출이 요구
되고 있는 것이다.

따라서, 국가보안법으로 인하여 양심 및 표현의 자유가 침해
된다는 논리는 이론적으로 뿐만이 아니라, 실제적으로도 잘못
된 것이라고 본다

o 서기관

현재, 한국정부는 남한사람이 북한을 방문해서 그곳 사람들과
접촉하였다면, 국가보안법으로 처벌하고 있는 것이 아닌가

7   0192

o 과 장

현재 정부는 북한과의 접촉을 원하는 사람을 위하여 남북교류
협력법을 제정.시행하고 있는 데, 이 법상 허가를 받도록 되어
있다. 따라서, 사전에 허가를 받으면 처벌되지 않는다.
그리고, 허가없이 북한을 방문하여 그곳 인사와 접촉했다고
해서 그 자체만으로 국가보안법으로 처벌되는 것이 아니고,
위와 같은 행위가 북한을 이롭게 할 목적으로 의도적이고 불순
한 동기에 의하여 수행되었다는 것이 엄격한 증거자료에 의해
입증될 경우에 한해서 비로소 국가보안법 위반으로 처벌받게
되는 것이다

o 서기관

남북한이 분단되어 대치하고 있는 상황이 종전 동서독의 분단
현상과 여러면에서 비슷하다고 한국 외교관을 봄에 들은 적이
있다.
그렇다면, 남한이 북한보다 체제적으로 우월한 입장에서 각종
매스컴 즉 TV, 라디오 등을 상호 자유 시청토록 하고, 또한
남한사람이 자유롭게 북한사람과 접촉할 수 있도록 해야 한다고
생각하는 데, 귀하의 견해는 어떤가

o 과 장

한국정부는 북한에 이미 상호 뉴스의 교환 둥 각종 매스컴의
교류를 제안 한 바 있다.

그런데, 귀하가 믿을지 모르겠지만, 북한은 현재 TV, 라디오의
모든 채널을 고정시킨 채, 그들 선전선동과 세뇌공작의 도구
로만 활용하고 있다.

따라서, 북한은 남한의 매스컴 교류제의를 계속 거부하고 있다.

그리고, 한국을 독일과 같은 상황에 있는 나라로 평가해서는
안된다.

무엇보다도 독일은 서로 총을 맞대고 피를 흘리며, 동족상잔의
비참한 전쟁을 치른 경험이 없다.

동.서독의 분단도 서방세계와 동구의 커다란 이념적 대결구조
속에서 단지 그 지리적 위치가 그 경계선에 있다는 것일 뿐,
휴전선을 사이에 두고 북한과 대치하면서, 한국민이 피부로
느끼고 있는 급박한 위기감을 느끼지 못하고 있다고 본다.

정부는 우리의 자유민주주의체제를 수호하기 위해 정부를
유일한 대북한 접촉창구로 하는 국가정책을 수립. 시행하고
있는 것이다.

그러므로, 개인의 대북한 접촉허용범위 확대문제는 앞으로
남북한 주위여건의 변화에 따라 정부가 결정해야 될 정책
판단의 문제라고 본다.

현재, 정부는 남북한 주위의 국제관계 변화 및 남북한 직교류
가 활발해짐에 따라 남북교류에관한법률을 제정하는 등 조심
스럽게 접촉허용범위를 확대하고 있다

○ 서기관

잘 이해하겠다.

귀하가 앞서 언급한대로, 현재 남북한은 점차 그 교류의
범위를 확대하고 있고, 또한 이러한 변화에 발맞추기 위하여
지난 5월 국가보안법도 일부 개정한 것으로 알고 있다.
그런데 이와 같은 변화에도 불구하고, 국가보안법상 북한은
여전히 반국가 범죄집단으로 규정되어 있는 데, 이는 현실과는
모순되는 것이 아닌가

○ 과 장

보는 각도에 따라서는 모순이 된다는 주장도 가능하다고 본다.
집단 (Organization)이라는 용어속에는 실체를 인정하는 뜻이
내포되어 있는 것으로, 집단으로 인정받기 위하여는 조직의
우두머리와 간부 및 그 하부조직 등이 존재해야 하는 데,
순수한 법적 개념은 아니다.

그리고, 헌법은 한반도 영보내에 유일한 한개의 국가만을 인정
하고 있을 뿐이다.

앞으로, 한반도의 상황변화 복히 북한의 무력적화통일정책 포기
등 중대한 변화가 발생할 경우에는 국가보안법의 관련조항도
변경 여부가 논의될 수 있을 것이다.

o 서기관

동감이다.

분단의 기본이 되는 상황에 변화가 오게 되면, 이에 따른
법개정이 필요하다고 생각한다.

독일의 경우는, 과도기 과정에 우선 봉서독 기본조약을 체결
한 다음 양국에 연락사무소를 설치하였고, 계속해서 실질적인
접촉을 확대시켜 나가는 절차를 밟았다.

그러나, 그 당시에도 서독은 국가보안법을 갖고 있지 아니
하였다.

한국은 복일과 상황이 다므다고 보는가

o 과 장

가장 큰 차이점은 진정하고도 절박한 침략의 위협이 존재하고
있느냐는 것과, 이에 대항하기 위한 국민들의 공감대가 형성
되어 있는가 하는 점이다.

앞서 언급한 바와 같이, 북한의 남침야욕과 북한공산당의
잔인성을 6.25사변 등으로 몸소 체험한 한국민에게 있어서
무력적화통일정책을 고수하고 있는 북한정권의 존재야말로
절박한 생존권의 위협 그 자체이다.
따라서, 국가보안법과 관련해서 문제가 될 부분은, 그 존재
여부가 아니라, 오히려 일부 규정중 포괄적인 개념정의로
인하여 법 적용상 남용될 위험성에 관해서라고 본다.
그런데, 이와 같은 법적용상의 문제점에 관해서는 지난 5월
법개정으로 인하여 남용의 소지가 사라졌다고 본다.

O 서기관

절박한 위기감에 대한 귀하의 설명에 진정으로 동감하고,
특히 한국이 처한 특수한 상황에 대해서 깊이 이해하게
되었다.
방향을 바꾸어서, 지난 5월 KNCC가 발표한 시국사범의 구속
통계 숫자에 대하여 어떻게 생각하는가

O 과 장

KNCC를 포함한 소위 재야인권단체들은 각자 필요에 따라서
자기들 나름대로의 기준에 따라 일방적으로 각종 통계를 작성
해 발표하고 있다.

12   0197

귀하가 언급한 KNCC의 지난 5.24자 시국사범 구속자 현황도
그 중의 하나로, 그 명단중 표본으로 100명을 선정하여 현재
구속여부를 확인하였는 데, 작성일인 5.24 현재 구속자 수는
명단인원의 절반에도 못 미치는 40명에 불과하였고, 37명은
이미 석방된 사람들이었으며, 6명은 이중으로 중복등재 되어
있었고, 17명은 인적사항 자체가 불확실하여 구속여부조차도
확인되지 아니한 실정이었다.
그리고 명단 전체로 보면, 동일인이 명백한 사람들을 이중으로
등재한 것이 57군데에서 발견되었고, 시국사범 명단중에는
공갈기자, 상해치사사건 관련자 등도 포함되어 있었다.
이와 같이 임의적이고 공신력이 전혀 결여된 일개단체의 통계
에 관해 언급한다는 것 자체가 우스운 일이다

O 서기관

그와 같은 내용에 관해서는 미처 몰랐다.
AI는 한국내 양심수로 분류된 200명의 명단을 발표하였는 데
이에 대한 의견은 어떠한가

O 과 장

우선, AI가 소위 양심수라고 분류한 구속자 수는 발표할
때마다 30여명에서부터 200여명까지 달라지는 데, 이는
AI가 한국의 재야인권단체를 통하여 그들이 임의로 만들어

13

0198

낸 왜곡된 해외홍보용 자료를 아무런 검증절차도 밟지 않고
그대로 수용한 결과라고 할 것이다.

그리고, 양심수로 분류하는 과정을 살펴보면, AI는 각 구속자
에 관련된 사건기록 전체와 이를 뒷받침하는 각종 증거자료에
대한 충분한 검토를 결여한 채, 국내 반체제세력 집단들이나
재야인권단체들의 일방적인 주장과 왜곡된 정보를 그대로 수용
하고, 결론부분만을 근거로 하는 잘못을 저지르고 있다.

따라서, AI보고서에 언급된 사람들 중 일부는 폭력을 사용한
간첩행위를 하면서 폭력을 옹호한 자들이 포함되어 있는 데,
이들은 AI의 양심수 개념정의에 따르더라도 명백히 양심수라
할 수 없는 자들이라 할 것이다.

또한, AI의 양심수에 대한 개념정의 자체도 불명확하여
"폭력을 옹호한 경우"와 "양심"의 개념을 설정하는 데
각 나라마다 많은 차이가 발생하는 문제점이 있다는 것을
지적해 두고 싶다

○ 서기관

AI의 양심수 개념정의 자체에 많은 문제점이 있다는 귀하의
의견에 전적으로 동감한다.
입음은 어떤 종류의 폭력을 옹호하느냐와 그로 인해 어떤
위험이 발생되느냐가 기준이 될 수 있다고 보는 데, 귀하의
견해는

14   0199

o 과 장

좋은 의견이다. "명백하고 현존하는 위험이론"이 많은 경계
선상에 있는 문제들에 대해 기준이 될 수 있다고 본다.

이 때 현존하는 위험에 대한 판단은 그 문제들 주위의 특수
상황을 반드시 고려해서 해야 하며, 한국의 경우는 남북분단
대치상황과 적화무력통일정책을 고수하고 있는 북한정권의
남침위험 가능성이 반드시 평가 참작되어야 한다고 본다.

이는 또한 국가권력 행사의 한계문제와도 직결되는 것으로서
같은 맥락에서 이해되어야 할 것이다.

현재 한국정부는 폭력혁명을 전제로 한 공산주의를 불용하는
정책을 취하고, 이에 저촉되는 행위를 국가보안법으로 처벌
하고 있다.

이와 같은 경계선상의 문제들과 관련해서, 본인의 경험을
말하자면, 약 20년전 대학시절 본인도 반정부 집회나 시위에
가담한 경험이 있는 데, 당시는 돌을 사용하였고, 시위동기나
양상도 오늘날 좌익폭력세력들이 조직적으로 선동하는 체제
전복시위와는 전혀 다른 것이었다.

오늘날 좌익폭력혁명세력들은 현 체제를 부정하고, 사회주의
국가 건설을 공공연히 표방하면서, 학원가는 물론 노동계,
출판계 각 분야에 침부하여 화염병과 사제폭탄으로 무장하고
공공기관을 습격함으로써 그 폭력성이나 위험성이 극에 달하고
있다 할 것이다.

15

이는 명백히 AI의 양심수의 개념이나 귀하가 언급한 위험의
한계를 벗어난 것이다

O 서기관

최근 사노맹의 박노해(박기평) 피고인에 대해 검찰로부터 사형
이 구형되고 법원에서 무기징역을 선고한 것으로 알고 있다.
그런데, 독일의 경우, 수백명의 인명을 살상한 극소수의 극렬
테러리스트에게만 무기징역형이 선고되는 것과 비교해 볼 때,
박노해의 경우 상당히 중형이 선고된 것처럼 보이는 데, 귀하의
견해는

O 과 장

법원의 판결에 대해 공적으로 평가할 위치에 있지 않은 점을
이해하기 바란다. 굳이 본인의 개인적 느낌을 이야기 한다면
합당한 형이 선고되었다고 본다.
이 사건의 실상을 파악하기 위해서는 무엇보다도 우선
박노해가 중앙위원으로 활동하는 사노맹이라는 조직의 목적
및 활동내용과 박노해의 구체적인 관련행위에 관해 명백한
이해가 있어야 할 것이다.
수십장에 달하는 공소장의 범죄기재내용만 살펴 보더라도,
결국 사노맹이나 박노해의 최종목적은 무장폭력혁명을 통한
현 자유민주체제의 전복과 노동자사회주의건설에 있다 할
것이다.

그리고, 박노해는 위 조직의 수괴급으로서 위 폭력혁명의
이론적 근거를 제시하고, 혁명선봉을 목적으로 각종 유인물,
책자를 저술·배포하였으며, 각종 학생 노사분규 및 불법집회
등을 배후 조종하여 파출소방화 등을 일삼은 자이다.
따라서, 박노해는 4,000여만명 남한사람의 생존권을 박탈
하려는 살인마집단의 두목이라 할 것이다.
이를 북한의 남파간첩사건과 비교해 볼 때, 남파간첩보다
죄질이 훨씬 더 중하다고 할 것인데, 남파간첩의 경우 주로
무기징역형이 선고되어 왔으므로 사노맹의 수괴인 박노해에
대해 무기징역을 선고한 것은 개인적으로 볼 때 국민의 법감정
에 괴리가 없다고 느낀다.

o 서기관

독일의 경우, 공산당의 활동이 가능한데, 한국은 어떤가

o 과 장

이론적으로 마르크스-레닌주의 자체만을 연구대상으로 삼는
경우, 순수학문적 연구는 가능하다.
그러나, 공산주의 속성상 폭력수단의 동원이 필수불가결한
것이므로, 한국내에서는 공산당의 활동이 전면 금지되어 있다

17   0202

o 서기관

사형제도에 대한 견해는 어떠한가.

그리고 이를 폐지해야 한다는 입장에 대한 견해는

o 과 장

사형제도의 존폐문제는 한국내의 가장 치열한 논쟁거리중의
하나이다.

그런데, 최근 사형선고는 가정파괴사범 등에 대해서만 지극히
일부 선고되고, 전체적으로 줄어 들고 있다.

입법적으로도 1990.12.31 특정범죄가중처벌등에관한법률과
특정경제범죄가중처벌등에관한법률 등을 개정하여 15개 조문
에서 사형을 폐지하였다.

그리고 사형제도의 존폐문제에 대한 본인의 의견은, 평온한
가정에 5,6명이 떼를 지어 야간에 침입하여 강도한 후 남편
이나 가족이 보는 앞에서 부녀자를 윤간하는 소위 가정파괴
사범 등 인륜을 저버리는 흉악범죄가 빈발하는 우리 현실 및
법감정에 비추어 사형폐지는 시기상조라고 본다.

18   0203

최근 한 여론조사 결과도 대다수의 국민은 사형제도의 필요성
에 공감하고 있고, 오히려 일부 범죄자에 대하여는 공개처형
까지도 필요하다는 의견이었다.

다만, 인간의 존엄과 가치의 보장 헌법정신 등을 고려해 사형
선고에 신중을 기할 필요가 있다고 본다

O 서기관

법원이 재판의 독립성을 보장받고 있는가

O 과 장

물론이다.

헌법은 법관의 신분을 명백히 보장하고 있고, 6공화국에 들어
와 법관 임명절차를 개선하여 법관인사에 대한 민주성과 정치
적 중립성을 제도적으로 한층 강화하였다.

재판진행을 방청해 보면 알겠지만, 모든 구속영장 발부에서
부터 시작하여 보석결정, 재판진행 및 판결선고까지 판사는
오직 법률과 양심에 따라 거의 전권을 행사하고 있다.

또한 사법부 스스로가 그 어느때보다 사법권 독립결의를 확고
히 다지고 있고, 이로 인해 대다수 국민들의 사법부에 대한
신뢰도 아주 높아졌다

0204

ㅇ 서기관

한국 법원의 판결에 관한 통계에 따르면, 기소한 사건의 90%
이상이 유죄로 선고된다고 알고 있는 데, 독일의 경우 50%
이상이 법원에 의해 증거불충분 등의 이유로 기각되거나 무죄
선고를 받고 있다.
한국 법원의 유죄선고율이 너무 높은 것이 아닌가

ㅇ 과 장.

매우 흥미있는 질문이다.
우리나라 검사는 사건의 기소여부결정에 전적으로 자유재량권
을 가지고 이를 행사하고 있는 데, 평균 배당사건중 약 10%
정도만을 법원에 정식 기소하고 나머지 약 90%는 약식기소
하거나 불기소 결정으로 처리를 한다.
그리고, 학생이나 미성년자 관련사건에서 초범이고 뉘우치는
빛이 뚜렷하여 개전의 가능성이 있다고 판단되는 경우에는
유죄증거가 충분함에도 기소유예결정으로 용서해 주고 있다.
사건처리과정을 보면, 각 검사들이 철저한 책임의식을 가지고
유죄증거자료에 대한 수사를 완료한 후 유죄의 확신을 갖게
되면 비로소 기소를 하게 되는 데, 이때에도 상급의 검사들로
부터 다시 증거자료 등에 대한 검토를 받게 된다.
따라서, 사건처리에 매우 신중하고 엄격한 절차를 거치게
되므로 90% 이상의 유죄선고를 받을 수 있다고 본다.

0205

20

이는 일본의 경우도 우리와 거의 비슷한 실정이다.

이에 비해 독일의 경우는 법원의 판단을 받아 봄 만하다고
생각될 때, 한국과 같이 엄격한 수사 및 증거수집절차를
거치지 아니한 채 기소하는 것으로 알고 있다.

이는 오히려 우리 시각에서 볼 때, 좀 무책임한 업무수행이
아닌가 하는 느낌이 든다

ㅇ 서기관

귀국 검사의 업무처리에 관해 잘 이해하겠다.

독일의 경우, 유죄증거가 확보되면 반드시 기소하게 되어
있는 데, 귀국에서는 소년범 등에 대해서 기소유예결정을
한다는 것이 매우 흥미롭다.

그리고 배당사건의 약 10% 정도만이 정식 기소되는 사실에
대해서는 처음 알았다.

다시 한번, 귀하의 성의있고 진지한 설명에 감사드린다.

앞으로도 계속 접촉하면서 상호 관련자료를 교류하고,
관심사에 대해 논의를 했으면 하는 바램이다

ㅇ 과 장

이런 면담을 해 오면서 느끼는 점은, 한국내의 인권상황에
관하여 많은 외국인들이 국내의 급진좌익, 반체제세력집단
들이 자의적으로 왜곡하여 해외홍보용으로 유포한 정보를

마치 진심인 것처럼 믿고 상당한 오해를 하고 있다는 것인데
오늘 대화가 상호간에 진정한 이해를 증진시키는데 도움이
되었으면 한다.
그리고 귀국에서 인권문제와 관련해서 발간하는 레포트
놈이 있으면 본인에게도 보내 주었으면 한다.

O 서기관

잘 알았다.
독일 정부에서는 두종류의 인권관련 보고서를 발간하는 데
간행즉시 귀하에게 송부해 주겠다.
오늘 바쁜 업무시간중에 면담시간을 할애하여 준 것에
다시금 감사를 드린다.

분류기호 문서번호	구일 202- 37324	기 안 용 지	시 행 상 특별취급	
보존기간	영구.준영구 10. 5. 3. 1	장 관		
수 신 처 보존기간				
시 행 일 자	1991. 10. 11.			

보조 기관	국 장	전 결	협조기관		문 서 통 제
	심의관				접얼 1991. 10 12 통세고.
	과 장				
기안책임자		장 시 정			발 송 인
경 유			발 신 명 의		발 송 1991. 10 12 외무
수 신		주 EC 대사			
참 조					
제 목		인권문제 관련 자료 송부등			

　

　

대 : ECW-0712(91.9.17)

대호, 인권문제 관련 법무부 자료를 별첨 송부하니 향후

관련 사안 대처에 활용바랍니다.

　

첨부 : 법무부 송부 인권문제 관련 자료

0208

KNCC 의 자료에 대한 입장

o 전국 검찰청의 사건통계는 죄명, 성별(여성), 검찰청, 검찰처분
  내용, 국적(외국인) 등과 같이 전국 검찰청의 모든 통계담당자가
  이해할 수 있는 객관적 분류에 따라 천산집계되고 있는 것임

o KNCC의 죄명별 통계는 1991.7.13 현채 구속되어 있다고
  하는 (구속시점이 언제전 관계없이) 정치범 1,630명을 죄명별로
  분류한 것으로 알고 있음.
  그러나 이 통계는 1,630명이 누구인지 또한 어떠한 기준에 의해
  분류하였는지를 밝히고 있지 아니함.
  KNCC는 정치범을 추출한 것 이라고 할지 모르나, 그것은 KNCC의
  자의적인 추출일 뿐이며 명단을 공개하지 않는 한 정부로서는
  그 당부를 판단할 수 없는 것임

o 그리고 위 정치범 분류자중 폭력행위 가담자, 계획자 등에 대한
  통계도 위 정치점의 명단을 제공해 주지 않는 한 확인할 수가
  없는 것임

0209

Highlights of Amendments to the National Security Law

As Passed by the National Assembly on May 10, 1991

0210

The amendments are designed to eliminate overly stringent aspects of the past National Security Law and to ensure that it provides for only minimal restrictions needed to defend freedom and democracy against external and internal subversion and sabotage. To that end, 14 of the 25 articles of the law have been rewritten to abolish 20 punitive clauses, which pertain, among other things, to meeting or communicating with or contacting foreign Communists or Communist organizations, misprision of clandestine travel to or from the territory controlled by an antistate organization and various forms of preparations and conspiracies to undermine national security.

A new paragraph (Paragraph 2, Article 1) has been created. It provides that in interpreting and implementing the National Security Law, only minimum necessary legal steps shall be taken to achieve its intrinsic purposes of preserving national security and survival and protecting freedom of the people and that there shall be no extended interpretation of the law. This provision is intended to prevent any abuse of the law, and thus end past controversies over its enforcement.

1

0211

Special care has been taken to make sure that human rights abuses will not be perpetrated under the law. In particular the amended statute much more narrowly defines an "antistate organization" as a group equipped with a "command and control system" so that there will be no room for arbitrary applications of the "antistate organization" clause.

In the past, the law prescribed unconditional punishment for the giving or receiving of money or goods to or from an antistate organization or its member (Para. 2, Article 5) ; clandestine travel to or from the territory controlled by an antistate organization (Article 6) ; the praising, encouraging or siding with an antistate organization or its members (Article 7) ; and meeting or communicating with or contacting a member of an antistate organization (Article 8). The just-revised National Security Law, however, punishes such acts only when they are committed "with the knowledge that this will imperil national survival and security or the basic free and democratic order." This revision is in keeping with the April 2, 1990 ruling of the Constitution Court that the National Security Law is "constitutional with certain reservations." The narrowing of the scope of punishment will end human rights controversies in connection with the enforcement of the law.

0212

2

Furthermore, the just-passed amendments have deleted the vague phrase, "otherwise gives aid and comfort to an antistate organization" from Article 7, which is intended to punish anyone who "praises, encourages and sides with" an enemy. This has eliminated a lattitude for arbitrary enforcement of that article.

The revised National Security Law is aimed at actively promoting and guaranteeing peaceful inter-Korean exchanges with a view to advancing the goal of national reconciliation leading to unification. This is the revised statute punishes such acts as the giving or receiving of money or goods to or from an antistate organization or its member, clandestine travel to or from the territory controlled by an antistate organization, the praising, encouraging or siding with an antistate organization or its member only when such acts endanger national security and survival. In that way, all legal obstacles to genuine peaceful inter-Korean exchanges have been eliminated.

In addition, the revised law exempts from punishment the above-mentioned acts in regard to foreign Communist organizations and their members with the aim of providing

0213

3

institutional guarantees for active exchanges and cooperation
with all former or present Communist countries, except North
Korea, in the political, economic, social and all other fields.

The amended National Security Law has other revised
provisions also designed to reflect the people's desire for
full democratization to the maximum possible extent with a
view to helping build a truly free and democratic nation
advancing into the 21st century.

In the provisions against espionage (Items 2 and 3,
Para. 1, Article 4), the revised law much more narrowly and
clearly defines "state secrets" as "knowledge access to which
is limited to authorized persons only in order to prevent
serious disadvantages to national security" that will stem
from its leakage or disclosure and other specific types of
information. This will promote freedom of information to
the maximum extent.

Whereas Article 14 of the old National Security Law
provided that anyone sentenced to imprisonment for a definite
term for treason should mandatorily be subjected to post-
imprisonment suspension of civil rights, the amended version

0214

4

provides that such suspension of rights may be waived in consideration of extenuating circumstances. This change aims to more effectively protect the civil rights of citizens.

Article 10, which punishes misprision, has been amended to limit its application only to failures to report acts (including espionage) committed to serve the purposes of an antistate organization by its member or any other person following its instructions. To elaborate, the amended version of Article 10 does not punish failures to report the giving or receiving of money or goods, clandestine travel, praising, encouraging or siding with the enemy, and meeting or communicating with the enemy, as defined earlier. In other words, misprision is now punishable only when unreported acts imperil national survival. The scope of misprision has thus been minimized.

Furthermore, the revised version requires a lightening or waiver of punishment for misprision when such an offense is committed by a relative of the person found guilty of treason. The old law provided that such leniency might be granted at the discretion of the judge. This revision is designed to protect freedom of conscience and thought to the maximum extent.

5

0215

It should be noted that the governing Democratic Liberal Party accepted most of the demands raised by the opposition in the course of negotiations with it over amendments to the National Security Law. The DLP thus revised its draft bill to extensively reflect the spirit of the ruling by the Constitution Court regarding the constitutionality of the old law.

In particular, unauthorized travel to or from enemy territory has been excluded from the list of offenses to which misprision is applicable. Furthermore, the DLP withdrew a proposed clause for permitting an additional extension of the pretrial detention of suspects charged with grave violations of the National Security Law.

In sum, the just-passed amendments represent the maximum relaxation of the law permissible under the prevailing security situation of the nation.

보 도 자 료
(KNCC 자료)

1991. 7. 15.

한국기독교교회협의회 인권위원회는 7월 15일 인권위원회를 개최하여 현 우리사회는 사상 최악(7월 13일 현재 시국관련구속자는 사상 최대수치인 1,630명 -- 구속자 자료 참조)의 인권상황에 직면하고 있음에 인식을 같이하였다. 이는 현정권이 광역선거이후 민자의승을 바탕으로 민주세력들및 학생,노동자들에 대한 대대적인 연행,구속,수배 등을 통하여 정치적 반대자를 무력화하여 집권말기의 통치권을 공고히함으로써 장기집권의 빌만을 굳히려는 것으로 판단된다.

현정권이 민주화운동,통일운동,인권운동의 탄압수단으로 국가보안법,집시법,노동법 등 제반 법률등을 이용하고 있는 상황에서 본회는 7.17제헌절을 기해 7월 14-21일까지를 악법철폐기도주간으로 설정하고 한국교회와 성도가 우리사회의 모든 반민주,반통일 악법철폐와 그로 인한 양심수들의 진정석방을 위해 합심하여 기도할 것을 같이하였다. 제헌절을 기한 악법철폐기도주간은 올해로 2회째를 맞이하고 있으며 7월 14일, 서울을 시작으로 부산,대구,대전,광주등 전국 10여개 지역에서 연합예배도 개최된다.

‡‡ 첨부자료 : 1991년 7월13일 현재 구속자 통계분석

한국기독교교회협의회
인 권 위 원 회
위 원 장 박 광 재

0217

87년 6.29선언 이후 연도별 특정 시점 구속자현황

87.8.12.	88.11.30.	89.6.30.	89.11.30.	90.5.30.	90.11.30.	91.3.27.	91.7.13.
760명	534명	849명	1055명	1159명	1217명	1149명	1630명

시국관련구속자의 수치와 인권상황은 항상 반비례하여 왔음을 상기될 때 현우리가치의 인권상황은 6공화국 이후 사상최악임.

1991.7.13일 현재 구속자현황 분석

** 총구속자수 — 1,630명

적용법률별 구속자현황(91.7.13.)

국가보안법	화염병등	집시법	특수공무집행방해	업무방해	노동쟁의조정법
580명-35.5%	258명-15.8%	245명-15%	166명-10.1%	137명-8.4%	113명-6.9%

직업별구속자 현황(91.7.13.)

학 생 - 833명(51%)	노동자 - 397명(24%)	장기수 - 97명(6%)	재 야 - 85명(5%)
군 경 - 39명(2.3%)	출판문화 - 33명(2%)	농 민 - 23명(1.4%)	성직자 - 6명

위의 통계를 통해 알 수 있듯이 화염병처벌에 관한 법률등과 집시법으로 구속된 사람의 수가 국보법 다음을 차지하고 있는 것은 국민의 기본권인 집회,시위등의 자유가 극심하게 차단되고 있음을 반증하는 것임. 노동쟁의조정법에 의한 구속자보다 업무방해로 인한 구속자가 많은 것은 현정권이 일방적으로 기업주측의 권익을 보호하고 있음을 시사한다.

국보법관련 구속자의 수가 지난 3월 27일(44.2%였음)보다 약 9%정도 줄어든 것은 지난 6월 석탄임 기석방의 영향으로 풀이된다. 그러나 지난 4월 국회서 날치기 통과된 국가보안법은 그 내용에 있어서나 적용에 있어서 기존의 국보법과 별다른 차이를 가지고 있지 않다는 점, 즉 사상의 자유, 결사의 자유, 학문의 자유, 표현의 자유등 국민기본권을 극심하게 제한하고 민주화,통일운동을 탄압하는 독소조항등은 그대로 유지되고 있다는 점이 아래의 통계로 확연히 증명된다. 또한 아래의 통계는 4월 임시국회의 국보법이 개정되었던 4월과 그 다음달인 5월에는 국보법구속자가 현저히 줄어들었지만 다시금 6월부터는 국보법관련구속자는 폭증하게 된다는 점을 보여준다. 이것은 현정권이 국보법을 통하여 국민 개개인의 인권을 유린하며 민주화운동을 탄압하고 통일논의가 민간차원으로 확산되는 것을 극심하게 차단함으로써 궁극적으로 정권유지의 수단으로 악용하고 있음을 증명한다.

91년도 2-7월 국보법관련 구속자 통계분석

	2월	3월	4월	5월	6월	7.13일
총 구속자수	51명	132명	75명	100명	150명	37명
국보법구속자	14(27%)	59(44.6%)	17(22.6%)	10(10%)	36(24%)	19(51.3%)

0218

KWANGHWAMOON P O BOX 134   RM 307 CHRISTIAN BLDG 136-46   YUNCHI-DONG, CHONGRO-KU SEOUL 110-701
TEL:784-0283, 744-3717   TELEX K 28840, KORENCC   CABLE:KOCOUNCIL   FAX:744-8119

HUMAN RIGHTS COMMITTEE
NATIONAL COUNCIL OF CHURCHES
IN KOREA

The Human Rights Committee of the National Council of Churches in Korea at its meeting on July 15, recognized that we are facing the worst human rights situation in history : as of July 13, 1991, there are 1,630 political prisoners, the largest number ever. In particular, there were mass arrests of students, workers and opposition persons following the ruling party's big victory in the local elections. This is designed to strengthen the power of the ruling group and solidifying the foundation for its endless grasp of power to make the opposition group impotent, thereby.

Situation of Prisoners of Conscience since June 29 Declaration in 1987

Date	87.8.12	88.11.30	89.6.30	89.11.30	90.5.30	90.11.30	91.3.27	91.7.13
No.	760	534	849	1055	1159	1217	1149	1630

The above statistics show that the present human rights situation in Korea is at its worst since the beginning of the 6th Republic entered.

By Law Applied   (as of July 13, 1991)

National Security Law	Anti-Firebomb Law	Law on Assembly & Demonstration	Obstruction of Police Duty	Interruption of Work	Law on Labor Dispute Mediation
580 (35.5%)	258 (15.8%)	245 (15%)	166 (10.1%)	137 (8.4%)	113 (6.9%)

0219

By Occupation   (as of July 13, 1991)

students	workers	long-term prisoners	opposition persons
833 (51%)	397(242%)	97(6%)	85(5%)
soldigers &. riot police	publishing & cultural movement persons	farmers	clergy
39(2.3%)	33(2%)	23(1.4%)	6

TOTAL 1,513

According to the figures, those imprisoned under the Anti-Firebomb Law and Law on Assembly and Demonstration are the second largest in number next to those jailed under the National Security Law. This proves that the basic rights of the people, such as the freedom of assembly and demonstration are interfered with severely by the government. There are even more prisoners convicted for interruption of work than there are sentenced under the Law on Labor Dispute Mediation, indicating that the government supports the profit of company owners. As of July 13, 1991, prisoners under the National Security Law were fewer than on March 27, due to many releases on parole on Buddha's birthday. But through the statistics below, we can realize that there is no significant difference between the former National Security Law and the revised one rushed through the National Assembly in April—despite the popular demand for its total abolition.

The figure below also reflects retriction of the basic rights of the people, such as freedom of ideology, freedom of association, freedom of study and freedom of expression, under the National Security Law, which still contains some articles interfering with and oppressing democratization and the reunification movement. In May, immediately after the National Security Law was revised in April, there is a remarkable decrease of arrests under the National Security Law, but from June the number of the National Security Law prisoners again jumps up.

The statistics reveal the 6th Republic's immoral trampling of the rights of personal liberty, its suppression of the democratization movement of opposition groups, and its blocking of the spread of the reunification movement, through the use of the National Security Law. It also exposes the ruling party's plot to prolong its power.

0220

Prisoners under the NSL from February to July, 1991

	February	March	April	May	June	July
total	51	132	75	100	150	37
National Security Law	14(27%)	59(44.6%)	17(22.6%)	10(10%)	36(24%)	19(51.3%)

0221

주 E C 대 표 부

이씨정 20524- 507   1991.10.17.

수신 : 장 관

참조 : 구주국장

제목 : 구주의회 인권 결의안

        연 : 이씨정 20524-457(90.12.20)

    1. 구주의회 사무총장 Enrico Vinci는 별첨 본직앞 서한을 통하여
구주의회가 지난 9.12. 채택한 89년도 및 90년도 세계인권에 관한 결의안을
송부하여 왔습니다.

    2. 동 결의안 내용중에는 90.12월 구주의회가 채택한 연호 한국관련
인권결의안에 비하면 상당히 완화된 것이지만 권위주의 국가정부로 아국이
포함되어 있는 바, 본직은 91.11월 중순 구주의회를 방문하여, 구주의회
지도자들과 광범위하게 접촉, 아국의 인권개선 현황을 적극 홍보할 계획
입니다.

    3. 한편, 동 결의안에는 북한을 폐쇄사회로 규정하고 있음을 첨언
합니다.

    첨부 : 상기 서한 및 결의안 사본.   끝.

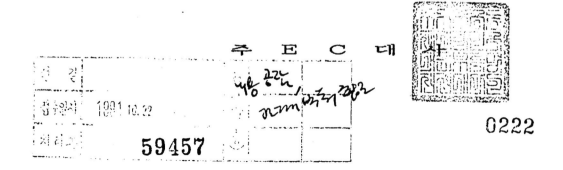

주 E C 대

0222

59457

Strasbourg, le

25.IX.91   26524

S.E. Monsieur Tong Man KWUN
Ambassadeur
Chef de la mission de la
République de Corée auprès des
Communautés européennes
249, Avenue de Tervuren
1150 BRUXELLES

Excellence,

Le Parlement européen a adopté, sur la base d'un rapport de sa commission politique,

une résolution sur les droits de l'homme dans le monde en 1989 et 1990 et la politique de la Communauté en matière de droits de l'homme,

et a décidé d'en transmettre le texte aux gouvernements de tous les pays mentionnés dans la présente résolution.

J'ai l'honneur de vous adresser en annexe, au nom du Président du Parlement européen, un extrait du procès-verbal de la séance en question contenant la résolution du Parlement et vous serais très reconnaissant de bien vouloir transmettre ce document au gouvernement de votre pays.

Conformément à l'article 107 paragraphe 4 du règlement du Parlement, le procès-verbal de la séance sera publié au Journal officiel des Communautés européennes.

Je vous prie de croire, Excellence, à l'assurance de ma haute considération.

Enrico VINCI

Annexe

0223

PARLEMENT EUROPÉEN

SESSION 1991 - 1992

EXTRAIT

DU PROCES-VERBAL

DE LA SEANCE DU

JEUDI 12 SEPTEMBRE 1991

PRESIDENCE: Nicole FONTAINE, Vice-président

RESOLUTION

sur les droits de l'homme dans le monde en 1989 et 1990 et la politique de la Communauté en matière de droits de l'homme

<u>Le Parlement européen</u>,

- vu les propositions de résolution déposées par:

    a) M. Staes, sur les droits de l'homme au Guatemala (B3-0003/90);
    b) MM. Arbeloa Muru et Ramirez Heredia, au sujet d'une amnistie interna- tionale en faveur des prisonniers d'opinion (B3-0062/90);
    c) M. Glinne, sur la prostitution enfantine (B3-0066/90);
    d) M. David, sur le sort malheureux des enfants dans le tiers monde (B3-0213/90);
    e) M. Arbeloa Muru, au nom du groupe socialiste, au sujet d'exécutions secrètes en Irak (B3-0497/90);
    f) M. Newens et autres signataires, au sujet des violations des droits de l'homme en Iran (B3-0655/90);
    g) M. Newens et autres signataires, au sujet de tentatives d'assassinat contre des réfugiés iraniens (B3-1101/90);
    h) Mme Fontaine, au sujet de la participation d'enfants à des conflits armés (B3-1479/90);
    i) M. Arbeloa Muru, au sujet de mesures contre la torture, les morts violentes et les disparitions (B3-0033/91),

- vu la résolution relative aux droits de l'homme dans le monde et la politique des droits de l'homme suivie par la Communauté, adoptée le 17 mai 1983 [1],

- vu la résolution sur les droits de l'homme dans le monde et la politique des droits de l'homme suivie par la Communauté, adoptée le 22 mai 1984 [2],

- vu la résolution relative aux droits de l'homme dans le monde et la politique des droits de l'homme suivie par la Communauté, adoptée le 22 octobre 1985 [3],

- vu la résolution relative aux droits de l'homme dans le monde et la

politique des droits de l'homme suivie par la Communauté, adoptée le 12 mars 1987 [4],

- vu la résolution relative aux droits de l'homme dans le monde et la politique des droits de l'homme suivie par la Communauté, adoptée le 18 janvier 1989 [5],

- vu le rapport de la commission politique et les avis de commission du développement et de la coopération et de la commission de la jeunesse, de la culture, de l'éducation, des médias et des sports (A3-0221/91),

---

[1] JO n° C 161 du 20. 6.1983, p. 58
[2] JO n° C 172 du 2. 7.1984, p. 36
[3] JO n° C 343 du 31.12.1985, p. 29
[4] JO n° C 99 du 13. 4.1987, p. 157
[5] JO n° C 47 du 27. 2.1989, p. 61

1

0225

A. considérant que le premier Parlement européen avoir été élu au suffrage
universel s'est engagé à élaborer un rapport annuel relatif aux droits de
l'homme dans le monde et à la politique des droits de l'homme suivie par
la Communauté,

B. considérant que l'attachement aux principes démocratiques de gouvernement
et à la protection des droits de l'homme et des libertés fondamentales
dans le cadre d'un régime de droit constitue un préalable à l'adhésion à
la Communauté européenne,

C. considérant que la Communauté a réitéré cet engagement dans la déclaration
interinstitutionnelle commune du 5 avril 1977, dans la déclaration sur les
droits de l'homme adoptée, le 21 juillet 1986, par les ministres des
Affaires étrangères des Douze, dans le préambule de l'Acte unique européen, stipulant que les Etats membres et les institutions de la CEE
s'engagent à promouvoir ensemble la démocratie en se fondant sur les
droits fondamentaux reconnus par les constitutions et les lois des Etats
membres, dans la Convention européenne de sauvegarde des droits de l'homme
et des libertés fondamentales ainsi que dans la Charte sociale européenne,

D. considérant que pendant la période soumise à examen, il a été fait référence aux droits de l'homme dans les conclusions du Conseil européen de
Dublin (juin 1990) relatives aux droits de l'homme et au bon usage gouver-
nemental en Afrique, du Conseil européen de Rome (décembre 1990) sur la
promotion de la démocratie et des droits de l'homme dans les relations
extérieures, ainsi que dans les conclusions de la session du Conseil du
19 décembre 1990 sur la restructuration de la politique méditerranéenne,
comportant une déclaration relative au respect des droits de l'homme et au
renforcement des valeurs démocratiques,

E. considérant que l'attachement de la Communauté européenne aux droits de
l'homme a également pour vocation de s'élargir à la protection des droits
de l'homme en dehors de la Communauté (1), les plus hautes autorités de la
Communauté ayant indiqué que les préoccupations manifestées au sujet de
violations des droits de l'homme perpétrées dans des pays tiers ne
sauraient être assimilées à une ingérence non fondée dans les affaires
intérieures d'un pays tiers, et considérant que les pays membres de la
Communauté européenne, tant individuellement que collectivement, ont pour
obligation de veiller à l'application du droit international en matière de
droits de l'homme,

_____

(1) Etant donné que les représentants de la Communauté ne disposent d'aucun
accès direct au régime juridique des pays tiers, les violations des droits
de l'homme perpétrées en dehors de la Communauté relèvent de la compétence
de la commission politique du Parlement, chargée des affaires extérieures,
alors que les violations perpétrées au sein de la Communauté et
susceptibles d'ouvrir droit à réparation dans le cadre des législations
nationales des Etats membres, de la législation communautaire et de la
Convention européenne des droits de l'homme et des libertés fondamentales
relèvent de la compétence de la commission juridique et des droits des
citoyens ainsi que de la commission des pétitions.

𝓁

0226

F. considérant que les droits de l'homme revêtent un caractère universel, quels que soient les régimes juridiques ou de gouvernement, les gouvernements ayant pour devoir d'en assurer la sauvegarde à l'intérieur tout comme au-delà de leurs propres frontières,

G. considérant l'évolution significative intervenue dans la perception par la communauté internationale de ses obligations d'intervention, par différentes méthodes, lors de toute violation grave des droits de l'homme, illustrée tout récemment dans la résolution n° 688 du Conseil de sécurité des Nations unies du 5 avril 1991,

H. considérant que l'action de la Communauté en faveur des droits de l'homme dans les pays tiers s'inspire du régime juridique propre à la Communauté, fondé sur les traités, la jurisprudence de la Cour de justice, la législation communautaire, les dispositions contenues dans la Convention européenne sur les droits de l'homme et les libertés fondamentales, ainsi que sur les constitutions et régimes juridiques des Etats membres,

I. considérant qu'en cas de violations des droits de l'homme dans la Communauté européenne, des instruments ouvrant droit à réparation dans un cadre juridique approprié (y compris celui du droit communautaire qui englobe désormais certains droits de l'homme traditionnels comme les libertés d'association et d'expression) existent normalement, et lorsque semblables instruments se révèlent inappropriés, des mécanismes permettant d'obtenir réparation sont en principe disponibles,

J. considérant qu'en dépit de la compétence désormais acquise par la Communauté en matière de droits de l'homme, la Communauté n'est pas habilitée, aux termes des traités, à exercer un mandat juridique spécifique en la matière, et n'a pas adhéré à la Convention européenne des droits de l'homme, en dépit des appels lancés par le Parlement en ce sens,

K. considérant que dans le cadre du prochain examen des dispositions relatives à la coopération politique européenne [1], ainsi que dans les nouvelles dispositions susceptibles de découler de la Conférence intergouvernementale sur l'Union politique, une référence explicite devrait être faite à l'obligation pour la Communauté d'oeuvrer au développement et à la sauvegarde des droits de l'homme,

L. considérant que les systèmes régionaux de protection des droits de l'homme dans différentes parties du monde revêtent de plus en plus d'importance, le poids de la "dimension humaine" devant également apparaître comme constituant un volet essentiel de l'architecture institutionnelle de la nouvelle Europe élargie,

M. considérant que dans ses rapports annuels le Parlement privilégie trois droits fondamentaux (droit à la vie, droit au respect de l'intégrité physique et morale de la personne, droit à être jugé équitablement par un tribunal indépendant), tout en reconnaissant l'indivisibilité et l'interdépendance de tous les droits de l'homme, politiques, civils, économiques, sociaux et culturels,

---

[1] prévu au titre III de l'Acte unique européen

3

N. considérant que ni l'absence de développement social et économique ni les croyances ou idéologies ne sauraient justifier les atteintes aux droits civiques et politiques, que ni les croyances et idéologies ne sauraient justifier les atteintes aux droits sociaux de l'homme ou au droit au développement, et que la Communauté européenne doit se garder de s'ériger en modèle et, dans le regard qu'elle porte sur les problèmes de droits de l'homme dans les pays tiers, prendre toujours en compte la relativité et le "contexte" culturels,

O. considérant que de graves menaces pèsent actuellement sur les droits de l'homme au sein de la Communauté, notamment à la suite de la résurgence de l'intolérance et du racisme, d'où l'adoption, le 11 juin 1986 de la déclaration contre le racisme et la xénophobie [1], une commission d'enquête du Parlement ayant élaboré par ailleurs en 1990 un rapport[2] qui demandait des mesures concrètes complémentaires,

P. considérant qu'au sein de la Communauté la convivialité démocratique demeure menacée par le terrorisme qui, pendant la période examinée, a entraîné des assassinats et autres actes criminels dans différents Etats membres, notamment en Espagne, Grèce, République fédérale d'Allemagne, France, parfois avec l'appui de forces politiques qui se drapent dans la légalité démocratique,

Q. considérant que les problèmes de droits de l'homme au sein de la Communauté européenne, notamment le droit d'asile et le traitement des réfugiés, figurent parmi les problèmes politiques les plus importants de la Communauté, dont de nombreux aspects ne sont pas visés par les conventions de Genève de 1951, et que la Communauté, au regard de l'achèvement du marché intérieur de 1992, doit trouver au niveau communautaire des solutions complétant les mesures nationales ou intergouvernementales,

R. considérant que la reconnaissance des droits de l'homme a considérablement progressé à l'échelle du globe, qu'une Communauté reposant sur le principe de l'Etat de droit et de la démocratie se voit conférer par là même une responsabilité mondiale, qu'elle se doit d'ancrer notamment dans la politique étrangère et que le Parlement européen, en tant qu'interlocuteur, à l'échelle planétaire, pour les problèmes liés aux droits de l'homme, se doit de rester à l'écoute de ces questions, d'en vérifier, autant que faire se peut, la véracité, puis de leur apporter son soutien par ses résolutions,

S. considérant que les ressortissants de la Communauté exigent à juste titre le respect scrupuleux des droits de l'homme par tous les Etats membres et demandent que le respect des droits de l'homme dans les pays tiers constitue un paramètre fondamental dans les rapports de la CEE avec ces pays,

T. considérant que le pluralisme et la démocratie contribuent à la consolidation des droits de l'homme et qu'un nombre croissant d'êtres humains estiment devoir bénéficier des droits de l'homme et prennent conscience de leurs droits individuels,

U. considérant que les droits de l'homme s'épanouissent au mieux dans un contexte de stabilité démocratique et que les organes de la Communauté,

---

[1] JO n° C 176 du 14.7.1986, p. 62

[2] Conclusions de la commission d'enquête sur le racisme et la xénophobie et résolutions du 10 octobre 1990 sur le rapport de cette commission (JO n° C 282 du 10.10.1990, p. 57)

0228

notamment son Parlement, se doivent d'encourager l'évolution sur la voie
·de l'Etat de droit, de la démocratie et du pluralisme politique,

V. considérant que, dans un nombre croissant de pays, bien que ce ne soit pas
encore le cas pour tous, les gouvernements sont de plus en plus sensibles
aux opinions extérieures et aux démarches effectuées au sujet de la
situation des droits de l'homme dans leur pays;

W. considérant qu'il est admis que l'engagement en faveur des droits de
l'homme constitue une activité internationale légitime ne pouvant être
assimilée à une ingérence déplacée dans les affaires intérieures de pays
tiers,

X. considérant que si la pression internationale n'est pas toujours opérante,
il est un fait avéré que même les gouvernements qui violent les droits de
l'homme y sont sensibles et qu'elle constitue en outre la seule protection
du prisonnier politique, bon nombre d'anciens détenus ayant certifié que
les mots peuvent avoir du poids et les documents être persuasifs,

Y. considérant toutefois que la Communauté européenne, tout autant que
d'autres membres de la communauté internationale, s'est montrée "sélective" dans son approche et que, parfois, sa politique des droits de
l'homme obéit à des considérations d'ordre stratégique, géopolitique et
commercial,

Z. considérant qu'au cours des dernières années, les droits de l'homme ont
été davantage mis en avant dans la politique étrangère de la Communauté et
de ses Etats membres et que des orientations claires doivent en être
tirées,

AA. considérant que, dans un monde dont les éléments deviennent de plus en
plus interdépendants, la paix peut être menacée par le fait que les
atteintes aux droits de l'homme augmentent en nombre là où des ordres
établis s'effondrent et où règnent la violence et la misère et que la
Communauté ne peut envisager la mise en place de conditions stables sans
respect absolu des droits de l'homme,

1. réitère les engagements, déclarations de principe et propositions formulés
dans ses précédents rapports sur les droits de l'homme;

2. estime que la période considérée (1989 et 1990) a suscité l'espoir que la
communauté internationale puisse progresser, de manière significative,
sur la voie d'un respect accru des droits de l'homme, notamment à la
suite de la fin de la "guerre froide" et de la possibilité qui s'ouvre
aux Nations unies de jouer un rôle plus important et plus efficace;

3. déplore toutefois que ces espoirs et aspirations, suscités par les
changements notables intervenus dans un certain nombre de pays, notamment
en Europe centrale et de l'Est, n'autorisent pas à conclure qu'à
l'échelle internationale, l'ampleur des souffrances résultant de
violations des droits de l'homme soit en déclin;

4. déplore qu'outre la guerre et les conflits civils, assortis des
violations abusives qui en résultent, la majorité des gouvernements du
monde pratiquent ou tolèrent différentes formes de violation des droits
de l'homme et que dans un nombre significatif de pays, y compris ceux qui
sont étroitement associés à la Communauté, les violations de ces droits
reconnus à l'échelle internationale soient flagrantes et systématiques,
telles la torture et d'autres atteintes aux droits de l'homme, à
l'existence et à la dignité;

5

5. relève que les principes fondamentaux du droit international portant sur la sauvegarde des droits de l'homme sont les plus communément bafoués dans des situations de conflits armés, y compris, entre autres, au travers des exécutions sommaires de prisonniers, des actes de terrorisme individuel ou collectif, de la torture et de l'exécution d'otages et de prisonniers, des bombardements aveugles et de l'utilisation d'armements prohibés;

6. estime à cet égard que les violations flagrantes des conventions de Genève sont plus fréquentes que jamais, et note que les organisations humanitaires de réputation internationale telles que le Comité international de la Croix Rouge jugent que les années 1980 ont donné lieu à une escalade de la violence à travers le monde, notamment dans des conflits internes non spécifiquement protégés par le droit humanitaire international;

7. rappelle avec tristesse qu'au cours des 45 dernières années, environ 105 conflits armés ont sévi, la plupart d'entre eux dans le tiers monde, et que ces dernières années, les guerres civiles et les conflits inter-ethniques notamment ont été plus répandus et que dans les années 80, on a relevé une progression nette du nombre de conflits, internationaux, internes ou les deux, à caractère prolongé pour bon nombre d'entre eux, plus de 80 % des victimes des conflits contemporains étant des civils, femmes et enfants en majorité écrasante;

8. note par ailleurs que 13 guerres se poursuivent en Afrique, notamment la plus ancienne, en Erythrée, qui dure depuis près de 30 ans et le conflit qui se prolonge également en Angola et au Mozambique;

9. est vivement préoccupé par le fait que l'utilisation de l'ypérite par l'Irak contre l'Iran, éventuellement celle de gaz au cyanure et d'agents innervants, a enfreint une règle internationalement reconnue, et note que 20 pays posséderaient actuellement des armements chimiques ou seraient en mesure de les utiliser, en violation du protocole de Genève de 1925;

10. déplore que la vague de libéralisation qui a balayé le monde au cours de la période considérée n'ait eu aucun effet significatif sur de nombreux pays; qu'avec des exceptions notables, par exemple la libération de Nelson Mandela, prisonnier politique le plus connu au monde, des milliers de prisonniers politiques de longue durée demeurent incarcérés dans différents pays, et que dans certains cas ils ont été maintenus en détention pendant plus de 20 ans, comme par exemple à Cuba, en Indonésie, au Malawi, en Syrie et au Maroc; qu'entre 40 et 60 pays dans le monde pratiquent, selon des sources fiables, la torture de manière courante, y compris dans certains pays proches de la CEE autour du bassin méditerranéen comme la Turquie; qu'une "législation d'exception" est maintenue en vigueur sans justification afin de garder en détention des prisonniers de conscience ni inculpés ni jugés, comme en Syrie, où une législation portant instauration de l'état d'urgence demeure en vigueur depuis 1963;

11. affirme que semblable phénomène est tout simplement imputable à certains gouvernements et à leur répugnance à respecter les pactes internationaux auxquels ils sont parties et à mettre en oeuvre des mesures préventives et palliatives;

EVOLUTION NEGATIVE

12. attire ci-après l'attention, tout comme ce fut le cas dans les rapports annuels précédents, sur les conséquences de conflits armés et politiques,

6

de gestions ⠀fastes et de famines, qui ⠀⠀ent entraîner de graves
violations des droits de l'homme:

I. Réfugiés et personnes déplacées

a) la progression constante de la population mondiale de réfugiés,
estimée actuellement à 15 millions, auxquels s'ajoutent 20 millions de
personnes déplacées, dont le plus grand nombre se trouvent en Asie du
Sud-Est, en Afghanistan, au Pakistan, dans la Corne de l'Afrique, en
Afrique australe et en Amérique centrale, des problèmes nouveaux se
faisant jour dans des pays comme la Somalie et le Libéria, pays où la
guerre civile de 1990 a provoqué l'exode, à l'intérieur du pays, de
500.000 personnes sur une population de 3 millions, 500.000 autres se
réfugiant dans des pays limitrophes,

b) l'apparition de nouveaux problèmes de réfugiés, à une échelle consi-
dérable au Proche-Orient, notamment à la suite de la guerre du Golfe,
touchant particulièrement les populations chiite et kurde d'Irak, et en
Europe centrale et de l'Est, où, par exemple, environ 1 million de
personnes aurait afflué en République fédérale d'Allemagne en 1990,
avec, selon certaines estimations de la Commission, la perspective de
voir 4 à 8 millions de personnes quitter prochainement l'Europe
centrale et de l'Est, y compris l'URSS;

II. Enfants

a) la marginalisation et la vulnérabilité accrues des enfants aux
violations flagrantes des droits de l'homme soulignées par le Sommet
mondial de l'enfance en 1990, 15 millions de nourrissons et d'enfants
mourant chaque année, selon les estimations de l'ONU;

b) l'existence de plus de 100 millions "d'enfants esclaves" dans le
monde, le plus grand nombre de ceux-ci se trouvant sur le sous-
continent indien, bien que l'exploitation de la main-d'oeuvre
enfantine soit également observée dans certains pays européens comme
le Portugal, l'Italie et la Grèce;

c) les violences perpétrées contre "les enfants des rues", comme au
Brésil et au Guatemala où, en 1990, on a enregistré une vague
d'assassinats d'enfants fauchés par des "escadrons de la mort"
composés, dans de nombreux cas, de policiers agissant hors service;

d) les souffrances endurées par les gamins de Bogota et autres villes
colombiennes, qui vivent et meurent dans les rues et qui parfois sont
capturés pour faire office de "sicaires", voire d'assassins par des
bandes de trafiquants de drogue;

e) dans plusieurs pays de par le monde, l'incarcération injuste, la
torture, les "disparitions" et l'assassinat d'enfants par des agents
de l'Etat, une illustration caractéristique étant fournie par l'Irak,
où des centaines d'enfants ont été maltraités, beaucoup ayant disparu
ou été torturés;

f) l'absence de protection des droits des enfants dans d'autres pays
comme le Guatemala, le Pérou, le Sri Lanka, la Turquie, les terri-
toires occupés et l'Afrique du Sud, où on estime à 9.000 le nombre
d'enfants détenus dans le cadre d'une législation d'exception de juin
1986 à juin 1989;

g) l'augmentation massive de la prostitution enfantine, qui apparaît
notamment dans les pays où le revenu moyen par habitant est largement

7

0231

inférieur à la moyenne mondiale, phénomè====qui se rencontre parfois, même de manière sporadique, dans certains pays membres;

III. Torture

a) la répétition de morts sous la torture dans des pays comme le Salvador, le Burkina Faso, le Soudan, l'Afrique du Sud, l'Indonésie, l'Irak, la Chine, l'Inde, Myanmar (Birmanie) et le Koweït, certains pays où le phénomène de la torture n'avait pas encore été observé de manière significative ayant été identifiés de manière fiable, notamment la Guinée équatoriale et le Kenya où, en 1990, des centaines de prisonniers d'opinion ont été torturés et maltraités;

b) la participation accrue de médecins à la torture du fait du caractère de plus en plus scientifique des méthodes utilisées, d'où une campagne internationale menée au sein du corps médical visant à frapper d'interdiction les médecins en question, notamment en Amérique du Sud (notamment au Chili) où, en 1990, près de 20 médecins ont été déclarés coupables de complicité de torture par les commissions d'éthique de leurs organismes professionnels;

IV. Droits syndicaux

a) les violations des droits et libertés syndicaux dans de nombreux pays, telles qu'elles ont été signalées par l'Assemblée générale de la Conférence internationale du travail de juin 1991;

b) la promulgation de lois et/ou de décrets visant à limiter les activités syndicales et à opprimer les dirigeants et militants syndicaux, ce qui s'est traduit par des disparitions, des pratiques de torture et des exécutions extrajudiciaires et de ces syndicalistes, en raison uniquement de leurs activités syndicales;

V. "Escadrons de la mort", exécutions sommaires et disparitions

a) la résurgence d'exécutions sommaires survenant souvent dans des situations de conflit armé international et interne, de violences entre groupes armés (guérilleros, trafiquants de drogue, police et armée), la réapparition des escadrons de la mort, qui semblaient déjà matés dans certains pays;

b) l'extension du phénomène à des régions où ces agissements n'avaient pas encore été rapportés avec fiabilité, comme dans certaines régions d'Asie (par exemple au Sri Lanka, en Inde, aux Philippines et en Birmanie); en Afrique: par exemple, les opérations d'escadrons de la mort en Afrique du Sud apparaissent au grand jour; au Mali où des membres de l'ethnie touareg ont été assassinés avec la connivence des autorités gouvernementales et où 55 prisonniers ont été exécutés sommairement par les forces de sécurité en août 1990; au Niger, au cours de la même période, où une centaine de targuis auraient été tués; en Somalie, où en juillet 1989, 46 prisonniers politiques ont été exécutés sommairement; en Mauritanie enfin où, en avril 1989, ainsi qu'en novembre/décembre 1990, les forces de sécurité ont procédé à des exécutions sommaires; au Tchad, où plus de 300 prisonniers ont été exécutés par la garde présidentielle en décembre 1990 ou condamnés à mourir de faim pendant leur détention; au Moyen-Orient, avec l'assassinat notamment, par les forces irakiennes d'occupation en 1990, de nombreux koweitiens sans armes;

c) le nombre croissant de menaces de mort proférées contre des personnes dans de nombreux pays, selon M. Amos Wako, rapporteur spécial des

8

Nations unies qui, en 1990, s'est adressé par écrit à 45 gouvernements pour leur demander des explications au sujet d'exécutions sommaires dont il avait été informé;

d) la pratique constante des "disparitions" au Pérou, en Colombie, au Guatemala, au Salvador, aux Philippines, au Sri Lanka et en Chine, où l'on demeure sans nouvelles de douzaines de personnes arrêtées en juin 1989; l'absence continue d'informations nouvelles ou d'enquêtes au sujet des "disparitions" à long terme, comme en Ethiopie, en Syrie, au Maroc, au Sahara occidental, en Guinée, au Tchad et à Chypre, de nombreuses affaires remontant à dix ou quinze ans;

e) l'incapacité à ce jour, de pouvoir rendre compte des personnes disparues au cours de l'invasion de Chypre par la Turquie;

f) la parution au grand jour de nouvelles informations au sujet de disparitions survenues dans des pays où le phénomène a été pour l'essentiel éradiqué, tout comme en Argentine, en Uruguay et au Chili, où la commission chilienne des droits de l'homme a fait savoir qu'elle détenait les preuves de 2.200 exécutions politiques et de 900 disparitions sous la dictature de Pinochet; la tendance à faire bénéficier de l'immunité de poursuites les auteurs présumés de violations des droits de l'homme, tout comme dans certains pays d'Amérique latine en ce qui concerne des membres de l'ancienne institution militaire;

VI. La peine de mort et les exécutions illégales

a) la perpétration d'exécutions illégales, hors du cadre juridique légal, ou au terme de procès grossièrement bâclés, dans un certain nombre de pays comme l'Irak, le Koweït, le Nigéria, le Soudan et l'Iran, où la période sous revue a marqué la fin des trois années au cours desquelles 5.000 personnes auraient été exécutées sans avoir eu accès à un avocat, sans avoir pu faire citer des témoins à décharge et sans droit d'appel, mais où, en 1989 seulement, plus de 1.000 prisonniers ont été tués dans le cadre d'éxécutions massives secrètes pour des crimes "politiques" et des crimes "de droit commun", nombre de ces exécutions ayant eu lieu en public, notamment par lapidation pour adultère, délits liés à la drogue, prostitution et subsistance basée sur des revenus immoraux;

b) l'application permanente de la peine de mort dans de nombreux pays, parfois à une grande échelle, tout comme en Iran et en Irak, où en 1989, des centaines d'exécutions sont intervenues sur la base de peines prononcées par des juridictions spéciales sans droit d'appel; en Chine, où l'on a enregistré une progression du nombre déjà élevé des exécutions après l'étouffement du mouvement démocratique; en Union soviétique, où les autorités ont désormais entamé la publication des chiffres annuels en matière de peines de mort et d'exécutions, qui s'élèvent à 190 pour 1990;

c) l'exécution de prisonniers politiques incarcérés de longue date, comme en Indonésie, où quatre exécutions de cette nature sont intervenues en 1990, alors que d'autres condamnés à mort demeurent incarcérés depuis plus de vingt ans;

d) les arrêts rendus aux Etats-Unis dans le sens du maintien de la peine de mort pour les jeunes délinquants, la Cour suprême ayant, en juin 1989, décrété que la Constitution américaine autorise l'exécution des jeunes délinquants et des handicapés mentaux et la Chambre des représentants ayant envisagé, en octobre 1990, l'élargissement de la liste des délits fédéraux passibles de la peine de mort et la

9

limitation des appels que peuvent inter_er les prisonniers d'Etat passibles d'une exécution;

e) le maintien de la peine de mort en Turquie, seul Etat membre du Conseil de l'Europe ayant perpétré des exécutions dans un cadre juridique dans les années 80, bien que le nombre de délits passibles de la peine de mort ait été réduit et que la peine de mort n'ait pas été exécutée pendant plus de 6 ans; en 1991, après la période sous examen, le parlement turc a commué les quelque 290 peines de mort;

f) la tendance à l'abolition de la peine de mort, qui ne saurait être jugée positive dans la mesure où les législations de 134 pays sur 178 prévoient encore la peine capitale et qu'elle demeure appliquée en fait dans 92 pays: en effet, si la peine de mort continuait à être abolie au rythme de 1990 (7 pays l'ont abrogée totalement: Namibie, Tchécoslovaquie, Irlande, Andorre, Sao Tomé et Principe, Mozambique, Hongrie et Népal où elle a été supprimée pour les seuls délits de droit commun), il faudrait attendre les années 2000 et plus pour voir un monde sans peine de mort; sans tenir compte des tentatives de réinstauration actuellement en cours dans certains pays, comme en Brésil en juin 1991, au Salvador, ainsi que dans certains pays orientaux pour les délits liés aux stupéfiants, et du fait que le discours en faveur de la réinstauration de la peine de mort apparaît également dans les législations communautaires;

VII. Peuples indigènes

a) la menace qui se précise sur l'existence et la survie des peuples indigènes qui s'efforcent de mettre leurs terres à l'abri des incursions des pionniers et des entreprises minières et sylvicoles, notamment au Brésil, au Canada, en Malaisie (Sarawak) et en Indonésie (Iran Jaya);

VIII. Conflits ethniques

a) la multiplication des conflits ethniques, religieux, intercommunautaires et tribaux, tout comme en URSS, en Roumanie, en Yougoslavie et en Irak pour le problème des Kurdes et dans les provinces septentrionales de l'Inde, au point de mettre en péril l'unité de ces pays, ainsi qu'au Libéria, en Birmanie, en Somalie, en Afrique du Sud, au Burundi et au Rwanda, le maintien et l'intensification de certains conflits durables, tout comme au Timor oriental et en Irian Jaya qui, depuis respectivement 15 et 29 ans, mènent une guerre d'indépendance contre l'Indonésie; en Ethiopie, au Liban et au Soudan où le régime militaire islamiste actuel pilonne régulièrement des cibles civiles dans sa guerre contre l'armée de libération des peuples soudanais, aurait maintenu en détention plus de prisonniers politiques que tout autre Etat d'Afrique l'année dernière et privé de denrées alimentaires les civils dans de nombreuses régions, 11 millions environ d'habitants étant actuellement menacés par la famine au Soudan; en Syrie, où vivent encore, dans trois ghettos, 4.000 Juifs qui sont privés des droits élémentaires et n'ont pas le droit de quitter la Syrie;

IX. Liberté du culte

les entraves à la liberté de culte mises en place par l'Etat dans de nombreux pays et la persécution des dirigeants religieux;

EVOLUTION POSITIVE

10

0234

13. attire l'attention sur les éléments positifs apparus au cours de la période examinée:

I. Elections et progrès sur la voie du pluralisme

a) l'apparition de gouvernements élus en Europe centrale et de l'Est où, en 1990, en l'espace de quatre mois, six Etats membres du Pacte de Varsovie placés sous la férule d'un parti unique pendant plus de 40 ans, ont eu la possibilité d'élire les gouvernants de leur choix;

b) une évolution apparue dans de nombreux pays africains sur la voie d'un pluralisme élargi, encouragé en partie par les changements intervenus en Europe ainsi que par la faillite politique et économique sans oublier la corruption et l'oppression pratiquées par leurs gouvernements;

 c) des pressions analogues exercées dans certains pays d'Asie, qui ne peuvent toutefois occulter le maintien au pouvoir de gouvernements autoritaires, en dépit des pressions populaires exercées en Birmanie, en Thaïlande, en Corée du Sud et en Chine;

d) le renforcement du processus démocratique à travers l'Amérique latine, notamment grâce aux élections libres et secrètes qui se sont déroulées au Chili, au Nicaragua et en Haïti, ne laissant que Cuba sous régime à parti unique, bien que la démocratie demeure extrêmement fragile dans de nombreux pays, comme au Pérou et en Colombie;

e) en Afrique du Sud, les avancées importantes qui ont été réalisées vers l'abolition de l'apartheid et la mise en place d'une concertation entre toutes les parties intéressées;

f) au Sahara Occidental, le plan de paix élaboré par l'ONU et accepté par les différentes parties, mais dont l'application risque d'être mis en cause par les incursions de l'armée marocaine au Sahara Occidental;

II. Diffusion accélérée de l'information

a) la diffusion de la révolution médiatique avec, pour résultante, qu'à l'exception de certaines sociétés et certains Etats très fermés comme la Corée du nord, une partie de la Chine ou la Birmanie, l'information au sujet des violations des droits de l'homme peut être diffusée à travers le pays ainsi qu'à l'extérieur; en outre, la diffusion du concept de respect nécessaire des droits de l'homme par tous les pays, les actions internationales dénonçant les violations et la pression de l'opinion publique là où cela est possible, la diffusion plus aisée des informations dans ce secteur également constituent autant d'éléments concourant à la réduction des violations dans le domaine des droits de l'homme;

III. Développement du mouvement des droits de l'homme

a) la progression constante, enregistrée tout au long des années 80, d'associations vouées à la surveillance et au développement du respect des droits de l'homme, en Amérique latine et dans des pays africains comme le Burkina Faso, le Cameroun, la Côte d'Ivoire, le Kenya, le Mali, la Mauritanie, le Nigéria, le Sénégal et l'Ouganda;

b) la création par les autorités gouvernementales d'organes officiels chargés d'examiner les plaintes au titre des violations des droits de l'homme, par exemple au Bénin, en Ouganda, au Zaïre, au Maroc, au Togo, au Mexique, au Chili, en Argentine, en Turquie, entre autres,

11

0235

organes dont les travaux ne font toutefois que débuter et qui ne
bénéficient pas toujours du soutien nécessaire;

c) le travail accompli par la commission des droits de l'homme des
Nations unies et par certaines organisations régionales (notamment
l'OEA) qui contribuent à signaler les violations des droits de l'homme
perpétrées dans de nombreux pays;

IV. __Règlement de conflits__

a) la mise en oeuvre ou la perspective de mise en oeuvre d'un règlement,
dans le cadre de certains conflits internationaux durables, comme au
Sahara occidental, en Namibie, au Nicaragua, au Salvador, au Cambodge,
en Angola, et le Sahara occidental, où le référendum sur l'indépendance
pour le peuple sahraoui aura lieu prochainement, et un règlement
partiel des conflits ethniques en Afrique du sud; dans certains cas, la
nouvelle entente conclue entre les Etats-Unis et l'Union Soviétique a
représenté un élément significatif;

V. __Elargissement de prisonniers politiques__

a) la libération en nombre de prisonniers politiques dans certains pays:
la Zambie (juillet 1990), l'Ouganda (avril 1990), le Burkina Faso (août
1989); l'Afrique du Sud (1989 et 1990), la Jordanie (septembre 1989),
le Bénin (août 1989) et l'Ethiopie, où les trois petits-fils d'Hailé
Sélassié, ancien empereur d'Ethiopie, ont été libérés en septembre
1989, au terme de 15 années de détention sans jugement;

__SYSTEMES REGIONAUX DE PROTECTION DES DROITS DE L'HOMME__

14. réaffirme sa conviction que les modalités régionales de protection des
droits de l'homme, prévues par la Convention européenne des droits de
l'homme et de la Charte de l'organisation des Etats américains pourraient
se révéler plus efficaces que d'autres instruments internationaux à portée
plus vaste, pour autant qu'elles prévoient des systèmes de contrôle et
d'application de sanctions éventuelles en cas de violation, ce qui n'est
pas le cas actuellement;

15. invite les Etats membres de la Communauté qui ne l'on pas encore fait:
   - à abolir la peine de mort prévue par leur législation (Grèce,
Belgique, Italie, Espagne et Royaume-Uni), ce qui est de facto le cas,
   - à ratifier le VIe protocole additionnel à la Convention européenne des
droits de l'homme ainsi que le 2e protocole facultatif au Pacte international sur les droits civils et politiques,
   - à ratifier la Convention européenne pour la prévention de la torture;

16. espère que la Commission africaine des droits de l'homme et des peuples,
organe de contrôle de l'OUA érigé aux termes de la Charte africaine des
droits de l'homme et des peuples, qui dispose désormais d'un siège permanent, pourra jouer un rôle accru à la suite des changements intervenant
en Afrique et qu'elle bénéficiera du concours des gouvernements
africains;

17. déplore que des organisations de ce type ne demeurent qu'à l'état
embryonnaire en Asie, les efforts visant à les instaurer au sein du monde
arabe ayant été contrariés par les gouvernements, en dépit des efforts
soutenus déployés par l'Union des avocats arabes et par l'Organisation
arabe des droits de l'homme;

18. relève qu'à travers le monde, au cours de la période considérée, on a
enregistré une prolifération d'organisations de défense des droits de

12

0236

l'homme militant en ce sens, phénomène significatif en Europe centrale et de l'Est, en Asie et en Afrique, et que la progression de ces organisations s'est poursuivie en Amérique latine, contribuant ainsi, de manière notable, au développement des droits de l'homme, à la fixation de normes et aux enquêtes sur les violations perpétrées auparavant;

19. estime que les dispositions contenues dans la quatrième Convention de Lomé qui portent sur les droits de l'homme représentent un progrès significatif et espère qu'elles inciteront les gouvernements des pays ACP à mieux réagir aux préoccupations et aux démarches de la Communauté au sujet de problèmes liés aux droits de l'homme;

20. considère que le problème fondamental, aux incidences appréciables sur le plan des droits de l'homme, porte sur la mise au point de mesures permettant à la majorité des habitants de la planète, y compris à des populations différentes vivant dans les mêmes pays, de se réunir dans le cadre de structures politiques communes, notamment en Afrique et en Union Soviétique où ce problème a revêtu une acuité dramatique au cours de la période considérée;

21. estime que les nouvelles démocraties d'Europe centrale et de l'Est qui se sont substituées aux régimes précédents doivent être aidées, dans la mesure où le maintien de situations économiques difficiles qui sont à la base du mécontentement populaire ne saurait engendrer la paix sociale nécessaire pour que ces pays qui découvrent la démocratie puissent véritablement combler le retard les séparant des pays occidentaux et garantir à leur population des conditions de vie satisfaisantes;

22. observe qu'avec la disparition de l'affrontement Est-Ouest, un nouvel affrontement Nord-Sud est apparu au cours de la période examinée, un "rideau de la pauvreté" séparant les hémisphères développé et en développement, et relève à titre d'exemple que le revenu réel de l'Africain moyen a chuté, en termes réels, au cours des vingt dernières années, que les pays d'Afrique ont accumulé à ce jour des dettes internationales équivalant à l'ensemble du PNB du continent, alors que l'aide fournie par le monde développé est en régression, d'où le constat qu'à défaut de pouvoir inverser la tendance, les nouvelles démocraties seront vraisemblablement balayées par les crises économiques;

23. estime que si la Commission a proposé au Conseil (octobre 1990) l'annulation des dettes des pays ACP vis à vis de la CEE (prêts spéciaux, transferts et rééchelonnements de crédits spéciaux), un plus grand nombre d'initiatives de cette nature pourraient être prises;

24. juge impossible de dissocier les efforts de développement de ceux nécessaires à l'instauration d'Etats démocratiques;

25. reconnaît que le respect de l'ensemble des droits de l'homme (politiques, économiques et sociaux) devra être le critère fondamental dans l'évaluation des politiques de développement des années 90;

POLITIQUE DE LA COMMUNAUTE

26. estime qu'au cours de la période considérée, l'optique de la Communauté au sujet de la politique des droits de l'homme [1] a notablement évolué, en partie à la suite des changements intervenus en Europe centrale et de

---

[1] SEC(91) 61, 25 mars 1991, "Droits de l'homme, démocratie et politique de coopération au développement" (annexe 4)

13

0237

l'Est et de la pression exercée dans d'autr— régions du monde dans le sens d'un pluralisme élargi;

27. se félicite de toute initiative tendant à conférer une cohérence accrue à la politique des droits de l'homme suivie par la Communauté vis-à-vis des pays tiers, et invite la Commission et le Conseil à veiller à ce que l'approche soit empreinte de cohésion à mesure que nous nous écarterons d'une politique "sélective" et "ad hoc";

28. estime que, dans le rôle que la Communauté souhaite jouer dans le processus de paix au Moyen-Orient, la situation des droits de l'homme dans les divers Etats arabes soit expressément abordée, notamment lorsqu'il s'agit des principes de l'Etat de droit, de la démocratie, de la protection de l'intégrité de l'homme et de la liberté du culte;

29. relève à cet égard, l'existence de nombreux exemples, au cours de la période considérée et ultérieurement, illustrant à l'évidence que la politique de la Communauté a été dictée moins par des considérations liées aux droits de l'homme que par d'autres intérêts comme, par exemple, en ce qui concerne la Birmanie, la Chine, la Syrie et le Maroc, entre autres;

30. se félicite de l'objectif consistant à incorporer des références à des engagements communs en matière de respect des droits de l'homme dans un nombre croissant d'accords conclus par la Communauté avec des pays tiers ou avec des groupes de pays, tout comme pour l'accord Lomé IV, l'accord entre la Communauté et les pays parties à l'accord général d'intégration économique de l'Amérique centrale, avec l'Argentine, le Chili et le Mexique, et les accords d'association actuellement en cours de négociation avec la Pologne, la Tchécoslovaquie et la Hongrie;

31. invite la Commission et le Conseil à insister pour que ces références soient incorporées, de manière formelle, dans l'ensemble des accords de cette nature conclus par la Communauté;

32. invite la Commission et le Conseil à veiller à ce que dans les cas où l'aide programmable est suspendue à propos du respect des droits de l'homme (tout comme pour le Soudan en 1990), une diminution de l'aide humanitaire ou d'autres formes d'aide ou de coopération prêtant un concours direct à la population locale ne s'ensuive pas, à condition de veiller soigneusement à ce qu'elle parvienne aux populations auxquelles elle est destinée;

33. estime que toute décision de suspension de l'aide ne doit pas être arrêtée uniquement aux niveaux administratif ou exécutif, mais doit toujours faire l'objet d'une délibération politique approfondie et transparente;

34. invite la coopération politique européenne à se montrer plus explicite au sujet des critères régissant l'étude des cas individuels;

35. relève que le volet droits de l'homme du processus d'Helsinki s'est largement étendu puisque de nombreux droits de l'homme importants ont été consacrés dans le document de Copenhague en juin 1990, y compris les droits des minorités et le droit à un gouvernement représentatif;

36. invite la Commission et le Conseil à veiller à ce que les considérations liées aux droits de l'homme constituent l'un des principaux piliers de la "nouvelle architecture européenne" et relève la priorité accordée au respect des droits de l'homme lors du sommet de la CSCE de novembre 1990 à Paris, à savoir que les activités de suivi prévues avant la prochaine

14

0238

conférence du bilan qui doit avoir lieu à Helsinki en 1992 portent sur les droits de l'homme, l'un des principaux engagements contenus dans la déclaration finale de la Conférence de Copenhague sur la "dimension humaine", en juin 1990, ayant été la création d'un espace juridique commun;

37. estime que, comme dans le cas de la Commission, le Parlement doit être représenté à toutes les conférences intérimaires appropriées (telles que la conférence sur la dimension humaine qui aura lieu à Moscou en septembre 1991) ainsi qu'aux conférences de suivi et rappelle son appréciation du concours apporté, dans le passé, par la coopération politique européenne à des délégations du Parlement ayant assisté à ces conférences de la CSCE;

38. estime, au regard du rôle que la Communauté doit jouer au sein de la CSCE, qu'il n'est plus raisonnable que la Communauté, en tant que telle, ne soit pas signataire de la Convention européenne des droits de l'homme, et invite le Conseil, sans retard, à répondre positivement à la proposition faite par la Commission au Conseil en novembre 1990 [1] dans le sens de l'adhésion de la Communauté à la Convention européenne, et de l'octroi à la Commission d'un mandat de négociation à cet effet;

39. note que si tous les actes juridiques des Etats membres sont soumis à l'examen de la Commission et de la Cour des droits de l'homme de Strasbourg au plan du respect des droits de l'homme, les actes communautaires ne sont pas assujettis à ces instruments, raison pour laquelle les institutions de la Communauté bénéficient d'une sorte "d'immunité" en échappant à toute surveillance au détriment du système de protection des citoyens;

40. relève par ailleurs qu'en raison de l'élargissement des compétences de la Communauté dans le domaine économique et d'autres secteurs, la législation communautaire a des incidences multiples en matière de droits de l'homme, par exemple les projets de directive relatifs à l'enregistrement de données personnelles et au droit de résidence;

41. estime que semblables considérations revêtent une importance particulière au regard des propositions dont est saisie la conférence intergouvernementale sur la citoyenneté européenne, et rappelle le document publié par les Douze en décembre 1990, avant le début de la Conférence intergouvernementale, stipulant que la grande majorité des délégations conviennent de l'opportunité d'incorporer le concept de citoyenneté européenne au nouveau traité, ainsi qu'un nombre de droits spécifiques à définir lors de la conférence, tels que les droits civiques, économiques et sociaux, l'égalité de traitement vis-à-vis de la législation sociale ainsi que la protection diplomatique dans les pays tiers;

42. invite la conférence intergouvernementale et d'autres réunions chargées de passer en revue les dispositions de la coopération politique européenne ainsi que la politique étrangère de la Communauté à énoncer clairement que l'intérêt pour les droits de l'homme constitue l'un des piliers de la politique étrangère de la Communauté;

---

[1] Communication de la Commission sur l'adhésion de la Communauté à la Convention européenne de sauvegarde des droits de l'homme et des libertés fondamentales ainsi qu'à certains de ses protocoles (SEC(90) 2087) (Annexe 5).

15

0239

43. demande aux ministres des Affaires étrangères réunis dans le cadre de la coopération politique européenne d'élaborer un rapport annuel sur les droits de l'homme dans le monde à l'intention du Parlement européen;

44. invite le Conseil et les Etats membres à envisager à nouveau l'élaboration d'une Charte européenne des droits ainsi que l'incorporation de la notion de citoyenneté européenne dans le futur traité par le biais d'une série de droits garantis par des mécanismes politiques et juridiques, et demande par ailleurs que la Communauté se voie octroyer la responsabilité en matière de contrôle de l'immigration et du droit d'asile;[1]

45. invite les Etats membres de la Communauté à réviser les législations nationales ou les règlements administratifs afin d'interdire l'exportation de matériels spécialisés, à des fins manifestement de sécurité, dont des gouvernements répressifs peuvent faire un usage abusif, ainsi qu'à ne pas coopérer avec ces gouvernements en mettant à leur disposition formation ou informations au sujet des techniques d'interrogatoire;

46. invite au développement d'une coopération plus structurée entre le Parlement et la Commission au sujet des droits de l'homme, en partie par le canal d'un groupe de travail interinstitutionnel (proposé d'ailleurs dans le rapport annuel précédent), ainsi qu'au travers de réunions périodiques destinées à examiner les priorités en matière d'action à entreprendre dans le domaine des droits de l'homme;

47. demande à la Commission d'étudier la possibilité de confier à un de ses membres la responsabilité spécifique des questions relatives aux droits de l'homme et du citoyen et de le faire assister par une task force spécialisée à cet égard;

48. demande qu'une référence explicite soit faite aux objectifs en matière de droits de l'homme lors de la présentation annuelle du programme de la Commission;

49. demande la tenue de réunions analogues dans le domaine budgétaire entre les représentants du Parlement européen et de la Commission, afin d'assurer une meilleure transparence en ce qui concerne les dépenses liées aux droits de l'homme et une meilleure coordination pour cibler les crédits dans le cadre d'une perspective globale équilibrée, ainsi qu'une meilleure coordination et plus d'équilibre entre les différentes lignes budgétaires;

50. demande une augmentation des crédits disponibles pour les activités et programmes mis en oeuvre dans différentes parties du monde en rapport avec les droits de l'homme, lesquels devraient également être accompagnés de moyens techniques et de personnel pour leur exécution, eu égard aux ressources extrêmement limitées de la Commission dans le domaine des droits de l'homme;

51. estime que les crédits devraient davantage être mobilisés en direction d'organisations régionales, d'une manière équitable et dans le respect d'un équilibre géographique;

52. demande qu'une partie substantielle du budget des Communautés européennes affectée aux droits de l'homme soit consacrée à l'éducation et à la

---

[1] Résolution du Parlement européen du 14 juin 1991 sur la citoyenneté (PV de cette date, partie II, point 18)

16

formation, dans le cadre d'un programme plur___uel de rotation, afin de permettre à des juristes, médecins, fonctionnaires, personnels d'établissements pénitenciaires, policiers et autres professions d'effectuer des stages dans les services des droits de l'homme des Etats membres ainsi qu'au sein de la Commission et du Parlement, lesquels devraient également organiser des stages spécifiques d'au moins trois mois en matière de droits de l'homme;

53. souhaite que la Fondation européenne pour les droits de l'homme d'Amsterdam, qui est financée par la Communauté, se voie assigner des objectifs bien définis et soit mieux intégrée, avec la participation du Parlement, aux activités de la Communauté;

NATIONS UNIES

54. déplore que seule la moitié des Etats membres des Nations unies aient ratifié les accords des Nations unies relatifs aux droits de l'homme, qu'un seul Etat sur cinq respecte ces conventions et invite les Etats membres de la Communauté n'ayant pas encore ratifié la Convention internationale sur les droits politiques et civiques ainsi que ses deux protocoles facultatifs, la Convention internationale sur les droits économiques, sociaux et culturels ainsi que la Convention contre la torture, à le faire, tout en reconnaissant dans le même temps avec regret qu'à elle seule la ratification n'est pas synonyme de respect de ces conventions;

55. se félicite de la coordination efficace réalisée entre les Douze aux Nations unies où, au début de la session 1990 de la commission des Nations unies pour les droits de l'homme, le Président en exercice a prononcé une déclaration marquante au nom des Douze, suivie également d'une déclaration au nom des Douze sur la situation des droits de l'homme dans certains pays suscitant de vives préoccupations;

56. relève que lors de la session de mai 1990 du Conseil économique et social des Nations unies, la présidence irlandaise a joué un rôle décisif dans le règlement du problème difficile soulevé par la conclusion d'un accord au sujet de l'élargissement de la commission des droits de l'homme, ainsi que par les mesures visant à renforcer l'efficacité de cette commission;

57. invite les Douze à poursuivre leurs efforts visant à rehausser la qualité et l'efficacité des travaux poursuivis par les Nations unies dans le domaine des droits de l'homme;

58. relève que la Communauté européenne n'a pas suffisamment développé ses liens avec les structures mises en place par le Conseil de l'Europe en matière de droits de l'homme, voire même avec les Nations unies ou ses institutions spécialisées, estimant qu'il conviendrait d'examiner attentivement la possibilité pour la Communauté d'obtenir au moins le statut d'observateur, par exemple auprès de certains organes comme le HCR;

59. réaffirme sa conviction que l'Organisation des Nations unies constitue par excellence l'organisation mondiale qui doit être autorisée à établir les normes de respect des droits de l'homme et estime par ailleurs qu'il convient de modifier le règlement de son Conseil de sécurité, fondé qu'il est sur une idée tout à fait dépassée, qui a été inspirée par la Seconde guerre mondiale et dont la conception doit donc être revue;

60. réitère sa préoccupation devant le fait qu'aux Nations unies, notamment au sein de la commission des droits de l'homme, les alliances régionales ont trop souvent contrarié la condamnation de pays où les violations des droits de l'homme sont manifestes, et que cette politisation et

47

0241

conclusion d'alliances ne reposant sur aucun principe demeure le trait dominant des travaux accomplis par les Nations unies en matière de droits de l'homme;

LES ACTIVITES DU PARLEMENT

61. réaffirme les engagements formulés lors de précédents rapports annuels et sa conviction que le Parlement, grâce aux liens noués avec les forces politiques dans des pays tiers, et en qualité d'unique parlement international élu, doit jouer un rôle actif en matière de sauvegarde des droits de l'homme, ce qui correspond aux voeux de millions de ressortissants de la Communauté et ne saurait être considéré comme un abus de pouvoir ou comme une ingérence dans les affaires intérieures de pays tiers;

62. s'engage à recourir plus largement aux instruments officiels et informels du Parlement pour défendre les droits de l'homme auprès des représentants des pays tiers;

63. estime qu'en tout état de cause, le rôle joué par le Parlement ne sera plus actif et efficace et qu'il ne perdra pas sa crédibilité qu'au prix de la nette amélioration et du renforcement de ses propres structures au sein du secrétariat général et de ses procédures de vote en séance plénière, et constate que, malgré les efforts consentis ces dernières années en ce sens, les exigences accrues à l'égard du Parlement européen ainsi que les succès indubitables enregistrés dans ce domaine imposent des améliorations efficaces; juge en outre nécessaire de garantir au Parlement européen la possibilité d'avoir toujours connaissance de toutes les violations des droits de l'homme survenues dans le monde, afin de lui permettre, avec l'autorité qu'il a acquise ces dernières années, d'intervenir là où cela est nécessaire en se fondant sur des informations avérées et incontestables;

64. décide de nouer des liens plus étroits de coordination avec d'autres organismes nationaux et internationaux concernés par les droits de l'homme, tant à l'intérieur qu'à l'extérieur de la Communauté européenne, ainsi qu'avec la Commission et la Coopération politique européenne;

65. invite la Commission et le Président en exercice du Conseil des ministres des Affaires étrangères réunis dans le cadre de la coopération politique européenne (conformément aux dispositions du paragraphe 7 deuxième alinéa de la décision du 28 février 1986), de formuler officiellement des observations au sujet de la présente résolution;

°
°   °

66. charge son Président de transmettre la présente résolution à la Commission, au Conseil, aux ministres des Affaires étrangères réunis dans le cadre de la coopération politique européenne, au Conseil de l'Europe, au Secrétaire général des Nations unies ainsi qu'aux gouvernements de tous les pays mentionnés dans la présente résolution.

Enrico VINCI
Secrétaire général

Siegbert ALBER
Vice-président

18

0242

분류기호 문서번호	구일 20005- 230	협조문용지 （　　　）	결 재	심의관 冰 담 당　과 장　국 장 씨나/ （서명）
시행일자	1991. 10. 26.			
수　신	국제기구국장	발　신	구주국장	
제　목	구주의회 채택 인권 결의안			

　　　　91.9.12. 구주의회는 89년도 및 90년도 세계인권에 관한 결의안을

채택한 바, 그중 우리나라 및 북한 관련 내용을 아래와 같이 통보하오니

귀업무에 참고하시기 바랍니다.

　　　　　　　　　　　- 아　　　래 -

ㅇ　구주의회 채택 인권 결의안중 한국 및 북한 관련사항

　1.　한국정부를 비마, 태국 및 중국정부와 함께 권위주의 정부로 예시

　　　하면서 다만, 선거 및 다원주의 진전에 따른 개선 조짐이 있음을

　　　인정

　2.　북한을 중국, 비마와 함께 폐쇄국가로 규정

　　　* 작년도 구주의회 채택 결의안 (90.12) 한국 관련 요지

　　　- 임수경, 홍성담등 방북 또는 북한인사 접촉 이유로

　　　구속된 인사의 석방 촉구

/ 계 속 ..

- 2 -

- 동 결의안 EC 정상회담, 집행위 및 한국정부에 전달

첨부 : 상기 결의문중 우리나라 및 북한관련 부분 및 번역문. 끝.

0244

구주의회 인권 결의안

(1991.9.12)

(p. 11)

긍정적 발전

검증기간(1989-90)에 나타난 다음과 같은 긍정적 요소들이 관심을 끈다.

I. 선거 및 다원주의 진전

a) 중·동부 유럽에 선거로 선출된 정부 출현. 40년이상 일당 독재에 있던 바르샤바조약기구의 6개 회원국가가 1990년의 4개월 동안 그들의 선택에 따른 정부를 선출할 수 있게 됨.

b) 아프리카 여러나라에서도 다원주의 확장추세; 유럽의 변혁과 동국들의 정치·경제적 실패 및 그들 정부의 부패 및 억압에 부분적으로 영향을 받음.

c) 버마, 태국, 남한 및 중국에서처럼 국민들의 저항에도 불구하고 권위주의 정부를 유지하고 있는 일부 아시아 국가들에도 유사한 압력

d) 칠레, 나카라구아와 아이티에서 실시된 자유·비밀 선거로 라틴아메리카에서 민주적 절차가 강화됨. 그러나 쿠바는 아직 일당 체제가 유지되고 있으며, 페루와 콜롬비아등 많은 나라에서 민주주의는 매우 취약함.

e) 남아연방에서 인종차별 정책 폐지 및 모든 관계 당사자 사이의 합의 도출을 향한 중요한 진전이 이루어 짐.

f) 서부사하라에서 UN이 제시한 평화계획을 여러 당사자들이 수락함. 그러나 동 계획의 실행은 모로코 군대의 서부 사하라 침입으로 무위로 끝날 가능성이 있음.

0245

II. 정보의 공개 확산

a) 북한, 중국 일부와 버마같이 극히 폐쇄된 몇몇 국가들의 예외가 있기는 하지만, 매스미디어의 발전에 따라 인권 침해에 대한 정보가 국내 및 외부에 알려지고 있음. 더 나아가서 외국의 인권 존중개념의 확산, 인권위반을 비난하는 국제적 움직임과 보다 손쉬운 정보 확산등이 인권 위반 사례 감소에 기여하고 있음.

0246

52613

분류기호 문서번호	구일 202-		기 안 용 지		시 행 상 특별취급	
보존기간	영구.준영구 10. 5. 3. 1		장	관		
수 신 처 보존기간						
시행일자	1991. 10. 26.					
보조 기관	국 장	전 결	협조기관		문서등제 검열 1991. 10. 2 9 장재관	
	심의관					
	과 장					
기안책임자	장 시 정				발 송 인	
경 유			발신명의			
수 신	법무부장관					
참 조						
제 목	구주의회 채택 인권 결의안					

91.9.12. 구주의회는 89년도 및 90년도 세계인권에 관한 결의안을

채택한 바, 그중 우리나라 및 북한 관련 내용을 아래와 같이 통보하오니

귀업무에 참고하시기 바랍니다.

- 아 래 -

ㅇ 구주의회 채택 인권 결의안중 한국 및 북한 관련사항

1. 한국정부를 버마, 태국 및 중국정부와 함께 권위주의 정부의

   하나로 예시하면서 다만, 선거 및 다원주의 진전에 따른 긍정적

   조짐이 있음을 인정

/ 계속...

0247

2. 북한을 중국, 버마와 함께 폐쇄국가로 규정

＊ 작년도 구주의회 채택 결의안 한국 관련 요지

- 임수경, 홍성담등 방북 또는 북한인사 접촉 이유로

   구속된 인사의 석방 촉구

- 동 결의안 EC 정상회담, 집행위 및 한국정부에 전달

첨부 : 상기 결의문중 우리나라 및 북한관련 부분 및 번역문. 끝.

0248

2과

報 告 畢

1991. 10. 30.
歐 洲 局
西 歐 1 課

長 官 報 告 事 項

題 目 : 人權問題 關聯

法務部側(人權課長)은 10.31(木) 駐韓 EC 諸國 大使館 政務擔當官들
에게 우리나라의 人權問題에 對하여 說明 豫定인 바, 關聯 事項을 아래
報告드립니다.

---

1. 會合 周旋 經緯

   ○ 주한 EC 제국 대사관측의 인권규약 문제등에 관한 설명 요청을
     법무부측에서 수락함으로써 이루어 짐.(관련 서한 별첨)

   ○ 금일(10.30.) 주한 영국대사관 Harrison 서기관, 법무부측 요청에 따라
     동 회합에 대한 우리부의 허가 요청

2. EC諸國 大使館側 說明 要請 事案

   ○ 인권규약상의 유보 및 고문방지협약 가입 문제 등

   ○ ILO 협약 및 한국 노동법 충돌 문제, 국가 보안법 재개정 및 동법위반
     사범에 대한 전향 조건 조기 석방 문제등

3. 問題點

   ○ 주한 EC 제국 대사관이 거의 모두 참여하는 등 상기 회합의 공식적 성격
     에도 불구, 우리부에 사전 통보 및 협의 절차가 없었음.

   ∨ * 외교관계에 관한 비엔나 조약 제41조 2항 위배

     - 법무부측은 동 회합에 대하여 우리부가 사전 협의 받은 것으로 이해하였다고 함.

   ○ 인권문제에 대한 EC 제국의 집단적 압력 행사로도 오해되어 질 수 있는
     가능성 있음.

4. 向後 措置計劃

   ○ 동 회합이 명일(10.31.)로 예정되어 있어, 취소 경우 야기될 영향등을 고려
     예정대로 시행보록 하되 법무부측으로 하여금 한국의 인권 현황에 대한
     이해를 제고하는 방향으로 적극 설명토록 함. 다만, 인권규약등 우리부
     소관사항은 제외토록 함.

   ○ 동 회합의 상기 절차상등의 문제점에 대하여 주선국인 영국대사관 및 의장국인
     화란대사관 담당관에 주의 환기

5. 言論 對策

   ○ 법무부로 하여금 적의 대처토록 협조

일반문서로 재분류(1991.12.31.)

첨부: 상기 서한 사본. 끝.

0249

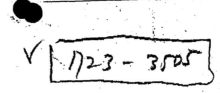

1991.10.28 11:58

(첨부 2)

To:	From:
Director Yoo Kook-Hyun	G A Harrison
Human Rights Division	
Ministry of Justice	Date: 25 October 1991

Fax No: 503 7045

No of pages, including this one: 3

존경하는 유 과장님!

...NG WITH EUROPEAN COMMUNITY POLITICAL OFFICERS ON HUMAN RIGHTS

...k you for your telephone call on 18 October. We fully
...rstand the Ministry's obligations to the National Assembly

...have discussed revised dates for the meeting with Community
...lleagues. Our preference is for a meeting at 3pm on Thursday 31
...ctober. I hope this date is acceptable. I enclose a list of EC
...bassy political officers taking part.

...should be grateful for information on the following issues.

a) **International Covenants on Human Rights**

i) What are the reservations made by the Republic of Korea on
    clauses of the International Covenant on Civil and Political
    Rights and the International Covenant on Economic, Social
    and Cultural Rights?

ii) Does the Republic of Korea intend to accede to the UN
    Convention against torture later this year?

...) Is the Republic of Korea becoming a party to the UN
    optional protocol on the Abolition of the Death Penalty,
    ado...d last year?

...) ILO

Given the appa...nt conflict betwe...n provisions of various Korean
labour laws and the ILO Convention, are any revisions of the lab...
laws planned, before joining the ILO?

c) **National Security Law (NSL) Issues**

i) Despite the revisions to the NSL in May, certain groups have
    commented that the law remains very strict. Are there any
    plans for further revisions, to encourage North/South...
    humanitarian exchanges?

0250

ii)   **The system of conversion letters**

We understand that there have been cases where prisoners who
have been convicted of crimes under the National Security Law
are offered an early release on the condition that they sign
so-called "conversion letters".   Does this practice continue?

iii)   **Long-term prisoners**

In view of the great changes in the political environment and
the length of time they have been imprisoned, would the
judicial authorities consider any kind of change in their
present attitude towards them?

Finally, my colleagues have several specific cases, on which they
would welcome information. I have sub-divided these into labour
law-related cases and NSL-related cases. In order to save time at
our meeting on 31 October perhaps you could provide any relevant
information (date of arrests, exact charges, trial dates,
sentences, details of appeals, etc) to hand over in written form.
This would be much appreciated. The list of cases is as follows:

Labour-related cases

Lee Eun-ku
Chung Yoon-kwang
Son Jong-kyu
Yoon Hyung-won
Hong Young-pyo
Park Chang-soon (died in hospital after attempted suicide in
                 unclear circumstances)
Park Song-in
Lee Un-kyong
Koh Song-bom

NSL-related cases

Hong Song-dam
Chong Song-hi
Oh Chin-hi
Choi Ik-kyu
Park No-hai
Cho Sang-nok
Park Soon-kyung
Seoul Social Science Research Institute researchers.

I look forward to seeing you on 31 October.

With thanks for your help.

Yours sincerely,

G A Harrison
Third Secretary

0251

POLITICAL OFFICERS

J Huber   ) Royal Netherlands
G J C Bijl De Vroe   )   Embassy

J-L Bodson   Belgian Embassy

. Thorsteinsson   Danish Embassy

S Miralles   Spanish Embassy

V Elbling   German Embassy

B Bourdon   French Embassy

P S Laro   Italian Embassy

Mr P Smyth   Irish Embassy

Mr G A Harrison   British Embassy

아국의 주요 인권관련 협약 가입 및 유보현황

1. 경제적, 사회적, 문화적 권리에 관한 국제규약

(Int'l Covenant on Economic, Social and Culture Rights)

o 90.7.10. 발효

2. 시민적, 정치적 권리에 관한 국제규약

(Int'l Covenant on Civil and Political Rights)

o 90.7.10. 발효

o 유보조항

- 제14조 5항 (상소권 보장)

- 제14조 7항 (일사부재리 또는 이중처벌금지)

- 제22조 (결사의 자유)

3. 시민적, 정치적 권리에 관한 국제규약 선택의정서

(Optional Protocol to the Int'l Covenant on Civil and Political Rights)

o 90.7.10. 발효

4. 국제 인종차별 철폐협약

(Int'l Convention on the Elimination of All Forms of Racial Discrimination)

o 79.1.4. 발효

0253

5. 여성차별 철폐협약

(Convention on the Elimination of All Forms of Discrimination against Women)

- o 85.1.26. 발효
- o 유보조항
    - 제9조 (국적취득, 변경)
    - 제16조(g) (성씨 및 직업선택권)

법무부 인권과

1991.

아래 문건을 수신자에게 전달하여 주시기 바랍니다.

제 목 : _____

수 신 : 서기과 서기과리실

(수신처 FAX NO: 720-2486)

발 신 : 법무부 인권과

○ 위의 내용 1991년 평가 중 유엔의 관심사항 결과보고 내용

입력자 1990년 일자

표지포함 총 ___ 매

위 문건 이상

○ 총체적 이용에서 검토의가 부여하기 등의 지난의 요해결 말 이내

[수신처 불명]

0255

배 부 치	법 무 부							대 검	청외대	기 타 기 관
	⊗⊗⊗⊗⊗⊗⊗							⊗⊗	⊗⊗	⊗⊗⊗○○○○
	장차법검기김 무첨회창 신국성 관리정장장							공 인 부 장	사정 (비환)	제안외공법 1 행기무보제 조부부치치

정 보 보 고

1. 제 목　　　　　　　　　　　**2. 출 처**

주한 E.C담당서기관(정치담당) 6명 당부방문 결과　　　인 권 과

3. 내 용　　　　　　　　　　　　　　(1991.11.14)

○ 주한구주공동체대표부 1등서기관 엔젤로스

　　판그테티스 (Angelos PANGRATIS) 외

　　E.C소속 5개국 1등서기관 6명이 11.8.

　　15:00, 당부를 방문하여 인권과장과 아국의

　　인권상황 등 전반에 관하여 면담하였는 바,

　　면담결과는 별첨과 같음

○ 첨부 : 면담결과 1부.

0256

주한E.C국가 정치담당서기관 6명
인권과장 면담내용

1991. 11

법 무 부 인 권 과

0257

1. 개 요

○ 일 시 : '91.11.8(금) 15:00-17:30

○ 장 소 : 인권과장실

○ 면담자 : Angelos PANGRATIS

  (주한구주공동체 대표부 1등서기관)

  GUY A. HARRISON

  (주한영국대사관 2등서기관)

  Govert Jan C. BIJL DE VROE

  (주한네덜란드대사관 1등서기관)

  Peter E. SMYTH

  (주한아일랜드대사관 1등서기관)

  Viktor Elbling

  (주한독일연방공화국대사관 1등서기관)

  Bruce BOURDON

  (주한프랑스대사관 2등서기관)

○ 배석자 : 인 권 과   정 기 용 검사

        보안제2과장   이 순 길 교정감

* 첨부자료 : 질문사항

1

2. 대화요지

O 네덜란드 서기관

본인이 E.C 회장국 대사관에 근무하므로 먼저 이야기하겠다.
원래 E.C소속 국가의 대사관 직원들이 모두 오려고 하였으나
각자의 사정이 있어 전원 참석하지 못하였다.
이번 방문은 특별한 의미가 없고 비공식적인 것이다.
평소에 각 국가마다 국회의원이나 당해국가 인권단체들로부터
질의 등을 받은 경우가 있어, 이 기회에 이러한 점에 대하여
설명을 듣고자 한다.
귀부에서 요청한대로 질문서를 송부하였으나, 굳이 그에 한정
하여 이야기 할 필요는 없다

O 과 장

그간 몇차례에 걸쳐서 모임이 연기된 것은, 국회가 개회중이
었고, 또한 외무부를 경유하는 과정에서 대사관측에 다소의
착오가 있었기 때문인 것으로 알고 있다.
본인은 적절한 기회에 귀하들을 면담하기를 기대하여 왔다.
공식적으로 만나는 것 보다 이번과 같이 실무자들간에 격의
없이 충분한 대화와 토론을 하여 상호 이해를 돕는 것이 중요
하다고 생각된다

2   0259

o 네덜란드 서기관

질문서 1번은 국제인권규약에 관련된 것으로, 우선 1항의 질문
은 귀국이 국제인권규약 B규약에 가입하면서 어떠한 조항들에
대해 유보를 하였는지와 그 유보이유에 대해 알고 싶다

o 과   장

1990.7.10 국제인권규약에 가입당시 "시민적 및 정치적 권리
에 관한 국제규약(B규약)" 중 4개조항에 대해서 유보를 하였
는데, 1991.3.15자로 1개조항에 대해 유보를 철회하여, 현재
에는 3개조항이 유보된 상태이다.
유보된 조항을 조문 순서별로 보면, 상소권 보장에 관하여
규정한 인권규약 제14조 5항이, 비상계엄하여서 일정한 범죄
에 대하여 사형의 경우를 제외하고 군사재판 단심제를 인정
하는 아국의 헌법 제110조 4항 및 군사법원법 제534조와 상충.
유보되었고,
인권규약 제14조 7항은 일사부재리 또는 이중처벌금지(double
jeopardy)에 관하여 규정하고 있는데, 법과 제도가 서로
상이한 국가간에 무조건 일사부재리 또는 이중처벌금지를
강요할 수 없다고 할 것이므로, 외국에서 받은 형은 감경
또는 면제할 수 있다고 규정한 우리 형법 제7조가 유지되는
것이 상당하다고 판단되어 위 규약 비준시 유보하였다.

3

0260

또, 결사의 자유에 관하여 규정한 인권규약 제22조는, 노무직
을 제외한 공무원 및 사립학교 교원의 집단행동을 금지한 한국
헌법 제33조 2항, 국가공무원법 제66조, 지방공무원법 제58조,
사립학교법 제55조와 정면으로 배치되어 유보하였다.

그리고, 인권규약 제23조 4항은 혼인중 및 혼인해소시 배우자
의 평등에 관한 조항으로서, 위 규약 가입당시 국내 민법과
상충되어 유보하였으나, 그후 민법을 개정하여 남녀간의 차별
적 요소를 수정하고, 금년 1.1부터 개정민법이 시행됨에 따라
위 규약 내용과 아국 법제와의 저촉문제가 해소되어 1991.8.15
자로 유보를 철회하였다

O 네덜란드 서기관

그러면 국제인권규약중 A규약에도 가입하였는가?
가입하였다면 유보한 조항이 있는가, 또 보고서는 제출하였는가

O 과 장

국제인권규약 A규약인 "경제적, 사회적 및 문화적 권리에
관한 국제규약"에도 가입을 하였는데, 유보한 조항은 없다.
그리고, 최초보고서는 1992.6.까지 제출하도록 되어 있다

4

0261

O 구주공동체대표부 서기관

노동조합 설립과 판련해서, 한가지 묻고 싶은 것은 공무원들
에게 인정되지 아니하는 것이 단결권, 단체교섭권, 단체행동권
중 어느 것인가.
그리고, 교사들에 대해서도 제한하는 이유는 무엇인가

O 과 장

공무원에 대해서는 노동조합을 결성하는 단결권이나 단체교섭
및 단체행동 모두가 금지되어 있다.
교사들에 대해 노조를 허용하지 아니하는 법규를 갖고 있는
점은 무엇보다도 한국의 유교적,윤리적 문화배경과 국민, 특히
학부모의 교육에 대한 인식(perception)을 이해하여야 설명이
가능하다. 예전부터 우리나라에는 선생을 부모와 같은 위치의
존경의 대상으로 인정해 왔지 정의를 하는 노동자로 생각하지
는 아니하였다.
최근 들어 교사들의 노조결성이 허용되어야 하는 것인가에
대해 논의가 있기는 하나, 궁극적으로 국민의 여론에 따를
문제이다.
정부는 현 시점에서의 국민여론이, 교사의 경우 노동쟁의를
전제로 하는 집단으로 인정하는 것을 거부하는 공감대가 형성
되어 있다고 확신하고 있다

5

0262

o 내덜란드 서기관

　다음은 질문서 1번의 2항인데, 고문방지협약에 가입할 용의가
　있는지 여부에 관해 한국의 입장을 알고 싶다

o 과　장

　귀하의 질문은 외무부가 주무부서로서 다루는 부분에 관한
　것이므로, 본인은 답변할 입장이 아님을 밝혀 둔다.
　다만, 한국정부는 인권관계 국제협약에 점진적 가입추진을
　기본입장으로 하고 있는데, 위 고문방지협약 가입여부 결정
　전에 우선 협약의 운용실태파악 등 충분한 검토를 위한
　시일이 필요할 것으로 알고 있다

o 내덜란드 서기관

　질문 1번의 3항과 관련, 사형제도 폐지를 위해서 국제인권규약
　B규약 제2선택의정서에 가입할 용의가 있는지 알고 싶다

o 과　장

　B규약 제2선택의정서에 가입하는 문제에 대한 최종결정 역시
　외무부에서 해야 하는 것인데, 아직 결정되지 아니한 것으로
　알고 있다.
　법무부로서는 현 시점에서 사형을 폐지하는 방향으로 형법 등
　관련법령 개정을 검토한 바는 없다.

6

0263

사형의 존폐문제는 여러 국제인권단체, 특히 유럽쪽의 인권
단체들에 의해 거론되는 가장 기본적인 질문중의 하나인데,
한국내에서도 논쟁거리중의 하나이다.

최근 한 여론조사의 결과에 의하면, 한국의 대다수의 국민들
은 인륜을 저버리는 흉악범죄가 빈발하고 있는 우리 현실에
비추어 볼 때, 사형폐지는 시기상조이며, 오히려 일부 가정
파괴사범이나 잔인한 강력 범죄자에 대하여는 사형 등 무거운
형벌을 과감하게 적용하여야 한다는 입장을 보이고 있다.

다만, 본인의 개인적인 생각으로는, 인간의 존엄과 가치보장
의 헌법정신을 고려해서 사형선고에 더욱 신중을 기할 필요가
있다고 본다

○ 네덜란드 서기관

다음, 질문서 2번 문제로 넘어가서, ILO 가입과 관련해 ILO
협약과 배치되는 노동관계법 조항들에 대해 개정할 용의가
있는지 알고 싶다

○ 과 장

ILO 가입에 관한 주무부서는 노동부이므로, ILO와 관련된 질문
은 노동부에 해 주기 바란다.

본인이 알고 있는 바로는, 현재 ILO에서 채택된 협약은 172개
인데, 각 개별협약에 관한 비준여부는 노동부가 충분한 시간적

7

0264

여유를 가지고, 우리나라 법령 및 현실을 신중히 검토한 다음, 노사단체 및 관계부처의 의견을 수렴하여 단계적으로 비준할 예정으로, 현재 상당히 깊은 연구가 이루어지고 있는 것으로 알고 있다.

세계 대부분 국가들도 위 172개 협약중 자국의 실정에 맞는 협약에 한하여 선별적으로 비준하고 있는 실정이다

O 네덜란드 서기관

질문 3번, 국가보안법과 관련해서, 지난 5월에 개정된 것으로 알고 있는데, 추가로 개정할 계획이나 용의가 있는지 알고 싶다

O 과 장

이 국가보안법 문제가 바로 법무부 소관업무로서 항상 논란의 대상이 되고 있는 부분이다.

국가보안법 추가개정에 관한 위 질문은 2가지 관점으로 나누어서 생각해 볼 수 있다.

첫번째가, 현재 남북관계가 남북대화를 통해서 긍정적인 방향으로 나아가고 있으므로, 이와 같은 추세를 반영하고 국가보안법 적용을 점차 줄이기 위해서 국가보안법을 재개정해야 하는 것이 아니냐라는 측면과, 두번째로 한국이 먼저 주도적으로 국가보안법을 재개정함으로써 한반도 주변상황과 북한에 긍정적인 파급효과를 거둘 수 있을 것을 예상하여 재개정해야 하는 것이 아니냐는 관점이다.

8

0265

먼저, 첫번째 관점에서 살펴보면, 무역. 경제협력 등을 통한 남북관계 개선은 매우 중요하고도 바람직한 현상이다.

따라서, 현재 우리 정부는 남북교류촉진을 위해 남북교류에 관한 법률을 제정. 시행하고 있고, 북한지역 합작개발, 이산가족 상호방문 등 다각적인 제의, 접촉을 통해 북한과의 교류를 확대함으로써, 폐쇄적인 북한을 개방시키려는데 최선의 노력을 경주하고 있다.

다만 분명히 해야 할 점은, 이와 같이 남북관계가 긍정적으로 발전하는 것과 국가보안법 개정 필요성 여부와는 전혀 다른 별개차원의 문제라는 점이다.

국가보안법은 대남적화통일노선을 고수하고 있는 북한의 위협으로부터 한국의 존립안전과 자유민주주의 및 자본주의체제를 보호하려는 자위적이고 방어적 성격의 법률이다. 즉, 이 법률은 남북교류에 관한 것이 아니라 대한민국이라는 한 국가의 기본체제를 지키기 위함을 목적으로 하고 있는 것이다.

따라서, 국가보안법을 위반한 행위에 대하여는 당연히 우리의 자유민주주의체제 수호를 위해 위 법에 의한 처벌이 가하여지는 것이며, 국가보안법 추가개정문제 역시 북한이 대남적화 무력통일전략을 포기하였는가라는 기본전략 변화여부와 관련되어 결정되는 것이다.

남북한 교류접촉 확대를 국가보안법 개정과 연결시키는 것은 우리의 현실을 충분히 이해하지 못한 피상적인 관찰의 결과라고 본다.

9

두번째로, 한국이 먼저 주도적으로 국가보안법을 재개정함으로써, 한반도 주변상황과 북한에 긍정적인 파급효과를 거둘 수 있을 것을 예상하여 재개정을 해야 하는 것이 아니냐라는 문제는 국민여론에 바탕을 둔 고도의 정치적 판단으로 결국 정치권에서 고려해야 할 성질의 문제이고, 또 이와 같은 결정을 내리기 위해서는 먼저 개정후 발생될지 모를 상황에 대해 철저한 분석과 책임문제 등이 반드시 검토되어야 하는 것이다.

잘 알다시피, 북한은 1953년 휴전이후 지금까지 약 40년간 남한의 무력적화통일을 궁극적 목표로 하여 계속 전쟁준비를 해 오면서, 호시탐탐 남침의 기회만을 노려 왔는데, 이와 같은 북한의 남침야욕과 무력적화통일의 기본전략이 변화하고 있다는 증거는 없다.

참고로 북한의 체제유지 및 대남전략과 관련해서 북한법률이 어떻게 규정되어 있는지 조사한 자료가 있는데, 이것은 비밀로 취급되어 공개되지 아니하므로, 그동안 신문, 방송을 통해서 간혹 나타나는 것들을 종합정리해 만든 것이다.

이 자료를 보면, 북한의 기본적인 대남무력적화전략이 일반형법에도 그대로 명시되어 있는데, 북한의 형법은, 남한을 "원쑤", "적"으로 규정하고 남한의 체제를 전복한 다음 위대한 김일성,김정일의 뜻을 받드는 인민독재의 위대한 국가를 건설하는데 그 목적이 있다고 명시하면서, 모든 무장혁명에 저해가 되는 모든 행동을 반혁명죄 (Counterrevolutionary Crimes)로 규정하고 이에 대해서는 사형과 전재산 몰수형으로 처벌하며 불고지죄도 아울러 처벌하고 있다.

10

0267

이와 같이, 전투적이고 위협적인 북한의 구체적인 자료들을 통해서, 한국민이 현재 느끼고 있는 한반도의 긴장감을 이해하는데 도움이 되리라고 생각하고, 특히 제3자 입장인 외국인이 갖기 쉬운 의문인 국민과 정부가 북한에 대해 과민 인식을 하고 있는 것이 아니냐라는 점에 대해 보다 분명하게 이해함에 도움이 되리라고 빈다.

위 자료는 외무부를 통해서 귀국 대사관으로 보낼 계획인데, 검토한 다음 보외할 내용이 있으면 언제든지 환영하겠다.

O 구주공동체대표부 서기관

내 조국인 그리스 역시 20세기 들어와 자유민주주의체제를 수호하기 위해서 공산주의 세력들과 여러차례 전쟁을 겪은 경험이 있는데, 전쟁에 대한 내 개인적인 경험에 비추어 볼 때, 현재 한국이 처하고 있는 상황에 대해 이해가 간다.

O 과 장

그리스가 많은 전쟁을 겪은 역사적 사실은 잘 알고 있다. 그런데, 그리스는 한반도와는 달리 국토가 분단된 것도 아니고 지정학적 위치나 인접국가들도 모두 유리한 편이다. 그와 비교해 볼 때, 한국은 세계에서 가장 폐쇄된 공산집단인 북한과 직접 대치하고 있는 불리한 주변 여건하에 있다.

11

0268

o 네덜란드 서기관

   다음은 질문 3번의 1항, 전향제도에 관한 질문인데, 국가보안
   법에 의한 구금자, 특히 장기수는 전향서에 서명하면 조기석방
   된다고 알고 있는데, 과연 사실인가.
   사실이라면 앞으로도 전향서 제도를 계속 유지할 것인가

o 과 장

   먼저 전향서 (conversion letters) 라는 단어의 의미를 알고
   있는지 묻고 싶다.
   이는 한국내 운동권, 재야 인권단체에서 정부가 좌익 장기수
   들에게 강제로 위 전향을 강요하여 양심의 자유를 침범하고
   있다고 주장할 때 사용하기 위하여 만든 용어이다.
   수형자에 대하여는 교정교육이 실시되는데, 이는 입소전 자신
   이 저지른 국민과 국가에 대한 잘못을 뉘우치는 반성(repentance)
   이 전제가 되고 건전한 국민정신을 함양시켜서 사회에 다시
   복귀시키도록 하는 것이다.
   장기수도 물론 사회에 복귀시킬 수 있도록 하는 교정교육의
   대상이므로 반성의 기회가 주어지는데, 반성은 자신볼 스스로
   자유로운 의사에 따라 입소전에 공산주의에 심취하여 북한의
   지령에 따라 대한민국의 공공건물을 파괴하고 국가전복을 기도
   하는 활동에 대해 잘못을 시인할 때만 의미가 있을 뿐이다.
   따라서, 전향서는 강요해서 작성될 성질의 것이 아니다.

11

0269

또한, 소위 "전향서"를 작성하였다 하여, 즉 전향하였다 하여 곧 조기석방되는 것도 물론 아니다.

전향한 후에도 일반수와 똑같이 법규에 정해진 일정한 복역기간이 경과하고, 법 소정의 가석방 요건에 해당하며, 재범의 우려가 없다고 판단될 때 소정의 심사를 거쳐서 가석방하고 있을 뿐이다.

그러므로, 미전향 장기수가 전향서에 서명만 하면 조기석방 된다는 말은 전혀 근거가 없는 잘못된 것이다.

O 독일 서기관

독일에도 가석방 제도가 있는데, 관계법의 해당요건이 충족되면 모든 수형자가 심사대상이 되고, 심사결과에 따라 가석방 여부를 결정하게 된다.

그런데, 한국에는 오직 좌익 장기수에게만 자신의 과거행위를 반성한다는 내용의 문서를 받는가

O 과 장

좋은 질문이다.

한국 행형법과 시행령에 규정된 가석방의 요건은 독일법 규정과 거의 유사한 것으로 알고 있다.

모든 재소자의 가석방 여부를 결정하기 위해서 재소자의 수형성적, 생활태도, 사회적응능력 여부 등이 종합적으로 평가 되는데, 자신의 과거비행에 대해 반성하는 것도 그중 하나의 요소가 된다.

13

0270

자신의 잘못을 뉘우치고 회개하는 재소자에 대하여는 사회에
대한 위험성이 그만큼 줄어든다고 평가하게 되는데, 미전향 장
기수의 경우도 자신의 잘못을 반성하고 전향하는지 여부가 다른
재소자들과 마찬가지로 하나의 요소로 평가되는 것일 뿐이다.
그런데, 일부 재야단체에서 미전향 장기수에 대해서만 유달리
소위 자신의 과거행위를 반성하는 내용의 "전향서"를 작성하는
것처럼 왜곡하여 이를 문제삼는 것은 잘못된 것이다.
소위 "전향서"라는 것은 일반 재소자들 모두에게 적용되는
"전비에 대한 뉘우침", 즉 "반성"과 같은 것이고, 또 별도의
형식이나 작성법이 따로 있는 것도 아니다

o 내덤반느 서기관

다음은 질문 8번의 8항, 장기수 문제인데, 이미 앞에서 언급한
전향제도와도 관련이 있는 것이다.
시대변천에 따른 정치환경의 변화와 오면 수형기간 등을 고려
해서 그들에 대해 사법당국이 별도의 조치를 위할 계획이 있는
지 여부에 관해 알고 싶다

o 과 장

미전향 장기 좌익수들은 정치범이 아니고, 1950년 한국동란중
에 국가기밀을 빼내는 등 대한민국 전복을 기도하다가 검거되
어 무기징역 등 중형을 선고받고 복역중인 자들로서, 현재의

14

0271

국제정치상황 변화와는 아무런 관련이 없는 자들이다.

또한, 그들은 현재까지도 자신의 범죄행위를 반성하기는 커녕, 오히려 정당화 하려는 태도를 고수하고 있는데, 이들에 대해 가석방 결정을 하여 조기석방하였을 경우에는 지하간첩활동을 재개하거나 북한으로 잠입하여 적극적인 공산당 활동을 할 위험성이 매우 높은 사람들이다.

그리고, 본인이 파악한 위 질문의 취지중의 하나는, 인도주의 적인 측면에서 40년 가까이 긴 수형생활을 한 점을 고려하여 조기 석방의 온정적 조치를 취할 수도 있는 것이 아닌가 하는 점인데, 40년 가까운 긴 세월동안 수감되어 있었다는 점에 대해서는 개인적으로 동정이 가지만, 앞서 언급한대로 조기석방 여부를 결정할 때는 반드시 석방후 지하간첩활동 재개 등 우리 사회에 직접 영향을 미치는 위험성에 대해 충분히 고려가 되어야 할 것이다

○ 아일랜드 서기관

최근 언론보도에 따르면, 한국내 좌익 장기수가 50명 있다고 하고, 또 다른 인권단체들은 수십명에서 수백명까지라고 주장하고 있는데, 좌익 장기수에 대한 정확한 통계를 한국 정부가 공식적으로 발표한 것이 있는지 여부와, 없다면 왜 통계숫자를 밝히지 않는지 그 이유에 관해 알고 싶다

15

0272

o 과 장

한국정부는 공식적으로 재소자 숫자에 대하여 정확하게는 발표
하지 않는 정책을 취하고 있다.
따라서, 정부가 확인해 줄 수 있는 숫자는 한국내 재소자 수가
약 5만명 정도이고, 미전향 좌익 장기수는 50명보다는 적은
숫자라는 것이다.
이와 같이 미전향 장기수에 대해 정확한 숫자를 밝히지 않는
것은 북한의 정치적 대남선전 및 석방요구 등 여러가지 정책
적인 상황 등을 고려해서이다.

o 구주공동체대표부 서기관

미전향 좌익 장기수중 60세 이상자나 70세 이상의 고령자가
석방되었을 때, 과연 비밀수집 등 간첩활동을 할 위험성이
있을지 의문이다

o 과 장

그것은 귀하가 한국의 특수상황을 이해 못하고 간첩활동을 서구
식으로 생각하여, 적극적인 첩보수집 등 활동적인 간첩을 연상
하였기 때문인데, 한국의 경우는 단일민족으로 미전향수의 친척
들이 한국내에도 많이 거주하고 있어 그들과 접촉할 수 있고,
또한 현재 활동중인 지하 간첩조직과도 손쉽게 연락이 가능한
형편이다.

0273

따라서, 가석방된 미전향수들은 이를 지하조직과 연계하여 각종 간첩활동에 관여할 위험성을 충분히 갖고 있는 것이다

o 영국 서기관

영국에는 모든 기결수에 대하여 가석방 심사제도가 적용되어 일정한 기간경과 후에는 자동적으로 심사대상이 되는데, 한국의 제도는 어떠한가, 그리고 미전향 장기수의 경우는 어떠한가

o 과 장

한국의 가석방 제도도 모든 기결수에 적용되어, 선고형량의 일정부분을 복역한 자는 전원 가석방 심사대상자로 되고, 각 교도소에 설치되어 있는 가석방 심사위원회에서 대상자를 상대로 심사하여 가석방 여부를 결정하게 되는데, 미전향 장기수의 경우도 일반사범과 동일한 절차를 밟는다.
다만, 미전향자의 경우 대한민국의 모든 체제를 부정하는 자이므로 국가에 위해를 끼칠 가능성이 높아 가석방 결정이 나지 않는 것이 현실이다.
가석방과는 별도로 미전향 장기수가 중한 병에 걸렸을 때 형집행정지 결정 등으로 석방되는 경우가 있다

17

0274

o 독일 서기관

　그러면, 가석방심사위원회 결정후의 절차는 어떻게 되는가

o 과　장

　가석방심사위원회의 결정은 법무부장관에게 품신되어 최종적
　으로 법무부장관이 기각할 수 있는 심사권한을 갖는데, 부인되
　는 예는 거의 드문 형편이다

o 복일 서기관

　법무부장관이 최종결정권자이면, 특정인에 대해 가석방심사
　위원회로 하여금 심사를 하도록 명할 수도 있는가

o 과　장

　이론상은 가능하다. 하지만 이제까지 그런 경우는 없었던 것
　으로 알고 있다

o 네덜란드 서기관

　끝으로, 국가보안법 및 노동운봉과 관련해서 현재 구속중인
　사범 약 10여명에 대해 개인별 자료가 필요해서 요청을 하였다

18

0275

ㅇ 과 장

귀하가 요청한 판련자료의 범죄사실이나 재판결과들은 모두
준비해 놓았는데, 외무부를 통해서 빠른시일내로 건네 주겠다.
이와 같은 신원이 정확히 밝혀진 개인별 자료의 요청은 언제
튼지 환영한다. 그리고, 한국의 개괄적인 인권상황 및 국가
보안법 문제 등을 설명한 개설서인 'FACTS AND FICTION, HUMAN
RIGHTS IN KOREA'를 줄 테니 업무에 참고하기 바란다(자료수교)

ㅇ 네덜란드 서기관

성실히 답변해 준 데 감사하다.
한국의 인권 및 판련상황을 이해하는데 큰 도움이 되었다고
본다

ㅇ 과 장

본인도 오늘 모임이 뜻이 있었다고 생각한다

19

0276

인권문제관련 외무부 조치사항(91.10.1-12.31)   오이며 민감
나진수 과장에 지시

1992.1.15.
외 무 부

1. 아국의 인권신장노력 홍보

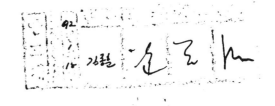

가. 국제사면위(AI) 대응활동

- 최근 아국정부의 사형집행문제

1) 내 용

o 91.12.18. 9명의 사형확정자에 대한 사형집행에 대해 AI 사무총장은
법무부장관 앞 서한을 통해 유감표명

2) 대응조치

o 법무부와 협의, 금번 사형집행의 배경 및 집행대상자의 범죄사실등
관련자료를 주영대사관에 송부, AI측에 설명토록 조치

나. "이인모"사건관련 북한책동 대응

1) 북한책동 내용

o 91년도 하반기부터 북한 언론매체, 해외 친북단체등을 통해 전인민군
종군기자 이인모의 북한송환을 주장하는 선전활동 적극 전개

2) 대응조치

o 북한의 대외활동에 대한 대응방안 검토를 위해 관계부처 담당관
협의회를 12.6. 개최

- 외무부(회의주관), 안기부, 통일원, 법무부, 공보처 담당관 참석

- 동문제에 대한 대외적 대응논리 및 구주지역 공관에 접수된
진정서 처리대책등을 협의

o 향후 유엔 인권위등에서 동문제가 제기될 가능성에 대비, 관련자료
준비

0277

2. 북한의 인권문제

가. 재소고려인 유가족 후원회의 진정서 유엔제출

1) 내 용
   o 91.11월 국제인권옹호 한국연맹은 재소고려인 유가족 후원회의
     탄원에 따라 북한에서 숙청된 소련파 인사 45명의 생사확인을
     요청하는 진정서를 유엔 및 AI등에 제출

2) 당부조치
   o 주소대사관등 재외공관을 통해 상기 사실을 확인, 동진정서 사본을
     입수함.
   o 향후 동진정서는 유엔 인권위원회 산하 실종자처리 실무위원회에
     회부될 예정임.   - 끝 -

0278

외교문서 비밀해제: 한국 인권문제 2
한국 인권문제 제 사안 2

초판인쇄 2024년 03월 15일
초판발행 2024년 03월 15일

지은이 한국학술정보(주)
펴낸이 채종준
펴낸곳 한국학술정보(주)
주 소 경기도 파주시 회동길 230(문발동)
전 화 031-908-3181(대표)
팩 스 031-908-3189
홈페이지 http://ebook.kstudy.com
E-mail 출판사업부 publish@kstudy.com
등 록 제일산-115호(2000. 6. 19)

ISBN   979-11-7217-056-1 94340
       979-11-7217-054-7 94340 (set)